MW00776249

# Lesbian Lives

---

## Psychoanalytic Narratives Old and New

# Lesbian Lives

◆

## PSYCHOANALYTIC NARRATIVES OLD AND NEW

Maggie Magee
Diana C. Miller

A̲P̲  THE ANALYTIC PRESS

1997    Hillsdale, NJ                London

The following material is reprinted here by permission :

Lines from "Transcendental Etude," Poem XVII of "Twenty-One Love Poems," *The Dream of a Common Language: Poems 1974–1977* by Adrienne Rich © 1978 by W.W. Norton & Company, Inc.; excerpt from "It Is the Lesbian in Us . . ." *On Lies, Secrets, and Silence: Selected Prose 1966–1978* by Adrienne Rich © 1979 by W.W. Norton & Company, Inc.; selections from *Breathless* by Kitty Tsui, published by Firebrand Books, Ithaca, NY © 1996 by Kitty Tsui; lines 220-221 from *The Wild Good: Lesbian Photographs & Writings O* by Bea Gates, used by permission of Doubleday, a division of Bantam Doubleday Dell Publishing Group © 1996 by Bea Gates; selected lines from "Making Tortillas" by Alicia Gaspar de Alba published by Doubleday Dell Publishing Group, ©1996 Alice Gaspar de Alba; the poem "Some Unsaid Things" by Joan Larkin from *Lesbian Poetry: An Anthology*, ed. E. Bulkin & J. Larkin, published by Persephone Press, Watertown, MA © 1975 Joan Larkin: pages 24–26 from *Epistemology of the Closet* by Eve Kosofsky ©1990 The Regents of the University of California; a prior version of chapter 3, "She Foreswore Her Womanhood: Psychoanalytic and Biological Theories of the Etiology of Female Homosexuality." *Clinical Social Work Journal*, 20:67–87 © 1992 Plenum Publishing Corp.; a prior version of chapter 5, "Coming Out: The Necessity of Becoming a Bee-Charmer" *Journal of the American Academy of Psychoanalysis*, 22:481–50 © American Academy of Psychoanalysis; a prior version of chapter 7, "What Sex Is an Amaryllis? What Gender Is Lesbian?" *Gender and Psychoanalysis*, 1:139–170 ©1996 International Universities Press.

Published by The Analytic Press, Inc.
Editorial Offices: 101 West Street, Hillsdale, NJ 07642


Typeset in Bulmer MT by Compudesign, Jackson Hts., NY

LIBRARY OF CONGRESS CATALOGING-IN-PUBLICATION DATA

Magee, Maggie, 1940-
    Lesbian lives : psychoanalytic narratives old and new / Maggie Magee / & Diana C. Miller
p.  c.m
    Includes bibliographical references and index.
    ISBN 0-88163-269-4
    1. Lesbianism—Psychological aspects. 2. Women and psychoanalysis. 3.
    Psychoanalysis and homosexuality. I. Miller, Diana C. , 1944- II.
I. Title
RC451.4.G39M34    1997                  97-335034
616.89'17'086643—dc21                    CIP


Printed in the United States of America
10 9 8 7 6 5 4 3 2 1

# ACKNOWLEDGMENTS

Many people helped us to begin this book and were there along the way at important moments to keep us to the task. Among those we remember at this time are David Susky, Charles Weiss, and Bruce Kahl, men whose lives with AIDS inspired us and whose deaths from complications of AIDS strengthened our resolve to write.

The members of our early writing group, Nancy Hollander and Bonnie Engdahl, discouraged us from editing a collection of previously published psychoanalytic papers on female homosexuality and sent us forth to find our own chapters. Linda Garnets, Allison Acken, and Grace Choi, our first suite-mates, offered congenial company in which to begin our private practices. Although Jessica Lehman and Peter Hirsch had two children during the time it took us to give birth to one book they still made time to keep us company here and in Kona. Phyllis and Richard Wasserstrom, dearest friends since the civil rights movement, were, like family, there at our beginning. Marlowe and Maryl Magee gave us their love and a new niece, Erin Hannah. Elizabeth McDonald, Diana's sister, sent care packages year after year filled with books, poetry, and always, her splendid artwork.

We have been sustained by steady friendships with Diane Wilson, Claudia Fonda-Bonardi, Chris Sekaer, and Litzi Engel. Jack Drescher, Gil Zicklin, David Schwartz, Terry Stein, Bob Cabaj, and Alan Blum were knowledgeable touchstones of sanity at the other ends of telephone lines and e-mail. Louis Gooren, Bill Byne, and Anne Fausto-Sterling gave generously of their time and expertise to help us understand biological studies. Jennifer Bleakley scoured the library for books we could read in order to avoid writing; Nina Jacobson, Gene Nakajima, and Howard Rubin lent us still more books and came to our presentations. Judd Marmor was always supportive of our work, even when he disagreed with our views on biology and homosexuality. Jeanne Axler, pain doctor extraordinaire, got us through the first years of physical fall out from writing with acupuncture, stretch exercises, bread, movies, and claufouti. Robert Forrester, physical therapist to professional athletes and to the rest of us, worked out our computer-generated muscle spasms; Pilates instructor Nancy Coleman kept Diana kayaking.

We thank those whose responses to our first papers helped improve these chapters: Donna Bassin, Peggy Buttenheim, Muriel Dimen, Jimmy Fisher, Virginia Goldner, Adrienne Harris, the members of the Southern California Psychiatric Society's Gay, Lesbian, and Bi Issues Committee, the members of the Association of Gay and Lesbian Psychiatrists, the 1994 seminar members at the Southern California Psychoanalytic Institute, the 1994 seminar members at the Los Angeles Institute and Society for Psychoanalytic Studies, the 1995 seminar members at the Institute for Contemporary Psychoanalysis, the National Committee on Psychoanalysis, the Southern California Chapter of the American Psychological Association, Division 39, the American Psychological Association's Division 39, Section 111 1995 Symposium "Perspectives on Lesbian Sexuality," the New York University Postgraduate Division in Psychoanalysis's 1993 conference, Perspectives on Homosexuality: An Open Dialogue," and the 1995 winter meetings of the American Academy of Psychoanalysis.

Patricia C. Willis, Curator of the Yale Collection of American Literature, and Cyrena N. Pondrom, Gertrude Stein scholar, encouraged our Bryher explorations. Perdita Schaffner generously commented on an earlier version of the chapter on Bryher. Sanford Gifford, Chair of the American Psychoanalytic Association's Committee on History and Archives, and David R. Pokross, Hanns Sachs's attorney, were graciously and promptly responsive to our questions.

We are particularly grateful to all those in LAISPS (Los Angeles Institute and Society for Psychoanalytic Studies) who accepted us as psychoanalysts and give us opportunities to present our work, to teach, to participate in the life of the institute, and to build friendships.

We thank Gary Yontef for saying firmly 20 years ago, "You have a real conflict, and you will have to decide which to follow, your experience or certain ideas about that experience." David Bender's quiet curiosity reached out to many things and especially to the thoughts and interests of his analysand. Jean Sanville, a steadfast believer in the power of the reparative intent, and a true supporter of beginning writers, introduced us to Paul Stepansky, who was willing to become our editor. His knowledge of psychoanalysis and its history and his understanding of our project rescued us from a moratorium that had begun to feel like a mortuary. We reamed that a good fit is as necessary in the editor–writer relationship as it is between analyst and patient. Lenni Kobrin shepherded our book through production. Because of Lenni we discovered the wondrous relief of having a fine copy editor take one's writing in hand. We thank Andrea Schettino for her book jacket design and Joan Riegel for her work in marketing.

Finally, we remember fondly our Annie Oakley Beagle, who snored beside the computers, brought us bones, and kept us calm.

# CONTENTS

# PROLOGUE

## TO MAKE OF OUR LIVES A STUDY

Adrienne Rich's (1978) poem "Transcendental Etude" describes how important it is for a woman who loves a woman to study her own experience. In order to undertake that study, she must turn away from her culture's ideas about homosexuality and must find or make new images and new language. Although Rich was not, of course, writing about psychoanalytic treatment, her poem does illustrate the challenges that face psychoanalytic therapists and lesbian patients. They must turn away from existing psychoanalytic formulations of female homosexuality. They must find and make new formulations, in new language.

In "Transcendental Etude," Rich plays feminist variations on a favorite theme of Romantic literature and poetry, the Study or Observation of Nature. For the Romantics, observing the natural world was the royal road to the human psyche, and poetry replicated the contemplative state of the Nature Observer. Created through the Imagination, poetry was a vehicle through which Man (the generic sex) might momentarily transcend his limitations and receive what Wordsworth called "intimations of immortality." As Rich's poem begins, a woman drives through the green August Vermont countryside. She observes the fragile peace and beauty of the natural scene. She watches a doe with her fawns. She reflects upon the coming violence of winter, the deer hunters of November. All around she sees nature

> . . . so dense with life,
> minute, momentary life . . .
> a lifetime is too narrow
> to understand it all, . . . [p. 73].

She realizes that for women

> no one ever told us we had to study our lives,
> make of our lives a study, as if learning natural history
> or music, . . . [p. 73].

To pursue that particular nature study, the woman turns from thoughts of the deer mother and her fawns to thoughts of a human mother and her infant, a subject also of much analytic attention. Rich notes, as have analytic observers, how that relatively brief relationship, which begins even before birth, has lengthy and impressive affective consequences.

> At most we're allowed a few months
> of simply listening to the simple line
> of a woman's voice singing a child
> against her heart. Everything else is too soon,
> too sudden, the wrenching-apart, that woman's heartbeat
> heard ever after from a distance,
> the loss of that ground-note echoing
> whenever we are happy, or in despair [pp. 73–74].

Rich compares the process of creating (such as writing a poem or thinking a new thought) to birth, that first dramatic separation. In both processes, there is pain in leaving familiar positions, however cramped and unsuitable they have become to sustain life or thought. Such separations bring fears of exile and annihilation, although it would be certain stagnation and death to continue as we are.

> . . . there come times . . .
> when we have to take ourselves more seriously or die;
> when we have to pull back from the incantations,
> rhythms we've moved to thoughtlessly,
> and disenthrall ourselves, . . .
> . . . We cut the wires,
> find ourselves in free-fall . . . .
> No one who survives to speak
> new language, has avoided this:
> the cutting-away of an old force that held her
> rooted to an old ground
> the pitch of utter loneliness [pp. 74–75].

Rich's woman protagonist/narrator labors, in spite of fear and intellectual loneliness, to give birth to new thoughts about her love for another woman. To achieve this, she must separate herself from the incantatory power of a set of ideas prevalent in the general culture and in much analytic thinking. She must "disenthrall" herself from the notion that lesbian relationships are psychologically immature because they originate in or replicate early mother–child emotional intimacy. She must pull back from the internal thoughts and external incantations that insist "it is unnatural, /the homesickness for a woman, for ourselves." By remembering and affirming a child's sensual experience with its mother, the narrator is able to affirm as natural her sensual love for another woman. And, from this new perspective, she becomes able to see, instead of pathological development and immaturity,

> . . . two women, eye to eye
> measuring each other's spirit, each other's
> limitless desire,
> > a whole new poetry beginning here [p.76].

The poem now moves in a new direction. The woman sits alone at a kitchen table, quietly, by lamplight, "feeling" her way through assorted bits of materials. Instead of examining the variety of the natural world outside her window, she begins to study the variety of shapes and textures inside.

> Vision begins to happen in such a life
> as if a woman quietly walked away
> from the argument and jargon in a room
> and sitting down in the kitchen, began turning in her lap
> bits of yarn, calico and velvet scraps,
> laying them out absently on the scrubbed boards
> in the lamplight [p.76].

Although it is never possible to free ourselves so easily from the "arguments and jargon" of our culture, nevertheless, a certain kind of "vision" also may "begin to happen" for those in analytic therapy who make of their own lives a study. When old incantations, old "rhythms moved to thoughtlessly," are recognized and understood, new psychic compositions may take form.

> Such a composition has nothing to do with eternity,
> the striving for greatness, brilliance—

only with the musing of a mind
one with her body, . . .
pulling the tenets of a life together
with no mere will to mastery,
only care for the many-lived, unending
forms in which she finds herself [p.77].

## Psychoanalysis as Kitchen-Table Collage

Rich's woman, sitting alone with her thoughts, feeling her way through varied fragments, assembling a collage of the "unending forms in which she finds herself," is a literary descendant of the many spinners, "spinsters," weavers, and quilt-makers of folk tales, literature, and history, women whose creations, unlike those of Romantic poets, frequently had "nothing to do with eternity, the striving for greatness, brilliance." Unsigned textile compositions, usually domestic articles for practical daily use, were the anonymous creations of unknown artists, often women.[1] Freud (1933a) once suggested that women invented woven materials out of shame in order to cover their inferior genitals, but there is nothing necessarily "female," nor necessarily defensive, about weaving, and Freud (1930) also used weaving as a metaphor for the sublimation of artistic creation.[2] Spinning wool thread from animal hair, turning used scraps of cloth into warm bed coverings, turning fine silk threads into a cloth that tells a story in pictures, all are processes through which simple materials are gradually, through careful, repeated movements, transformed into new objects for daily use.

Weaving/quilting/collage assemblage all make fitting metaphors for psychoanalytic treatment, a relationship process through which multiple strands of variously textured experiences, of various origins, are repeatedly felt their way through and examined. Apparently disparate or unexamined materials are reseen or rearranged to form a new psychic composition more useful to its maker. Psychoanalysis provides a relational and intrapsychic opportunity for the patient to appreciate and know her "many lived" dimensions.

Stephen Mitchell (1988) has used weaving as a metaphor for psychic processes. He recalls the story of that famous weaving wife, Penelope, whose husband, Odysseus, had been away from home for 19 years and given up for dead. Penelope conceived a scheme to keep her besieging suitors at bay while she awaited her husband's return. She said that she could not marry until she had woven a shroud for her father-in-law. Penelope wove by day and tore out her weaving each night, a labor of love, loyalty, and clever deception, the last a talent for which Odysseus was famous and that he greatly admired in his wife.

While acknowledging Penelope's poignant dedication, Mitchell nevertheless asserts that "she is not interested in entering this world of new possibilities and wants to wait for Odysseus's return" (p. 272). Mitchell goes on then to compare "the relational matrix within which each of us lives [to] a tapestry":

> Like Penelope, each of us weaves and unravels. . . . Like Penelope in the seeming purposiveness of her daytime labors, we experience our lives as directional and linear. . . . Yet, like Penelope in her nighttime sabotage, we unconsciously counterbalance our efforts, complicate our intended goals, seek out and construct the very restraints and obstacles we struggle against. Psychopathology in its infinite variations reflects our unconscious commitment to stasis, to embeddedness in and deep loyalty to the familiar [pp. 272–273].

We share Mitchell's belief that unconscious commitment to stasis works deadly sabotage. And, while it is true that one can be too tightly strung ("the tenacity and complexity of psychopathology, the tightness and durability of Penelope's weave," p. 291), Mitchell's metaphor ignores significant aspects of Penelope's situation that are also pertinent to psychic tapestries. Penelope's suitors were not inviting her to a "world of new possibilities." They simply wanted Odysseus's estate. They were eating Penelope out of house and home, plotting the murder of her son Telemachus, whose inheritance she was trying to protect, and in general being thoroughly rowdy and unwanted houseguests. Those insistent suitors—the goddess Athena calls them "a gang"—seem more appropriate candidates for the "infinite variations" of pathology than does Penelope's tight weave or her "embeddedness" in "the familiar." With guests like these in residence, one sets up repetitive defenses, until, at least in epics, a hero, aided by divine assistance, finally arrives to put the house in order.

In contrast to Penelope, Rich's collage-maker/weaver has a room of her own, a quiet kitchen table at which she sorts her materials into new compositions. She can silence the voices that would disturb her internal peace. Many, however, do not have the equivalent of that quiet constructive state. Their internal worlds resemble Penelope's: under siege, in forced stasis, their resources consumed and their energies spent holding the fort against uninvited, demanding pests whom they are unable to banish. Some intervention, not necessarily heroic or divine, is needed.

Psychoanalysis provides a relational equivalent to that quiet room and kitchen table. It offers a relational process through which patients may settle down to sort themselves out. Rich's collage maker lays out her materials "absently." That is, she explores semiconsciously, unconsciously. In Winnicott's terms, she "plays" with her materials and thereby creates the potential for the "spontaneous gesture," that moment in which something *new* can happen. Jean Sanville (1991) believes that the analyst's first task is to help patients lessen their rigid patterns of thinking and relating—Mitchell's "unconscious commitment to stasis"—so that they may also be able to play with their materials. Sanville has described how, with sufficient patient–therapist fit and clinical care, transference becomes a relational playground in which a patient unconsciously constructs, from memory, fantasy, and experiences with the actual therapist in the here-and-now, new editions of old fears and longings, conflicts, achievements, stalemates, dilemmas, strategies (Shor and Sanville, 1979). Over the course of treatment, through repeated encounters with her own unconscious transference creations and with her analyst's responses, a patient comes to recognize herself in many forms, as a woman with her own jagged sharpness, as well as her own abilities to soothe and to mend,

> becoming now the sherd of broken glass
> slicing light in a corner, dangerous
> to flesh, now the plentiful, soft leaf
> that wrapped around the throbbing finger, soothes the wound;
> and now the stone foundation, rockshelf further
> forming underneath everything that grows [Rich, 1978,
>     p. 77].

Ideally, when patients leave treatment having internalized the analytic relationship and its functions, they have greater access to their own quiet kitchen tables for their continuing self-analyses.

## An Orlando Psyche: "Selves Like Plates on a Waiter's Hand"

But what is "the self" of any analysis? The term self can imply that behavior, experience, and identifications, including sexual desire and object choice, are relatively stable or fixed or that, at least, there is a basic or primary "core" of identity to be discovered or more fully articulated through treatment. Freud sometimes compared psychoanalysis to an archeological or geological enterprise that probes deeper and deeper until it reaches the core of the neurosis. At one time Freud believed that the "unpenetrable" psychological bedrock upon which female development rested was a disappointed desire for a penis. Freud (1931) later glimpsed what he believed to be an even deeper and earlier, "Minoan," layer of female psychic development. He speculated that women might have better access than men to the unfortunately named "preoedipal" period.

But searching for a primary, essential, bedrock psychological layer— including the search for a core "sexual orientation"—may also be a premature defensive foreclosure thrown up against the discomforts of uncertainty, complexity, variety, and ambiguity. Some patients, such as Hannah in Chapter 6, preoccupy themselves with the search for etiology and bedrock and in so doing defend against the anxieties of choice. For some women, "lesbian" feels like bedrock identity; for some women who love women, other aspects of their identity, such as being a mother, or a journalist, or a poet, contribute as much or more to their sense of who they "really" are. Rich describes "the stone foundation" as "further forming underneath everything that grows," an image suggesting that even what might be seen as core is itself still in the process of becoming.

Freud (1887–1902) once wrote Fleiss that he was "accustoming myself to the idea of regarding every sexual act as a process in which four persons are involved" (p. 289). Leonard Shengold (1989) suggested that "Freud's 'four' was pitifully inadequate."

> One's identity is a multidimensional web, consisting of myriad introjected images from early childhood of one's parents, modified by later editions of them and their successors. These images are in all states of transformations into pictures of one's former and present selves, and of coalescence with these pictures. These composite, time-transcending, kaleidoscopic images are somehow held together by the synthesizing structure of our minds, our cinematic historical museums. My inadequate metaphor attempts to evolve this complicated dynamism, which wavers between transient organization and near chaos [pp. 35–36].

In our own search for useful metaphors for the dynamic unconscious processes that shape subjective experience, we turn to the work of Freud's English publisher, Virginia Woolf, who with her husband Leonard owned and operated the Hogarth Press. In 1924 the Woolfs began to publish Freud's work, in translations by their Bloomsbury neighbors and colleagues, Alix and James Strachey and Joan Riviere. Might psychoanalytic theory have developed somewhat differently if Freud had read the work of his publisher?

In many novels Virginia Woolf developed a theme quite consonant with Freud's assertion that subjective experience is unconstrained by time, place, or sex and that mentally and emotionally we wander freely through wide-ranging identifications. *Orlando* (Woolf, 1928) is a story about the multiple psychic "times" coexisting within what is called "the present moment." To know one's own mind, for Woolf, was not simply a matter of knowing what various times one is experiencing, sometimes simultaneously; it was also realizing the various "selves" one is "being" from moment to moment, also simultaneously.

> For if there are (at a venture) seventy-six different times all ticking in the mind at once, how many different people are there not—Heaven help us—all having lodgment at one time or another in the human spirit? . . . So that it is the most usual thing in the world for a person to say, directly they are alone, Orlando? (if that is one's name) meaning by that, Come, come! I'm sick to death of this particular self. I want another. Hence, the astonishing changes we see in our friends [p. 201].

Woolf stressed the influence of contexts on subjectivity. Instead of describing a "self," or even "an internal world," Woolf emphasized the simultaneous existence of multiple nascent states that shift in intensity and importance in response to external context as well as internal cues.

> For though one may say, as Orlando said (being out in the country and needing another self presumably), Orlando? still the Orlando she needs may not come; these selves of which we are built up, one on top of another, as plates are piled on a waiter's hand, have attachments elsewhere, sympathies, little constitutions and rights of their own, call them what you will (and for many of these things there is no name) so that one will only come if it is raining, another in a room with green curtains, another when Mrs. Jones is not there, another if you can promise it a glass of wine—and so on; for everybody can multiply from its own experience the different terms which his different selves have made with him—and some are too wildly ridiculous to be mentioned in print at all [pp. 201–202].

Some might see in Woolf's analogy of the waiter's hand a representation of a core self or primary identity. We prefer to see the waiter's hand as a necessary background, that is, unconscious, ego function. Just as the most skilled waiters carry multiple (although not limitless) plates "without thinking"—that is, they carry them unconsciously—the most psychologically flexible psyches manage multiple (although not infinite) identifications, and move among numerous (but not infinite) affective states, with ease. When this function has been insufficiently developed, or has become momentarily overwhelmed, all states and identifications feel precarious and dangerous. Rigid structures arise to keep things in order; physical as well as psychological flexibility, fluidity, and balance are diminished.

Perhaps if Freud had read Woolf, in addition to revising his original two-layer topographical model of the psyche into a three-part system of structural conflict, he might have imagined an even more complex "mental apparatus," one whose multiple structures each had "attachments elsewhere, sympathies, little constitutions and rights of their own" and each called up by external contexts as well as internal cues. Such a design offers greater dynamic possibilities than binary and three-part models. With such a dynamic model of mental functioning, psychoanalysis might have more quickly broken free from crippling dichotomous thinking—conscious/unconscious, latent/manifest, active/passive, masculine/feminine; homosexuality/heterosexuality—all clumsy lenses through which to observe subjectivity. Rather than telling and retelling two narratives of early development, "the oedipal" and "the preoedipal," developmental theory might have more easily stressed the significance of multiple, simultaneous narratives. Analysts might have more easily recognized transferences and countertransferences in shifting emotional time zones. Psychoanalysis might have had better access to more subtle dimensions of psychic experience and better theories to explain the access it does have, many of which are still "things for which there are no name."[3]

Freud did read the work of Woolf's Bloomsbury neighbors, such as her brother-in-law Lytton Strachey's *Elizabeth and Essex*, which was published in the same year as Woolf's *Orlando*.[4] And the Stracheys and their circle read Freud, as did much of intellectual and bohemian London in the 1920s and 1930s.[5] If Freud did indeed ignore the work of women writers such as Woolf, his gender-bound reading would not have been seen as an intellectual handicap. It was simply evidence of the literary discrimination to be expected of an educated man of his day, and of all days. Until pressure in the 1970s from feminists in college and university "women's studies" departments, the literary canon contained few works by women authors. The novels of Woolf, of the Brontes, of Austin remained "women's fiction," works whose plots and characters did not represent that generic "Man." The authors, narrators, and protagonists of literary narratives have been, until quite recently, predominantly male.

Ironically, that female *exclusion* actually set in motion certain *gender expanding* experiences for literate women. Women who read, of necessity, imagined themselves undertaking the adventures of the central character, a male hero. A reader, whether male or female, becomes Ulysses, bewitched by Circe, becomes Oedipus blind to his own beginnings, becomes Hamlet, catching the king's conscience, or Candide, determined to tend *his* own garden. Because she was female, Virginia Woolf was denied an education at the universities her brothers and husband and male friends attended. Woolf educated herself, through reading. *Orlando* is, among other matters, a playful depiction of reading as a gender-expanding experience. Late 19th- and early 20th-century male gynecologists feared the social and physical consequences of such reading. They warned that higher education for women would lead to physical illness and female infertility.[6]

Women writers, of necessity, also experimented with cross-gender identifications, "passing" as men in order to be published. George Eliot and George Sand wrote under male pseudonyms, finding in this strategy, according to Carolyn Heilbrun (1988), an enlarged psychic space in which to create, as well as a way to get their work read by male publishers and readers. Flaubert could not envision George Sand, whom he admired greatly, as a mere female. He addressed his letters to Sand "Dear Master" and "Oh you, of the third sex," expanding her gender to reflect what he saw as her enlarged capacities. Hilda Doolittle enjoyed the sexual ambiguity of her *nomme de plume*, "H.D." She found its "pattern of letters" "a good signature for a writer." H.D.'s partner, Annie Winifred Ellerman, who introduced her to psychoanalysis and to Freud, legally changed her own name to the equally sexually ambiguous, Bryher. Elaine Showalter et al. (1993) point out that American women writers of the modern period were less likely than their European and English counterparts to take male names, although they note that *Mary* Flannery O'Connor and *Lula* Carson McCullers "dropped their girlish first names when they began to write" (p. x).

To widen their horizons, women may hide their sex and display behaviors, functions, and capacities previously gendered masculine. But a similar process has not been necessary or available for men. Male readers, for example, never had the same need—and thus opportunity—to cross-sex read as did women. Freud missed the possibilities that reading the work of his female publisher might have brought.[7] Although Flaubert might say, "*Madame Bovary; c'est moi*," male readers did not feel their intellectual horizons enlarged by imagining themselves Emma Bovary, stuck in the provenances (literally "places of origin"). If most men did not find it psychologically or intellectually broadening to imagine themselves Flaubert's Emma Bovary or Tolstoy's Anna Karenina, heroines whose passions led to social isolation and suicide, even less did they think it worthwhile to identify with the female protagonists created by women writers. The limited adventures possible for the Bronte sisters' fictional governesses, or Austin's Emma, or Elliot's Dorothea Brook were only too apparent. Nor would male writers have expected their work to have a greater chance of being published and read if they took a feminine pen name. Ezra Pound, H.D.'s one-time fiancé, who helped her find her writing name, would never have considered writing under a name that hid his sex.

These pervasive social realities contribute more to the ways gender identifications are internalized and maintained—as well as undone, expanded, and revised—than psychoanalytic developmental theories have yet managed to appreciate. Preoccupied with noting the early emotional consequences of discovering genital sexual differences, psychoanalysis has given short shrift to exploring other important ways gender works psychically. And psychoanalytic theory has been further handicapped by a persistent conflation of "gender identity disturbances" with homosexuality. Some who are currently rethinking gender understand that psychoanalysis must revise its understanding of male and female development as well as related notions about object choice.

The following chapters explore themes introduced in this prologue. We examine psychoanalytic formulations of female homosexuality. We review biological models of the etiology of female homosexuality that have gone in and out of psychoanalytic fashion. We turn away from biological and psychological arguments to assemble other kinds of materials for examination. We examine the historical backdrop for Freud's abbreviated treatment of an 18-year-old feminist in love with an older independent woman in Vienna in 1920. We compare Freud's patient's understanding of her love to that of her fictional contemporaries, Ruth and Idgie in Flagg's (1987) *Fried Green Tomatoes*, set in the American South of the late 1920s and 30s. We read unpublished letters between Bryher, an English heiress, lesbian patient, and would-be analyst in Weimar Berlin, and her analyst, Hanns Sachs. We compare the challenges facing women with lesbian identity in the United States several decades ago with the choices available for such women today. We discuss clinical examples from the published psychoanalytic literature and offer others from our own practices. We skim the headlines of contemporary news articles about gay and lesbian issues. We read poetry and cultural criticism by lesbian writers. Our composition, like that of Rich's absently playing woman with her kitchen table collage, "has nothing to do with eternity"—with illustrating any universal, essential, psychological or sexual entity called "female homosexuality." On the contrary, we assemble these materials to provide psychoanalytic readers heightened appreciations of the "many-lived forms" of women who love women.

# INTRODUCTION

## PSYCHOANALYTIC, HISTORICAL, AND LITERARY NARRATIVES OF FEMALE SAME-SEX RELATIONSHIPS

> Whatever is unnamed, undepicted in images, whatever is omitted from biography, censored in collections of letters, whatever is misnamed as something else, made difficult-to-come-by, whatever is buried in the memory by the collapse of meaning under an inadequate or lying language—this will become, not merely unspoken, but *unspeakable*.
>
> *[Adrienne Rich (1976, p. 199)]*

> Whosoever shall be guilty of Rape, Polygamy, or Sodomy with man or woman shall be punished, if a man, by castration, if a woman, by cutting thro' the cartilage of her nose a hole of one half inch diameter at the least.
>
> *[Thomas Jefferson, 1779, Revision of Virginia Law][1]*

When we began psychoanalytic training, we each believed that through seminars, clinical supervision, and our own training analyses we would come to understand the etiology of female homosexuality. We believed that psychoanalysis could help explain why, in spite of severe stigma, some women claimed lesbian identities and established lesbian relationships. We shared Eve Kosofsky Sedgwick's (1990) hope that "psychoanalytic theory, if only through the almost astrologically lush plurality of its overlapping taxonomies of physical zones, developmental stages, representational mech-anisms, and levels of consciousness, seemed to promise a certain becoming amplitude into discussions of what people are like . . ." (pp. 23–24). We hoped, in the words of Diane Hamer (1990), "to move towards a psycho-analytic understanding of lesbian identity . . . a contingent identity con-structed from individual biographical details rather than as something authentic, natural, pre-given—without pathologizing it, without making it a symptom of a sickness" (p. 135).

We knew that many of our gay and lesbian colleagues doubted that psy-choanalytic developmental theory, in which normative development was by definition heterosexual, could ever be useful for understanding lesbian rela-tionships. Psychoanalysts from Ernest Jones (1927) to Elaine Siegel (1988) have described female homosexuality as a consequence of pathological development, unconscious conflict, and disturbed object relations. As psy-choanalytic theories evolved from early drive theory through ego psychol-ogy and object relations models, there were corresponding changes in the particular developmental disturbances thought to produce female homo-sexuality, as well as corresponding changes in the particular psychological characteristics ascribed to homosexual women. Only a few exceptional ana-lysts, such as Stephen Mitchell (1978), Judd Marmor (1980a, b), and Robert Stoller (1985), were critical of the prevailing psychoanalytic practice of attributing common denominators of etiology and character to homosex-ual persons.

Some colleagues insisted that biological research rather than psychoan-alytic developmental theory would help answer the vexing questions of who was homosexual and why. Some gay male therapists felt that their own expe-riences and their patients' experiences of early, persistent sexual attraction to other males indicated a constitutional predilection to homosexuality. Richard Isay (1989), for instance, sees "sexual orientation . . . as immutable from birth" ( p. 21). The popular press reports "findings" of hormonal, genetic, and chromosomal differences between "homosexuals" and "het-erosexuals." Simon LeVay (1991), one of the most media-celebrated gay sci-entists, concluded that his research had established "that sexual orientation in humans is amenable to study at the biological level, and this discovery opens the door to studies of neurotransmitters or receptors that might be involved in regulating this aspect of personality" ( p. 1036). Many hope that biological research will end the association of pathology with homosexual-ity, an association to which psychoanalytic formulations have consistently contributed.

In our analytic work we found that we could not distinguish the early psychological developments of our lesbian patients from the early development of other patients. Our lesbian patients did not fit the developmental profiles described by any of the psychoanalytic theorists of female homosexuality. Nor did we find transference presentations or structural conflicts in our lesbian patients that in any way differentiated them as a group from other patients. But we discovered that biological studies of female homosexuality did not offer alternatives to pathological formulations about etiology. In place of psychoanalytic theories about disturbed early object relations, biology hypothesized homosexuality as a product of disturbed prenatal hormones. In place of psychoanalytic assertions of a "masculinity complex" or a "gender identity disturbance," biological researchers measured mounting behaviors in female rats and speculated about "latency rough and tumble play" in girls born with congenital adrenal hyperplasia (CAH).

We began to see that the apparently simple question "What causes female homosexuality?" contained unquestioned assumptions about the feelings, behaviors, and relationships of women who love women. Psychoanalysis has been a major contributor to these assumptions and has profoundly influenced contemporary understanding of what it is to be lesbian. Although Freud and his sexologist contemporaries disagreed about whether lesbian relationships were psychologically or biologically determined, they all saw women who loved women in sexual terms. This new practice of sexualizing women's relationships was to have radical and far-reaching consequences. In the two previous centuries women, or at least some women, had intimate and passionate attachments that had been understood to be natural as well as asexual (Faderman, 1981). Only prostitutes, women of the lower classes or lesser races, or women otherwise "degenerate" had sexual relations with one another. Freud's (1920) apparently simple description of his patient as a "beautiful and clever girl" from "a family of good standing" was actually a radical allegation. In those simple phrases Freud asserted that the daughters of respectable families, women who were neither physically, socially, or mentally degenerate, could sexually desire other women.

Unfortunately, however, the newly ascribed sexuality of women who loved women was understood to be a function of their essentially (psychologically or constitutionally) *masculine nature*. Women who loved women were *inverts*; that is, they were the sexual and psychological *opposites* of women who loved men. Although that assumption has undergone various revisions and refinements, its basic structure remains unchanged and continues to pervade psychoanalytic discussions of female homosexuality. One consequence has been that women in lesbian relationships must continually struggle to affirm the qualities and capacities they often share with women in heterosexual relationships, such as the ability and desire to bear and to raise children. Another consequence of psychoanalytic and sexologist definitions of same-sex relationships is that other powerful relational motivations were ignored or devalued. Freud's patient insisted that her love was not based on sexual attraction. Freud dismissed her statement as a reflection of societally induced sexual repression. To suggest that relationships of lesbian women (as well as those of other persons) are sustained by significant drives and powerful longings other than, or in addition to, simple sexual attraction still sounds to many like psychological naiveté and sexual repression.

## Twenty Centuries of Historical Omissions and Silences

Relying on sexual desire as the measure of, and defining characteristic of, female same-sex love has created, however, curious problems for historians, biographers, and literary scholars. By that measure, few examples of female same-sex love or relationships can be found in historical records. It is not that homosexual behavior was unknown in previous periods of history. In premodern Europe both religious and civil laws forbade female as well as male same-sex sex acts, and the penalty for disobedience was often death. But ecclesiastical and secular court records reveal that, unlike men, few women were actually found guilty of such acts and fewer still faced the death penalty.[2] It is not that women in those centuries were not seen as sexual persons. In premodern Europe women were actually considered the lustful sex. Closer to "nature," and therefore deficient in the "higher" functions of logic, rationality, and intellect, women were thought to fall prey more easily to temptations of the flesh than were men. Were the women of those centuries more surreptitious in their sexual encounters with one another, more clever at avoiding detection? Judith Brown (1986b) maintains that the historical silence about female same-sex behavior is evidence of societal censorship. She argues that, even more than male same-sex love, female same-sex love became "the silent sin." It was considered so detestable, so thoroughly against God and nature that it could scarcely be mentioned or written about. "Crimes that cannot be named, thus, literally had no name and left few traces in the historical record" (p. 75).[3]

That argument could find support in the court decisions of later centuries. When in 1811 two Scottish school mistresses were accused of "unnatural acts" together, English justices could not find them guilty, even though the charge against them was made by the granddaughter of a woman with impeccable social connections. The justices simply could not believe school mistresses capable of such vile acts and feelings (see Faderman, 1981, 1983). A century later, in 1921, when the English Parliament debated whether to include lesbianism in the new laws against homosexuality, the authorities again wanted to keep the very existence of female homosexuality a secret.

> "You are going to tell the whole world that there is such an offense, to bring it to the notice of women who have never heard of it, never thought of it, never dreamt of it. I think that is a very great mischief." said Lord Desart.
> The lord chancellor concurred: "I would be bold enough to say that of every thousand women, taken as a whole, 999 have never heard a whisper of these practices" [quoted in Hart and Richardson, 1981, p. 105].

Lynda Hart (1994) observed that the "British legislators thus found themselves confronting a rather odd predicament—should they formally prohibit something that virtually did not exist?" (p. 3).

The silences of the historical records are matched by similar silences in literary history. The words of women writing about their sexual longing for other women begin, and all but end, with a few fragments of poetry, all that remain of the work of Sappho, a 6th-century B. C. E. lyric poet from Mitylene. Sappho probably ran a girls' school or cultural salon on the island of Lesbos. Sappho was the mother of a "priceless" daughter, "golden Cleis," and was respected among her contemporaries for her passionate lyric verses, especially her *epithalamia*, or songs written to celebrate marriages.[4]

A long silence falls after Sappho speaks. For over 20 centuries few women write of same-sex love. So few, in fact, that when the sexologists wanted a name for sexual passion between women, they had no names to use but Sappho's and the name of her island. Gay and lesbian historians have added the names and voices of other women. Jeannette Foster (1956) rediscovered Mary Wollstonecraft's *Mary, A Fiction*. The novel was written several years before Wollstonecraft's famous *Vindication of the Rights of Women*. It is based on her love for Fanny Blood, a love that Wollstonecraft's husband, William Godwin, called "the ruling passion of her mind" (cited in Foster, 1956, p. 56).[5] John Boswell (1980) translated love letters between two nuns in a 12th-century Bavarian monastery. Judith Brown (1986a) examined lesbian sexuality in a convent in Renaissance Italy. Lillian Faderman (1994) added poets from the 17th century.

But where are the words of women other than Sappho and a few clois-tered nuns? Where are the texts other than some fragments of poetry, a few letters, and an out-of-print novel by Mary Wollstonecraft? Historian Martha Vicinus (1989) points out that women who loved women have always been "hidden from history." She has suggested certain "parameters" of historiog-raphy, which we see as relevant to analytic researchers trying to understand lesbian women: "We must first decode female sexual desire, and then within it, find same-sex desire. By necessity we need to be sensitive to nuance, masks, secrecy, and the unspoken. If we look to the margins, to the ruptures and breaks, we will be able to piece together a history of women speaking to each other" (p. 434).

Female homosexuality cannot be understood without reference to the position and status of women in culture. Only in recent history have some women had the economic means, legal rights, and social sanction to live independently from their fathers, husbands, or other male relatives, much less the economic means, legal right, or social sanction to establish primary relationships with one another. Over the centuries a few women did obtain some measure of financial, legal, and social independence. Some came to such power through inheritance. A daughter who was an only child might, in some periods, inherit her father's kingdom or his guild membership. A few women gained independence by crossing gender boundaries and actu-ally "passing" as men. Such a woman's relationship with another woman "passed" as a heterosexual marriage. If the nature of that marriage was dis-covered, the punished transgression was seldom the sexual behavior between the women. The considerably more consequential behavior of women who passed as men was their assumption of male economic and social privilege. Passing as a man by wearing men's clothing allowed a woman to do "men's" work and to earn "men's" wages, to travel freely, and to live independently. These behaviors actually contributed more to "the passing woman's" status as social deviant than did any sexual behavior.[6] By the mid-19th century, some women in Europe and the United States had begun to acquire certain measures of economic and social independence. Many women who longed for such independence and longed to establish primary relationships with one another did not use the language of sexual desire to describe what they wanted. They spoke in language such as that which in 1836 Charlotte Bronte wrote to Ellen Nussey: "Ellen, I wish I could live with you always. I begin to cling to you more fondly than I ever did. If we had a cottage and a competency of our own I do think we might love until Death without being dependent on any third person for happiness." (Quoted in Foster, 1956, p. 133). Bronte's desire was for independence, a relationship of equal partners, and meaningful work for herself and the woman she loved. Many contemporary lesbian women would share Bronte's longings for cottage and competency.

By the late 19th century, some middle-class women who had acquired their independence either through access to education or through inheritance of economic resources established partnerships sometimes called "Boston marriages," so named because these primary relationships between women were common in Boston, a center of middle-class prosperity and higher education for women. As women began to be admitted for the first time to American colleges and later to graduate schools, their friendships with one another later developed into female social networks that supported women's independence. Some of these college graduates, known as "New Women," made their living teaching, writing, publishing. Others established settlement houses, or organized for women's rights, children's issues, and married couples' access to birth control. Some emigrated to European capitals such as Paris and Berlin. Some became anthropologists in the American Southwest. Some formed female partnerships that flourished during the first three decades of the 20th-century.[7] Like the Boston marriages, those female unions did not enter the historical record as female love relationships. Histories and biographies described those writers, teachers, social workers, political activists, and anthropologists as "single" women, intellectually bright but romantically impaired bluestockings, or admirably hardworking, selfless, asexual, and lonely "spinsters." Their female relationships were erased from the records or made inconsequential and devalued.[8] Working-class lesbian relationships are even more invisible during this period.[9]

Therefore, in the 1940s and 1950s, when women who loved women looked for earlier women who had loved as they did, they found those 20 centuries of silence. They found fictional descriptions of female-female sexual behavior written by male writers, such as Cleland's (1749) *Fanny Hill: Memoirs of a Woman of Pleasure*, Theophile Gautier's (1835) *Mademoiselle de Maupin*, and Henri Balzac's (1835) *The Girl with The Golden Eyes*. In Balzac's novel the beautiful heroine kills her female lover, an early version of the violent, borderline lesbian.[10] They found contemporary pulp fiction descriptions of lonely, depressed, and suicidal women whose lives had been ruined by their inverted sexual desires. They found Krafft-Ebing's descriptions in *Psychopathia Sexualis* (1886), complete with detailed physical measurements of his subjects' genitals. They found sexologists' descriptions of women with "masculine" bodies and "masculine" minds.[11] They found psychoanalytic descriptions of "forsworn womanhood," penis envy, revenge against men, and disturbed mother–daughter relationships. What they did *not* find, however, were the female relationships that sustained some of the most respected members of the first generations of modern women.

In the late 1960s, women from the "second wave" of feminism began to examine women's history and literature. Some researchers were shocked by the intimacy and the passionate attachments to women revealed in the letters, diaries, and contemporaneous records of many women leaders. Some wanted to censor the passion described in those documents in order to save the reputations of respected women. How could such respected women have been homosexual? They did not resemble Balzac's sexual libertines or the illustrations in sexology texts of prostitutes, criminals, psychotics, and social outcasts. And even though two women shared cottage and competency, and often the same bed, could one call such relationships "sexual"? Was there proof of genital sex between the women? If not, then how could the women or their relationships be called lesbian?

Feminist biographers of women such as social activists Nobel Peace Prize winner Jane Addams and her companion, Mary Rozet Smith, and of educators such as Mount Holyoke President Miss Woolley and her teacher companion, Miss Marks, and of psychoanalyst Anna Freud and her companion Dorothy Burlingham faced a peculiar problem. What should they call the primary relationship of their subjects' lives? What names should be given to two women who may have lived together for 40 or 50 years, raised children together, established and run institutions together, and shared their lives and fortunes in sickness and health until parted by death? To call their relationship "homosexual" or "lesbian" sexualized the relationship and might be seen as an insult to the subject of the biography or at least might give the subject a name she did not call herself. But to call that relationship a "friendship" because of the absence of, or deemphasis on, specific sexual behaviors would once again grant secondary significance to the women's lifelong physical, emotional, and intellectual intimacy and would constitute a new kind of silencing by granting emotional primacy only to a woman's sexual relationships—or her lack of such relationships—with men.[12]

## Omissions from Psychoanalytic Histories and Narratives.

Although historians and literary scholars have been struggling for some decades with such conceptual issues and with the omissions and distortions of previous biographies and histories, psychoanalysts have been largely ignorant of these issues. They have only recently begun to address their own conceptual problems, historical silences, and omissions on the subject of homosexuality. In the course of our research we read psychoanalytic articles and books on homosexuality and female development. We read feminist, and gay and lesbian, fiction, poetry, biography, literary criticism, history, and cultural analyses. If these works were arranged on our bookshelves by their author's primary identifications, those bookshelves would speak volumes about certain psychoanalytic silences.

Imagine three standing bookcases. The first bookcase contains works by psychoanalysts; the second contains works by feminists; the third contains the work of gay and lesbian writers. A few texts can be shelved in either the first or second bookcases because their authors identify as psychoanalysts and as feminists. Some works can be placed in either the second or third cases because their authors identify as feminists and as lesbian. When we began our own writing, not one book could be filed on either the first or third bookcase as the work of a homosexually identified psychoanalyst.[13]

Although the practice has always been officially denied, psychoanalytic institutes have excluded open homosexual therapists from training. Homosexual therapists have trained at and graduated from psychoanalytic institutes, but they had to manage various degrees of closetedness during the admissions process and throughout training and afterwards. Some never discussed their gay or lesbian relationships in their training analyses. In 1988, over 100 years after Freud's first publications, Kenneth Lewes (1988), writing on male homosexuality and psychoanalysis, could still state: "There has not been in the history I have sketched a single analytic writer who could identify himself as homosexual" (p. 238). The following year, Isay's (1989) *Being Homosexual* was published. Isay did not identify himself as gay in that text. In Isay's (1996) second book *Becoming Gay*, he describes his experiences coming out as a gay analyst.

One result of the often denied but persistently administered barrier to analytic training is that analysts who treat homosexual patients have had little opportunity for consultation with gay or lesbian clinical colleagues and little access to gay and lesbian literature and historical and cultural criticism. Theoretical and clinical discussions about homosexuality have taken place among heterosexually identified analysts. Lachmann (1975), Mitchell (1978), Kwawer(1980), Stoller (1985), Eisenbud (1986 ), and Marmor (1980a, b, c; 1996) have described the prejudices against homosexuality in analytic theory and practice; Stoller and Marmor were instrumental in the struggle within the American Psychiatric Association to depathologize homosexuality and to remove homosexuality as a diagnostic category from the *Diagnostic and Statistical Manual of Mental Disorders*. Marmor, Roughton (1996), and others continued to challenge American

Psychoanalytic Association policies prejudicial to homosexual therapists (see also Marcus, 1992; Nardi, Sanders, and Marmor, 1994). These significant contributions still left in place a fundamental split within psychoanalysis: analysts who treated homosexual patients did not claim homosexual identity; therapists who claimed homosexual identity could not have psychoanalytic training. This pervasive split affected psychoanalytic treatment, training, and publication.

## Gay and Lesbian Psychoanalysts

Our relationship has made our writing about psychoanalysis and lesbian women both possible and necessary. When we applied for psychoanalytic training in 1984, we knew of no openly gay and lesbian therapists who had ever been admitted to any psychoanalytic institute. We knew openly gay and lesbian therapists who had applied and been rejected. We knew therapists who had been admitted to analytic training, some of whom later identified as homosexual during or after their training. Over the next few years at meetings of the Association of Gay and Lesbian Psychiatrists we met a handful of gay and lesbian psychiatrists who were training at nonmedical psychoanalytic institutes. We learned that the first "coming out" by a homosexual analyst at a psychoanalytic conference was said to have taken place in 1982. On a panel presentation on group therapy, in an unplanned, spontaneous moment, Bertram Schaffner identified himself as homosexual, prompting another panel member, Norman Levy from the Horney Institute, to acknowledge that he too was homosexual. Recently, in some institutes, the barrier against admitting and training openly gay and lesbian therapists has been lifting, allowing a long-needed theoretical and clinical conversation to take place about homosexuality. For instance, academic psychoanalyst Elisabeth Young-Bruehl (1988) brought her psychoanalytic and historical training, as well as her feminist and lesbian perspectives to her biography of Anna Freud and to her commentaries (Young-Bruehl, 1990) on Freud's writing about women. In 1989 we saw, for the first time on a psychoanalytic panel, analysts who publicly identified as homosexual. Two of the four male panelists at that American Academy of Psychoanalysis presentation were from the William Alanson White Institute; the woman panelist was a Jungian analyst.[14]

Nineteen-ninety-three was a watershed year for gay and lesbian analysts. Mark Blechner (1993), Ronnie Lesser (1993), and David Schwartz (1993b) critically discussed the clinical work of Jeffrey Trop and Robert Stolorow

(1992) in a historic exchange in the journal *Psychoanalytic Dialogues*. English therapists Noreen O'Connor and Joanna Ryan (1993) published *Wild Desires and Mistaken Identities*, an extensive review of psychoanalysis and lesbianism, a work that might be filed in any of those three hypothetical bookcases, a text by writers who identify as psychoanalytic, feminist, and as lesbian. The first psychoanalytic conference on homosexuality to include gay and lesbian analysts was sponsored by the New York University Postdoctoral Program in Psychotherapy and Psychoanalysis. See *Disorienting Sexuality: Psychoanalytic Reappraisals of Sexual Identities*, (Domenici and Lesser, 1995), the collection of papers from this conference, to which Jack Drescher, April Martin, and Bertram Schaffner also contributed descriptions of their experiences in psychoanalytic training.[15]

## An Overview of This Narrative

Most psychoanalytic discussion of the treatment of lesbian patients have seen female homosexuality as a psychological consequence of early developmental disturbances. We also are interested in psychological development and its difficulties, but our project differs from previous analytic discussions of female homosexuality. We focus on the developmental and psychological consequences of identifying as homosexual and of having lesbian relationships. This text offers no *lesbian-specific* psychology, no *characteristic* family history, structural conflicts, internal object relations, or psychological developmental lines that lead to, or even make more likely, female same-sex relationships or sexual attraction. Readers who wish to know why any of our patients became homosexual will be disappointed. We do not believe that any psychological biography can reveal as clearly as some may wish what motivates any person's attraction to another. We do not believe, as did Freud in 1920, that it is possible to provide "the narration of a single case . . . in which it was possible to trace its origin and development in the mind with complete certainty and almost without a gap . . ." (p. 147).

Instead of gapless, causal explanations, we offer descriptions of some of the psychological consequences of being lesbian, given various psychodynamics, in specific social contexts. Furthermore, we believe that analytic therapists of lesbian patients would do well to set aside their search for a categorical etiology (or etiologies) of female homosexuality. Divested of categorical assumptions about homosexuality, analytic therapists will be better equipped to offer psychoanalytic treatment to their lesbian patients.

Divested of such preoccupations, they are better situated to examine what some analysts call the "internal world" of each individual patient, her ego strengths, narcissistic assets and vulnerabilities, characteristic conflicts and defenses, and internal object relationships. Lesbian patients may come to treatment with a variety of early developmental histories, but these disturbances will be indistinguishable in their content or severity from those of patients who are not lesbian. Psychoanalysts will find disturbed lesbian relationships, but they will also find lesbian relationships quite different from those previously described in the psychoanalytic literature. Finally, we believe that the psychoanalytic treatment of lesbian patients requires therapists to understand and appreciate certain aspects of the "external world," namely, the ideas, attitudes, and assumptions about same-sex relationships that *both* patient and therapist have received from family, class, ethnic, religious, institutional, legal, and cultural affiliations.

Chapter 1, "Superior Guinea-Pig," is our contribution to filling certain gaps in psychoanalytic history. It is the story of Annie Winifred Ellerman, who called herself Bryher. Brhyer was a contemporary of Freud, a lover of women, books, adventure, and psychoanalysis. The daughter of one of the richest men in England, Bryher had the financial independence to establish cottage and competency for herself and her lifelong companion, the American poet H. D. Heiress, writer, publisher, film producer, and for much of her life a generous financial supporter of psychoanalysis, Bryher was an analysand of Hanns Sachs, who actively encouraged and tried to arrange for her psychoanalytic training. If circumstances had been different in Europe in 1933, Bryher might have become the first lesbian psychoanalyst. Chapter 1 tells the story of Bryher and psychoanalysis through her unpublished letters to H. D., Sachs, Walter Schmideberg, and others.

Chapter 2, "The Story of Our Lives Becomes Our Lives," examines certain assumptions about homosexuality prevalent in Western culture and prominent in psychoanalytic theory. It examines certain motivations behind many persistent attempts to establish a sexual, or biological, or clinical category: homosexual. Psychoanalytic developmental theorists have constructed such a clinical category through polarizing theories of sexual development, gender identity, and object choice. We believe these models are problematic for the treatment of all patients and particularly limiting for understanding lesbian women. Throughout this book we use images and metaphors from lesbian literature to illustrate the kind of alternative psychoanalytic principles we find more useful for thinking about homosexuality. We like to call these principles *lesbian rules*, having found that term, to our surprise, in the *Oxford English Dictionary*. The *O.E.D.* defines a lesbian rule as "a principle which allows flexibility," a theoretical and clinical quality sorely missing in psychoanalytic formulations of homosexuality.

Chapter 3, "She Forswore Her Womanhood," critically reviews the major psychoanalytic and biological theories about female homosexuality. We argue that psychoanalytic as well as biological formulations are driven by categorical assumptions about etiology and development and by attributions of masculine (sexual or hormonal or psychological) characteristics to lesbian women. Richard C. Friedman and Jennifer Downey (1993) have proposed "that psychoanalytic theory can grow and profit from a careful consideration of new findings in the psychobiology of sexuality" (p. 1159), specifically homosexuality. Our review of that research finds little reason for such optimism.

Chapter 4, "Assaults and Harassments: The Violent Acts of Theorizing Lesbian Sexuality," explores a wilderness region on psychoanalysis' dark continent of female sexuality. Psychoanalysis has no model of psychologically mature sexuality between members of the same sex. Moreover, in spite of decades of revision, psychoanalytic discussions of female sexual development are still riddled with phallocentric assumptions. Some feminist theorists replace that phallocentrism with another sexual essentialism based on female anatomy. Some feminist psychoanalysts, as well as some lesbian therapists, suggest that female-female desire has its origins in an early mother–daughter relationship. They emphasize the sensual, "nonverbal" intimacies of that relationship and believe that the identifications established through this relationship produce a special capacity for emotional intimacy and communication between women. Other theorists fear that such "primitive" origins leave in their wake a developmental quicksand, an ever-threatening, regressive pull, a relationship ooze of failed psychological separation. In our attempt to chart the territory of lesbian sexuality, we rely on some maps suggested by Eve Kosofsky Sedgwick (1990). These well-known but little acknowledged aspects of sexual experience may help readers appreciate the variety of erotic possibilities in lesbian relationships.

Chapter 5, "Coming Out: The Necessity of Becoming a Bee-Charmer," attempts to redress one consequence of the historical refusal to train homosexual therapists. Psychoanalysts have been ignorant of the one phenomenon that clearly and dramatically distinguishes the psychosocial development of contemporary lesbian women from other women, namely, the continual challenge of *identifying as homosexual to self and others.* "Coming out" is not a one-time event; it is a daily and lifelong interpersonal and intrapsychic process that simultaneously reveals, creates, and limits identity. Its effects on development have had almost no psychoanalytic attention. How a woman manages these challenges depends on her age, class, race, and culture; her economic and social assets and vulnerabilities, and on her ego strengths, narcissistic supplies, characteristic defenses and conflicts. Images from *Fried Green Tomatoes at the Whistle Stop Cafe* (Flagg, 1987) illustrate the anxieties of identifying as homosexual. Case descriptions by Freud (1920) and Khan (1964) demonstrate the effects of these fears and confusions on patients and analysts alike. To *come out* is always a matter of *coming out into* a particular social/cultural context, with its particular beliefs about and attitudes toward homosexual relations. We discuss Freud's 1920 case in terms of its context, namely, the early 20th-century scientific and political debates about homosexuality and women's roles.

Chapter 6, "Moratoriums and Secrets: Searching for the Love of One's Life," offers extended clinical material from the analysis of an adult woman. Hannah's search for love is made doubly difficult as her narcissistic issues become entangled and confused with her fears of being lesbian. In this chapter we again examine interactions between individual psyches and specific social contexts. We compare the life choices available to Hannah, who was 18 years old in 1965, with the choices available to Freud's patient, who was 18 years old in 1920, and with the choices available to young women who identify as lesbian today.

Chapter 7, "What Sex Is an Amaryllis? What Gender Is Lesbian?" examines some problems and paradoxes of current psychoanalytic gender identity models. Although few contemporary psychoanalysts still attribute a "masculinity complex" to their lesbian patients, the long-standing psychoanalytic association of female homosexuality with masculinity persists. "Gender identity disturbance" and "homosexuality" have become synonymous in much analytic thinking. Illustrations from clinical work with a lesbian patient and with a heterosexual man illustrate multiple, shifting, and changeable states of gendered and gender-free subjectivity, experience too often reduced to sex and gender shorthand by theorists of gender identity, as well as by therapists and their patients.

Chapter 8, "When the Psychoanalyst Is Lesbian: A Certain Idealization of Heterosexuality," addresses some clinical dilemmas when the analyst is known to be lesbian. Many analysts question the appropriateness of training lesbian and gay therapists. Many more would be critical of gay and lesbian analysts disclosing their homosexuality. And still others might doubt whether a patient of an analyst known to have a homosexual relationship could develop the necessary transferences for a therapeutic analysis. We offer several illustrations of transference development when the analyst is known to be lesbian.

In 1987, Richard Isay proposed that the American Psychoanalytic Association take a position similar to the one taken 15 years earlier by the American Psychiatric Association, namely, that it go on record opposing discrimination against homosexuality. It took five years of internal debate before, in 1992, the American Psychoanalytic Association finally endorsed the American Psychiatric Association position. The final chapter describes some of our experiences in training, summarizes briefly the history of American institutional psychoanalysis and homosexual therapists, and looks forward to future changes in the policies and practices of psychoanalytic training.

## Contemporary Texts and Contexts

Unlike those of the previous, silent centuries, the words of women who love women are easily available today. Publishers' catalogues and bookstores are filled with works by lesbian-identified writers. Electronic bulletin boards, forums, web pages, and data bases provide national and international communication. One can download bibliographies of lesbian artists and writers, can e-mail lesbian academics or astrologers. An electronic search of newswire references to "lesbian" will accumulate scores of entries a week, an impressive, if overwhelming, registration of the social/political/religious/legal context of contemporary psychoanalytic work with lesbian patients. Psychoanalysts, however, may be scarcely aware of such information. Most psychoanalysts have had little occasion to take notice of the legal and social institutions and practices that affect their lesbian patients' lives. Therefore, the final section of this text, the Appendix, summarizes selected contemporary political and social developments under such index entries as child custody, reproductive rights, domestic partnerships and same-sex marriage, education, and religion. Browsing the Appendix may help readers unfamiliar with the often paradoxical challenges of being homosexual today to appreciate the impact of social context on psychological development.

Although our Appendix appears, conventionally, at the end of the book, it is not merely supplemental to the text, an organ that could be removed or ignored without significant loss. It is, on the contrary, a crucial feature of this narrative, as is the information relegated to footnotes. If this text were electronic, a reader might, with the click of a mouse, have instant access to fuller versions of such materials. If this text were hypertext, readers of Chapter 3, for instance, might call to their screens Freud's 1920 paper on female homosexuality and Fannie Flagg's (1987) *Fried Green Tomatoes*, and might view images from the film made from that novel. Reading hypertext narratives may replicate aspects of subjective experience familiar to analysts. Reading in hypertext increases our capacity to proceed by way of digressions; it increases the possibility that what is context can become foreground and give way to new digressions and new context.

## The Limitations of Clinical Narratives

But whether printed on paper or hypertext, all narrative accounts finally remain static, limited, and less than satisfying depictions of psychoanalytic treatment. Freud (1905a) subtitled one of his case descriptions a "Fragment of an Analysis of a Case of Hysteria," therein acknowledging that any description, of whatever length or detail, can convey only a "fragment" of the experience of the treatment. Seeing reality as composed of decentered, context-influenced fragments of meaning supposedly characterizes a "postmodern" perspective. But some women writers were interested well before the postmodern period in the significance of subjective bits and pieces, what Virginia Woolf (1941) in her last work, *Between the Acts*, called "scraps, arts, and fragments."[16] And some analysts know that, rather than providing proof for any particular theory, case reports are simply examples that illustrate the writer's ideas. Stoller (1985), for instance, used the topic of homosexuality to illustrate the limitations of all case illustrations: "[U]nwilling to display uncertainty, we try to create validity from persuasive sentences. We coerce" ( p.181).

　　Like all psychoanalytic case illustrations, our clinical narratives reflect our sense about which particular moments in treatment have significance. Like all clinical narratives, ours are motivated by our own desires to persuade, to hide, to reveal, and finally to prove, or at least affirm, our belief that analytic treatment can be a productive enterprise for lesbian patients and analytic therapists. Like all writers who want to illustrate their ideas while protecting their patients' identities, we have experimented with various strategies of fiction. We have changed names, occupations, places, relationships, and, that most regrettable but most necessary of fictions, we frequently have changed metaphors and images most particular to the patient, which have therefore the greatest potential to identify her.

　　Many psychoanalytic case descriptions of lesbian patients, such as those by Charles Socarides (1978), Joyce McDougall (1980), and Elaine Siegel (1988) propose to demonstrate the transference patterns and psychodynamics the writers believe to be characteristic of lesbian patients. Stoller

(1985), on the other hand, made a point of emphasizing that his case, carefully entitled "One Homosexual Woman," was not intended to represent other lesbian patients. Nor should our cases be used to form a composite picture entitled "The Lesbian Patient." Other lesbian women will have histories and dilemmas different from those of the patients we describe. Our patients have been, for the most part, economically independent women managing with varying degrees of success and conflict to find satisfying love and sustaining work. Many came to adulthood or to their first lesbian relationships before the rise of the contemporary gay and lesbian movement in the United States. A few of our patients were lesbian women of color who faced double discriminations and the tasks of integrating often conflicting group identifications and loyalties. Each patient has her own particular family, class, religious, and social adaptations that have shaped her expression of her homosexuality and contribute to her way of understanding her sexuality.

## When Patients Read Psychoanalytic Narratives

Many lesbian patients and would-be patients have been interested readers of psychoanalytic literature. What part, if any, can patients play in the publication of psychoanalytic narratives? Ruth-Jean Eisenbud (1986) has described the impact on her own thinking when she heard a patient's reaction to her work. Stoller (1988) described his method of including patients in the publication process.[17] Lipton (1991) discussed the various motives patients may have for wanting or not wanting their analysts to write about them and "the vicissitudes of asking a patient's permission to use clinical material in public and other reports" (p. 967). For several of our cases we have had the benefit of the patients' reading.[18]

Knowing that the subject of a clinical biography will read one's writing does affect what and how one writes. In fact, once we began this process, whether or not we actually discussed the writing with the patient involved, that patient became part of our mental audience as we wrote, and her imagined responses played their part in organizing our writing. We became aware of discrepancies between what we might say if the patient were listening over our shoulder and what we might say if we knew she would never hear. These discrepancies were of course instructive. For instance, imagining our patients reading our writing helped curb our wishes to reduce into tidy, clear patterns clinical exchanges that had actually remained confusing for both analyst and patient. Having patients as readers also encouraged us to find language that could be useful to both patient/readers and therapist/readers.

We thank our patients for all they have taught us. We also thank them because, as our first readers, they, through their willingness to risk reading, strengthened our willingness to risk writing.

# SUPERIOR GUINEA-PIG

## BRYHER AND PSYCHOANALYSIS

I did think once of getting an analyst's collar. . . . [I]t was just the time when Turtle left for the States. . . . So I think it is much better to have become a sort of superior guinea-pig, able to sympathise with analyst and guinea pig alike!

*[Bryher to Walter Schmideberg, October 8, 1936]*

The imagist poet H.D. (Hilda Doolittle) had a short analysis with Sigmund Freud. Psychoanalysts and literary scholars have examined H.D.'s poetry and her *Tribute to Freud* (Doolittle, 1956), an account of her analysis, for what they reveal about the effect of the analytic treatment on H.D.'s writing, as well as the effect on Freud of his relationship with the modernist poet. H.D.'s analysis with Freud was encouraged and financially supported by her lifelong lesbian partner, Annie Winifred Ellerman. Ellerman, who called herself Bryher, is all but unknown to psychoanalysts today, although she played an interesting role in the early psychoanalytic movement, to whose support and survival she contributed in significant ways. She was a prolific letter writer whose correspondents included Sigmund and Anna Freud, Havelock Ellis, Hanns Sachs, and Annie Reich. Her unpublished correspondence is housed at the Beinecke Rare Book and Manuscript Library, Yale University. It offers perspectives on early analytic practice in London and Berlin, the conflict over lay analysts, and the 1930s forced emigration of many European analysts. This chapter uses Bryher's memoirs and correspondence to make her life and work better known to the psychoanalytic community she helped sustain. Had circumstances been different in Europe of 1933, Bryher might have become the first lesbian psychoanalyst.[1]

Annie Winifred Ellerman was born in 1894, the first child of Sir John Reeves Ellerman, one of the wealthiest men in England. Ellerman was a shipping tycoon, as well as the major stockholder in *The Times* of London and the owner of numerous London magazines. As a young child, Bryher traveled with her parents to Italy, Greece, Sicily, Spain, and Algeria. Bryher wanted to be a boy, and she longed for a life of adventure. She admired her father, who called her Dolly, and she wanted to run his shipping company when she grew up. But Sir John believed that a woman would always be at a disadvantage in the financial world. John Ellerman did not legally marry Hannah Glover, Bryher's mother, until a son, John II, was born when Bryher was 15 years old. Bryher's autobiographical writings and letters do not reveal her feelings about these family dynamics, but they must have contributed to an idea that it would have been better to have been the son of John Ellerman than to be his daughter.

When Ellerman died in 1933, he left a fortune of £30,000,000, the bulk of which English law prevented Bryher from inheriting. Nevertheless, her share of her family's wealth did enable Bryher to live independently and to have considerable adventures. She traveled frequently and widely, including trips to Egypt, Greece, America, and Iceland. She founded the first magazine devoted to film as an art form. She made an experimental psychoanalytic film. She wrote poetry and film criticism, three novels, several travel books, a children's geography book, two memoirs, and ten historical novels. She owned and edited the journal *Life and Times Today* for 15 years (1934–1950). She supported artists and writers and was especially supportive of independent women with interests similar to hers but with less income—Paris bookstore owners and publishers, Adrienne Monnier and Sylvia Beach of Shakespeare and Company.[2]

## Fido, Kat, Dog, and Pup: Marriages and Menageries

Perdita Schaffner believed that her mother and Bryher were platonic lesbians (Friedman, 1986, p. 220), and Barbara Guest (1984), H.D.'s biographer, believed, "It is certain that she [H.D.] never felt [for Bryher] the physical passion she had experienced toward Frances Gregg" (p. 120). Bryher and H.D.'s 43-year relationship began as a mutual rescue operation. Its terms and form were to be continually reinvented by the two women, who shared longings for independence and recognition.

Bryher was a frustrated 24-year-old when she met H.D. She wanted to write; she devoured poetry magazines and literary reviews. She wanted to go to New York, to visit Marianne Moore and Amy Lowell, whose poetry she loved. She was suicidally depressed by the social restrictions she felt from her family.[3]

> Complete frustration leads to a preoccupation with death. I could think of nothing else. There was plenty of vitality in me but this only made the situation worse. I found a bottle of rat poison in a cupboard and the only thing that prevented me from swallowing it was that I did not want to hurt my parents. For myself, death seemed infinitely preferable to the subexistence that we had to endure. The rat poison became my talisman. I could struggle on as long as I knew that it was mine for the taking. . . . Under such circumstances, I am always amazed now that I survived.
>     Sometimes the gods toss us a laurel berry to keep us still afloat [Bryher, 1962, p. 182].

Bryher's laurel berry was the opportunity to review books for the *Saturday Review*. She also began writing *Development* (1920), an account of her much-hated school days at Queenwood, "at the rate of about a phrase a day, written almost with blood. . . . Yet I could hardly read or think; my one overmastering passion was to be free. There will always be one book among all others that makes us aware of ourselves; for me, it is *Sea Garden* by H.D. (Bryher, 1962). I learned it by heart from cover to cover" (p. 182). When Bryher discovered that the author of *Sea Garden* was a woman poet and that the poet was living near her, she wrote and asked if she might visit. H.D. invited Bryher to tea. In Bryher's (1923) novel *Two Selves*, Nancy expresses her hopes before that meeting. "Was something going to happen to her at last? . . . If she had a friend something would burst and she would shoot ahead, be the thing she wanted and disgrace them by her knowledge. Because she would care for no laws, only for happiness. If she found a friend, an answer, the past years would vanish utterly from her mind" (quoted in Hanscombe and Smyers, 1987, p. 36).
    Bryher (1962) was terrified that her knowledge of poetry would be inadequate for conversation with H.D.

> I was waiting for a question to prove my integrity. . . . "I wonder if you could tell me something," H.D. began, "have you ever seen a puffin and what is it like?"
>     "They call them sea parrots and there are dozens of them in the Scillies. I go there almost every summer, you must join me next year. . . . Say that you will come with me," I pleaded. It was the moment that I had longed for during seven interminable years [p. 183].

Bryher felt she had found that friend she had longed for and had found a reason for living. She wanted to take H.D. to her favorite place, the Scilly Islands off Cornwall. She wanted to take her to Delphi and Athens and Egypt.

H.D. was 32 years old when she met Bryher. She had been engaged to Ezra Pound, had had an affair with Frances Gregg, married Richard Aldington, lost her first child, who had been stillborn, and published her first book of poems. She was separated from her husband, living with Cecil Gray, and pregnant. Her affair with Gray came to an end, and very late in her pregnancy she became ill during the deadly influenza epidemic of 1919. Bryher helped H.D. obtain nursing care. H.D. recovered and gave birth to Perdita on March 31, 1919. In "Asphodel," H. D. gives her account of the pact she made at that time with Brhyer. When the Bryher-based character threatens suicide, H.D. makes "her promise . . . to grow up and take care of the little girl." She describes Bryher as she gives her answer. "The eyes were wide eyes, bluer than blue, bluer than gentian, than convolvulus, than forget-me-not, than the blue of blue pansies. They were child's eyes, gone wild and fair with gladness." (Quoted in Hanscombe and Smyers, 1987, p. 39).

H.D. and Bryher often lived apart and sometimes lived with others. H.D. would have other brief sexual affairs with men. Nevertheless, in the words of H.D. scholar Rachel Blau Duplessis (1986), Bryher and H.D. were "bonded for life" (p. xx). When separated, they wrote frequently, sometimes several times a day. Bryher's letters to H.D. (variously addressed as "Lynx," "Cat," "Kat") were signed "Fido," a signature of her steadfast faithfulness. Each year they celebrated July 17, the anniversary of their meeting, with special gifts and grateful acknowledgments. H.D. wrote: "Every year I thank you for saving me and Pup [Perdita]" (Guest, 1984, p. 110). And Bryher was always equally grateful for having been rescued. "I shall be thinking of you with much gratitude for all the years, especially the blitz years, London would have been quite unendurable without the Kat and I doubt if I would ever have found my way to our work sans Kat" (p. 277). Bryher's wealth supported various homes and enterprises, assuring both women ample cottage and support for their competencies. Bryher (and Kenneth Macpherson) legally adopted Perdita in 1929, and Bryher financially and emotionally supported H.D., until H.D.'s death in 1961.

Bryher gives no indication in her letters or autobiographical writing that she was ever surprised, conflicted, or apologetic about the nature or strength of her emotional attachment to H.D. Bryher found Havelock Ellis's ideas about inversion helpful in understanding her attraction to H.D. as well as her childhood desire to be a boy. Ellis believed that inversion was an incurable congenital condition and was distinguishable from female homosexuality, which he believed to be acquired and contagious.[4] Bryher visited Havelock Ellis for the first time in 1919. They talked of America (which he advised her against visiting), of her phobias, of sailing and other adventures:

> Then we got on to the question of whether I was a boy sort of escaped into the wrong body and he says it is a disputed subject but quite possible and showed me a book about it. . . . We agreed it was most unfair for it to happen but apparently I am quite justified in pleading I ought to be a boy,—I am just a girl by accident. (To H.D., March 20, 1919)

Given Bryher's family dynamics, it is not hard to understand her plea that she ought to have been a boy and that only an "accident" of biology had made her female. Her self-chosen androgynous name, taken from one of her favorite Scilly Islands, led readers who did not know her to assume that she was a man. She was delighted that in Russia she was considered "an earnest young man" because of her book on Soviet films. Ellis's ideas about sexual inversion made sense to Bryher. Although physically Bryher was smaller and shorter than H.D., psychically she saw herself as Fido, the masculine protector and provider for H.D.'s feminine "Cat." Her friend Adrienne Monnier (1940) described Bryher 20 years later:

> She is small, slender—slender is not the word: you do not come to think about her body. You grasp only certain aspects of it: her hands, which habitually close into little energetic fists from which her thumbs thrust out like thick buds; the movement of her head, always a bit bent as if for study, and above all her eyes, which are sky blue—it is there you see all the mischief, all the insight, all the goodness of "the happy few" to whom she belongs [pp. 204–205].

Bryher and H.D. became friends with Ellis, whom they nicknamed Chiron, after the teacher of Achilles. Ellis accompanied them to Greece in 1920, and Ellis and Bryher corresponded until his death in 1939.

> Freud made the discoveries but it was Ellis who was a friend. He had replied to my letters within twenty-four hours of receiving them, told me about books and advised me about writing for twenty years. A myth has grown up that he was a fussy old man who compiled lists but had no original ideas. It is a false picture of a very great Englishman. . . . Ellis opened new ways and relieved the anxieties of hundreds of uneasy minds [Bryher, 1962, pp. 285–86].

In 1920, against the advice of Ellis[5] and her family, Bryher sailed to America, accompanied by H.D. and Perdita. There she finally met Marianne Moore and Amy Lowell[6] and Robert McAlmon, a young American writer who wanted to go to Europe. Bryher proposed marriage to McAlmon, and they married on Valentine's Day in 1921. As "Mrs. McAlmon" Bryher had greater social legitimacy and increased independence from her family as well as the necessary camouflage for her relationship with H.D. Bryher's father generously financed a publishing company for his new son-in-law, through which McAlmon met and published and, in the case of James Joyce, financially supported, many of the avante garde writers of 1920s Paris, including Hemingway, Fitzgerald, and Barnes. McAlmon thought Bryher's family insufferably repressed and neurotic, and Bryher disliked Paris and McAlmon's friends. They lived apart for almost all their marriage.[7]

In 1927 Bryher divorced McAlmon to marry Scottish filmmaker Kenneth Macpherson. Macpherson was at the time H.D.'s lover, and the Bryher-Macpherson marriage helped H.D. hide her affair from her long-estranged husband. It also provided Bryher with a more compatible male companion than McAlmon. This marriage was an evolving menagerie of animals, intimate relationships, and work colleagues.[8] Macpherson became known as Dog or, more appropriately, Rover, for his wandering ways in love relationships. Bryher and Macpherson raised monkeys in their London home. (Macpherson's film *Monkey's Moon* starred his pet douocoulis monkey). They built Kenwin (named for Kenneth and Winifred), a wonderful Bauhaus house overlooking Lake Geneva, much against the opposition of their architecturally conservative Swiss neighbors. Bryher, Macpherson, H.D., and their friend psychoanalyst Mary Chadwick were members of The POOL Group, a small film production company in London and Territet, Switzerland. POOL published Bryher's (1929) *Film Problems of Soviet Russia*, an extended discussion of Eisenstein, Pudovkin and other Russian directors, complete with film stills selected by Macpherson and ample infusions of Bryher's ideas about everything from airplanes to education. Bryher and Macpherson started *Close-up*, the first serious film journal.[9] POOL Productions also made several experimental films, including *Borderline* (1930) directed by Macpherson and starring Paul Robeson, his wife, Essie, H.D., and Bryher. *Borderline* used psychoanalytic concepts to explore racism and what today would be called homophobia.[10] Bryher once compared the creative pleasures of film production to childhood play.

> I think it is because studios are nurseries on a large scale, with full size blocks, trains, people, etc., to play with. (Turtle [Sachs] once suggested I ought to write on this, perhaps for Imago, but that would be too per-

turbing. Bad enough to write in the ordinary way and to cope with one's analyst, one doesn't want an audience of fifty analysts all barking at one's unk [unconscious].) [to Walter Schmideberg, February 24, 1937].

Aided by a letter of introduction from Havelock Ellis, Bryher met Freud for the first time in 1927. "I met Freud through flying and not through any serious consideration of the soul! H.D., Kenneth Macpherson and I happened to be in Venice together for a few days during May, 1927. I saw a flight to Vienna and back, advertised at a moderate price, and smelt adventure" (Bryher, 1962, pp. 241–242). When Bryher told Freud about seeing a storm from the plane, she observed, "I knew that he wished that he had been with us himself" (p. 243).

## Analysis While Riding on an Elephant

In 1927 Bryher and Macpherson also met the famous filmmaker G.W. Pabst. At Pabst's home in Berlin, Bryher found herself talking to his friend Hanns Sachs, another admirer of progressive films. Sachs, at the time a leading training analyst of the Berlin Psychoanalytic Institute, had consulted, against Freud's wishes, on Pabst's 1926 film, *Secrets of the Soul* (see Alexander, Eisenstein, and Grotjahn, 1966). Bryher told Sachs that she had met Freud and was interested in analysis but was not certain she could accept it completely.

> He confessed that he had had a daydream that a desperately neurotic maharaja would invite him to a remote palace in India where, after the daily hour of treatment which he agreed with me could easily take place on the back of an elephant, he could study one of his favorite subjects, the philosophy of the East. It was a strange ending to a fantastic evening. . . . A few months later, after a long correspondence, I began the analysis that I have always felt to be the central point in my life [p. 251].

Bryher's analysis with Sachs took place, with numerous interruptions, from 1928 until 1932 in Berlin. She also had sessions in Switzerland when Sachs vacationed near her home. After Sachs moved to Boston in 1932, Bryher visited him several times and had sessions during these visits. Her letters describe an analysis that was, by today's standards, an entirely unorthodox arrangement. It was, in fact, rather like Sachs's fantasy of an elephant ride, with time out for stimulating diversions and excursions. Their relationship was a shared adventure into the unconscious as well as into the culture and cinema of "golden" Weimar Berlin, the city about which Christopher Isherwood wrote the stories that inspired *Cabaret*, the city where Lotte Lenya sang Bertolt Brecht and Kurt Weil's *The Threepenny Opera* and *Mahagonny*, the city in which experimental director Piscator's use of photography, posters, and phonographs created "high tech revolutionary cabaret" (see Friedrich, 1972; Kaes, Isay, and Dimendberg, 1994). Berlin at that time had a strong homosexual civil rights movement. Homosexual civil rights activist Magnus Hirschfeld had opened the Institute for Sexual Research in Berlin in 1919. Hirschfeld had been, albeit briefly, among the original members of the Berlin Psychoanalytic Society. Hirschfeld's biographer, lesbian psychiatrist Charlotte Wolff, was a medical student in Berlin in the 1920s and a physician there in the early 1930s. Wolff (1986) described some of the connections among the film, psychoanalytic, and homosexual circles of Weimar Berlin.

> The psychoanalyst Hanns Sachs, a favourite of Freud, was a close friend of Casparius [Pabst's cinephotographer for his film *The Threepenny Opera* and a documentary filmmaker who photographed Freud]. He also knew Hirschfeld, and was a welcome visitor at the Institute [for Sexual Research]. He lived on the Kurfürstendamm, near Casparius, and the two saw each other daily. He had introduced him [Casparius] to G. W. Pabst, and the three men had a common interest in producing progressive and unusual films. Hanns Sachs admired Hirschfeld, in spite of the fact that the latter's attitude to psychoanalysis was by that time already ambivalent. Some of Pabst's films made in cooperation with Casparius were inspired by Hirschfeld's work and ideas [pp. 442–443].[11]

Lesbian-themed films such as Pabst's *Pandora's Box* and Leontine Sagan's *Mädechin in Uniform* were popular with the general public. In 1928, when Joseph Goebbels wanted to convey the corruption and vice of Berlin, he pointed to deviant women on the Kurfürstendamm. Goebbels described "the worldly lady, *garçon* from head to toe with a monocle and smoking cigarette, tap[ping] on high heels across its walkways and disappear[ing] into one of the thousands of abodes of delirium and drugs that cast their screaming lights seductively into the evening air." Goebbels spoke of a man openly selling a lesbian magazine, *Die Freundlin*. "'The Girlfriend, back issues only ten cents!' cries a resourceful hawker. It does not occur to a single passer-by that this is out of place. It is not out of place at all. The man knows the milieu" (Kaes et al., 1994, p. 56).[12]

Meisel and Kendrick (1985) have suggested that Berlin's milieu, which provided an "aura of moral and intellectual freedom allowed, in addition to indulgence in vice, the flourishing of rather suspect pursuits like psychoanalysis" (p.37). And Peter Gay (1988) characterized The Psychoanalytic Institute of Berlin, begun in 1908, as "the most vital" institute of its time, "the nerve center of world psychoanalysis" (p. 460). The Institute's Polyclinic was established in 1920 by Ernst Simmel and Max Eitingon. Ex-lawyer Hanns Sachs, another member of Freud's inner circle, came from Vienna to join the Institute that year. The psychoanalytic training program included auditors as well as candidates. Candidates had a mandated training analysis of at least one year, an experience that Sachs compared to that of a novitiate in a church.[13] Abraham analyzed Sándor Rado, Helene Deutsch, Edward and James Glover, Theodore Reik, and Melanie Klein. Sachs analyzed, among others, Franz Alexander and Erich Fromm and was briefly the second analyst of Karen Horney, herself a prominent teacher and member of the training committee. Michael Balint, Heinz Hartmann, and Otto Fenichel also trained in Berlin. Candidates found Berlin's culture and night life disturbing as well as stimulating. They were likely to encounter their training analysts and teachers at dance halls and parties at all hours of the night. Alix Strachey described such meetings in her letters from Berlin to her husband, James, during her analysis with Abraham in 1924–1925 (Meisel and Kendrick, 1985). Bryher's letters to H.D. during her analysis evidence similar titillation and anxiety about such encounters.

> Berlin Nov 8, 1929
> Dear Lynk, . . . Sachs said he would come for dinner at 8:30, so we waited til 8:30 and then he ambled up having HAD his dinner, so took us to a confectioner's opposite Zoo where we had eggs in cups as in America and a ham sandwich apiece and then went to the Hungarian Rhapsody .

The elephant ride was particularly fast paced from 1929 to 1931. Bryher shuttled between analysis in Berlin, working on *Borderline*, and writing and editing *Close-Up* in London, building her new home in Switzerland, and planning to become an analyst, a process she called getting her "dog-collar." Sachs actively encouraged all these projects. Bryher's letters during this period were a mixture of analytic gossip, film news, her ongoing plans to get everyone she knew into analysis, and her loneliness when separated from Sachs, who had been given the nickname Hop-toad.

Chadwick says some of the English women a's [analysts] are MOST destructive but this is absolute secrecy. They try to keep her from working too. She says NOBODY except perhaps Freud has been like Hop-Toad. That he puts work and inclination first, and that the English a's often wont allow work nor inclination to be spoken of, and definitely even will break it down. . . .

I MISS THE HOP TOAD HORRIBLY. . . . WE MISS BERLIN—yes, not Sachs, not apes, not Trude, BUT THE LIGHTS ON THE KUR-FURSTENDAMM and the air, . . . and suddenly for all one may have said one's heart is empty simply for the long street with the lights and funny animals (Bryher to H.D., December 1929 [?]).

Sachs wrote Bryher monthly in the spring of 1930 while she was in London still working on *Borderline*. He encouraged her to stay with the film. "I think it quite out of question that you should go away while you are still needed for the film work. I should feel 'inhibited' myself, working with you while you wouldn't be able to concentrate on our work feeling that you have 'deserted the cause'" (Sachs to Bryher, April 8, 1930). Commenting on psychoanalytic politics, he agreed with Bryher that "not all is well in the English ps. a. society" but stressed that one of the characteristics of democracy was that all opinions were taken into consideration. He believed that "respectability and ps.a. are not to be reconciled; it's not accidental that ps.a. sprang up among Jews in antisemitic countries—i.e. among people who, being treated as outcasts didn't care much about respectability" (Sachs to Bryher, February 9, 1930). In later letters, Sachs assured Bryher that it was all right to see Chadwick "to get rid of the instant pressure; she is certain not to interfere with our work and I'm sure you want at least a bit of free talk with someone who is not relying on your helpfulness" (Sachs to Bryher, December 14, 1930). He encouraged her to be patient about her treatment and reminded her that, although she preferred to be the helper, in order to do so she must learn first to take help.

Be patient, don't forget that you have a *therapeutic* end in view, that you want to heal and to help. I know it is hard to say such a thing to you— nobody knows better than I do that all your past life, all the difficulties of your development. . . . [ make it hard for] you to get help, and not to give it—but after a long experience—I'm just past my 50th birthday—I must say that this is the regular course: only the sufferers bring a readiness and understanding for the suffering of others. It's a queer thing that the strong ones stand aside and the weak ones help each other—but you know that this is a great sociological truth—it is a psychological truth as well (Sachs to Bryher, January 25, 1931).

A few weeks later he chided her: "Having managed everyone else's analyses I hope you won't forget your own" (Sachs to Bryher, February 8, 1931).

## Plans to Get a Dog Collar

In April 1931, H.D. was in London starting her first analysis with her friend and POOL group associate, Mary Chadwick.[14] Kenneth Macpherson, no longer sexually involved with H.D., was now also in treatment with Chadwick. Macpherson and H.D. sometimes met for tea after their analytic appointments. Bryher, who was paying for both H.D.'s and Macpherson's analyses with Chadwick, was in Berlin at her favorite hotel, busily arranging the Berlin premier of *Borderline* and running from film showings to psychoanalytic sessions. Sachs's nickname in her letters to H.D. had been changed to Turtle: "I arrived at Exquisit [Hotel]. . . . Rang up Turtle. . . . I am to go at 4 for an hour's analysis and then for half an hour to talk! . . . There's the Garbo on at the Capitol in Anna Christie, Chaplin at the Ufa Palast, and didn't see what the Gloria had" (Bryher to H.D., March 1931 [?]).

To satisfy the social proprieties, Bryher did not travel alone to Berlin. She brought a companion, Miss Lewin, an elderly English woman, whom she tried to keep ignorant of her political opinions and activities.

> 16th April 1931
> Dear Kat,
>
> EXCITEMENT isn't the word—Lotte Reiniger's husband [Lotte Reiniger was an actress and pioneer of animated films], a perfect example of a fat and elderly always smiling Fido, says Borderline is not only the film of the year, but one of the greatest films he has ever seen, he is threatening dire things to the Press for merely stating it is an excellent and psychological film when it is beyond all the films this year and in general fur flies every-where. . . . I like Lotte Reiniger so much— imagine she and her husband are rather like Dog and self, the right way round as the little Fido is most cute, barking at me from round glasses. This afternoon we go to see them and I shall ask them to dinner next week. . . . Miss Lewin is pathetically happy but it appears she cuts people for one sin only, that of being "left"; I am waiting for the debacle. I have hidden my Film problems [Bryher's book, *Film Problems of the Soviet Union*] under underclothes and hope. She is on one side very pleasant to travel with, doesn't get tired. On the other more conventional than one had thought. Of course she appeals to the "motherlove" of people on buses, taxis etc. so in that way is excellent but I fear she would die of shock did she know what I really thought.

> 19 April . . . Tragedy; I have box of cigars I DARE NOT smoke
> wegen Lewin. Turtle teases me daily about it but agrees only possibil-
> ity would be to rise at mid-night and smoke them. As a matter of fact
> I think it was a good move to bring her as apart from Henselmann and
> young Germany and the Turtle, all the others seem much easier about
> asking one around if one has a duenna mit. . . . Once established I
> think they won't mind so much if I turn up alone.
>
> The only difficulties are she won't go to Russian films and hates left
> stuff and one has to be very careful.

All Bryher's friends and Sachs attended the Berlin premier of *Borderline*.
Meanwhile, in her analytic sessions Bryher examined her "problems with
aggression." Bryher's positive transference to Sachs encompassed all of Berlin
but did not extend to the training lectures of anthropologist Geza Róheim.

> I am rather at a standstill I feel, Turtle thinks not. At any rate all prob-
> lems for me centre in aggressiveness. At moment. Literally it does come
> down to the fact that I should have been a contented professional
> boxer! Which is as comic and so silly. But at any rate the idea now of
> fighting about C.U. [Close-Up] appeals and I do think I have got things
> moving here about the film. . . .
>
> Berlin is very lovely; there's been a new moon and the sky is very
> electric blue and deep. I had a lovely walk up to the institute last night
> about seven, just before it got quite dark. It is very stimulating here and
> electric and I like this. And the sense of people. I don't know Germans
> as I know English which makes everything more exciting. . . .
>
> Fear this is a dull letter but I don't imagine that my experiences at
> the Róheim lecture with Papuan-English-German words all jumbling
> would be of much interest. I was bored, most of the time. Passive
> again—don't want to listen to other people on p.a. but want to get on
> the job myself! (To H.D., April 25, 1931)[15]

On April 15, 1931, Bryher announced, "I am being fixed up for a lot of
lectures in case I do become a lay analyst." The letters give the impression
that Bryher was curious, but neither distressed nor conflicted about her masculine identifications. "My analysis sticks because almost as far back as
memory I am 'male' but there must have been one point Turtle says, where
I decided to be 'male.' And til we find out why, we are stuck. It might come
to-day and it might be months. And then afterwards only can I [be] prod-
ded towards some definite attitude" (April 27, 1931?).

It is unclear if or how Sachs was expecting the analysis to affect Bryher's
homosexuality, or what the Psycho-analytic Institute of Berlin's position was

at that time on admitting homosexual candidates. In 1920 the Dutch Psycho-analytic Association had asked Ernest Jones for advice on admitting a known homosexual applicant for membership. Jones advised against it and wrote to Freud for his opinion. Freud and Rank disagreed with Jones in a now frequently cited letter.

> Your query, dear Ernest, concerning prospective membership of homosexuals has been considered by us and we disagree with you. In effect we cannot exclude such persons without other sufficient reasons, as we cannot agree with their legal prosecution. We feel that a decision in such cases should depend upon a thorough examination of the other qualities of the candidate [Lewes, 1988, p. 33].[16]

Sachs, Abraham, and Eitingon then wrote from Berlin diplomatically disagreeing with Freud and Rank. They felt that homosexuality should be analyzed and were concerned that neurotic homosexuals often did not let their analyses go deep enough. "We agree that we should only accept homosexuals into our membership when they have other qualities in their favor."[17]

Bryher was impatient to be finished with her analysis so she could begin to analyze others.

> I have come to the bones as it were avec Turtle. There was apparently never question of compromise—there is with most—I said I wanted codpiece or nothing always in the unconscious and we have worked back this layer right to three. The thing that won't come up is what happened before three to make this so definite. . . . Turtle says it might come up to-morrow and it might not come up for years and until the situation is remembered remedial measures can't be applied. It all hinges on that one thing. It is a nuisance though as I do want to get through and experiment on other people! [Bryher to H.D., April 28, 1931]

Her letters describe Sachs's curious recommendation that both Bryher and 12-year-old Perdita take up smoking, a pleasure he himself enjoyed in sessions and out.

> I am typing very hard to induce the Lewin to think I am working and thereby not to come in as I am also smoking a large fat cigar, a special Turtle gift. Last night went to final Róheim lecture and was asked if I minded the back view of the male genital for Close Up to the consternation I think of one or two female and neighbouring Fidos. I observed that I had no objection to front or back view—my only care was the

censor. You see I was after C.U. material. Róheim made a film in Papua
and Australia [April 28, 1931].

In May 1931 Bryher was absolutely happy in Berlin and hated to think
of leaving for a holiday break.

> It is too upsetting. I have to leave next week. I don't feel I can. Berlin
> to me gets more wonderful every day. Last night I went to the old
> Tauentzient kino to see the Garbo in Anna Christie and hear her in
> German . . . . I love Berlin so much, like a person I think. It is so peace-
> ful here and at the same time so quick and so exciting. . . . It is very
> sad. I LOATHE leaving [to H.D., May 1, 1931].

Writing about those days 10 years later to Walter Schmideberg, she
recalled the inextricable blend of progressive art and politics that were for
her the essence of Berlin and inseparable from her analysis.

> You did not like Berlin, I know, but for us there seemed so much hope
> there, and possibility of change in those 1927-31 years. The Institute,
> and Turtle's lectures, and Pabst making his best films, and seeing things
> like *Ten Days that Shook the World*, down in a cellar of the Russian trade
> place. . . . discovering Brecht's poems, and sitting on the floor of Lotte's
> studio while she cut out silhouettes or going to market with her, and
> hearing Berlin slang, which I never understood, but had an exciting,
> harsh quality, that I have always desired [February 18, 1937].

Meanwhile, in London the complicated dual relationships among
Macpherson, H.D., Bryher, and Chadwick were taking their toll on the
analyses. Chadwick complained about the effect on H.D.'s analysis of her
constant letters to Bryher. Freud was later to make the same complaint.
Bryher explained to H.D. the psychological function and difficulties of
"leaks" in analysis.

> You remember an occurrence in childhood, and this brings up a whole
> scheme of life you have repressed. Naturally it cannot all turn up in
> one hour. Well, it's a favorite trick of one's unconscious to look around
> as it were for a brick to stem the leak. You tell the story over again to
> a friend—*who is not an analyst.* The thing that your unconscious is
> afraid of saying, comes out to the friend who does not know the link,
> and thereby you have said it and eased the other part of you who might
> say it to the analyst who would use it as a lever to get at the other part
> of what the circumstance meant to you as shock or fear.

I think if you could possibly think of it as a kind of fairy tale it would be easier. Do anyway what you feel like doing. And I never mention to Chaddie in letters anything you or K write except in the broadest possible terms. It is always much better not, just as the Turtle has told me a lot of interesting and also rather depressing stuff about my own analysis but I thought better to hold it over until I see you at any rate. Depressing as apparently it is so difficult for me to compromise unconsciously. But I shouldn't worry [May 3, 1931].

Bryher attended Sachs's lectures. He took her to dinner and told her stories about his wife's family and about Freud. "Turtle is now I think quite keen on training me and thinks, I fancy, I must have positive work" (May 5, 1931). But she was not sure she wanted to go "even to him again for a short stretch." Again she was responding to an upcoming separation. It is unclear whether Sachs understood the strength of those feelings.

If I must go from here it is better it is swift. But it is like dropping from life into a pool for retired lobsters!
Love, my dear Kat,
Fido
I was in my dreams always most agreeable towards you [May 5, 1931].

On June 1 she wrote again from the Pension Exquisit. She had flown back to Berlin from London. She attended Sachs's lecture, dined with him, heard more analytic gossip, and explored the possibility of treating a clinic patient, a bright, talented, but disturbed 15-year-old girl from Berlin's slums: "The young 'genius' is considered too temperamental for me probably. Her family is mad and about four of them are living in one room on twenty five shillings a week" (June 2, 1931). "The small pup's [the child's] drawings are quite wonderful, and there is a selbst porträt. . . . Her name is Erna. Amazing color sense, less sense of form" (June 3, 1931).

When Bryher met Erna and saw the conditions of the poor in Berlin, she became even more eager to be an analyst.

Yesterday was interesting but pretty appalling. Think of it, a thousand pups in about half the space of Tavistock Square, with a syph [syphilis] treatment hut in the middle and the barracks for the unemployed behind. No beds only disused army stretchers (they sleep home nights, go to this place early in the morning ) for the tiny pups to rest on, no toys, no anything. They get sixpence a day per pup from the state and give them two meals. They get a place to do their homework and of sorts, to play in. The pup that paints was there, . . . her father is dying

of cancer, her mother is a waitress now out of work, the family is separated, the mother won't let her leave home because she says she plays
with boys, and they want her now to go to work as she would then
earn a pound a month. I cannot take her unless I agreed to take her
altogether, as once she left the slum she couldn't go back, and we
agreed that that is quite impossible, given the state of the world. . . .
So I am making an allowance of five pounds a month which will prevent her from going to work and keep her either at school where she
might eventually become a teacher or send her to an advertising-art
school. It is simply appalling though the conditions of life, hardly one
of the thousand children knows what it is like to sleep in a bed of its
own, the whole district is so over-crowded that in each room is a whole
family, and they have practically no heat in the winter in these tin huts.
It is perfectly dreadful.

Fraulein Pincuss, who is also an analysand of the Turtle, says the
conditions for teachers are terrible. . . . She says, with me, the schools
are terrible, that they murder the children wholesale, and that it is so
awful, she doesn't understand how people can stand the work. If the
opposition get in here, even the sixpence a day will be taken from
them. The political groups by the way, won't admit the pup because
she paints. It is all too hopeless.

. . . I am very eager now to get permit to analyse. It seems to me it
is the only constructive thing I know. You cannot attack these masses—
it is simply overwhelming [June 6, 1931].

By July of 1931 Sachs was signing his letters to Bryher with a sketch of a
turtle. He sent Freud's books to the writer Norman Douglas, whom he had
met through Bryher and Macpherson.[18] He saw Elizabeth Bergner, a film
actress to whom Bryher was attracted and whom she was bent on saving. He
encouraged Bryher's psychoanalytic interpretation of Shakespeare's plays. "To
enable you not to be afraid of your 'second sight' and make full use of it
should be the real aim of ps.a" (Sachs to Bryher, October 21, 1931). Sachs's
letters also conveyed his increasing concern about the political situation.

In June 1931 H. D. was joyful about the plans for the new house. She
thanked Bryher for helping her have the analysis with Chadwick. She had
recently been astonished to recover, through analysis, memories of a frightening childhood experience. She was impressed with how that forgotten
experience with her father had been influencing her behavior with
Macpherson. She said she wanted to stay in London for her analysis.
"London is MY OWN, just as Berlin is your own" (H.D. to Bryher, June 24,
1931). Nevertheless she stopped seeing Chadwick in July and never
returned to treatment with her.

In November and December 1931 and early 1932, H.D. had sessions in Berlin with Sachs, while Bryher, in London, tried to smooth Chadwick's feelings. But Sachs was not the right analyst for H.D. She was overwhelmed by his style of mixing film discussions, social talk, and unsettling interpretations. Sachs suggested that H.D. go to Vienna in December and have sessions while he was there. H.D. was suspicious. She wondered to Bryher if his suggestion was motivated by "your dollars, my analysis, or my beaux yeaux-es?" (H.D. to Bryher, December 4, 1931). In Vienna she was even more uncomfortable to find that she was staying on the same floor of the same hotel as Sachs. H.D. reported that Vienna was neither as "ramshackle" as London, nor as poverty stricken and filled with beggars as Berlin. Meanwhile Bryher listened to fears about the English economy and to growing pro-German/anti-French sentiment.

Letters from the spring of 1932 find Bryher, Macpherson, and Chadwick all together in the new house in Switzerland, while H.D. is in Delphi and Venice. Bryher wrote of plans to go and "finish" with Sachs. But she continued to delay her own return to analysis. As always, others needed help first. Two women house staff were pregnant; the house and garden needed tending. She sent Freud's books to a friend and offered to pay for another friend's analysis with Sachs. She encouraged H.D. to see Sachs again. Hanging over everything now was the fear that Sachs would have to leave Berlin. Bryher was finding it very difficult to return from that "pool for retired lobsters" into which she had fallen. When she finally did return to Berlin she found a changed city.

> June 13, 1932
> Equisit to let
> many shops empty
> Dear Kat
>
> I am told I must not send any political news but things are not pleasing.
> Turtle is very ill I think: he is going [to] Boston. If he can bear it there he will live there permanently. But he is heartbroken at leaving Berlin, and things are in the most appalling mess avec G. [his wife]. . . . No books being printed, no films being made, . . .
> I am very anxious and worried about Turtle. I was not allowed to have analysis to-day, we just talked.
> Gather he is worried about future of analysis too—it is all going medical-moral, etc., all most worrying. . . . I should be careful not to mention any politics in your letters.

On June 14 she noted for the first time that there are "a lot of brown uniforms about. It is all disquieting."

Sachs prepared to leave for Boston. He increased his efforts to obtain analytic training for Bryher. In the face of the increasing restrictions against non-medical analysts, Sachs, a lay analyst himself, was having difficulty getting Bryher accepted as a candidate.[19] Bryher described the problems to H.D.

June 15, 1932

> After such a long discussion and various hair-raising bits of analytical secret history being given me under such a solemn oath of secrecy I feel quite alarmed [when] I hear them. Turtle has agreed that if I behave these next weeks, he will endeavor to persuade the Swiss Society to admit me at Zurich in September, subject to my undergoing in Switzerland, Vienna or Berlin, three months clinical training in the autumn, which has alas to be spent studying in a lunatic asylum. He says, and no doubt he is right, that they always insist on this now for personal safety, because one must be able to tell at a consultation, if the person is borderline and apt for analysis or if they are really insane in which case they might try to kill one if precautions were not taken.
> And one cant learn from books
> Only—please under no circumstances speak of this in London or I may be refused admittance as there are some very queer things that have happened—analytically speaking—and it has been impressed on me to say no word not even of the possibility of being admitted until it has happened. There is a split on so to speak between the moralists and the strict Freudians.
> I said I would train in Vienna, unless I can train at Geneva or Lausanne, because if Turtle, Pabst, Metzner, and everyone one knows have left Berlin, it would be dismal and in Vienna I could . . . maybe get to work with Freud himself.
> I am also to study slang and colloquial German because Turtle says it is useless having a knowledge of the fine points of German literature when you are up against the ravings of a maniac waiter from a Viennese slum.

Sachs dreaded leaving Berlin. He feared he would be lonely in the U.S., but his doctor believed that his health was not good enough for England's climate.[20] He told Bryher more and more about his marital problems. His wife did not share his view of political developments. She was unwilling to leave Berlin. Forced to leave behind his life in the city he loved, Sachs could not have been able to attend fully to Bryher's feelings about their separation. The analytic elephant ride became even more precarious as the rich maharanee-analysand increasingly took up her familiar role of confidante and caretaker.

> Turtle had asked me to dinner and a film. . . . Turtle walked me miles into a very lovely part of Berlin, all allotment gardens with white flowers, daisies, marguerites, lilies, under hedges of white may and lime blossom. Telling me of these hair raising quarrels and difficulties and of his terror of Boston. He hopes to make sufficient during the nine months to retire and live in one room in Paris for the rest of his life. But I am so scared if he will be able to save as much as he thinks, in America. They want to park him in a University club. He says he is not at all sure he can stand the loneliness as he knows nobody there but his analysands whom he cant see but it is an opportunity to train six or eight in pure technique so he feels he ought—moral principles—to do it. I said if a couple of hundred would help him he had only to say but I thought his work must be the deciding factor and he cant work openly anywhere but Germany, Austria or America on account of the beastly restrictions about aliens working. Finally I was walked back to Reimann's and given—along with Turtle—ice cream. Perhaps American ices at least will be some help to him. . . .
>
> Koch tells me that Clare With, who did those nice geography books Kat liked so much, is half mad because she is head of a training college and her students throw books at her and shout "we dont want to be taught by a bitch, we want a man." In the brown uniform of course and under the new regime no woman may be employed in any government service. It is quite awful. They say it will be like Italy the first years under the duce.
>
> Everywhere, everywhere, men in brown [June 15, 1932].

Sachs took Bryher to "a full analysts meeting au institute, great honor but I do wish I hadn't a sense of humor on these occasions, . . . and I know, I know, I'll never be earnst [sic] enough to do analysis. They all talked technique hard. In Hungarian and Polish German. So that I didn't understand more than 50% and longed for a sketch book" (June 17, 1932). She took more seriously what was happening outside the institute meetings. In Germany, 6 million workers were out of work; Berlin's artists were now starving. "The new N uniforms appeared yesterday, rows upon rows of marching brown young males and woe betide you, if you happen to look dark. Rather like after a lynching in a south town if you happened to be a Negro" (June 17, 1932).

Sachs was to leave for Boston at the end of August. Bryher was to meet him in Zurich in order to gain admission to the Swiss Psycho-analytic

Society. Meanwhile she arranged for Sachs to have an outside stateroom on his trip to the U.S. On June 26, 1932 she wrote to H.D.: "I can't believe it is my last 'hour' in Berlin. It's too awful." Finally, on August 31, on her way to see Sachs off to America, an excited Bryher announced the news.

> Kat darling
> Turtle says
>     IF
> I am good
> I may be accepted on probation for *TWO* years. And then if accepted mentally, morally and politically so to speak I may then about end 1934-5!!! get dog-collar. If I make one bark during same period I get kicked out. Words cannot express my feelings. I think I'll certainly try the business with one ear *BUT*. I won't say at all what my other ear will do in the meantime. I shall apply then to become a probation pupil at Zurich but in the meantime I may get up to mischief on my own.

Sachs and Bryher continued their correspondence. He advised her about her relationship with Pabst.[21] He cautioned that a prospective case Bryher described was probably paranoid psychotic, "not psychoneurosis and those people are apt to become quite seriously dangerous. . . . I do not recommend analysis, the chance of any therapeutic result being practically nil. It is, as you guessed, a consequence of repressed homosexuality, but of a more primitive narcissistic type" (Sachs to Bryher, December 4, 1932). When H.D. wanted to see Freud, Sachs wrote to Freud "to fill him in" about her.

Sachs also wrote Bryher a lengthy discussion about censorship and its psychological functions—"to deny the existence of certain facts which are not in accordance with the code of life which censorship tries to uphold as the only existing one." His first example was of a trial against a book about lesbian love.

> A few weeks ago I read about a trial against a book describing a form of human love not acknowledged hitherto neither by acts of parliament nor by popular story writers: the love relations between two women. A modern witch trial is bound to have its modern ways: the attorney for the prosecution admitted that the book in question was a serious work of art, far from frivolity or lasciviousness, but—and in this culminated everything that was said in favor of the prosecution—we must think of those who are in danger of falling, those who waver between virtue and vice and may, by the impression of such a book wrought on their weak minds, be tempted away from normality and flung into everlasting perdition. Judge and jury and the court of appeal applauded

this sane argument and damned the book unhesitatingly—which, I sincerely hope, has done something to enlarge its circulation [Sachs to Bryher, undated, 1932?].

## Kenwin to Vienna

H.D. began her analysis with Freud in March 1933. When H.D. wrote that Freud would see her, Bryher wrote encouragement: "There is a wonderful sentence in Abraham about how he wondered if p.a. were really doing good when he could only take 10 patients a year, and then he saw the effect those 10 patients had on their groups and he knew it was" (Bryher to H.D. December 31, 1932).

Freud was apparently fascinated by H.D. and by the Bryher/Macpherson menagerie. Freud may have forgotten that he had met Bryher. When H.D. showed him her picture, Freud said, "It might have been a page in an Italian fresco."

> The Professor said, "She is *only* a boy." Then he said, "It is very clear." Of another photograph, he said, "She looks like an Artic explorer." He liked another snapshot of my daughter with Bryher on the terrace of the house at La Tour. I told the Professor that they both might be coming later to Vienna. He said, "I would so like to see them." This made me very happy.
> He said Bryher's letters were "very kind, very pliable," though she herself looked in the pictures, "so decisive, so unyielding." I told him how staunch Bryher had been and loyal, and how she arranged everything on our numerous journeys [Doolittle, 1956, p. 170].

Bryher, at Kenwin, sent books and dog questions to Freud. She commiserated with H.D. when Freud's chow, Yofi, suffered a painful pregnancy, which reminded H.D. of her own first pregnancy in which she had lost the baby. Bryher dryly contrasted her domestic dilemmas with H.D.'s analytic explorations. "I'm glad I'm a 'male' in your unc. MY unc keeps losing the key of wine cupboard" (March 16, 1933). She commiserated with H.D. for her sibling rivalry with Dorothy Burlingham, "now in her tenth year" of analysis with Freud. She sent Yofi congratulations on the birth of her puppies.

Sachs wanted Bryher to meet him in Vienna when he came from Boston to visit Freud. He believed that if "you and Anna Freud and I are for some time on the same spot something good—for your ps.a. career and something good in general—is likely to come" (Sachs to Bryher, April 21, 1933).

But Bryher held back. She kept making plans to go to Vienna and then changing them. She had various excuses, including that her mother needed her to visit. She insisted that "I shall miss the garden: it is my Yo-fi" (to H. D., March 26, 1932). But Bryher finally went to Vienna together with Perdita and her governess. Freud welcomed Bryher at her hotel, he sent flowers, a photograph, and thanks from Yofi (Guest, 1984, pp. 214–215).

But at the end of April 1933 Bryher had a major psychoanalytic dilemma on her hands. Freud, knowing Bryher's love for dogs and wanting to repay her for her many gifts to psychoanalysis, offered her one of Yofi's puppies. But neither Bryher nor Macpherson liked chows, and they were trying to limit their menagerie. Macpherson had just restrained himself from getting another monkey. By letter Bryher and H.D. discussed how to refuse the puppy without offending Freud. Finally Bryher wrote to Freud using her father's ill health as an excuse for declining his gift. She explained carefully that she feared having to leave Kenwin at any time to go to London and that she could neither take the puppy with her nor provide proper puppy-sitting at Kenwin.[22]

The brown uniforms made their presence increasingly felt. On May 6, 1933 the Nazis destroyed Hirschfeld's Institute of Sexual Science in Berlin. A few days later Freud's works were burned in the University of Berlin square, together with the writings of Havelock Ellis, Margaret Sanger, Gide, Proust, and Zola. H.D. had planned to finish her analysis with Freud at end of June, but when, on June 12, a tram she was riding on almost hit a bomb on the tracks, she abruptly left Vienna.[23]

On July 16, 1933 Bryher's father died. One of the first projects she undertook with her inheritance was to establish the Hanns Sachs Training Fund. It was intended to help provide financial assistance both to needy analytic candidates and to refugee analysts arriving in America. Sachs wrote his thanks.

Dear Bryher,

You will not hinder me to thank you for your gift to p.a. I consider it to be an excellent idea—helping perspective analysands and at the same time good analysts who are hard up. I felt at first inclined to "bawl you out" on account of the name of the fund but on second thought I found you were right. You see it may give added weight to my influence in the IPA especially in the problem of lay analysis—and everything that helps in that way is welcome. So thanks for that too [September 12, 1933].[24]

Bryher continued to financially support many of her friends' analyses. She also took financial responsibility for getting four Viennese candidates through their training.[25]

## Refugee Worker

And she increasingly turned her efforts to refugee work. She smuggled passports and papers into Germany for those trying to flee and used her home in Switzerland as a way station for those on their way to England. Bryher found the refugee committees poorly organized, slow, and fearful. She thought the Quakers were prompt and efficient: "The very lucky ones got on their lists."

> A few of us who had been interested in psychology organized a private group. The leading psychoanalysts had been rescued by their colleagues, we started with students but our lists soon widened to include people from a wide variety of occupations. . . . I was the receiving station in Switzerland. . . . Besides this, I looked after a group of medical students studying at Lausanne and had them come to see me whenever they wanted to talk over a problem. I thought one or two would go crazy before their final examinations because we all knew they had no second chance [Bryher, 1962, pp. 276–278].

She reported helping a total of 105 persons escape. Only two of those she helped were lost. One was Walter Benjamin, who committed suicide when he was detained by the Nazis. She developed the capacity to listen and to grow "a tough hide," because if one were to be able to continue to help, "even sympathy had to be rationed."

> Once you know that a moment's carelessness may cost a life, you yourself alter in a dozen subtle ways. I learned watchfulness, never to say a word on a telephone that could not safely be overheard or to leave notes where they might be read. I carried the particulars of my refugees in a tiny notebook that I usually wore suspended around my neck and inside my clothes. I had to suspect every stranger and as the years went on it was difficult to remain humane as well as alert [Bryher, 1962, p. 281].

Not all Bryher's energies in those years were spent with refugees. She attended the IPA Congresses at Lucerne in 1934, Marienbad in 1936, and

Paris in 1938. Her letters from Lucerne report the current gossip about analytic splits.

> Barbara [Low] phoned, very anxiously, and said could Glover come
> with to dinner, and Turtle is furious as they are opposition camps and
> I think Glover wants to get me for the English group to give them dol-
> lars. The intrigue that has already begun reminds one only of a hareem
> or some Eastern court. . . . Holland has split into two camps. The
> English are lonely. Wien and U.S.A. hang together, the Frogs are aloof
> [to H.D., August 26, 1934].

A few days later she describes her ongoing difficulties listening to the Congress papers and her meetings with psychoanalytic luminaries.

> Anna to lunch, she is most friendly now account of some seeds I sent
> to her. But Jones has declared war on me. The Jones-Klein group are
> as mad as they can be that the dollars have gone to Sachs-Anna. . . .
> The Princess [Marie Bonaparte] is black with white flowers and an
> enormous hat and the manner of one who had had her men (why did-
> n't I think of it in time, of course she's Mae West) read a short paper [to
> H.D., August 28, 1934].

Bryher was acutely aware of the anxiety and disapproval many of the English analysts felt about homosexuality, attitudes she had not encountered in Berlin. Even close colleagues, like Dorothy Townshend, disappointed her by their prejudiced ideas.

> I get more and more distrustful of the English group. I went to see
> Dorothy T yesterday—she has been continuously ill since Christmas
> and [she] asked me why I didn't have a little one as the aim of all analy-
> sis for women was to have a little one, and there was nothing so dread-
> ful as lesbianism. . . . This is most discouraging from Dorothy but it
> seems part of the technique here (to H.D., May 26, 1933).

When Barbara Low told Bryher that she had mistaken lesbian novelist Radcliffe Hall for a man, Bryher dryly noted, "I am apparently considered by the group as their Radcliffe. . . . I rather like the new conception of me and I was asked seriously about my trousers. I think by the time I get to be 80 I'll be just right" ( to H.D., November 5, 1934).[26]

At the Lucerne Congress, Bryher "lost her heart to Dr. Jekels," who at almost 70 had moved to Stockholm and was learning Swedish because he "values only one thing in life, liberty of thought." She thought the Americans "swept the field" with their paper presentations, Zilboorg's on suicide and Menninger's on "accidents as suicide preventions."

> I like Anna very much when you get alone with her, and she drops the analytical manner. She's so proud she got twenty five pounds for the hay on her farm. . . . Did I tell you an old dame bustled up to me yesterday and asked me if I was the clerk in charge of the excursions. I did feel triumphant but apparently I can't pass as an analyst.
> My ears ring with Traum—Trieb—Uber Ich and Masochismus [to H.D., August 30, 1934].

Travel continued. Perdita sent postcards to Freud from her cruise to Trinidad.[27] When H.D. returned to Vienna to see Freud in November 1934, Bryher again sent encouragement.

> I shouldn't worry about being "finished," technically one is never, one can't be, because there is always the fresh material to analyse, Turtle is not nor even Papa [Freud] himself, but there's a state which most people loosely call finished and that is apparently what you have reached. I was vaguely supposed to have reached one of those states about 2 years back with Turtle but we still march on cheerfully. I think that in p.a. everything is fluid even the matter, and probably that is why people hate it so much, one cant put on labels [to H.D., December 4, 1934].

Kenneth and Bryher visited the U.S., where Bryher observed the differences between analysis there and in England, met the president of the Boston Psychoanalytic, and was quite taken with Katherine Hepburn's films. Bryher continued to believe in psychoanalysis and to support those analysts she respected. In a letter to H. D., Freud reported the use to which he put one of Bryher's gifts.

May 19, 1935
Dearest H.D.

> Unnecessary to say how much I enjoyed your kind birthday letter! Will you make it easy for me giving my best love to Bryher and Perdita and tell Br. of the use I am making of the cheque she sent me as a present. You may have heard that Dr. Jones appeared at Wien and gave us an interesting lecture at a meeting introducing our people into the somewhat startling novelties of English psychoanalysis. He asked for an exchange-lecturer to be sent over to London from our side to continue

the discussion. We chose Dr. Walder to undertake this trip and Bryher's ten [?] pounds will meet part of the expenses. So the money goes back to where it came from.

Bryher paid for H.D.'s treatment with Walter Schmideberg in London. Bryher and Schmideberg, who became known as "Polar Bear," corresponded about analysis, the political situation, and her visits to America. Later he would become a live-in guest at Kenwin.[28] Visiting the U.S. again in November of 1936, Bryher discovered that Sachs had become very Bostonian; and his practice was so full that she could get only a few hours and could not get on "the regular list" until January. She and Macpherson attended a party for the Negro magazine *Challenge*.[29] Sachs gave a Thanksgiving dinner lecture on early American history. Perdita, Bryher, and Sachs saw some bad movies. Bryher was afraid she would never be "earnst" enough for Boston.

In a long letter to Schmideberg in 1937, Bryher expressed her fear that psychoanalysis was not growing. She cautioned that "anything alive has to grow." Bryher had strong opinions about how that growth should take place.

> 1. I feel too much is founded on the Victorian idea of the family. It is very strong and it is very powerful but it is not everything.
>
> I know that Freud himself was very happy with his family, that there is always the tendency to re-create childhood.
>
> . . . The Victorian idea of a female marrying and be[ing] content with that and pups [children], simply is lamentable to-day. . . . Yet analyze analytical writings and at least three quarters are based really on the nice Victorian picture of an old gentleman, his wife, and half a dozen pups all taking a walk in the woods on Sunday. . . .
>
> 2. Absolutely no research has been made in p.a. with regard to the girl who is really a boy. Freud made one study, and there are a few occasional references, that is all. . . . Turtle knows much but never writes about it.
>
> 3. I don't ask p.a. to clench its fist and march in political demonstrations but I do ask it not to go, as has happened in England, fascist.

Bryher detested what she saw as the English policy of long analyses for a selected few: "This cuts it entirely I feel from the life, the living part, of to-day. I don't want them to preach communism, I only want it to be possible for workers, and this includes many badly paid intellectuals, to come in contact with p.a." She regretted the Left's association of psychoanalysis with bourgeois ideas, an association she also blamed on the English analytic group. She favored short analyses, at low fees, for as many as possible, in many clinics: "For highly neurotic people, for those who wish to become analysts, for the wealthy if they want, let them take their two or three or four years." She also wanted to limit the number of "highly neurotic" and time-consuming cases: "I think one quite mad individual a year might be allowed each analyst."

Finally, she was a strong proponent of lay analysis: "I would not allow more than one in ten analysts to be doctors. They pretend to be impartial scientists, actually they want to reduce things to formulas, photograph them, label them, and suddenly everything is dead (Bryher to Schmideberg, July 6, 1937).

The following year she wrote a prophetic warning to Schmideberg: "This is in confidence, for I don't know if Turtle meant me to speak of it or not, but Boston has voted for—(my unk slip)—voted *against* lay analysis. We shall have to establish a centre for it somewhere for if analysis becomes entirely medical it will freeze, and no development will be possible" (March 14, 1938).

In March 1938, Sachs wrote, frantic about the situation in Europe, warning her to tell everyone to get out. In May, Sachs, with Bryher's assistance, helped several of his relatives get out of Germany. On May 18 he wrote to Bryher. "[M]y American colleagues—lead by 'Europeans'—have tightened down still more on the lay problem, intending evidently to give no sort of help to any 'lay'-emigrant who tries to make a living by therapeutic analysis—as inevitably they must do or starve."

When Bryher arrived again in New York in November 1938, Sachs wrote her from Boston: "I am glad you are here and we can have the talk or talks which I need so much. Curious thing to say for your ps.a. isn't it?" Several months later he wrote to her after she had returned home: "Dear Bryher, I think you know how I miss you and therefore need not say more about it. Let's hope that we will have some weeks near each other next summer in Europe. At present I disbelieve in both" (January 2, 1939).

The brown uniforms continued their march. Bryher continued to help refugees and to support psychoanalysis. She loaned Paula Heimann money to get a British medical degree in Edinburgh. Martin Freud, who was managing the gift of securities Bryher had given Freud for psychoanalytic publishing, feared the Nazis' invading London. In May 1940 he transferred those securities from London to Boston to be used by Sachs.[30] On June 19, 1940, Bryher wrote to Annie Reich to say that Anny Katan was now safe, but she herself felt "beautifully trapped, I am afraid. I expected to be able to get out across the hills, but in two days the Germans were at the borders."

It is most curious, I feel as if I were back in remote childhood. Somebody should write a paper on the therapeutic value of suicide! I feel well, if they do come in here, there is always that resource and in consequence, remain calm for all the rest of the time. A curious apathy descends on one, of which I have read, but in which I had not believed, till sometimes one feels that if one's life depended upon walking to the station, one would not go. Actually I have been rather energetic! It is what one observes, however, not only in one's self but all around one.

Finally, thinking that Germany was going to invade Switzerland, Bryher burned her refugee notebook and at the last moment, before the borders were sealed, made her way to London, where she spent the war years.

The second war was better for Bryher than the first had been. This time she was independent and among friends. She edited *Life and Letters Today* and set about to learn Persian.

Why Persian? Because . . . at such a time of utter despair we fall back on childhood and that to me meant galloping in complete freedom across the desert. Those days had been dreaming come alive and I have read since in many biographies that children who had had similar experiences to my own were marked by them for life. . . . [M]y lessons impelled me to read book after book about the history of the Near East. . . . I saw our world through the barbarian invasions of the past and I studied these volumes not to escape but to understand our extremely difficult present of gunfire and crashes [Bryher, 1972, pp. 55–58].

Practical Bryher was frustrated by English bureaucracy and critical of England's too little and too late response to the German threat. H.D. worried that Bryher would take her life during the war. But Bryher survived.

Any ability that I had had to endure was due to two reasons. One was that I had foretold the conflict in 1932 and therefore had no guilt feelings. The other was my Freudian analysis with Dr. Hanns Sachs. . . . This helped me to put up with many privations because my energy was free to fight the enemy and from time to time the authorities; I did not have to fight my own mind. I can recommend the European type of analysis (it seems to have changed its direction in America) as the best antidote to bombing, frustration and hardship although one must not expect a miracle. What makes me angry is that we have the tools in our own hands to prevent a great deal of mass stupidity yet we seldom use them. Psychoanalysis is less for the neurotic than for the tough and healthy who can really use it to make the world a gayer and happier place in which to live. We should not ask too much from it; it cannot prevent the great oppositions of life where there are frequently several people involved, but it can answer some of the riddles of life and death and help us to understand our obstructions whether these are artificially imposed by the State or ones we invent ourselves. Once we know and comprehend our motives, we can often make the people round us happier [pp. 178–179].

When H.D. had a severe breakdown in 1946, Schmideberg and Bryher took her to the Kunach Clinic in Switzerland. Bryher returned to nearby Kenwin, which would be her base until her death in 1983. Bryher never saw Sachs again. On December 7, 1946, he wrote full of hope because she was coming to visit in January "after a separation of more than 7 years." But he died on January 10, 1947, just before she reached America.

Bryher amicably divorced Macpherson in 1947. She tended her garden, cared for her dogs, and wrote, completing 12 books between 1952 and 1972.[31] She traveled to Cornwall, to Capri to visit Macpherson, to Paris for a Sylvia Beach celebration, and to America to visit Perdita and her husband, literary agent John Schaffner and their four children, whom she considered her grandchildren. Her interest in the development of psychoanalysis continued. Her files contain a *New York Times* article in 1971 on the 27th IPA Congress. She saved Adrian Stokes's obituary in 1972 and in 1974 saved articles on Lacan, psychoanalytic jokes from the *New Yorker*, and reviews of Juliet Mitchell's recently published *Psychoanalysis and Feminism*.

## The Hanns Sachs Training Fund

In 1964 Bryher wrote to Annie Reich wondering if Reich might find out what had happened to that Sachs Training Fund.

At the time of the emigration, I think it was about 1936, I deposited some funds in America through Dr [sic] Hanns Sachs, that were intended for the assistance of young analysts in training who had had to break their training off because they had to emigrate. At that time, Dr E. Glover and Anna Freud were put on the board together with myself. Actually I think Dr Sachs directed the employment of the income while he was alive and through the war. It was put into the charge of a lawyer, Mr D. Pokross. . . . The last ten or twelve years nothing has happened. Dr Glover is too preoccupied with the prolonged illness of his wife and daughter even to reply to letters. . . . I myself am on the board and can give some directions but I am seventy and I feel it would much better if the income and possibly, eventually, the capital were used up for the training of young analysts. Or have you any other idea? If you think it should be for training, would you, yourself, suggest candidates or recommend somebody to suggest them. It is not much, I think the income is only a few hundred dollars annually but it may be possible . . . to use up the capital gradually. Mr Pokross is a fierce watchdog and from his admiration for Dr Sachs has never increased his fees during these many years. . . . I think only that as nobody in the analytic world in Boston is interested, and I am interested in classical Freudian analysis, it would be so much better to use up this money for training purposes while some of us are still around who knew Sachs. It is only a few thousand dollars. But I don't want to add to your burdens. . . . I wish we could meet and dismiss the matter in five minutes and then talk about things nearer to us [October 28, 1964].

What happened to that Hanns Sachs Training Fund? Sanford Gifford, Chair of The American Psychoanalytic Association's Committee on History and Archives, was interested in Sachs's 1933 letter to Bryher, which he said was "exactly the kind of thing that our archives lack, despite his having been our first permanent training-analyst"[32] Gifford had no information about the Training Fund. He suggested that we contact David R. Pokross, Sachs's lawyer, and he generously gave us Pokross's address and telephone number, as well as contacting Pokross to let him know we would be writing.

Pokross was equally generous in his written response. He recounted his meeting with Bryher and his arranging for Macpherson's visa to remain in the U.S. He enclosed a copy of a speech he had given at the Boston Psychoanalytic Society and Institute's First Hanns Sachs Symposium in 1989 and a copy of an article in which he described some experiences in the early days of the Boston Psychoanalytic. He described the securities he had received in 1940 from Martin Freud, which had been a gift of Bryher to the Verlag (personal communication, May 28, 1996).

But, Mr. Pokross wrote, "I have never heard of the 'Hanns Sachs Training Fund.'"

We suspect that the original purpose of Bryher's gift may have gotten lost, as, for many years, did the training of lay analysts.

## Superior Guinea Pig

Perdita Schaffner suggested that for Bryher psychoanalysis was like a religion, which she wanted everyone around her to believe in and to experience (personal communication, January 9, 1996). Bryher's letters and memoirs certainly support that assertion.

> A classical, Freudian analysis in the right hands is perhaps the sternest discipline in the world, the hardest form of intellectual activity and a great spiritual experience. It offers, as reward, liberty and understanding. There is probably no movement about which more popular misconceptions exist, largely because it threatens the irrational. . . . We surrender nothing of what we desire, we learn why we want it and occasionally find that it was simply a cover for something that we wanted more [Bryher, 1962, p. 253].

Bryher idealized the founders of her religion and was disturbed by what she saw as the reactionary tendencies of the later generation and what she saw as the unfortunate tendency for most analysands to

> become drearily good, adaptable citizens. . . . The gay excitement of the early days died with the founders, the second generation was engaged in obtaining official recognition, they aspired to become part of 'the Establishment.' They succeeded and yet because in the deepest way they thus betrayed some of their leader's ideas, they tended in compensation to make laws of what Freud had suggested were points worth investigation [pp. 256–257].

On the way to the Marienbad Congress she had been impatient with analysts for being so slow about fighting human stupidity.

> "You cannot treat the psychoanalytic movement like a boxing match," Sachs admonished me gently, "Things have to go slowly."
>    I believed in speed. "If only they would get a move on," I grumbled, "we could change the world" [p. 267].

If Bryher believed in psychoanalysis so much, why didn't she pursue the analytic training that Sachs had tried so hard to secure for her? Sachs's encouragement of her analytic training was undoubtedly motivated by his identifications with Bryher, the progressive film maker and lover of languages and literature, by his gratitude toward his rich patient, and by his wish to give a favorite analysand something he treasured. Although Bryher idealized both Sachs and Freud, finally, however, she declined Sachs's analytic dog collar just as she had earlier declined Freud's puppy, another gift proffered by a grateful analyst. In a letter to Schmideberg, Bryher offered some reflections on why she did not continue to pursue analytic training.

I did once think of getting an analyst's collar. . . . [I]t was just the time when Turtle left for the States . . . and shortly afterwards my father died, . . . Then too, the political troubles began, and I should probably have got arrested. And there was trouble about a group: Switzerland, with its usual caution, admits no one who has not been analysed in Switzerland, no matter how long they may have had elsewhere, and Vaud forbids lay analysis. However, I could have got round it, because Geneva affiliates or did, to the Paris group, and I could, at that time, have got in there. I expect had I really wanted to get over the difficulties, I could have, but I think perhaps it is just as well I did not, now. I never could have kept the rules, not even Freudian ones, I should have wanted to make experiments. I'd have been very good with some people, driven others to distraction, and broken off eventually and founded a school of my own. So I think it is much better to have become sort of a superior guinea-pig, able to sympathise with analyst and guinea pig alike! [October 8, 1936]

Bryher was indeed well suited to sympathize with both analyst and analysand.

I do not believe in dignity in an analyst. It's inhuman work, and unless one gets right away from it, outside hours, there is eventually (I've seen it happen) no flexibility in dealing with analysands. It's hopeless of course, if the analyst isn't impartial (I've seen the results of that as well) but there is that curious not-to-be-in-words-described edge of difference between a comprehending impartiality and cold judgment, that the unk at once interprets as condemnation or a refrigerator. I had three experiences with analysts (English) pre Turtle, so KNOW [to Schmideberg, March 10, 1937].

Had Bryher gotten that dog collar she would have been the first analyst able to acknowledge the primacy of her lesbian relationship. Bryher loved to watch prize fights and felt her analysis had freed her aggression. But she was obviously ambivalent about training for herself, and she was probably not eager to fight for training against such formidable opponents as the increasing restrictions against lay analysts, the attitudes most analysts held about female homosexuality, and the brown shirts who had forced her analyst to leave his beloved city. The enriching connections between the analytic and homosexual communities that had flourished in Weimar Berlin were destroyed by the rise of fascism. The brown shirts wiped out a world just coming into existence. The Nazis extinguished the German homosexual civil rights movement in 1933. Homosexuality became increasingly pathologized in analytic theory and treatment. Training institutes closed their doors to lay analysts. It would take decades before nonmedical therapists began to establish their own training centers, a necessity Bryher had foreseen in 1938. And it would be still more decades before analytic training began to become available to openly gay and lesbian candidates. Bryher's letters and memoirs help illuminate these important developments in the history of psychoanalytic training and treatment. Her letters are, therefore, one more gift to psychoanalysis from a rebel patron, grateful patient, and most superior guinea pig.

# 2

# "THE STORY OF OUR LIVES BECOMES OUR LIVES"

[ADRIENNE RICH, 1978, P. 34]

If we are forced to talk about our lives, our sexuality and our work only in the language and categories of a society that despises us, eventually we will have eaten enough bitterness that we will be unable to speak past our griefs.

*[Dorothy Allison, 1992, p. 218]*

Certain assumptions about homosexuality are prevalent in Western culture and fundamental in psychoanalytic theory. Trying to catch sight of the foundational beliefs of one's own culture, it has been said, is like "trying to push the bus in which one is riding" (Berger and Luckmann, 1966, p. 12). Others have compared the task to "trying to look out of the rear window to *watch* oneself push the bus in which one rides" (Hubbard, Henifin, and Fried, 1979, p. 33). Persons with racial, ethnic, sexual, or other minority status have special perspectives from which to observe the cultural vehicle. Frequently ignored, or relegated to marginal sections, they are by their circumstances forced to see phenomena that passengers more comfortably culturally situated are in no position to notice. During our psychoanalytic training we had repeated opportunities to observe aspects of psychoanalytic theory and practice that our fellow candidates and analytic colleagues had less opportunity and motivation to recognize. We could not avoid seeing the pervasive normative heterosexuality of developmental models from which our own lesbian relationship was so consistently and graphically excluded. In their *Wild Desires and Mistaken Identities* (1993) discussion of the psychoanalytic literature on female homosexuality, O'Connor and Ryan describe their situation as British psychoanalytically oriented therapists who are also women in lesbian relationships, forced to feel their alienation from theory and practice: "Psychoanalysis, as a body of theory and practice, has not been able to integrate homosexuality into itself. Instead homosexuality remains largely split off, inadequately discussed and understood, subject to rigid and sometimes attacking theorising, and to excluding practices" (p. 9).

Gay and lesbian therapists who undertake psychoanalytic training must find their way past these splits and that alienation. They must claim a place within psychoanalysis and cherish their identification as psychoanalysts in the absence of institutional psychoanalytic tradition or theory to support their relationships and in the face of considerable psychoanalytic culture and theory that pathologize them. Although we remain critical of much psychoanalytic developmental theory, we enjoy the practice of psychoanalysis and psychoanalytic therapy. We believe in the therapeutic efficacy of psychoanalytic treatment, and with Jane Flax (1990) believe that "for all its shortcomings psychoanalysis presents the best and most promising theories of how a self that is simultaneously embodied, social, 'fictional,' and real comes to be, changes, and persists over time" (p. 16). But our relationship has also made us painfully aware of the limitations of psychoanalytic knowledge about homosexuality. From our peculiar position we see the cognitive and emotional chasms that exist between gay and lesbian theorists and most psychoanalytic writers. The writing of many gay and lesbian cultural historians and critics reveals their engagement with psychoanalytic texts, but, although psychoanalysis has traditionally enriched itself through cultural studies and literature, psychoanalytic texts do not as yet reveal much engagement with the burgeoning gay and lesbian literature of recent decades. In an attempt to build a few intertextual bridges, we use images from lesbian literature to illustrate principles we find most useful in thinking psychoanalytically about homosexuality. We call these principles *lesbian rules*. A lesbian rule was originally a mason's rule made of lead "which could be bent to the curves of a molding." Thus, figuratively, it became, in the words of the *New Shorter OED* (1993) "a principle allowing flexibility." The O.E.D. (1989) provides examples of the term's use in the 17th century: "*fig.* a principle of judgement that is pliant and accommodating . . . . That Lesbian square, that building fit, Plies to the worke, not forc'th the worke to it. . . . Thou goest not by a straight rule, but by a leaden Lesbian rule."[1]

Clinical psychoanalysis uses many such lesbian rules. Free association, the concept of psychic determinism, the principle of over- or multiple determination of all psychic phenomena are all tools that help analysts follow the psyche's "curved surfaces." Lesbian rules such as therapist neutrality and anonymity are necessary for the construction and maintenance of the relational frame and for the creation, development, and interpretation of the various dimensions of transference. Clinical concepts such as empathy, projective identification, countertransference, and intersubjectivity are tools that help analysts "ply" closely to their patients' experience. For its understanding of sexual development, gender identity, and object choice, psychoanalysis still relies too much, however, on "straight-edge" formulas, problematical for the treatment of all patients and particularly limiting for understanding lesbian women. In the following sections we examine some assumptions about homosexuality that would benefit from the applications of more lesbian rules.

## The Story of Our Lives Becomes Our Lives, Part 1
## Making Up People: Cultural Contributions
## to Perception and Identity

We understand ourselves by affirming—as well as by rejecting—various culturally defined characteristics of culturally designated categories of persons. When new categories of persons or new definitions of persons become available, through the introduction of new images or newly attributed characteristics, we may use these new forms to discover or affirm aspects of our "nature" that previously were unarticulated. Ian Hacking (1986) calls this process, in which cultural categories and definitions organize perception as well as shape identity, "making up people."

> Social change creates new categories of people, but the counting is no mere report of developments. It elaborately, often philanthropically, creates new ways for people to be. People spontaneously come to fit their categories. . . . Making up people changes the space of possibilities for personhood. . . . [N]umerous kinds of human beings and human acts come into being hand in hand with our invention of the categories labeling them [pp. 70, 79, 87].

Before examining how this process affects perceptions about homosexuality, we begin with another, perhaps more familiar, example of making up people. In the 1960s in the United States, "the space of possibilities for personhood" expanded for many African Americans, as the Negro civil rights movement created new political and subjective identities. While organizing voter registration drives, integration sit-ins, and demonstrations in the cities and rural communities of the South, some civil rights workers began to read the previous generation of African American activists such as W. E. B. Dubois and Frederick Douglas. Some began to study African history and contemporary African and American politics. In such works as *The Wretched of the Earth*, Franz Fanon's (1963) description of the French colonization of Algeria, they saw reflections of American cultural colonization of African Americans. They put aside the suits and ties and polished shoes they wore to school and to church and began to wear the jeans, denim shirts, and rough boots of the laborers and sharecroppers they were registering to vote. They wore dashikis and combed their hair into "Afros" or "naturals." Against assertions that to be "Black" was to be dirty, physically lazy, mentally slow, oversexed, primitive, ignorant, childlike, and dependent, the civil rights workers insisted "Black Is Beautiful!" They demanded "Black Power!" The articulation of these new images and definitions shook the national social and political order as forcefully as did the voter registration drives, sit-ins, and national civil rights legislation. The "nature" of what it was to be *Black* changed. Previously denied and devalued qualities of African Americans were made visible and significant. The new Black identity, in turn, "created new ways for people to be."

A similar process has been underway for over a century around homosexual identity. McIntosh (1968), Weeks (1977, 1991a, b), Foucault (1978), Hacking (1986), and others have described the particular combination of medical-psychiatric-sexologist-homosexual activist discourses beginning in the mid-1800s through which the identity of "the homosexual" was established.[2] Previously, of course, same-sex sexual behavior and same-sex sexual relationships existed. These authors argue, however, that what was new in the 19th century was the belief that, by certain moral, mental, psychological, or physiological characteristics, *persons* who had sex with members of their own sex could be distinguished from persons who did not. A categorical Other, The Homosexual, was established, a person whose presumed moral, mental, psychological, or physiological characteristics, it was believed, could then be defined and studied. Lesbian psychoanalyst April Martin (1994) describes some of the consequences of this new construction. "[T]he invention of the homosexual minority . . . had profound effects, not only on how people label themselves, but also on what they do sexually, and on what they think, feel, dream, and fantasize about—in short, shaping the very nature of desire itself. These effects in turn influence and reinforce our observations that there seem to be two kinds of people in the world" (p. 12).

The belief that there are two kinds of people, homosexuals and hetero-sexuals, is today so deeply a part of the general culture and much psycho-analytic thinking that it may seem sometimes simply a description of the reality of human nature." "Nature," it is said, requires and supports het-erosexuality; homosexuality "goes against" nature. People live in male–female pairs (and in groups headed by such pairs), it is believed, because "the survival of the species" depends on that arrangement. Since male–female sexual intercourse is necessary for conception, male–female union is obviously the necessary arrangement for other human projects, such as raising children.

Examination of any society reveals numerous relationship patterns and practices that contradict such assumptions. Throughout history and across cultures men and women have lived in varying degrees of physical and emo-tional separateness. For instance, Freud (1920) described the lives of men and women in bourgeois Vienna, that center of family values: "[T]he bach-elor gives up his men friends when he marries, and returns to club-life when married life has lost its savour" (p. 158). Throughout history and across cul-tures children have been cared for and raised by women working together in various combinations: mothers with their other children, grandmothers, sisters, aunts, friends, village members, servants, and slaves. Abundant phe-nomenological examples as well as statistical data demonstrate that, how-ever much we may ideally wish to see ourselves as arranged in groups headed by male–female pairs, the daily emotional and physical arrange-ments of humans have always been more complicated. Persistently, across class and culture, the human species has also depended for survival on same-sex contacts and connections. But the Noah's Ark narrative, the story of two-by-heterosexual-two, organizes perception. In that narrative male–female pairs are Mother Nature's favorite children. And, as in any fam-ily where one child is favored, it is hard for the family members to become aware of their favoritism, and its effects, and to realize that their preference, however long-standing, may not be based on particularly accurate infor-mation about the other children's characters, behavior, or potentials.

## Untouchables and Eta: *"My Nature Was Created by Others"*

Sometimes those outside a culture can more easily see its foundational assumptions. The 3000-year-old caste system of India appears to an observer like a socially created and economically maintained system of inequity. But for many within that system caste is neither socially con-structed nor socially changeable; it is the product of *karma*, a process with which neither individuals nor society should interfere. Being homosexual in contemporary American culture has some similarities to being Harijan, or Untouchable. To identify as, or to be identified as, a homosexual marks one indelibly as a member of a stigmatized sexual class. One becomes subject to pervasive, powerful, distorted, and distorting descriptions of one's moral and psychological nature. As Foucault (1978) pointed out, in the "nineteenth century homosexual became a personage, a past, a case history, and a childhood, in addition to being a type of life, a life form, and a morphology, with an indiscreet anatomy and possibly a mysterious physiology. Nothing that went into his total composition was unaffected by his sexuality. . . . It was consubstantial with him, less as a habitual sin than as a singular nature" (p. 43).

Being homosexual in contemporary America has several obvious advantages to being Harijan. Harijan is both unchosen and unchangeable, a birth-to-death social assignment that determines residency, education, marriage, and employment. Being homosexual can often remain hidden. And as long as homosexuality is hidden and one can "pass" as heterosexual, one enjoys the same social privileges as others of one's race and class and sex.

On the other hand, Harijan grow up with certain advantages not available to homosexual persons. Whereas being homosexual is rarely a shared family identity, Harijan children grow up among similar family members and friends. Harijan youth have a ready-made community, however despised and devalued, in which to find support and in which they will find others like themselves to love and to marry. Homosexual children and adolescents undergo the painful and lonely discovery that they are different from their family and that their difference, if discovered, may result in their exclusion from family and community. No society prepares its youth for being homosexual. However liberal and tolerant their views about homosexuality, parents do not want their children to grow up gay and lesbian. However liberal and tolerant their views about homosexuality, few parents offer their children any cognitive or emotional supports for emerging homosexual feelings. They do not include the possibility of same-sex relationships in their descriptions of their children's futures. Few parents would comfortably and sincerely tell their children, "Some day you will grow up and find someone to love and marry. Maybe that will person will be a man or maybe that person will be a woman."

The irrationality of the discrimination and stigma experienced by gay men and lesbian women can also be compared to that endured by Japanese *burakumin*. Burakumin are persons whose ancestors several centuries ago were *eta*, the "filthy, nonhuman" outcasts at the bottom of the feudal-era class system. Eta were forced to live in ghettos and do the dirty work of society. Today their descendants continue to be discriminated against, although just who is burakumin can be difficult to establish. "No one in modern Japan can identify a descendant . . . by skin color, speech, religion, nationality, ethnic origin or any of the other landmarks of discrimination. Only by learning the address of a person's ancestors and determining that it was located in one of the feudal-era ghettos can a *burakumin* be identified today" (Jameson, 1993).[3]

Like many with homosexual feelings and relationships, many Burakumin pass as legitimate in their society while living in closeted fear that their identity will be discovered. "A sign made by holding up four fingers—symbolizing four feet, as if referring to an animal—can destroy in an instant the standing and respect of a lifetime."[4] When a business colleague makes that sign toward him, Shikimoto comes to realize that his wife's family is burakumin and he discovers that he himself is a member of a group he has been taught to abhor.

> When I saw that gesture, I cannot describe my shock. . . . A chill came over me. . . . The realization that the woman I loved and married was a *burakumin* and the place I lived was *buraku* community destroyed my hopes for the future.
>
> I understood, in rational terms, that people should not discriminate against other people. I tried to suppress my feelings, but for weeks, in my heart, I could not find a solution. . . . Nobody taught me to discriminate against *burakumin*, but in the years in which I grew up . . . it just became a part of me naturally [Jameson, 1993, p. 24].

Only through understanding "that my nature had been created by others" could Shikimoto overcome his shock.

Shikimoto describes experiences painfully familiar to many gay men and lesbian women. They have felt that shock of recognition: "I am that person I have been taught to despise. My sexual feelings are a perversion I have been taught to hate." Like Shikimoto, gay men and lesbian women see the disgust and fear in friends and colleagues when they identify as homosexual. Like Shikimoto, gay men and lesbian women, as well as their family and friends, wish they did not feel such disgust and fear. Some homosexual persons and their friends and families come to understand that their shock and disgust became a part of them "naturally," by virtue of growing up in the world. But many families never manage the process of recovering from the shock. Many friendships do not survive the revelation.[5]

## Ideologies of Homosexual Etiology and Their Consequences

Contemporary narratives about the nature of homosexuality revolve around questions of etiology and choice. Is one born homosexual, made homosexual, or does one choose to be homosexual? If homosexuality is a choice or a "sexual preference," then individuals can choose whether to practice certain sexual behaviors. From this position, the Roman Catholic Church maintains it does not discriminate against homosexual persons, while at the same time refusing the sacraments to persons who choose to "practice" homosexual behavior. The U. S. Department of Defense maintains that it does not discriminate against homosexual persons, while at the same time dismissing from the Armed Services persons who choose to identify themselves as homosexual.

Others argue that people do not choose to be homosexual. They have no choice about their "sexual orientation" because biology determines sexual preferences, just as biology determines eye color or handedness. Therefore, just as it is irrational to discriminate against persons with blue eyes, or persons who are left handed, it is unreasonable to discriminate against homosexual persons. Since biology/nature rather than nurture determines homosexuality, parents should no more be blamed for failing to raise heterosexual children than for having left-handed or brown-eyed children.

Some gay activists believe that such biological analogies will help end social and political discrimination against homosexuality. Similar analogies were used by the first homosexual rights activists as they tried to overturn German laws against homosexuality in the early 1900s. But relying on biology can be a problematic civil rights strategy. On the issues of "race" and "sex," biological arguments have frequently been used to establish and maintain "separate but equal" categories, that is, to justify and continue discrimination. The biologically determined chromosomal and genital differences between the sexes certainly did not lead to women's social or political equality. On the contrary, women have had to insist that, *in spite* of biological differences, they are not inferior to men and have rights to fair treatment and equal opportunity. The analogy between homosexuality and eye color also seems politically naive. Skin pigmentation, certainly a physical characteristic one is "born with" and has no "choice" about, continues to function as a primary marker to maintain stigma and discrimination.

Rather than rely on biological analogies, we prefer to address the various issues about "nature" and "choice" by comparing how people think about homosexual feelings and relationships with how they think about religious and political beliefs and feelings and practices. It would be extra-

ordinarily freeing for everyone if the notions most people have about homosexuality were more like those they have about religion and politics.

For instance, legally, the United States does not have a national public
policy of "Don't Ask; Don't Tell" regarding political and religious beliefs. In
fact, *both* the right of personal privacy about one's religious and political
opinions *and* the right of public and private expression of such practices are
culturally supported and legally protected. Although religious and political
stereotypes and prejudices obviously exist, legal and constitutional protections against discrimination also exist. These protections have yet to be
established for persons who identify as homosexual. Discrimination in hiring and promoting homosexual workers and in renting to homosexual ten-
ants is legal in the United States and in most states (see Appendix). Openly
gay and lesbian persons are dismissed from military service where they have
performed with merit. Divorced mothers raising children with their lesbian
partners risk losing custody of their children if their relationship is discovered (see Appendix). Private consensual sexual behavior between same-sex
adults remains illegal in many states. In 1996 the U.S. Supreme Court struck
down a Colorado law that discriminated against homosexual persons. The
Court argued that "a State cannot so deem a class of persons a stranger to
its laws." Unfortunately, however, gay and lesbian persons remain a class of
persons who are strangers to the law. State by state, city by city, gay and lesbian organizations and their legal supporters must engage in protracted legal
battles to end such legal alienation.

Conceptually, religious and political beliefs and practices are understood
to be important elements of some persons' identities, but their importance
does not suggest either essential innateness or unchangeability. For some
persons, spiritual or religious or political beliefs and feelings and practices
are so much a part of their lives and identities that they are willing to endure
all manner of societal abuse and intolerance rather than give them up. Some
people are even willing to die rather than renounce them. We usually consider such passionate positions evidence of character and integrity, whether
or not we share the individual's particular beliefs. We do not resort to spec-
ulations about innate biological drives or genes to explain the intensity of
such feelings and behaviors. In spite of news headlines to the contrary, at
present there is no biological evidence of a "gay gene" or of a "homosexual
hormone," and there are no known "biological markers" for homosexuality
any more than there are biological markers for being Republican or being
Methodist. A person may be born into a family with certain political and
religious beliefs and yet grow up to have a different religion and different
politics than parents and siblings. When this happens, we neither blame

parental nurturing nor search for hormonal or genetic explanations for such differences among family members.

Conceptually, religious or political beliefs and practices are considered matters *neither of conscious choice nor of inborn disposition*. On the contrary, political and religious beliefs are believed to develop, change, and fluctuate in their importance in any given society over time, as well as to develop, change, and fluctuate in importance in any individual over the course of that person's lifetime. Religious and political beliefs and practices are considered phenomena affected by history and social context. We understand that Roman Catholics in New York in 1997, for instance, did not believe and act as they did in England in 1697 and that they may not believe in 1997 Milwaukee as they do in 1997 Dubrovnik. We understand that Republicans and Democrats are not the same political beings in 1997 as they were in 1897, and that a Democrat from Boston may have different political desires than a Democrat from Iowa does. A woman who changes from being Roman Catholic to being Methodist does not think that her Methodist disposition was previously "latent." Nor need she explain her change by saying she is actually "bireligious."

Most significantly, the current reductionist debate over choice versus nature distracts attention from more obvious and significant issues, namely, that whether one is born homosexual, made homosexual, becomes homosexual, or chooses to be homosexual, as long as homosexuality is hidden, *being* homosexual does not affect one's abilities to care for children, defend one's country, preach the gospel, interpret the Torah, run for public office, or analyze patients. It is the *disclosure* of one's homosexuality that seriously affects one's opportunities to do any and all of these. My nature does not change when my homosexuality is revealed. But the perceptions of others about my nature and their attitudes and behavior toward me may dramatically change following such disclosure. The following example from a patient's life illustrates this all too common phenomenon.

## Ann

Ann, 23, came to treatment because of a troubling habit. She was so ashamed of her inability to control the behavior that she did not tell me (MM) its specific nature in the first sessions. She knew nothing about my personal life, but she had sought assurances from her referral source that I would be able to hear about her lesbian relationship with Jill without prejudice. Ann suffered daily defeat trying to end her compulsion. Her harsh self-criticism about this failure, which she saw as evidence of her "lack of will power" and her "weakness," left its marks on her psyche as surely as her compulsion left its mark on her body, but Ann had no interest in examining that particular harshness. She had at first tried to hide her habit from Jill, as she had also wanted to hide the parts of her body that she felt were "scarred and disfigured" by her habit. She had enlisted Jill's help to control the hated behavior, but when neither Jill's love nor vigilant policing worked, Ann decided reluctantly to seek professional help. She believed that "to tell the secret" would stop the behavior. After telling me, finally, the nature of her habit—a behavior in the family of acts that includes nail biting, cuticle tearing, and the like—and discovering that this disclosure, although momentarily cathartic, had no effect on her behavior, she was depressed and discouraged. She pressed me for behavioral strategies but settled into exploring her feelings and history.

Ann's parents had divorced when she was four. Ann and her mother lived next door to her maternal grandmother. She saw her father in annual visits, always accompanied by her mother. Ann's mother was a diabetic who did not manage her diet or her insulin. Her mother had many medical complications and hospitalizations during Ann's childhood. Ann recalled going into her mother's room at night to watch her chest move to see if she was still alive. A responsible, observant, care-giving child, Ann grew up a responsible, nurturing adult, and entered one of the "caring professions," a woman better able to pay attention to the body and needs of others than to her own.

Her compulsive behavior had begun at puberty. When I questioned how her family had responded, she recalled that her mother sometimes said, "I know what you are doing, and you must stop," but she did not otherwise try to interrupt Ann's behavior. Ann recalled once seeking help from a doctor, but said she had been told, "There is nothing I can do for you if you don't stop." She resisted seeking medical help because she believed the doctors would be as critical of her behavior as she was herself.

From time to time Ann berated me for my ineffectiveness. She considered going to group therapy for "addictive or self-mutilating personalities." Gradually she became aware of her own reluctance to focus on the only issue she said she wished to change. She became aware of how difficult she found it to tell me much of anything about her habit or even to describe under what conditions it was most likely to occur. As we examined this difficulty, she realized that the closed bedroom door behind which she had always hidden her compulsive behavior had at the same time created a private world where she could be alone without obligations or responsibilities. But being in that private room and that special internal emotional state had other, more disturbing characteristics. In that state Ann's feelings did not shape up into connections with specific thoughts. The compulsive behavior was therefore experienced as "mindless," as unconnected to any mental content. The most meaning she could find was that the compulsion seemed a response to her fear that something inside her was wrong or dirty and that it must come out. Ironically, instead of helping her rid herself of what she feared inside, her compulsion threatened to expose her difficulties for all to see. Ann feared that her urgent physical attempts to rid herself of what was inside had caused her to leave a permanent record of "scars and disfigurements."

In addition to developing the troubling compulsion, Ann had attempted to manage the emotional intensities of adolescence by joining a fundamentalist Christian church. She taught Sunday school and was active in youth groups. She met a born-again Christian family into which she emotionally "adopted" herself. Ann became a caring sibling to the family's two young daughters and confidante to their parents, Irene and Ed, who each separately disclosed to her their concerns about their children, their unhappiness in their marriage, and their troubled sexual relationship. Ann and Ed had long conversations about religion and philosophy.

Ann's mother died while Ann was in college. Ann moved from her hometown after graduation, but through many visits, weekly phone calls, and letters she maintained the relationships with her grandmother and with Irene and Ed. She felt that she could never tell her grandmother about Jill, but she longed to share her feelings with Irene and Ed, with whom she had shared some of the most important experiences of her life. She was always somewhat saddened by her sense that she and I did not share evangelical Christianity, a spiritual experience that, although not central in her life now, had had its strongest influence in her adolescence.

Ann knew that Irene and Ed would initially be shocked by her lesbian relationship. She knew well the Biblical texts they would cite in support of their position. But she believed that the long-standing intimacy of their relationship with her and their history of soul-searching discussions would, in time, allow their loving friendship to continue.

She prepared carefully for her disclosure. She and her "friend" Jill visited on several occasions so that Irene and Ed might know Jill first as a person, not as "a homosexual." Finally, she told them about Jill in a letter, a form of communication Ann chose deliberately to allow Irene and Ed maximum time to react, reflect, and respond.

Irene immediately cut off all communication with Ann. Ed first tried to save Ann, revealing to her more of his own sexual past in an attempt to help her identify with him and thereby turn from her sinful choice. When he became convinced after many long telephone calls and in-person discussions over several months that Ann was not going to give up the relationship with Jill, he told Ann that he and Irene had decided that they could no longer have her in their home or around their children because, as he said, "Everyone knows that psychologists show us that homosexuality is a case of arrested development."

Ann had been prepared for many arguments, but not this one. She had never suspected that her fundamentalist Christian friend, who had been actively opposed to her psychotherapy, would mount a psychological argument against her. Ed could so easily articulate a basic psychoanalytic tenet about homosexuality—it's a case of arrested development—not because he believed in or valued psychoanalysis, but because the texts that sustain Christian theology and those that sustain psychoanalytic developmental theory share fundamental assumptions about homosexuality. Whether development is understood to be divinely or biologically or psychologically ordered, primary same-sex relationships are not considered an expectable, potentially satisfying human developmental outcome.

## Sin, Abomination, Taboo

For most fundamentalist Christians (as well as for many contemporary Protestants and Roman Catholics) male–female sexual attraction and behavior is *natural*; that is, it is God's design for humans. Same-sex behavior or attraction is *sin*, that is, it is a turning away from God's commandment that humans express sexual desire only within relationships sanctioned by heterosexual marriage. From many psychoanalytic perspectives, same-sex attraction is *libidinal malfunction or a disorder of object choice*—a regressed or deviated or arrested expression of human desire, a turning back from, or turning away from, or failure to develop the *biologically based* imperative to discharge sexual energy in relationships that can lead to species reproduction. Freud (1905b) saw the final outcome of sexual development as the pursuit of pleasure coming under the sway of the reproductive function. Socarides (1978) built his formulations of homosexuality on expansive elaborations of Freud's psychobiological drive theory.

> [T]he male–female design is taught to the child from birth and is culturally ingrained through the marital order. This design is anatomically determined, as it derives from cells which evolved phylogenetically into organ systems and finally into two classes of individuals reciprocally adapted to each other. This is the evolutionary development of

human beings. The male–female design is perpetually maintained, and
only overwhelming fear can disturb or divert it [p. 5].

Heterosexual relationships are the expected and natural outcome of constitutional or biological rigging, which, unless impeded by too many infantile
disturbances or oedipal level conflicts, makes behavior leading to species
reproduction more *satisfying* than other sexual activity. Same-sex libidinal
attractions and feelings exist, but in mature development these become integrated into male–female relationships or sublimated into friendships.

Of course, neither theology nor psychoanalytic theory believes humans
capable of perfect development. Moral and psychological conflicts are considered fundamental to human nature. Through prayer, God's grace, or psychotherapy, people redeem, repair, or ease their souls or psyches. Some
psychoanalysts will maintain that homosexuality is not being singled out
for special treatment; it is simply one variety of psychological disturbance.
We believe that in most analytic writing and conference presentations, as
well as in the language and attitudes of the general culture, homosexuality
has a *special* quality of not-rightness and that homosexuality arouses feelings that other conditions, even those considered more severe, such as psychosis, do not elicit. Thomas Szasz (1970) noted the special position of
homosexuality in psychiatry and the general culture: "Our secular society
dreads homosexuality in the same way and with the same intensity as the
theological societies of our ancestors dreaded heresy" (p. 242). He saw
homosexuals as psychiatric "scapegoats" and likened homosexuality to "a
kind of secular (sexual) heresy" (p. 245). He equated the status of homosexuals in the United States to that of Jews in 15th-century Spain during
the Catholic Inquisition: "As the man with Jewish religion was considered
not fully human because he was not Christian—so the homosexual is considered not fully human because he is not heterosexual" (p. 244).

Many Americans of all ethnic groups, classes, and religions distance
themselves and their children from homosexual persons. They also distance
themselves and their children from murderers, rapists, thieves, and addicts.
But the fears aroused by criminals and persons whose behaviors are influenced by drugs or destructive passions are of a different quality than the
feelings aroused by homosexuality. The intensely negative visceral feelings
about homosexuality resemble the feelings set off by contact with that which
is *taboo*. They are similar to the disgust of those Japanese who avoid living
near or marrying the unclean *eta*, or the feelings of those who avoid intimate contact with Harijan or the nausea aroused by eating ritually unclean
foods. In the Jewish Torah as well as the Christian New Testament, same-
sex behavior is an *abomination*: "Thou shalt not lie with mankind, as with

womankind: it is abomination" warned Leviticus (18:22). "And if a man lie with mankind, as he lieth with a woman, both of them have committed an abomination: they shall surely be put to death; their blood shall be upon them"(Leviticus 20:13).

The laws of Leviticus were designed to bind the Jewish people together and to give them a group identity against the Canninites and others. Therefore Boswell (1980) and others have argued that homosexuality was seen as abominable and dangerous because it was a behavior practiced by some tribes neighboring the Jews: "The Hebrew '*toevah*' . . ., here translated 'abomination,' does not usually signify something which is intrinsically evil, like rape or theft, . . . but something which is ritually unclean for Jews, like eating pork or engaging in intercourse during menstruation" (p. 100).[6]

Homophobia is usually defined as a fear of homosexuality, and it is usually analytically understood to arise from a person's fears of repressed same-sex desires. This interpretation is too limited. Homophobia's literal meaning, fear of sameness, more aptly describes the underlying anxieties of contamination and contagion, anxieties heightened to terrifying intensities by the associations of the deadly AIDS virus with homosexuality. The socially constructed category of homosexual functions as a projective depository for numerous *unarticulated* feelings; its particular negative valence arises precisely because so many unarticulated feelings have been condensed into it and can be represented by it. Through the mental mechanisms of splitting and projection we can unconsciously assign feared and hated aspects of our self to an Other, or to a whole category of Others. We then fear that whatever we have hated in ourselves and projected into Others—people who are Jewish, homosexual, African American, Harijan, burakumin—will be returned to us and that these disowned attributes will be discovered to exist in ourselves. Erikson (1963) described various groups who have been targets of this kind of primitive and common social projection: "Psychoanalysis shows that the unconscious evil identity (the composite of everything which arouses negative identification—i.e., the wish not to resemble it) consists of the images of the violated (castrated) body, the ethnic outgroup, and the exploited minority" (p. 243). Sartre described the result of such projections and splitting in regard to homosexuality. "The homosexual must remain an object, a flower, an insect, an inhabitant of ancient Sodom or the planet Uranus, an automaton that hops about in the limelight, anything you like except my fellow man, except my image, except myself" (quoted in Szasz, 1970, p. 257)..

Women, minority ethnic groups, physically handicapped people, and persons with class-stigmatized ancestors—as well as those who identify as homosexual—bear the consequences of our human abilities to engage in massive, pervasive, societally accepted and supported splitting and projection. Those who have been the target of such projections must come to recognize how culturally disavowed characteristics have been made part of one's identity—"my nature had been created by others." This is an arduous intellectual and psychological task, a task about which psychoanalysis has been remarkably and significantly silent. Donald Moss's (1992) article on homophobia within psychoanalysis, which Moss chooses to call simply *hatred*, was the first such article on the subject in psychoanalytic literature.[7] Stanley Leavy (1988) is unique in his understanding of psychoanalysis's failure to appreciate homosexual love.

> Only lately has the world (or a small part of it) reluctantly become willing to see that sexual desire may have nothing at all to do with procreation. I refer to homosexuality, while regretting the word, since giving a "scientific" name to love and desire within one's own sex extends to it a clinical presumption. . . . It has not yet become common opinion that the capacity for homosexual love is an extension rather than a restriction of loving. Here, too, the ancient call to hatred is readily awakened: whatever feels bad inside is linked to a bad source outside. . . . While psychoanalysis has enlightened us in respect to the universality of homosexual strivings and feelings, it has harmed many homosexual people by convincing them, as well as their society, that their strongest impulses and greatest pleasures are symptoms of disorder [pp. 37–38].

## Clinical Double Bookkeeping

It is not so surprising, then, that, failing to convince Ann with Biblical citation, Ed sought to justify his decision to keep her away from his children, whom she had previously cared for, by using a psychoanalytic concept, "developmental arrest." Ann's disclosure may have stimulated Ed's anxieties about various aspects of his own sexuality and of his own relationships. Precisely because he and Ann had once shared such intimate closeness through their spiritual identifications, he now needed to insist on extreme physical and psychological distance. He needed to insist that she and he were irreconcilably different and that her contact with his children was dangerous to their development. Ann's nature had not changed, but Ed's view of her nature had dramatically transformed following her disclosure. Her spiritual and psychological soundness were now called into question.

And, of course, in Ann we *could* see a case of "arrested development." The psychic histories of all patients—as well as the stories of many persons who never seek treatment—are tales of blocked and arrested psychological movement. Unfortunately, however, in the particular kind of cognitive and emotional double bookkeeping achieved by the splitting and projective processes that take place about homosexuality, a characteristic of *all* who seek treatment, and many who don't, becomes a different order of disturbance when the person is homosexual. We assume that Ann's way of being homosexual has connections (but not necessarily causal connections) to her fears about what is "inside" her—including what some psychoanalysts would call her sexual and aggressive drives—and we assume that her way of being homosexual has been shaped by many factors, including too early or unfinished mourning for lost parental caretakers. Her way of being lesbian, like her choice of profession and her compulsive habit, has been shaped by intrapsychic conflict, defense, and adaptation arising from the circumstances of her psychosocial history and by how she has consciously and unconsciously constructed her own understandings of that history and of relationships.

Ann did not wish to be relieved of her profession, although that did change during treatment. Nor did she wish to leave her lesbian relationship, although she thought a great deal during treatment about her sexual feelings and about her past relationships with both men and women. She found her adolescent journals, filled with lists of rules, goals, and motivational promptings, records of her many attempts to deal with the habit. In one journal she found a fragment of a short story she had written and forgotten. In it the heroine looks forward happily to spending summer at camp with her girlfriends but discovers sadly that her friends are no longer interested in and excited by their relationships with one another. They are now intent on attracting boys. In one scene the heroine moves suddenly away from a chance encounter with some boys and goes into a "woman's room" to talk with her girlfriends.

Ann understood that as an adolescent she must have been as anxious as the girl in her story, and she explored many aspects of that anxiety. The more of her own history and feelings she felt she understood, the more she felt able to have an intimate relationship. She began to acknowledge some longstanding dissatisfactions about her relationship with Jill. Ann's decision to leave that relationship increased her self-confidence, and she began openly identifying as lesbian to friends and colleagues. She became increasingly engaged in gay and lesbian social and political activities. She also began a new phase of mourning for her mother. Her compulsive behavior never entirely ceased, but she came to have less harsh views of her behavior and her body and was finally able to care for herself and her own body by seeking medical care.

Should we see Ann's development at the end of her treatment as still arrested because she was not achieving the "mutuality of orgasm with a loved partner of the other sex" as Erikson (1963) maintained? Was Ann clinging to a "fictitious sexual identity" (p. 87) in order to "ward off states of depression or depersonalization and thus act as a bulwark against suicide or psychic death," (p. 92) the motivation that McDougall (1980) has ascribed to female homosexuals? Most analysts would agree that heterosexual desire, fantasy, genital orgasmic behavior, and sexual relationships are not sufficient measures of psychological development.[8] Rapists and serial murderers are capable of each and all. Instead, most analysts would examine the subjectively experienced qualities of their heterosexual patients' sexual experience and relationships. We state the obvious because the obvious, in various forms, is precisely what is frequently lost sight of when psychoanalytic discussions turn to women whose sexual or intimate partners are other women. In treating patients such as Ann, analysts must use the same measures of psychological functioning they would use in treating other women, rather than attributing prima facie pathology of any particular kind to homosexual relations.

We are often asked, when we make this kind of statement, "So, do you believe that homosexuality is just one normal variant of human nature?" Like George Groddeck (1923), who more joyfully than Freud celebrated his own "bisexuality," we suspect that if stigma and shame were removed from homosexuality, people (maybe most people, but probably not all people) would have the potential for meaningful emotional and sexual attractions with various (but certainly not all and may be not even many) persons of both sexes. We believe that homosexual relationships can be as rewarding and integrative, as productive and anxiety relieving, and as alienated, disruptive, disturbed, and defensive as heterosexual relationships. Homosexual feelings, behaviors, and relationships do not serve categorically different psychological functions than do heterosexual feelings, behaviors, and relationships.

About the "cause" or "origins" of homosexuality, we are at present what Boswell (1989) calls "agnostics," unconvinced by any of the various hypotheses of causality. Our bias is to believe—although we too have no proof—that any individual's attraction to and motives for being attracted to any other individual develop from conscious and unconscious processes such as memory, fantasy, and other symbolic orderings, all with their significant emphases and omissions, all of which make important contributions to the formation of attachments and desire. Clinically our interest is in the intrapsychic contributions that shape an individual woman's *way of being lesbian*. That clinical orientation leads us to be attracted to conceptions of any phenomenon, including same-sex love and sexual desire, that permit the most thorough articulation of shaping influences, supporting as well as disturbing, some of which may be, or may have become, unconscious, and which at the same time allow for the potential within an individual for continuing change and adaptation. *Therefore, we are interested in the ways in which an individual's psychodynamics interact with existing socially constructed definitions of same-sex relationships and lesbian identity.* For instance, individual women, depending on varying and changing intrapsychic factors, will react in various ways to the attribution of deviant femininity. A woman may joyfully, defiantly, or shamefully embrace, protest, deny, affirm, or emphasize that attribution as evidence of her difference, uniqueness, specialness, or defectiveness. And she may, over time, shift back and forth among these feelings and responses, as a function of both her own changing psychological issues and the changing cultural context in which she lives.

Women such as Ann may come to treatment with psychic conflicts, disturbances in object relationships and attendant ego inhibitions; with anxieties about their sexual functioning and body image; with narcissistic deficits and superego impairments; and with troublesome conscious and unconscious identifications with one or both parents. *As any woman may.* To know that the patient is in homosexual relationships or identifies herself as lesbian is to know nothing about her specific developmental issues, the nature of her sexual experience, or her conflicts, nor about the quality of her external or internal object relations. To understand those matters one must, as with all patients, do the work of analytic treatment rather than rely on formulas or assumptions about the nature or etiology of homosexuality.

## The Story of Our Lives Becomes Our Lives, Part 2: The Power of Naming

From the multiple facets of our experience we make intentional and conscious only those which language enables us to recognize as having existence and form. Clinically this means that *what we name* is made available for treatment; *what we leave unnamed* is made unavailable for therapeutic examination; how we name influences how and what we treat. Schafer (1974) has described "the problem of naming":

> To designate is also to create and to enforce. By devising and allocating words, which are names, people create entities and modes of experience and enforce specific subjective experiences. Names render

events, situations, and relationships available or unavailable for psychological life that might otherwise remain cognitively indeterminate.
Consequently, whether or not something will be an instance of masculinity or femininity, activity or passivity, aggression or masochism,
dominance or submission, or something else altogether, or nothing at
all, will depend on whether or not we consistently call it this or consistently do not name it at all. . . . Similarly, to the extent that we link
or equate such names as, for example, femininity and passivity, we
exert a profound and lasting formative influence on what it is said to
be like to be feminine or passive [p. 478].

Psychoanalysis has exerted a profound and lasting influence on what it
is said to be like to be homosexual. To the extent—and it has been a very
great extent—that female homosexuality is linked and equated with penis
envy, masculinity, gender identity disorder, narcissistic disturbances, preoedipal disturbances, and oedipal conflict, psychoanalysis has influenced
what is said to be lesbian. Chapter 3 explores the various ways psychoanalysis has named female homosexuality. To the extent—and it too has
been a very great extent—that psychoanalytic theory has focused on categorical etiologies rather than on the experiences of individual homosexual
patients and the developmental challenges attendant on homosexual identification, it has rendered significant aspects of psychological life unavailable for therapeutic examination.

When we apply lesbian rules to certain particulars of clinical writing,
we find it is often neither helpful nor accurate to use the words homosexual, heterosexual, gay, or lesbian as nouns. Although it may be rhetorically
convenient to call certain women patients homosexuals or lesbians, it also
reaffirms the notion that a category of persons exists—lesbians—whose
characteristics (sexual or psychological) are categorically different from (and
usually considered opposite from) those of another categorical set of characteristics belonging to women called heterosexuals. Those in the process
of pursuing social legitimacy and political equality use such language to
establish group identity (e.g., Blacks, African Americans, Gays, Queers), just
as those in the process of creating or maintaining social illegitimacy and
political inequality use such language (nigras, niggers, queers, spics, kikes).
But social, political, and economic categories do not equate with psychological distinctions.

Of course, using homosexual, gay, and lesbian as adjectives, as descrip-
tive modifiers of persons or things, does not solve the problem of reifying
categories. The category "lesbians" can simply be replaced by the category
"lesbian women." But using adjectives and modifying phrases sometimes

does allow greater flexibility and accuracy. Such usage allows us to distinguish, when necessary, for instance, between women who experience sexual attraction to other women, women who claim lesbian identities, and women with nonsexual but deeply bonded, lifelong, intimate partnerships with other women.

Many women feel that they fit comfortably into contemporary sexual categories and feel comfortable claiming membership in these sexual identities (heterosexual, homosexual, bisexual). But other women find these stifling. Sometimes a woman's rejection of being called "a lesbian" reveals what gay and lesbian psychologists call "internalized homophobia" or self-hatred. Sometimes a woman's distaste for calling herself " a lesbian" may express her narcissistic difficulty committing to *any* sexual or relational choice. And sometimes a woman's reluctance to call herself "a lesbian" expresses her resistance to having her identity reduced to one highly charged term and her refusal to be so categorized for others' rhetorical or political convenience. For such women, the difficulties associated with "coming out" often have as much to do with their frustration at such reductions as with any anxieties about discrimination and rejection. Most of our patients complained about the lack of satisfying language to describe themselves and their relationships. Speaking of her long-term relationship, one woman might say "my girlfriend"; another might say "my partner." One woman happily called herself "a gay girl." Several women said simply, "I live with and love a woman."

Although we prefer the terms same-sex and other sex (not opposite sex), sometimes we use the adjective homosexual in an attempt to reclaim, if possible, its neutral meaning of sexual or emotional contact, connection, desire, or interest toward a person of the same biological sex as oneself. We rarely use the term sexual orientation. Some use this term to assert the normality (as in "biological naturalness") of homosexuality. By nature (biology), one is oriented or attracted to persons of one's own sex or to persons of the other sex, usually unfortunately conceived of as the "opposite" sex. If one is bisexual, sexual attraction swings back and forth to either sexually magnetized pole. From this perspective, many hope and expect to find a biochemical, hormonal, chromosomal, or other biological basis for homosexuality. As we discuss further in the next chapter, polarized taxonomies (male–female; homosexual–heterosexual; active–passive; butch–femme; top–bottom) are common in the general culture, easily understood and accepted, and prominent in much psychoanalytic thinking. Their widespread acceptance does not, however, make them accurate. Clinical concepts derived from binary polarities are also not theoretically consonant with other psychoanalytic

concepts we find useful, such as a dynamic unconscious, multiple identifications, and the overdetermination of all psychic phenomena.

Finally, every woman's names for herself must be understood in relationship to the particular social/historical context in which she lives and its
prevailing narratives about homosexuality. In the late 19th and early 20th
century, complex social interactions came into being around the newly
socially constructed category of homosexual. In the late 20th century,
socially constructed identifications are continuing to develop as the discourses of contemporary gay and lesbian associations interact with contemporary medical forensic social religious biological labeling. Although
such processes create new possibilities of personhood, other possibilities
are at the same time diminished. As new categories become established,
their characteristics come to be seen as "natural," making other expressions
suspect or invalid. All narratives shape perception, while simultaneously
limiting the emergence and perception of other possibilities.[9] It is important, therefore, who gets a place before the microphones and cameras of culture to relate and depict the narratives and images of homosexuality.

## The Stories of Our Lives Become Our Lives, Part 3: Missing Narratives

The Heisenberg Uncertainty principle holds that the act of observation
affects the phenomenon observed. The implications of this tenet from sub-
atomic physics, namely, that reality is partly a function of the observer, have
been liberally applied in the social sciences. For instance, Galen Cranz
(1980) studied the role of women in the newly developed urban parks of
the late 19th century. Cranz found that the lithographs and paintings of the
period expressed public ideals about park usage. In these depictions women
were represented as spectators at the park athletic events; men were the athletes. Photographs of the period, however, provided different perspectives.
In the photographs, women appeared as active participants in the park activities rather than as the audience to male sport.

> [W]omen, especially young women, were responsible for much of the
> burgeoning interest in athletics. They began to play lawn tennis, cro-
> quet, and basketball and to ride bicycles in the 1890's . . . [but] the artis-
> tic images of women's role in public parks were slow to acknowledge
> the reality of their active sports life. . . . Lithographs of skating in Central
> Park express the ideal of heterosexual civility. Men teach women to
> skate, but only men suffer the indignity of falling down. . . . In pho-

tographs of the same scene, the ideal is betrayed by reality: Women are in pairs, teaching each other how to skate. Ideally, women are escorted by men, presumably their husbands, and learn from them; in practice, women learned from each other and probably fell down, too [pp. S82–S83].[10]

Historically most psychoanalytic descriptions of female homosexuality have resembled those urban park paintings and lithographs. Their images of lesbian women have been derived from theories of normative femininity; female homosexuality is, by definition, femininity's obverse. Psychoanalytic literature also contains a handful of clinical snapshots or images of lesbian patients and their analysts more equivalent to those urban park photographs. For instance, we see Helene Deutsch (1932) meet her once depressed and suicidal ex-patient on the street. We see a moment between Joyce McDougall (1989) and her patient Bendedicte; when McDougall leaves the consulting room, Benedicte suddenly recovers memories of her early father. Freud (1920) describes a family crisis as an 18-year-old girl falls in love with an older woman in bourgeois Vienna. He shows us one moment between himself and the patient: "Once when I expounded to her a specially important part of the theory, one touching her nearly, she replied in an inimitable tone, 'How very interesting', as though she were a *grande dame* being taken over a museum and glancing through her lorgnon at objects to which she was completely indifferent" (p. 163). Those are the only words Freud allows us to hear his nameless patient speak, but they convey the unfortunate dynamics between an earnestly expounding analyst and an outwardly compliant but unmoved patient.

Turn of the century women did not always fit painters' theories about feminine park deportment, as the period's photographs demonstrate. And in psychoanalytic discussions of female homosexuality, some patients have behaved in ways that did not fit their therapists' theories. Freud's patient brought him her dreams. Freud noted that the dreams were "distorted according to [the] rule [of dream construction] and couched in the usual dream-language" (p. 164), but he declared that they "could nevertheless be easily translated with certainty" (p. 165). Freud did not describe the dreams' images. He simply asserted that the dreams conveyed her "longing for a man's love and for children" (p. 165). Since, in Freud's theory, homosexual women did not dream such dreams, he told his patient that her dreams were "false or hypocritical" and intentionally deceptive. The patient brought him no more dreams.

Deutsch (1932) hardly recognized an ex-patient when they met a year after the analysis had ended. The patient, who had been chronically suicidal and depressed since adolescence, was now a " vivid, radiant person." Attracted to women since "an early age," the patient had always been too fearful to follow that desire. The patient told Deutsch that she had recently left her husband and found happiness "in an uninhibited sexual relationship with a woman." Deutsch was impressed with the patient's transformation. She understood that the analysis had "freed up" the patient's anxiety and had relieved her hostility toward female figures, feelings that had originated in her relationship with her mother. As a result of the analytic work, she felt capable, finally, of forming a relationship with a woman. But Deutsch could not see this as a successful outcome of analytic treatment.

Masud Khan (1964) treated a college student. He described the patient's sexual pleasure in her lesbian relationship and even attributed "ego-enhancing" benefits to the experience. Khan's writing demonstrates that he liked his patient and that he was impressed by the depth of her feelings in the lesbian relationship. Probably as a consequence of these feelings, he found it difficult to see the young woman as "a true homosexual pervert." He preferred to see her as passing "through a phase of homosexual perversion en route to health and a true integration of her femininity" (p. 256 ). Khan lost an opportunity to revise his ideas about lesbian women.

Other images of lesbian women, those provided by diaries, journals, letters, poetry, fiction, autobiography, and biography of women in sexual or intimately committed relationships with other women, may be unknown to analysts. Such depictions may be discounted or dismissed because, however much they reveal unconscious processes, they are not the product of analytic transference, the primary means through which analysts acquire psychic information.[11]

The issue of how psychoanalysts acquire evidentiary support for interpretations or theories is beyond the scope of this book. We do not suggest that either a clinical description or a theoretical formulation has better access to any objectively ascertainable reality. Nor do we believe that only a "lesbian therapist" can understand a "lesbian patient." Such arguments would contain the categorical assumptions and splitting to which we object. But we do insist that major impediments to analytic understanding existed as long as none of the theoretical discussions and none of the clinical cases in the literature could be written by analysts who had had lesbian relationships.

In addition to the effects of the historical exclusion of homosexually identified therapists from psychoanalytic training, there is another reason for the limitations and biases of psychoanalytic discussions of homosexuality, namely, that analysts whose lesbian patients did not fit psychoanalytic theories about female homosexuality rarely presented their work or published such cases. We do not share Mitchell's (1981) once sanguine assumption: "Most psychoanalysts approach homosexual material . . . as they would any other experiences of their patients. . . . Such analysts are not likely to write about psychoanalytic approaches to treating homosexuality, since they would tend to feel that homosexuality does not pose particularly distinctive or unique features in terms of analytic work" (p. 63 ).[12]

On the contrary, we believe that a publication and presentation closet has existed for certain analysts. Often they have chosen to keep silent about their patients and their work—not because they found the work so unremarkable, but because they feared being criticized, especially if their patients did not end their analyses as heterosexual, or at least no longer practicing "manifest" homosexuality. They kept silent because they feared that most deadly of psychoanalytic criticisms: *what you do is not real analysis.* Analysts have been afraid to speak openly with one another about other theoretical and clinical issues. For instance, there have been differences between what some analysts privately believed about the importance of external factors in child development and what they publicly said they believed about such factors: "Until recently psychoanalysts showing such interests [in external factors] were considered suspect by their colleagues. . . . Psychoanalysts remain sensitive to threats of exclusion and abandonment by colleagues, and research progress requires individual courage to withstand them" (quoted in Dewald and Kramer, 1976, p. 406). We believe that similar fears of exclusion and abandonment by colleagues have existed surrounding the treatment of homosexual patients. And we believe that these fears have affected analytic progress in understanding homosexuality.

Where does a woman who wishes to make her life with another woman find stories to live by? Where does she hear about, or read about, or observe the lives of women whose lives are not shaped by what Carolyn Heilbrun (1988) calls the only female narratives available, the conventional marriage plot or the story of "the fallen woman?" As we saw in the Introduction, the first 2,000 years of history and literature provided few narratives by women who loved women. Bryher's life certainly offers such a narrative, but her life was made possible by tremendous wealth and social privilege. And, even having those advantages, Bryher remains relatively unknown in the psychoanalytic literature. As we shall see in the next two chapters, psychoanalysis has developed two basic narratives about female homosexuality. In the first story, a woman who makes her emotional and intimate life with another woman is seen as having "fallen" from the path of true feminine development, expressing masculine not feminine identifications and desires. Freud's assertion that his patient had "forsworn her womanhood" expresses the central plot of this story.[13] In the second and related psychoanalytic narrative, a lesbian woman is psychologically immature, in the grip of "pre-oedipal" object relations, the same pathological mother–child "fixation" tale from which Rich's collage maker worked to free herself.

# "SHE FORSWORE HER WOMANHOOD"

## PSYCHOANALYTIC AND BIOLOGICAL THEORIES OF THE ETIOLOGY OF FEMALE HOMOSEXUALITY

If you don't know the kind of person I am
and I don't know the kind of person you are
a pattern that others made may prevail in the world
and following the wrong god home we may miss our star.

[William Stafford, 1977, p. 52] "A Ritual to Read to Each Other"

## Psychoanalytic Theories of Female Homosexuality 1920–1995

Several interrelated conceptual problems have influenced psychoanalytic understanding of female homosexuality: 1) a phallocentric bias; 2) a reliance on polarities and binary categories (male–female; active–passive; homosexual–heterosexual); 3) the division of lesbian patients into subtypes based on these binaries; and 4) the assumption that lesbianism is a "condition" for which a specific etiology, distinguishing developmental lines, and clinical characteristics can be discovered.

To understand the development of psychoanalytic thinking about female homosexuality, one must begin with the development of psychoanalytic theory about female sexuality, a history marked by frustrated but persistent attempts to articulate the experience, desires, anxieties, and vicissitudes particular to female development (Horney, 1924, 1926, 1932, 1933; Jones, 1927; Kestenberg, 1975; Stoller, 1968, 1976; Strouse, 1974; Schafer, 1974; Chasseguet-Smirgel, 1976; Galenson and Roiphe, 1976; Fast, 1984; Fliegel, 1986; Schwartz, 1986) . In early psychoanalytic theories of female sexual development, women's sexual anatomy was compared with men's and found wanting. It was claimed that women's "inferior" sexual organs forced them to envy or deny sexual difference. Because of their "castrated" body images, women were believed to have excessive narcissistic needs and to make object choices based on those needs. Because those already "castrated" do not fear loss of the penis, women, lacking castration anxiety, were thought to lack the motivation for superego development. Several generations of interested analysts revised male-centered models of female development so that penis envy, ego and superego impoverishment, passivity, dependency, and masochism are no longer considered defining female characteristics. As these characteristics, however, lost their power to define normal female development, they became instead the defining psychological characteristics of homosexual women. And there were no lesbian-identified analysts to protest this reassignment and its assumptions.

We can see this reassignment of negative characteristics take place in one of the earliest papers about female homosexuality, Jones's (1927) "The Early Development of Female Sexuality." Jones, who supported Karen Horney's revisions of Freud's models of normal female development, began his discussion by noting "the bias . . . common to the two sexes" regarding female development and by hoping that "analytic investigation will gradually throw light on the prejudice in question and ultimately dispel it. There is a healthy suspicion growing that men analysts have been led to adopt an unduly phallo-centric view of the problems in question" (p. 459). Jones said that what Freud took to be a "phallic stage" in girls, marked by activity and masculine identifications, was not evidence of penis envy. Jones suggested that boys and girls alike experienced "aphanisis," the fear of the total and permanent extinction of the capacity for sexual enjoyment. Jones thus proposed a model of oedipal-level anxiety and its related superego development that did not depend on male sexual anatomy or castration fears. Girls also had something to lose. In the process of redressing the bias against female sexuality, Jones went on to describe a group of women for whom he made no attempt to dispel prejudice. Having had "the unusual experience" of treating five cases of "manifest" homosexuality in women, Jones asked, "What differentiates the development of homosexual from that of heterosexual women?" (p. 460).

Identification with the father is thus common to all forms of homosexuality. . . . There is little doubt that this identification serves the
function of keeping feminine wishes in repression. It constitutes the
most complete denial imaginable of the accusation of harboring guilty
feminine wishes, for it asserts, "I cannot possibly desire a man's penis
for my gratification, since I already possess one of my own, or at all
events I want nothing else than one of my own. . . ."

As this identification [with the father] is to be regarded as a universal phenomenon among young girls, we have to seek further for the
motives that heighten it so extraordinarily and in such a characteristic
way among those who become homosexual. . . . The fundamental—
and, so far as one can see, inborn—factors that are decisive in this connection appear to be two—namely, an unusual intensity of oral
eroticism and of sadism respectively. These converge in an *intensifica-
tion of the oral-sadistic stage*, which I would regard, in a word, *as the central characteristic of homosexual development in women* [pp. 468–469].

Jones's paper illustrates several features of much analytic writing on the
subject of female homosexuality: 1) Jones took a formulation—penis envy—
which he had just discredited as an explanation of feminine development,
and used it to explain the development of female homosexuality; 2) he
divided his lesbian patients into subtypes, as if by so doing he was gaining
diagnostic clarity: "one type who set their hearts on being accepted by men
as one of themselves" and "those who have little or no interest in men, but
whose libido centres on women . . . [as] a vicarious way of enjoying femininity" (p. 467); 3) he postulated dichotomous etiology-based categories:
homosexual women–heterosexual women and proceeded to define the
developmental markers that distinguish women in these two categories; 4)
like many who would follow him writing on this subject, Jones saw the
developmental disturbance that supposedly characterized female homosexuality as taking place *earlier* in development—Jones suggested it is
innate—and of having greater intensity than whatever disturbances exist in
heterosexual women.

There have been other psychoanalytic accounts of the etiology of female
homosexuality. Female homosexuality has been described as:

- a disorder of drive/object caused by penis envy at the oedipal stage
  which leads to a repulsion toward heterosexual relations and a
  regression to a fixation of an earlier object: (Freud, 1920; Fenichel,
  1945)
- a disordered identification with the father in which identification
  replaces object relationship (Freud, 1920; Jones, 1927)

- an identification with the father in order to prevent psychotic symbiosis with mother (McDougall, 1964)
- failed identifications with mother—maternal envy interferes with identification (Freud, 1920) or the masochistic, debased life of mother interferes with girl's identification (Romm, 1965) or a narcissistic mother interferes with daughter's identifications (Siegel, 1988)
- a disturbance of early object relations characterized by masochism (Deutsch, 1932; Brierley, 1932; Socarides, 1978)
- a disturbance in separation-individuation (Socarides, 1968)
- a narcissistic disturbance (Siegel, 1988)
- a body-ego disturbance (Khan, 1964; McDougall, 1964)
- a premature genital awareness (Khan, 1964)
- a precocious turn-on of erotic desire, which "occurs when the child has been excluded from 'good enough' or long enough primary bliss and seeks inclusion by a sexual bond and sexual wooing" (Eisenbud, 1982)
- a disturbance with constitutional contributions (Freud, 1920; Jones, 1927; Socarides, 1963, 1968)
- a disturbance with no fixed etiology (Freud, 1920)
- a disturbance arising out of pathogenic family constellations (Deutsch, 1932; McDougall, 1964; Siegel, 1988)
- a symptom of other underlying disorders (Thompson, 1947)
- a borderline phenomenon characterized by defenses against psychotic as well as oedipal anxieties (McDougall, 1964; Quinodoz, 1989)
- behavior that occurs when there are no available men (Thompson, 1947)

A few analysts criticized such attempts to find a common etiological denominator in homosexual persons. Stoller and Marmor stressed the multideterminant nature of any psychic phenomenon. Both pointed out the prejudices in most psychological theories about female homosexuality. For Stoller (1985) "Homosexuality, like heterosexuality, is a mix of desires, not a symptom, not a diagnosis. . . . [N]o single clinical picture with common underlying dynamics and etiology holds for all homosexual women" (pp. 184, 185). Marmor (1980a, b) asserted that "clearly we are dealing with a syndrome that has multiple and diverse roots. . . . [Seeing] the development of homosexual preference as a form of 'disordered' sexual development is simply a reflection of our society's disapproval of such behavior" (pp. 7,

396). Fritz Morgenthaler (1988) criticized the psychoanalytic practice of polarizing heterosexuality and homosexuality. He challenged the assumption that "the selection of a homosexual partner . . . indicated a symptom, [and] that homosexuality as such makes an individual psychically ill" (p. 73). He described three stages of "undisturbed, normal development into homosexuality" in men. He acknowledged that "the simplifying formula—that everything would be alike in females if the conditions were reversed—is an assumption. . . . [F]emale homosexuality requires a separate examination" (p. 75).

Such views are not, however, representative of most analytic writing past and present on the subject of female homosexuality. On this subject, analysts have shown less interest in the examination of multidetermined phenomena than in distinguishing between supposed sexual and developmental polarities, homosexuality and heterosexuality.

Schafer (1974) has pointed to the difficulties Freud had working "within a nineteenth-century biological-medical tradition" that emphasized "great natural polarities or dichotomies" (pp. 482–483). Freud's thinking is riddled with such polarities: activity–passivity, manifest–latent, masculine–feminine, homosexual–heterosexual, secondary process–primary process. When nature and reality are conceived as composed of great natural polarities—male and female as "opposite" sexes, homosexuality as the "inversion" of heterosexuality—it is easy to conclude that traits or characteristics applicable to members of one sexual category—that is, male or heterosexual—must appear in some opposite form, or must be lacking altogether, in members of the other and opposite sexual category, that is, female or homosexual. Freud (1905b) attempted to redress the limitations of this kind of thinking in his qualifications within *Three Essays on the Theory of Sexuality* through his revisions of this work from 1910 to 1924 and in his writings on female sexual development (Freud, 1925, 1931, 1933a). In footnotes and disclaimers, Freud tried to escape the reductive implications of categorical thinking by assuring himself and his readers that he was not disparaging women or by insisting that "psycho-analytical research is most decidedly opposed to any attempt at separating off homosexuals from the rest of mankind as a group of special character" (Freud, 1905, p. 145*n*) or by maintaining that we are all have evolved from one sexual category, "bisexuality"; that we have all made and make homosexual choices; that we all have both active and passive characteristics within us.

In one of Freud's most creative attempts to avoid certain confining binaries he argued that "the nature of inversion is explained neither by the hypothesis that it is innate nor by the alternative hypothesis that it is acquired" (p. 140). In this statement Freud positioned himself in opposition both to his contemporaries who saw homosexuality as evidence of innate constitutional or biological degeneracy (innate or inherited immorality), and to those who believed homosexuality to be a product of social contagion (acquired immorality).[1]

## Zwischenstufen

But Freud's stated protest against separating homosexuals off as "a group of special character" also always conflicted with his wish *to use the existence of a difference as evidence of a boundary between opposites* and his belief that a fundamental etiological difference did exist between homosexual persons and heterosexual persons, a belief he shared with the sexologists and homosexual activists. For there were men of Freud's time who were quite willing to identify themselves as belonging to a group with "special" character.[2] Although some in the early homosexual movement, such as Benedict Friedlander, refused to separate themselves from other men by the assertion of innate differences, their views were outnumbered. The movement came to be led by such men as Magnus Hirschfeld, founder of the Scientific Humanitarian Committee, for whom persons attracted to others of the same sex were indeed a class with special character. They were *Zwischenstufen*, members of a third, or intermediate, sex. The Yearbook of the Scientific Humanitarian Committee (*The Yearbook for Intermediate Sexual Types, with particular attention to homosexuality*) published illustrations showing the differing physiologies of heterosexual men, heterosexual women, and intermediate-sexed persons (Lauritsen and Thorstad, 1974, p. 48).

Thus we can see the context in which Freud's ideas about homosexuality developed. Freud's (1905b) *Three Essays on Sexuality* developed in a discourse of sexologists, men who were interested in categorizing humans by their sexual behaviors, and homosexual activists, men who were trying to establish social and political legitimacy based on constitutional difference. Freud (1920) later cautioned: "The literature of homosexuality usually fails to distinguish clearly enough between the questions of the *choice of object* on the one hand, and of *the sexual characteristics and sexual attitude of the subject* on the other, as though the answer to the former necessarily involved the answer to the latter" (p. 170, italics added).

The "literature" Freud was criticizing was that of Hirschfeld's Institute for Sexual Research. Freud's (1905b) first footnote in *Three Essays on the Theory of Sexuality* was to "the well-known writing of Krafft-Ebing, Moll, Moebius, Havelock Ellis, Schrenck-Notzing, Lowenfeld, Eulenburg, Bloch and Hirschfeld, and from the Jahrbuch fur sexuelle Zwischenstufen, put out under the direction of the last-named author" (p. 135). Freud supported the political aims of the homosexual civil rights movement, namely, the abolishment of paragraph 175 of the Penal Code, which made homosexuality a criminal offense. He contributed to the 1928 Festschrift for the 60th birthday of Hirschfeld (Lewes, 1988), but he disagreed with Hirschfeld's assertion that a male homosexual was "a feminine brain in a male body." Freud (1905b) wished to distinguish *physical* sexual characteristics from what he called "mental qualities" (p.142), which, unlike the brain, he found no problem seeing as gendered masculine or feminine. Ironically, while Hirschfeld was intent on seeing homosexual men as having "feminine minds" in male bodies, Havelock Ellis and Freud were trying to rescue homosexual men from being seen as feminine. A primary motivation of Freud's seems to have been his desire to rescue homosexual men from being seen as having feminine mental qualities: "It is only in the inverted woman that character-inversion of this kind can be looked for with any regularity. In men the most complete mental masculinity can be combined with inversion" (p. 142).

## Lesbian = Masculine

What Freud, the male homosexual activists, and the male sexologists all could agree on, however, was the "masculinity" of homosexual women.[3] Freud (1920) described the case of a "beautiful and clever girl of 18, belonging to a family of good standing, [who] had aroused displeasure and concern in her parents by the devoted adoration with which she pursued a certain 'society lady'" (p. 147). He noted that the girl had "intellectual attributes [that] . . . could be connected with masculinity: acuteness of comprehension and her lucid objectivity" (p.154). Freud noted that to call these qualities masculine was merely "convention." He did not, however, think it was merely convention to characterize as "masculine" her behavior toward her loved one: namely, her "humility" and her "sublime overvaluation of the sexual object" (p.154). Speaking of the girl's bitter disappointment upon discovering that not she but her mother was to have a baby from the father, he claimed that "she forswore her womanhood and sought another goal for her libido. In doing so she behaved just as many men do who after a first distressing experience turn their backs forever upon the faithless female sex and become woman-haters. . . . She changed into a man and took her mother in place of her father as the object of her love" (pp. 157,158).

Freud's language here illustrates a major psychoanalytic assumption about female homosexuality: one who loves a woman must be like a man. Although Freud, at that time, found it difficult to see a man who loved a man as sexually or psychically feminine, he easily attributed *maleness* to a

woman's love for a woman. In summarizing the various factors contributing to his patient's homosexuality, he included oedipal disappointment
renewed at puberty, an original infantile fixation to mother, the advantages
for the girl of her "retiring" from heterosexual pursuits in favor of her envious mother, and the girl's "masculinity complex." As evidence of her masculinity complex, he said she was "a spirited girl, always ready for romping
and fighting, she was not at all prepared to be second to her slightly older
brother. . . . She was in fact a feminist; she felt it to be unjust that girls
should not enjoy the same freedom as boys, and rebelled against the lot of
woman in general" (p. 169).

An attribution of masculinity—variously defined as times and theory
changed from masculine *physical characteristics* to *masculine mental qualities*
to *masculine identifications* or *failed feminine identifications*—has haunted analytic depictions of female homosexuality. Even those who rejected the concept had to address it in their discussions. Helene Deutsch (1932), writing
about her experience with 11 cases of female homosexuality, began by stress-
ing "the fact that none of these eleven women presented physical signs
which might indicate that there had been a constitutional deviation, phys-
iologically, in the direction of masculinity. . . . [T]he patients showed no
physical signs of masculinity" (p. 208). Khan (1964), writing about a young
woman patient in a sexual relationship with a woman, who, he continues
to assure the reader, was not a "true pervert," still felt it necessary to point
out that "it would be a misrepresentation of the emotional experience of this
patient to conclude in this context that she was behaving in a 'masculine
way,' was being a man or that the behavior was unfeminine. That phallic
identifications (with the analyst-father-brother) helped her to find her way
to this 'infantile state of bliss' is true. But the aim was certainly feminine,
tender and passive" (p. 251). To rescue her from the charge of masculinity
Khan asserted that she was properly feminine—that is, tender and passive—
in her sexual aims.

If these definitions of masculine and feminine seem dated, new versions
of the supposed masculine component of female homosexuality may be
more resonant to some contemporary clinicians. A major shift in psychoanalytic theory occurred when "masculine identification" changed from
being a describer of supposed mental qualities—such as acuteness of comprehension or lucid objectivity—to being a manifestation of "disturbed gender identity." Many therapists today who would never apply Freud's term
"masculinity complex" to their homosexual women patients have adopted
the notion that female homosexuality is synonymous with a "disturbance
in gender identity." McDougall (1989), for instance, discusses "sexual iden-

tity formation and its inversions." For McDougall homosexuality is an "inversion" of gender identity which occurs because of the different oedipal crisis that she believes besets homosexuals.

> [W]hile accepting their biological sex as an inescapable reality, [others] refuse the sexual role that society attributes to masculine or feminine identity. This is the homosexual response to an internal conflict regarding sexual role and object choice. The reasons for this deviation in gender identity are various and highly complex. . . .
>
> [T]he heterosexual oedipal crisis . . . involves, among other important factors, the wish to possess in the most literal sense of the word the parent of the opposite sex while wishing death upon the same-sex parent. But there is also the homosexual oedipal drama which also implies a double aim, that of *having* exclusive possession of the same-sex parent and that of *being* the parent of the opposite sex [pp. 205–206].

Although she has argued for "a measure of abnormality" (McDougall, 1980) in us all and has reminded her readers that there are many kinds of homosexuality, McDougall has also persistently and variously distinguished heterosexuals from homosexuals, as if they were distinctive psychological categories. In her attempt to explain female homosexuality, McDougall says that, for a homosexual woman, "the father's penis no longer symbolizes the phallus and she herself embodies the phallic object. Through unconscious identification with the father, and by investing her whole body with the significance of the penis, she is now able in fantasy to fulfill a woman sexually" (p. 133).

This formulation has implications for women in lesbian relationships that McDougall may not have considered. If the unconscious intrapsychic arrangements McDougall describes—"she herself embodies the phallic object"—is present in both women, then, at least unconsciously, lesbian women are psychologically *homosexual men*. McDougall's thinking here is reminiscent of Freud's notion that the little girl is a little man who desires her mother, who she also believes has a penis. In such theories of female same-sex love, females wish to be men or they want male genitals or they love other women, who they believe have male genitals. A woman's sexual desire for another woman disappears in these discussions. McDougall (1980) like Hirschfeld, put homosexuals in an intermediate group which she calls "third structure people" or "neosexualities" (McDougall, 1985), who are neither psychotic nor neurotic, but are characterized by the overall frailty of their psychic functioning.

## Other Views of Female Development and Their Implications for Female Homosexuality

Stoller (1968, 1985) reversed Freud's idea that masculine identity was primary for both sexes and that a female child had the difficult psychological task of establishing femininity out of disappointment in discovering "the poverty of her sexual equipment." Stoller insisted that little girls have an early primary femininity, namely, a sense of themselves as female. He further suggested that femininity may even be easier to establish than masculinity.[4] Kirkpatrick and Morgan (1980) used Stoller's theory of primary femininity to explain the relatively greater ease women feel than men do in shifting the sex of their object. Kirkpatrick and Morgan (1980) hypothesized that if core female gender identity were a more stable formation than male, then sexual object choice would need to be less firmly fixed for women.

> [I]ntimacy with women on some level may be continuous as a natural part of a woman's emotional life. The sexualization of these experiences may not represent as much psychological distortion as in the male. In women, homosexuality and heterosexuality do not appear to be at opposite ends of a continuum as Kinsey et al (1953) suggested they were. Rather, the two trends might be seen as running a parallel course, capable of intermingling and of changing positions of ascendancy in consciousness and behavior under certain circumstances [p. 360].

The observation that women may be relatively freer in their object choices than men had early psychoanalytic expression in the writing of Georg Groddeck (1923), a little-known contemporary of Freud.

> [T]he woman's erotism is much freer than the man's in relation to the two sexes: it seems to me as if she had a fairly equal capacity of love for either sex, which can at need be transferred from one to the other without any great difficulty. In other words, it appears that, in her, neither homosexuality nor heterosexuality is very deeply repressed, that such repression as there is is pretty superficial.
>
> It is always dangerous to assign opposite qualities to men and women; one ought not to forget in that connection that in reality there is neither man nor woman, that everyone is rather a mixture of man and woman [p. 201].

For Groddeck, the unconscious mind was a continual script writer, its narratives expressed through the body in physical symptoms and through culture in creative acts. Instead of focusing on gendered or sexual distinctions among such scripts, Groddeck delighted in observing the variety of narratives both men and women could create. "Even before I went on to psychoanalysis there was as a basic in my medical thinking the conviction that in the human being, aside from the psyche with which science occupies itself, there exist thousands and millions of more or less independent inner lives which group themselves sometimes this way, sometime another, working together or in opposition, and are even quite independent at times."[5] Groddeck's image is reminiscent of Woolf's Orlando's psyche of multiple selves arranged like plates on a waiter's hand, each with its own constitutions and sympathies, a dynamic unisexed, multigendered universe.

## Turning to Science to Solve the Puzzle of Homosexuality

Some might explain the conceptual difficulties in analytic formulations of female homosexuality by pointing out that psychoanalysts are not, after all, hard scientists. Psychoanalysts must construct theory on the shaky sand of small clinical "samples." Their "data"—mental processes, feelings, associations, transferences—cannot be counted and measured in replicable, double blind studies conducted by uninvolved observers. Nor are psychoanalysts empirical psychologists. They can not engage in the kind of research done by Evelyn Hooker (1957). Hooker showed the results of Rorschach and other psychological tests to expert test interpreters and asked them to distinguish the test results of homosexual men from those of heterosexual men. To their thorough surprise, the expert test analysts could not make that distinction any better than could chance. One examiner, believing he could do better the second time, pleaded to redo the experiment.[6]

　　Some, believing that biology will eventually articulate the nature of homosexuality and distinguish homosexual women from other women, dismiss psychoanalytic explanations of homosexuality entirely. In his argument with the literature of the homosexual activists, Freud (1905b) ended by cautioning that psychoanalysis could not be relied upon to "solve the puzzle of homosexuality." That task, thought Freud, must be left to biology, which was beginning to have "very important results" and "remarkable transformations."

> Psycho-analysis has a common basis with biology, in that it presupposes an original bisexuality in human beings. . . . But psycho-analysis cannot elucidate the intrinsic nature of what in conventional or in biological phraseology is termed "masculine" and "feminine". . . . When one compares the extent to which we can influence it ["a modification

of inversion"] with the remarkable transformations that Steinach has effected in some cases by his operations, it does not make a very imposing impression. But it would be premature, or a harmful exaggeration, if at this stage we were to indulge in hopes of a "therapy" of inversion that could be generally applied [p. 171].

Steinach's experiments to which Freud was referring were based on the assumption that homosexuality was a pseudohermaphroditic biological condition. Steinach experimented first with rats and then on human males. He found what he believed to be female sexual cells, "F-cells," in the testes of homosexual men. Under his direction, surgeons such as Lichtenstern removed one of the "hermaphroditic testes" of a homosexual patient and replaced it with the undescended testes of a "normal" male. Steinach claimed that his research was successful in curing homosexuality, but that even greater success would have been possible if both homosexual testes could have been removed. That procedure was problematic, however, because, although it would have made the patient heterosexual, it also would have rendered him sterile.

Freud was impressed with this line of research, but he was not confident that similar surgical intervention would have such impressive results with homosexual women.

> If it were to consist in removing what are probably hermaphroditic ovaries, and in grafting others, which are hoped to be of a single sex, there would be little prospect of its being applied in practice. A woman who has felt herself to be a man, and has loved in masculine fashion, will hardly let herself be forced into playing the part of a woman, when she must pay for this transformation, which is not in every way advantageous, by renouncing all hope of motherhood [p. 172].[7]

Steinach's cure for female homosexuality would have also rendered the female patient sterile. Freud believed that homosexual women would not be willing to make the exchange. "Being forced to play the part of a woman," a change "which is not in every way advantageous," was too high a price to pay for a woman who "has felt herself to be a man and has loved in masculine fashion," especially if the normal compensation for women's not being able to be men—motherhood—would be unavailable. Since Freud equated female homosexuality with masculinity, nothing short of motherhood could compensate for its loss.

Barry Magid (1993) has summarized Freud on Steinach's scientific researches into homosexuality. We share his conclusions, although we might state them without Magid's self psychology emphasis.

That the then most fashionable and "scientific" research into the biological basis of sexual orientation sounds so bizarre to us today should serve as a caveat that the only appropriate avenue for psychoanalytic investigation is the subjective experiences of our patients. . . . When we explore the experience of our homosexual patients, we must take as our sole guide the ongoing function that sexuality serves. . . . A sexual orientation that makes available a range of positive, stable selfobjects is not in need of any further justification, and is neither stigmatized nor redeemed by looking for its origins either in early development trauma or biological predispositions [p. 431].

But other analysts still look optimistically toward biology for help in understanding homosexuality. And when biology looks at homosexuality *Plus ça change, plus c'est la même chose*. In the following section we examine major biological theories about female homosexuality. We discuss reviews of biological research by Richard C. Friedman and Jennifer I. Downey, two psychoanalytic examiners of biological research on homosexuality whose writings are becoming known to those psychoanalysts looking for alternatives to psychoanalytic explanations of etiology.

## Biological Theories of the Etiology of Female Homosexuality 1920–1995

While Hirschfeld was studying *Zchwisenstufen* and Steinach was searching for "F- cells" in the hermaphroditic testes of homosexual men and Lichtenstern was transplanting "heterosexual testes" into homosexual men, the lesbian psychiatrist Charlotte Wolff (1971) was in medical training in Berlin.

I can trace my first attempts to understand lesbianism back to those early days. . . .

The pioneer work of Hirschfeld and Steinach gave a strange glamour to the study of sexual deviation. . . . I was fascinated by the new views on the subject provided by the budding science of endocrinology. The books by Krafft-Ebing, Havelock Ellis and others . . . also pointed to a physiological cause of homosexuality. . . .

I must have already understood in those early days that many lesbians did not fit into the biological concept of Hirschfeld and others, who identified the intersexes with homosexuals. Intersexual people are hermaphroditic in the widest sense of the word, with secondary characteristics of the opposite sex. They may or may not be homosexual as well [pp. 44–45].

But the assumption that homosexuals are pseudohermaphrodites or intermediately sexed persons has always been a central component of psychoanalytic and biological models of homosexuality. Homosexual women are believed to have more maleness or greater levels of masculinity than other women, for example, more male hormones, more libido, increased paternal identifications, or increased masculine gender identity. At first, researchers believed that one could tell simply by looking at gross anatomical signs who was homosexual and who was heterosexual. Early editions of Krafft-Ebing's *Pychopathia Sexualis* contained illustrations that distinguished the toes of heterosexual women from the toes of prostitutes and the toes of female inverts. Later researchers claimed anatomical distinctions that had escaped the notice of Hirschfeld and Krafft-Ebing. Henry's (1948) *Sex Variants: A Study of Homosexual Patterns* contains illustrations of the enlarged labia and clitoris thought to be typical of homosexual women (p. 1102).

By the 1970s, scientists studying homosexuality had left behind such crude measures. By then they believed that the essential differences that made the difference, such as hormone levels and brain structures, would not be visible to the unaided eye. Sex steroids had been discovered and were now believed to be the operative agents in homosexuality, and they were used, therefore, in attempts to "cure" homosexuality. But by 1954, Swyer (cited in Birke, 1981) concluded that "there is no convincing evidence that human homosexuality is dependent upon hormonal aberrations. The use of sex hormones in the treatment of human sexuality is mainly disappointing." But research continued into the 1980s, searching for differences in the circulating levels of androgens and estrogens in heterosexual persons and homosexual persons. In 1984, Meyer-Bahlburg, reviewing 27 of these studies, concluded that they "in fact, showed no difference between the testosterone or estrogen levels of homosexual and heterosexual men." (cited in Burr, 1993, p. 58).

## Prenatal Hormone Exposure: Günter Dörner

Current hormonal research into the etiology of homosexuality hypothesizes that prenatal hormone exposure is the "predisposing" agent. Günter Dörner, a Berlin endocrinologist, was an early expounder of this hypothesis. Dörner (1979, 1989) described homosexuality as a pseudohermaphroditic phenomenon, an illness within the more general area of what he called "teratophysiology, the study of what causes physical damage and malformation." He believed that homosexual men were prenatally exposed to "unphysiological concentrations of hormones" that acted as "teratogens" during brain differentiation, resulting in "permanent disorders of mating and non-mating behaviour associated with permanent structural alterations in discrete regions of the brain" (Sigusch et al., 1982, p. 445). The notion that homosexuality had a biological basis first occurred to Dörner while he was watching ballet on television and noticed that "there were some homosexual dancers with typical female behavior . . . gestures that couldn't be performed by heterosexual males" (quoted in De Cecco and Parker, 1995, p. 3).

Charlotte Wolff (1971) also discussed the work of Dörner.

> [T]he most far-reaching and detailed investigation of the phenomenon has been undertaken by Professor Guenther Doerner, Director of the Institute for Endocrinology at the Humboldt University of East Berlin. . . . According to Doerner there can be no doubt about the fact that a disorder in the development of the sex glands in foetal life alters permanently an eroticizing zone, seated in the hypothalamus, which is a part of the mid-brain mainly responsible for man's emotional responses. This disorder produces male responses in a female and the opposite in a male individual [pp. 45–46].

Friedman and Downing (1993), reviewing genetic, hormonal, and brain study research on "sexual orientation," also enthusiastically cited Dörner's work: "Research on the sexual differentiation of the brain (Goy and McEwen, 1980) carried out in good part during the past 25 years, has yielded psychoanalysts and other behavioral scientists interested in the origins of sexual orientation provocative new findings (Dörner, 1983, 1986, 1989; Dörner et al., 1975; Meyer-Bahlberg, 1984)" (pp. 1163–1164).

Since few readers of that article probably had either the time or the interest to read the cited references, most were probably not aware that those provocative findings of the past 25 years (Goy and McEwen, 1980) came primarily from research on the brains of rodents. Even if curious readers had read Dörner's work, as cited by Friedman and Downey, they would not have learned, from those references or from Friedman and Downey's review, the nature of the experiments conducted on homosexual men between 1962 and 1979 in East Berlin, which used Dörner's rat research as their scientific basis.[8] Neurosurgeons inserted probes into the brains of homosexual patients and coagulated the hypothalamic area, which Dörner believed contained the "female sex center." Those experiments were stopped after both scientific and public protest.[9] Although Friedman and Downey (1993) propose that their review is an "attempt to discuss the significance of nonpsychoanalytic data for a psychoanalytic clinical readership" (p. 1165), *JAPA* readers also would not learn from their review that Dörner believed that wartime stress on pregnant women was responsible for the birth of homosexual sons (see Dörner et al., 1980, 1983) or that he suggested the use of prenatal endocrine screening and intrauterine sex hormone treatment of fetuses found with inappropriate sex hormone levels (i.e. homosexual levels).[10] Moreover, readers who followed up on Friedman and Downey's references to Meyer-Bahlburg would have been surprised to discover that Meyer-Bahlburg, in several reviews of hormonal research, actually concluded that biological research, including Dörner's, had yet to provide evidence for a biological etiology of sexual orientation.[11]

Why do Friedman and Downey (1993) use these references to Dörner and Meyer-Bahlberg to support a claim of provocative biological findings? And why do they make assertions such as the following? "We believe that enough evidence has accumulated from various sources to support the strong likelihood of primary biological factors shaping and influencing the emergence of homosexuality in some individuals. We infer this to be the case, despite the fact that no biological test reliably discriminates between groups on the basis of sexual orientation (Gooren et al., 1990)" (p. 1164).

That statement implies that some "biological tests" do discriminate between groups based on sexual orientation, albeit unreliably. But no "biological tests" discriminate in any way between these groups, as the writers referenced in Friedman and Downey's citation, Gooren, Fliers, and Courtney (1990), point out.

Friedman and Downey (1993) dispute Freud's notion of constitutional bisexuality and its clinical implications, namely, that unconsciously every homosexual man also is sexually attracted to women, and every heterosexual man is also unconsciously attracted to men.[12] Friedman and Downey apparently hope that biological explanations of homosexual etiology may redress the pathologizing of psychoanalytic explanations and lead to some clinical revisions. If exclusive homosexuality and heterosexuality are constitutional, analytic therapists could stop trying to change homosexuality by resolving unconscious conflicts. As Friedman and Downey assert, "We disagree with the view that homosexuality necessarily arises in reaction to pathological maladaptive intrapsychic conflict, or that heterosexuality should be assumed to be a universal developmental norm" (p. 1164). Friedman and Downey want to reserve the possibility of constitutional homosexuality "for some individuals."

> [T]he data in toto suggest that some people may well be strongly constitutionally predisposed to develop a homosexual or bisexual or heterosexual object for one reason or another. By this we mean that the conscious experience of specific types of erotic fantasies, initially experienced during childhood, is the consequence of constitutional influ-

ences in subgroups of individuals. Admittedly, this involves an induc-
tive leap, but not, in our view, a wild one [p. 1181].

Their motivation resembles that of Hirschfeld's Scientific Humanitarian
Committee, whose motto, "Per Scientiam ad Justitiam" (Through Science
to Justice), expressed the hope that, if science could prove that some persons were innately, biologically, constitutionally homosexual, social prejudice toward homosexuality would diminish.

If, however, as we believe, irrational and primitive fears and projections
are the primary obstacles to acceptance of homosexuality, as they have been
on issues of race and gender, then history offers little justification for believing that justice will necessarily be obtained through scientific research. No
particular scientific research was necessary to show that physical differences
existed among individuals, for example, differences of pigment coloration,
hair texture, eye color, and eyelid formation. No scientific studies were necessary to establish that such characteristics were "constitutional" rather than
matters of individual choice or control, conscious or unconscious. Just as
obviously, even without scientific studies, the physical anatomical differences between the human sexes are obvious, as are other easy to observe
phenomena, such as, for example, that adult females menstruate and males
do not, that females give birth and lactate and males do not. Scientific
research has enabled us to discover other sex differences not observable to
the unaided eye, such as, for example, that testes produce sperm and that
ovaries release eggs, that females have two xx chromosomes while males
have one x and one Y chromosome. But increased knowledge of these constitutional differences between males and females neither ended sex discrimination nor insured women fair or equal treatment. Such differences
have just as readily been used to justify unequal treatment and unequal
opportunity. For decades published scientific research found sex and "racial"
differences in cognitive, behavioral, and moral capacities.[13] Such findings
were accepted because they fit existing beliefs about "race" and gender.
Sustained and collected energies have been required to point out the inadequacies and errors of such reports, their design flaws, their biased assumptions, and their overgeneralizations.[14]

The question about differences, as Carol Tavris (1992) observed is not what
are the differences, but "Why is everyone so interested in differences? . . . What
functions does the *belief* in differences serve?" (p. 43). Some aspects of difference attract little interest. For instance, little attention is given to the fact
that the two sexes have more in common than that which distinguishes
them and that various racial and ethnic populations share more similarities
than differences. Or that there are more differences within racial categories

and within sexual categories than between each. Or that there are more differences among individuals than among groups. Research studies that find no difference where differences are culturally believed to exist do not make the headlines. And research studies that find differences where difference is desired are cited in "the literature" long after their assumptions have been discredited and their data found to be unreplicable, witness Friedman and Downey's citing Dörner's biological research.

## Brain Research on Sexual Orientation

Contemporary brain research on "sexual orientation" unfortunately follows in the tradition of earlier brain research on sex and race, searches that, as Stephen Gould (1981),[15] and Carol Travis (1992) have pointed out, were driven onward by their prejudices and by the problematic nature of their own findings. Anne Fausto-Sterling (1985) summarizes some of the researchers' dilemmas.

> Early studies, which discovered that male brains were larger than female brains, concluded that the female's smaller size resulted in her inferior intelligence. This logic, however, ran afoul of the "elephant problem": if size were the determinant of intelligence, then elephants and whales ought to be in command. Attempts to remedy this by claiming special importance for the number obtained by dividing brain size by body weight were abandoned when it was discovered that females came out "ahead" in such measurements. The great French naturalist Georges Cuvier finally decided that intellectual ability could best be estimated by the relative proportions of the cranial to the facial bones. This idea, however, ran aground on the "bird problem," since with such a measure birds, anteaters, and bear-rats turn out to be more intelligent than humans. Some brain scientists believed that the frontal lobe of the cerebrum . . . was an important site of perceptive powers and was less well developed in females than in males. Others argued that even individual brain cells differed in males and females, the cerebral fibers being softer, more slender, and longer in female brains [p. 37].

With the advent of the concept of "brain lateralization," researchers looked with renewed vigor for sex dimorphic specialization. Carol Tavris (1992) explains:

> According to one major theory, the male brain is more "lateralized," that is, its hemispheres are specialized in their abilities, whereas females

> use both hemispheres more symmetrically because their corpus cal-
> losum is allegedly larger and contains more fibers. . . . Geschwind and
> . . . Behan, maintained that this sex difference begins in the womb . . .
> [when] testosterone in male fetuses washes over the brain, selectively
> attacking parts of the left hemisphere, briefly slowing its development,
> and producing right-hemisphere dominance in men. Geschwind spec-
> ulated that the effects of testosterone on the prenatal brain produce
> "superior right hemisphere talents, such as artistic, musical, or math-
> ematical talent" [p. 45].

Tavris and other feminist scholars painstakingly continue to point out the
inaccuracies, false findings, poor research designs, and inflated findings of
such studies. "The observed differences are very small, the overlap [between
men and women] large, and abundant biological theories are supported
with very slender or no evidence" (p. 49).[16]

Although it is no longer so scientifically fashionable to speak of corre-
lations between brain size and intelligence, current research into the
assumed "sexually dimorphic brain" remains plagued by cultural stereotypes and prejudices similar to those which misled earlier research to
hypothesized associations between brain structure and racial superiority or
brain structure and masculine or feminine traits. Findings that homosexual
persons and heterosexual persons are more alike than different in their abilities and in their brains do not make the news; findings of essential differences make headlines.

## Simon LeVay

In August 1991 *Science* published Simon LeVay's "A Difference in
Hypothalamic Structure Between Heterosexual and Homosexual Men."
Various media portrayed LeVay's research as a scientific breakthrough. Its
assumptions fit cultural stereotypes about homosexuality, namely, that
homosexual men are more like women than they are like other men.

LeVay's work was based on work by Roger A. Gorski, who in the 1970s
had found a group of cells in a rat's hypothalamus that were larger in males
than in females. Because the area they were found in was thought, at that
time, to be significant in regulating the sexual behavior of rats, the cells were
called "sexually dimorphic nucleus." One of Gorski's team, Laura Allen,
looked for similar sex differences in the human hypothalamic area. In the
anterior hypothalamus Allen found four potential groups of cells, *INAH*
(interstitial nucleus of the anterior hypothalamus) 1, 2, 3 and 4. Two of these
nuclei, INAH 2 and INAH 3, Allen found to be sexually dimorphic, that is,

significantly larger in men than in women.

LeVay extended the search from sex difference to differences between homosexuality and heterosexuality. He hypothesized that Allen's nuclei were involved in the generation of "male-typical sexual behavior," defined by LeVay as being sexually "oriented" toward women. "I tested the idea that one or both of these nuclei exhibited a size dimorphism, not with sex, but with sexual orientation. Specifically, I hypothesized that INAH 2 or INAH 3 is large in individuals sexually oriented toward women (heterosexual men and homosexual women) and small in individuals sexually oriented toward men (heterosexual women and homosexual men)" (p. 1035). LeVay examined brain tissue from routine autopsies of 41 persons who had died in hospitals in New York and California: 19 presumed homosexual men who had died from AIDS (one bisexual male is counted in this group); 16 presumed heterosexual men, 6 of whom died of AIDS secondary to IV drug abuse; and 6 presumed heterosexual women, one of whom died of AIDS. There were no brains belonging to women who were identified as lesbian.

LeVay found that "the volume of this nucleus [*INAH 3*] was more than twice as large in the heterosexual men . . . as in the homosexual men" (p. 1035). Additionally, LeVay found similar volumes in INAH 3 between women and homosexual men. From this LeVay concluded that "the discovery that a nucleus differs in size between heterosexual and homosexual men illustrates that sexual orientation in humans is amenable to study at the biological level" (p. 1036).

*Criticisms of LeVay's Study* Following the publication of LeVay's research, there was wide acceptance of its implied linkage of homosexuality with brain structure, particularly hypothalamic structure. Criticisms of the study received less attention. These criticisms included sample size, various methodological procedures, LeVay's basic research assumptions,[17] his method of identifying his research subjects, including his control group,[18] his use of men who had died of AIDS,[19] various procedural issues, his reading his own slides instead of having them read by independent assessors, his assessing the volume of cells instead of counting the neurons,[20] his relying on group averages to distinguish groups,[21] and the fact that the study has not been replicated.

LeVay acknowledged many of these points but continued to maintain that a brain difference between homosexual and heterosexual persons had in fact been discovered. He went on to suggest that homosexuality is consolidated prenatally or very early in infancy: "I am saying that gay men have a woman's INAH 3—they've got a woman's brain in that particular part. In a brain region regulating sexual attraction, it would make sense that what you see in gay men is like what you see in heterosexual women" (quoted in Spanier, 1995b, p. 61). Frederick Suppe (1994) and others have argued that "the binary labeling of regions of the brain or behaviors as "male-typical" or "female-typical" is unwarranted when the phenomena are known to exhibit considerable diversity" (p. 231). Edward Stein (1994) pointed out that LeVay's focus on the hypothalamus as potentially related to "sex-drive" and specifically connected in some way to "sexual orientation" also was not well founded. Prior attempts to link the hypothalamus to sexual orientation have either not been proven, or if initial support was claimed, it later was not confirmed (p. 303).

Finally, William Byne (1994) observed that LeVay's work was founded on "an imprecise analysis of the relevant animal research." LeVay believes that INAH 3, like the *SDN* of the rat, is located in a brain area that generates sexual behavior in males. But Byne points out that Gorski and Arendash found that they could destroy the SDN on both sides of a rat's brain with no impairment of sexual behavior (p. 53).

Discussing LeVay's work and noting these and other qualifications, Friedman and Downey (1993) conclude: "These qualifications notwithstanding, LeVay's observations have generated much interest and will either be replicated in the near future, or not. If they are replicated they will stand as an empirical finding that mandates explanation in terms of a general theory of psychoneurobiolgical functioning of human sexual behavior" (p. 1178). That is a large mandate for a small study with significant problems. Unfortunately, even if LeVay's findings are never replicated, that study will undoubtedly continue to be cited, as Dörner's research was cited by Friedman and Downey. The use of such citations implies more solidity to the research results than yet exists.

## Female Homosexuality and CAH

The sexually dimorphic brain hypothesis and the role of prenatal hormones play featured roles in biological research that sees female homosexuality as a pseudohermaphroditic condition. Here we review this research and discuss Friedman and Downey's review of the research.

Biological researchers in female homosexuality began, as we have seen, by measuring the size of the sex organs of homosexual and heterosexual women. Homosexual women's organs, because they were thought to be more "masculine," were assumed to be larger than heterosexual women's. When these assumptions could not be supported, researchers moved on to measure circulating testosterone in adult lesbian women. Failing to find evidence that adult lesbian women had more circulating testosterone than other women (see Gartrell, Loriaux, and Chase, 1977; Downey et al., 1987), biologists, like their analytic counterparts, searched ever earlier in development for the hypothesized determinants or predisposing factors. Current hormonal theory holds that in female homosexuality, or at least in some "varieties," the prenatal brain has been "masculinized" by exposure to excessive androgen. This "masculinized" brain produces what researchers call "cross-sex" behaviors believed to be associated with female homosexuality. These cross-sex behaviors are divided into 1) sexual behaviors (or mating behaviors) and 2) nonsexual behaviors ("aggression," "maternalism," and "cognition"). These behaviors are taken from animal research on rodents and rhesus monkeys that had been either prenatally or perinatally exposed to excessive androgen.[22]

There is no way ethically to devise a research protocol in which pregnant human mothers are given testosterone and the behaviors of their daughters later observed for signs of cross-sex behaviors. So certain experiments of nature have been studied, such as congenital adrenal hyperplasia (CAH). Beginning with Money and Lewis (1966), girls born with CAH have been viewed by researchers as "in many respects a human analogue to genetic female rats, guinea pigs, and monkeys who were experimentally exposed to androgens during the prenatal and/or neonatal critical period of central nervous system differentiation" (Ehrhardt and Baker, 1974). Prenatally CAH female fetuses, who are chromosomally XX, were exposed to increased androgen levels—not soon enough to induce masculinization of the internal reproductive ducts (the Wolffian ducts), but in time to masculinize the external genital anlagen so that the babies are born with an enlarged clitoris or a genital that may look like a penis with undescended testes. From 1968 through 1995 ten studies explored the relation of prenatal hormonal exposure to female homosexuality by examining CAH girls for signs of the supposedly sexually dimorphic behaviors of animal research—aggression, maternalism, cognition, and "masculine" mating behavior (Ehrhardt, Epstein, and Money, 1968; Erhardt, Evers, and Money, 1968; Ehrhardt and Baker, 1974; McGuire, Ryan, and Omenn, 1975; Money, Schwartz, and Lewis, 1984; Slijper, 1984; Mulaikal, Migeon, and Rock, 1987; Dittmann et al., 1990a, b; Dittmann, Kappes, and Kappes, 1992; Berenbaum and Snyder, 1995).

We will summarize first some of the research predictions and findings associated with the "nonsexual" cross-sex behaviors (aggression, maternalism, and cognition).

*Energy Expenditure and Aggression*  Money and Ehrhardt (1972) believed that "the common denominator of many tomboyish activities in girls is a high level of physical energy expenditure, especially in the vigorous outdoor play, games, and sports commonly considered the prerogative of boys. Such activities correspond, it would appear, to the rough-and-tumble play of prenatally masculinized female rhesus monkeys" (p. 99). He therefore predicted a high energy expenditure in CAH girls. In three of the studies (Ehrhardt, Epstein, and Money, 1968; Ehrhardt and Baker, 1974; Slijper, 1984) CAH girls were reported to exhibit "a high level of intense physical energy expenditure in comparison with the other groups" (Ehrhardt and Baker, 1974, pp. 40–41). Ehrhardt and Baker reported that "This behavior was long-term and specific in the sense of a high degree of rough outdoor play rather than a general elevation of activity level" (p. 41). McGuire et al. (1975) and Dittmann et al. (1990a, b) did not find significant differences in energy expenditure.

Since androgenized rhesus monkeys also showed more "threat" behavior, Money and Ehrhardt (1972) speculated that "fetally androgenized girls might have evidenced more aggression against their playmates than did their matched controls" (p. 99). But when he discovered that "in point of fact, this did not prove to be true," Money suggested that researchers should assess dominance assertion, the striving for position in the dominance hierarchy of childhood, and he predicted that CAH girls would show increased dominance assertion.

Ehrhardt and Baker (1974), McGuire et al. (1975), and Dittmann et al. (1990a, b) could not find increased dominance assertion in CAH girls. Money and Ehrhardt (1972) invoked a cultural explanation to understand such results: "Quite possibly, they [the CAH girls] may have exempted themselves from competitive rivalry with boys, sensing that, because they were socially identified as girls regardless of their skills and accomplishments, they were obliged not to trespass on the culturally defined right of male superiority" (p. 100).

*Maternalism* The second set of "nonsexual" behaviors taken from animal research has been called maternalism. It was predicted that fetally androgenized females would have decreased maternal behavior, as measured by a decrease in doll play, a preference for playing with boys' toys, interest in a career over marriage, and a reduction in fantasizing about marriage and having children (Ehrhardt and Baker, 1974, pp. 38–39).

Of the 10 studies cited, only four examined doll and baby interest and marriage fantasies. McGuire et al. (1975) found no significant difference among CAH girls in these areas. Dittmann et al. (1990a) reported that "with regard to expectations for the future, *CAH* patients had less of a 'wish to have their own children' and a higher preference for 'having a career versus staying at home'" (p. 401). In their sample of 16 CAH girls, Berenbaum and Snyder (1995) found an increased preference for boys' toys and activities.

As early as 1977 Quadagno, Briscoe, and Quadagno had suggested an alternative explanation for any decrease in "maternalism" found in CAH girls:

> We propose that the . . . [CAH] girls were unsure of their role as poten-
> tial mothers due to their biological problems. Hence, they were less
> likely to verbalize aspects of maternalism. We feel that the information
> conveyed to the CAH girls had a profound negative effect on them in
> terms of their verbalization of interest in infants, pregnancy, and child
> care [p. 77].

*Cognition* The third nonsexual cross-sex behavior assumed to be influenced by prenatal androgen exposure is cognition. It was predicted that CAH girls, because of their masculinized brains, would have higher intelligence than would other girls. In 1966, Money and Lewis measured IQ in 70 CAH girls; the mean IQ was 109.9 with a range from 38 to 154. These results were compared with the presumed normal IQ distribution curve of the general population with a mean of 100. When 60% of the patients, rather than the expected 25%, scored higher than 110, Money speculated that the "elevated androgen, characteristic of the syndrome, may in some way be responsible" (p. 372).

Ehrhardt and Baker (1974) found the IQs of their sample of CAH girls only a little higher than the IQ of the general population. Bleier (1984) suggested that "the modestly elevated IQs in these families have nothing to do with prenatal exposure of the brain to excess androgens" (p. 103). She believed that any difference could be explained by the socioeconomic or intellectual factors of the sample, a "population of families that had access to sophisticated medical care in a major teaching and research medical center," namely, Johns Hopkins (p. 102).

But the notion of higher intelligence in a "prenatally masculinized brain" has not disappeared. Although the CAH subjects in a 1994 study showed *lower* rather than higher IQs, the study's authors, Helleday et al., suggested that cortisol treatment prevented the higher IQ they had predicted: "A potential for a more 'masculine' cognitive profile may not have been fully revealed, because of the suppressed adrenal androgen synthesis" (p. 353).

*Criticisms of CAH Studies* CAH research has been criticized from various directions. McGuire et al. (1975) and others note the use of sex-biased concepts: a girl should not rate "career" higher than marriage; a girl should not expend too much energy in rough-and-tumble sports; a girl should play with dolls; female IQs will be lower than male IQs. Methodological criticisms have included inadequate data collection, absence or inadequate control groups, and inadequate statistical analysis. The gender nonconforming play has usually been measured not, as one might expect in biological research, by on-site blind observers, but by retrospective questionnaire reports made by CAH girls or women and their parents.

There is another compelling omission in these studies, one most alarming to an analytic reader interested in human psychological development. The researchers emphasized the early exposure to excessive androgen and ignored or minimized other significant aspects of the condition CAH. CAH girls are not simply little girls who prenatally were exposed to increased levels of androgens. A CAH girl is born with an enlarged clitoris that may resemble a small penis; or she may even be born without a vagina. Parents of the newborn are told that the child is female and that later surgery will make their child look like a normal girl. Some CAH girls undergo multiple genital surgeries to construct a vagina and reduce the clitoris. Some clitoral reductions leave the woman incapable of orgasm. In addition, since with CAH the adrenal gland does not make cortisol, CAH girls must take cortisol daily for life, and, even with early intervention, they are chronically ill and must be closely monitored medically because the side effects of cortisol are multiple. Medication management is often difficult, and when the adrenal gland also does not produce aldosterone, life-threatening crises may result. These important aspects of CAH certainly must have psychological and developmental consequences for the child as well as psychological consequences for her family.[23] But these factors are barely mentioned in research reports, and they are not addressed at all by Friedman and Downey (1993) in their review of this literature and its implications for understanding female homosexuality.

Slijper (1984) is the only researcher who has taken into account the effect of chronic illness on the behavior of CAH girls. She compared CAH girls and diabetic girls with their nonchronically ill peers. She suggested that the increased activity of CAH and diabetic girls was more closely correlated to their being chronically ill than to any prenatal androgen exposure. Slijper noted that "chronically sick children . . . tend to react to a feeling of insufficiency with compensatory behaviour of a self-assured and bustling kind (Tavormina et al., 1976)" (p. 418). Regarding the decreased "maternalism" reported in CAH girls, Slijper remarked, "One also frequently finds an anxiety for the future in these [chronically ill] children which expresses itself in a low level of interest in marriage, motherhood and caring for small children (Schowalter, 1979)" (p. 418).[24]

Finally, the parents of CAH girls are affected by the chronicity of their daughters' illness. They face the challenge of raising a child as a girl whose external genitals look male. They must help their child through multiple surgical procedures and daily medication regimens. How parents meet these challenges must be important factors influencing the girls' development, behaviors, and future expectations. Ehrhardt and Baker (1974) acknowledged: "It is undoubtedly a traumatic experience for parents to have a baby girl born with a genital abnormality." Nevertheless, they claimed that, when they interviewed the parents later in life, "Most parents had little persistent concern about the genital abnormality at birth, especially since the appearance of their daughter's genitalia had been normal for so many years" (pp. 48–49).

Although early diagnosis and cortisol treatment may prevent further virilization and early surgeries correct virilization, many of the subjects in these studies had, nonetheless, considerable virilization due either to late treatment or to compliance difficulties. Dittmann et al. (1990a) observed that "a long-term experience of virilized genitalia for patients and parents could potentially influence patients' attitudes and behaviors in diverse ways" (p. 417). Although Ehrhardt and Baker (1974) reported that "the masculinized external genitalia can be surgically feminized soon after birth" (p. 34), research reports reveal great variation in the timing of surgical intervention. Ehrhardt and Baker themselves reported that "surgical correction of the external genitalia varied as follows: in six patients within the first year of life, in seven patients between ages 1 and 3 years, and in four patients later in life" (p. 37). Vaginoplasties are performed during adolescence. Moreover, surgical outcomes are also variable. Mulaikal et al. (1987) reported that 28 of 80 CAH patients did not have "satisfactory introitus and vagina" after surgery (p. 179).

*Mating Behaviors* The second kind of behaviors taken from animal research and hypothesized to be sexually dimorphic and affected by prenatal androgen is known as mating behaviors. The hypothesis is that excess androgen exposure leads to masculine mating behavior in females. Masculine mating behavior is equated with female homosexuality. An illustration in Byne (1994) shows the kind of mating behavior examined in rat research. We see two rats. One rat is called "homosexual" because she is said to exhibit "male mating behavior"; that is, she is "mounting" the other female rat. The other female rat, although apparently engaged in sexual behavior with a female rat, is not called homosexual. She is considered a normal, heterosexual rat, because she exhibits "female mating behavior," or lordosis. There are no equivalents to human lesbian couples in rat research. In the rat couples there is only one "homosexual" rat.

Phoenix (1978) cautioned: "It is a long way from the rat to the monkey and an even longer way from the monkey to man" (p. 30). This is particularly true in the area of sexuality. Nevertheless, on the basis of this animal model, the prenatal hormonal hypothesis predicts increased homosexuality in CAH girls.

Five of the ten CAH studies (Ehrhardt, Epstein and Money, 1968; Ehrhardt, Evers, and Money, 1968; Money et al. 1984; Mulaikal et al., 1987; and Dittman et al., 1992) addressed homosexuality in CAH subjects. The first problem facing researchers has been which behaviors to measure, since human female homosexuality is not a matter of mounting and lordosis. The studies do not share a common definition of homosexual behavior or of homosexuality. They use various and differing definitions, ranging from lesbian identity, to homosexual relationships, to homosexual sexual experience, to same-sex sexual fantasy content in dreams, daydreams, and nightmares.

Ehrhardt, Epstein and Money (1968) studied 15 CAH girls, age 5 to 16, and noted that the "tomboyism" of the CAH girls "did not include implications of homosexuality or future lesbianism" (p. 165). The second study, by Ehrhardt, Evers, and Money (1968) examined 23 CAH women, aged 19 to 55, who had not received cortisone treatment until after they were eight years old. The researchers reported that "even a strong degree of tomboyism did not preclude the possibilities of future marriage, childbearing and family life." In this sample, 12 of 23 had had heterosexual relations only, three to four reported homosexual/bisexual relations; six had had no sexual experience; and for one no information was available. The researchers did note that "if homosexual dreams and fantasies can be taken as a sign of homosexual inclinations, the incidence in our sample is 48%—clearly elevated and closer to the corresponding incidence of 50% given by Kinsey for the male" (p. 120). Money et al. (1984) described the sexual relations of 30 CAH women, all over 17 years old. Twelve were exclusively heterosexual, four were labeled bisexual/homosexual; seven were not sexually active; and no information was available for the remaining seven.

Mulaikal et al. (1987) examined 80 CAH patients, age 18 to 69. Forty-six were described as exclusively heterosexual; 4 were defined as bisexual; 30 were reported as having had no sexual experience. Dittmann et al. (1992) examined 34 CAH girls and women, only 9 of whom were over 21, and compared them with 14 control sisters. They reported: "Although not of statistical significance, the following variable was of particular interest: 20% of our [CAH] patients and none of the sisters reported having had or specifically having wished for a 'relationship with a female partner'" (p. 159). In the nine patients older than 21 years, four expressed such an interest.

In summary, none of the five studies, which in all had approximately

152 subjects,[25] reported any of the CAH females exclusively homosexual. Curiously, in Money et al.'s 1984 study and in the Mulaikal et al. (1987) study, which examined some of the same patients, five women who identified themselves as lesbian were described by the researchers as bisexual.

In general, the researchers' conclusions are represented by Dittmann et al.'s (1992) comments: "Only a certain percentage of patients in the present study and in previously reported studies showed a bi- or homosexual orientation. Thus it is important to point out that prenatal hormone effects do not determine the sexual orientation of an individual." Nevertheless, the researchers clung to the assumption, concluding "that prenatal hormonal conditions play a significant predispositional role . . . in the development of sexual orientation" (p. 164). Although CAH girls have not been found to grow up to be lesbian in any significant numbers, a number of articles misrepresent these data and some researchers concluded that more CAH girls would have been homosexual, if early cortisol treatment had not intervened.[26]

*Play and Fantasies* Sometimes the lack of direct evidence for adult lesbian identity and relationship is minimized while concepts such as "cross-sex latency play and homosexual fantasies" are emphasized. Friedman and Downey (1993) stress that CAH girls have more cross-sex latency play and homosexual fantasies than do other girls owing to the influence of prenatal androgen.

> Prenatal androgens influence childhood play and interest in certain other sex-dimorphic activities. Indeed, this latter effect supports the conclusion that prenatal androgen influences postnatal nonsexual behavior, as well as postpubertal sexual behavior. Psychoanalysts who routinely use a developmental model of the origins of adult behavior in their clinical work will readily appreciate the importance of this point [p. 1169].

Three unproved assumptions are offered by Friedman and Downey as scientific facts: 1) play is a "sex dimorphic activity," which is 2) biologically determined 3) by prenatal androgens. Friedman and Downey also suggest that differing "developmental lines" may exist for various "subgroups" of lesbian women. For instance, they describe one group who arrive at a lesbian identity later in life.

> Although they have the capacity to be erotically aroused by males or females, they turn to women and adopt a lesbian lifestyle after disappointing or frankly traumatizing experiences with men in early adult

life. Such women not infrequently comment that they find men more erotically arousing in fantasy, but that the sexual relationship with a female partner is so much more gratifying emotionally (in a global sense) that they prefer it [p. 1189].

What is the meaning of the qualifying parenthetical phrase "(in a global sense)"? Does that mean "overall" gratifying? Friedman and Downey claim that "what is striking about this group of women is that their erotic capacities and experiences unfold in a nurturant, interpersonal context" (p. 1189). Why is this striking? Friedman and Downey also claim that there is a sex difference in the function of erotic fantasies.

With regard to the psychic and interpersonal context within which erotic fantasy is (consciously) experienced, males and females tend to differ. Men tend to be led by erotic fantasy. . . . Although this occurs in some women, many others, in this case homosexual women, seem "led" by a need for empathy, intimacy, connectedness, and caring. Their erotic fantasy life requires kindling in an intimate relationship before it becomes shaped. Such women may change the gender of the erotic object during their lives as a function of their intimate relationships [p. 1190].

Men can start their own sexual fires since they are "led" by internal fantasy. Although some women apparently can also be self-starters, "many women, including in this case homosexual women" require a relationship in order for their erotic life to unfold. Curiously, Friedman and Downey's kindling metaphor is the same metaphor that Freud (1905b) used to describe the sexual experience of women. For Freud, the clitoris was preliminary kindling to the real blaze, the vaginal orgasm (p. 221).

Friedman and Downey (1993) acknowledge that "the use of nonhuman animal data to make inferences about human sexual behavior has been criticized" (p. 1173) and that "there is an active debate going on among psychoendocrinologists today about whether the nonhuman mammalian sex research literature can be interpreted to indicate that sexual orientation in humans may be directly affected by prenatal androgen" (p. 1175). Nevertheless, they declare themselves convinced of the prenatal hormonal influence on "sexual orientation." "Despite all reservations and qualifications, the largely circumstantial evidence that a prenatal biological effect, probably hormonal, influences sexual orientation seems convincing to us. Too many different lines of research converge around the same common findings for the results to be dismissed" (p. 1179).

Where there is so much smoke, they believe, there must be fire. We suspect it's more a matter of smoke and mirrors. As William Byne (quoted in Burr, 1993) cautioned, "If the prenatal-hormone hypothesis were correct, then one might expect to see in a large proportion of homosexuals evidence of prenatal endocrine disturbance, such as genital or gonadal abnormalities. But we simply don't find this" (p. 62). To date there in no evidence of inadequate or in any way diminished reproductive capacities in homosexual persons.

The conceptualization of homosexuality as a pseudohermaphroditic condition is now over 100 years old and 1,000 studies deep.[27] We share Meyer-Bahlburg's (1990/91) conclusion about the findings: "The evidence available to date is inconsistent, most studies are methodologically unsatisfactory, and alternative interpretations of the results cannot be ruled out" (p. 281).

## Conclusion

How different conceptually, finally, are contemporary biological models of homosexuality from those of early homosexual activists and sexologists? How different are LeVay's (1991) assumptions from those of Karl Ulrich, who in 1865 postulated "a class of individuals who are born with the sexual drive of women and have male bodies"? (Quoted in Dannecker, 1981, p. 33). And how different conceptually are biological models of female homosexuality from psychoanalytic notions of forsworn womanhood, masculinity complexes, and gender identity disorders? Steinach believed he had found "F-cells" in the testes of male homosexuals. Lichtenstern surgically removed "hermaphroditic" ("homosexual") testes and transplanted single-sex ("heterosexual") testes into homosexual patients. Neurosurgeons, using Dörner's model of homosexuality, probed the "female sex centers" of the brains of male homosexuals. Money predicted that prenatal hormones contributed to "sexual dimorphic play" and higher intelligence in males or in "masculine" women. Friedman and Downey (1993) found brain research on laboratory rats and rhesus monkeys and studies of congenital hormonal abnormalities provocatively relevant to psychoanalysts trying to understand human homosexuality.

Freud saw homosexuality in various ways: as an "aberration" of the sexual drive (1905b), an "inversion" of sexual object relations (1905b), a "perversion" of the drive's aim, as "one variety of the genital organization" (1920, pp. 150–151). Clara Thompson (1947), objecting to Freud's drive theory, suggested that the term homosexuality had become a "wastebasket into which are dumped all forms of relationships with one's own sex." Then she threw in some of her ideas: she called homosexuality a symptom, like, she said, "a headache" [which] may be the result of brain tumor, a sinus, a beginning infectious disease, a migraine attack, an emotional disturbance, or a blow on the head. When the underlying disease is treated successfully, the headache disappears" (pp. 183, 187). As Mitchell (1978) has pointed out:

> The choice of analogies, again even among those questioning existing theory, tends to suggest pathology by offering conceptual frameworks for viewing the development of homosexuality that are derived from an understanding of ulcers (Friedman) or masochism (Lachmann). The problem is that even if one addresses secondarily adaptive or growth-enhancing aspects of the behavior, one is still employing a paradigm derived from a condition understood to be originally and most basically pathological [p. 260].

We offer two metaphors from two women patients, neither metaphor based on medical or biological analogies. One woman's conscious interest was in men; her sexual fantasies were of men. She saw herself as a heterosexual woman who suffered from major blocks to achieving satisfying relationships with men. Previous therapy had helped, but in her late 30s, before entering analysis, she had suddenly and with very little difficulty formed a deeply satisfying relationship with a woman. Although she explored from many directions in her analysis the possible causes for this surprising development, it always seemed other or more than the sum of any explanations she considered. One day she used a football analogy to describe her making the lesbian relationship. "It's like a lateral pass," she said. "The intended receiver is not open. So one passes off laterally. Progress is not interrupted, and movement can go forward." Although amused by her own football metaphor, she felt that it conveyed both the motivation behind her "change of object"—to allow emotional development and movement to continue—and the feelings she had experienced making it, namely, the deep satisfaction of having her moves responded to by an "open" receiver and the excitement in the moment the connection was made.

Another woman offered a different metaphor from her experiences. She had had a lesbian relationship in college and another in graduate school. She had been married for 10 years and, after her divorce had begun a fulfilling relationship with a woman. "It's like double Dutch in jump rope," she explained. "You just keep jumping. One partner may move out of the rope and another may move in. But you keep jumping. It's the motion of the rope, the movement of your partner, and how you relate to that person that enables you to stay in the game."

These metaphors offer images of interpersonal relationship rather than of pathological development. In the first, life is compared to a football field, where "forward progress down the field" can be impeded. A change of object allows for the possibility of further development. Of course, using this football analogy, one might also miss connecting with an intended lateral receiver, or that receiver may drop the ball, or defensive tackles may descend on both passer and receiver. There is the possibility for disruption, conflict, as well as further adaptive movement toward the "goal posts," defined by this woman as a satisfying and sustaining intimate object relationship. In the second image, life is also likened to a game, this time to the challenges of a girls' jump rope game. Our mastering of each challenge is determined by our own capacities for timing and balance, by the turns of the rope of fate, and by our ability to match our rhythms with those with whom we may share fate's turns.

Female homosexuality is not a clinical category characterized by distinguishing developmental disturbance, characteristic biological correlates, or different developmental lines. Female homosexuality has not been proven to be a matter of pre- or postnatal hormonal levels. Women with homosexual desires and relationships cannot be distinguished from other persons by the size and shape of their toes, the size and shape of their labia, or even the size and shape of their INAH, all hypotheses founded on the phallocentric attribution of masculine qualities to lesbian women.

In the next chapter, we examine the second major phallocentric assumption about female homosexuality: women who love women are like children, psychologically and sexually immature.

# 4

# ASSAULTS AND HARASSMENTS

## THE VIOLENT ACTS OF THEORIZING LESBIAN SEXUALITY

To alienate conclusively, *definitionally*, from anyone on any theoretical ground the authority to describe and name their own sexual desire is a terribly consequential seizure. In this century, in which sexuality has been made expressive of the essence of both identity and knowledge, it may represent the most intimate violence possible.

*[Eve Kosofsky Sedgwick, 1990, p. 26]*

[G]ender ontologies always operate within established political contexts as normative injunctions, determining what qualifies as intelligible sex, invoking and consolidating the reproductive constraints on sexuality, setting the prescriptive requirements whereby sexed or gendered bodies come into cultural intelligibility.

*[Judith Butler, 1990, p. 148]*

Clearly much work remains to be done by feminist lesbians to determine whether or not psychoanalysis can be fruitfully appropriated and elaborated for the purpose of theorizing lesbian sexuality, for articulating the specificity of lesbian desire.

*[Dianne Chisholm, 1992, p. 219]*

Is there a specificity of lesbian desire? Are the erotic pleasures of women who love women categorically different from those of other women? Some lesbian women insist on the existence of such specificity, as do many psychoanalysts. What do two women together do sexually? Psychoanalysts have often had difficulty getting their patients to talk about these matters, and difficulty understanding patients who did speak. Freud (1920) was keenly interested in his patient's sexual behavior. When she denied any interest in discussing what he thought should be her desires, he assumed she was simply defending against her wishes: "With none of the objects of her adoration had the patient enjoyed anything beyond a few kisses and embraces; her genital chastity, if one may use such a phrase, had remained intact. . . . She was probably making a virtue of necessity when she kept insisting on the purity of her love and her physical repulsion against the idea of any sexual intercourse" (p. 153).

In his *Clinical Diary*, Sándor Ferenczi (1932) noted that several of his female patients and women friends had complained: "'Men don't understand,' women say, and are (even in analysis) very reticent about their homosexual feelings. 'Men think women can only love the possessors of penises'" (p. 124). Ferenczi had earlier recounted having made a "psychoanalytic confession" to a woman patient: "(the disclosure of my never-before-expressed dislike of a homosexual relationship, perhaps accompanied simultaneously by a trace, on my part, of male and medical jealousy)" (p. 103). That same "trace" of male and medical jealousy may have led him to the following conclusion about homosexuality in women: "In reality, they [women] continue to long for a mother and female friend, with whom they can talk about their heterosexual experiences—*without jealousy*" (p. 124). Ferenczi had difficulty appreciating another "reality": some women want other women as primary partners not as confidantes about their heterosexual relationships.

Khan (1964) described what he called the "ego-enhancing" pleasures of one woman's sensual exploration of another woman's body: "Their dialogue of bodies and erotic love gave her a unique sense of aliveness and well being, a freedom from fear and inner nagging" (p. 252). Such descriptions tempt readers to identify with the young patient. "She now recounted how she adored licking the grooves around the neck of her friend, it always gave her a strange and uncanny feeling of her friend's wholeness and smoothness" (p. 259). But any temptations to identify are quickly thwarted by Khan's interpretations: "The impulse to eat and bite was only thinly veiled here. The fight with the oral-sadistic and anal-sadistic impulses now came to the fore" (p. 259). Following in the footsteps of Freud, Jones, Glover, and Deutsch, Khan looked at female homosexuality and saw infantile sexuality:

> The intensity and polymorph eroticism of the relationship, . . . con-
> sisted of kissing each other's breasts, masturbating each other. . . .
>     One particular body-organ and its use was rather significant: namely
> the tongue. . . . [T]he libidinization of the genitalia with the tongue
> [also] served a very positive function in increasing the narcissistic cap-
> ital of her body-ego. . . . Another rather interesting function of the
> mouth-tongue-breast-hand activities was, that combined with hand-
> caressing, it was helping to differentiate the body-organs with their sep-
> arate status and role. This extremely primitive function can perhaps be
> described as a sort of body reality-testing [pp. 85–86].

Would Kahn have described a man's sensual exploration of a woman's body
as "mouth-tongue-breast-hand activities" and interpreted such behavior as
fulfilling "extremely primitive functions"?

    The frustration Freud and Ferenczi expressed about their patients' reluc-
tance, resistance, or lack of interest in reporting their sexual behavior can
still be heard seven decades years later in the words of Quinodoz (1989):
"The psychoanalytic literature has little to say about the nature of the erotic
and sexual exchanges between homosexual women. The patients themselves
have little or nothing to say about them" (p. 58). Although he apparently
heard little or nothing from his patients about their sexual practices,
Quinodoz nevertheless had much to say himself about the specifics of lesbian desire.

> Erotization of the skin is particularly important and is often a form of
> defence against the painful feelings connected with mourning and sep-
> aration. Some women confine themselves to exchanges of this kind,
> while others use the fingers or the tongue as a substitute for the penis.
> Jones (1923) and Flügel (1925) investigated the use of the tongue by
> female homosexual patients for the achievement of an identification
> with the penis, this identification, according to Jones, reaching "a quite
> extraordinary degree of completeness. I have seen cases where the
> tongue was an almost entirely satisfactory substitute for the penis in
> homosexual activities." Jones had already noted in 1923 that fixation
> to the nipple militated in favour of the development of homosexuality
> in women [p. 58].

    The violence of such notions is far reaching. Individual experience and
individual meanings are obliterated. Skin sensitivity is pathologized: it
masks mourning or fends off psychosis. When a woman uses her fingers or
tongue or whole body to explore a woman's body, they become penis substitutes. When a woman uses her fingers and tongue or body to explore a

man's body, they remain her fingers and tongue and body. Women who find sensual delight in another woman's breast are infantile; men who find delight in women's breasts are sexually mature. If her skin, her fingers, her tongue, her breast and nipples, her whole body are seen as pathological, a woman has no way to touch another woman sexually.[1]

Two related aspects of psychoanalytic thinking contribute to psychoanalytic alienation from lesbian sexuality. First, psychoanalytic ideas about female homosexuality are byproducts of psychoanalytic perceptions of female bodies. Commenting once on Freud's anxiety about female sexuality, McDougall (1986) noted that "Freud was . . . a little afraid of the objects of his fascination. His metaphors constantly reveal a representation of the female genital as a void, a lack, a dark and disquieting continent where no one can see what is going on" (p. 213). Second, psychoanalytic metaphors about sexuality rely heavily on the use of synecdoche, a figure of speech in which a part of something is made to stand for the whole something. For instance, when we say, "There are a lot of hard hats on that job," we mean, "There are a lot of construction workers on the site." A characteristic of the hat—its hard toughness—is used to represent the whole person. When we call certain persons "hard hats," we mean their characters may have a certain impervious rigidity. In sexual theories, the genitals, or parts of genitals, are used as synecdoches. Idiomatic sexual synecdoches are common: "That guy's a real prick." "That really took *cajones*!" Genitals, or, rather, parts of genitals, come to represent, even determine, the whole person. Whatever characteristics are ascribed to these genital parts (e.g., penetrating, probing, firm) become the physical, moral, psychological, emotional, and intellectual characteristics ascribed to all persons who have such a genital. We will examine these anxious, phallocentric, and synecdoche-driven theories at work, first in contemporary psychoanalytic discussions of female sexuality and then in psychoanalytic discussion of lesbian sexuality. Such sexual theories are easy to construct. They seem simply "natural," obvious common sense to many people. They can be difficult to deconstruct and revise because they make reality seem so simple, so black and white, like night and day, left and right. Such notions are, however, violent acts that limit perception, distort experience, and restrict possibilities.

## Female Sexuality: Something Is Certainly Lacking

Although there is still disagreement about the onset and importance of vaginal sensations in young girls, probably few analysts would still agree with

Freud (1905b, 1933a) that the clitoris is masculine or that a girl's discovery of her vagina comes at puberty (Kleeman, 1976; Galenson and Roiphe, 1976). Nevertheless, for many analysts, it has been difficult to surrender their beliefs in the superiority of male sexual anatomy as a psychic and intellectual organizer. For instance, although Kestenberg (1975) disagreed with Freud's (1937) assertion that a "repudiation of femininity" in both sexes was "nothing else but a biological fact" (p. 101) she nevertheless held that men were better able, because of their anatomy, to externalize the "anxiety-provoking nature of inner-genital sensations." "By virtue of their outwardly oriented male sex anatomy and physiology [men] can learn much faster than women. Women require a great deal of priming of their principle sex zone, the vagina, because they lack direct experience with it earlier in life and because the vagina is an internal, visceral organ" (Kestenberg, 1975, p. 150).

Some analysts have attempted to amend such pervasive phallocentricism by offering more valorizing synecdoches of female sexuality. The dark void was replaced by the fertile inner space. For instance, Donna Bassin (1982) urged a conceptualization of that inner space that "goes beyond maternal/reproductive functions."

> Women's early experiences of inner space seem to contribute to the construction of a category of experience, like phallic activity and its representations, which serve as structures of knowing and creating the world. It is suggested that these symbolic images are connected with biological origins and provide a base for a mode of cognition that is available to women through appropriate analytic and environmental stimulation [p. 200].

Female bodies have no monopoly on "inner space." Significant inner spaces are also to be found in male sexual anatomy, however much psychoanalytic writing ignores their existence. The colloquial synecdoche, "That guy really has balls," honors the scrotum, the sac whose inner contents determine reproductive potency as much as does the penetrating penis. Penis-centric analytic discussions of "castration anxiety" so thoroughly ignore this aspect of male sexual anatomy that castration has all but lost its original meaning, namely, loss of the testicles. Anita Bell (1961) and Robert M. Friedman (1996) have pointed out the long-standing psychoanalytic defense against awareness of the importance of the testicles.[2] Furthermore, psychoanalytic metaphors that equate inner space with female coexist, paradoxically, alongside other equally pervasive psychoanalytic metaphors in which the psyches of members of both sexes are symbolized by various nonsexual metaphors of inner space. Skin makes a boundary between "inside" and "outside" and often serves as a somatic site for anxieties about contact and penetration. Various nonsexual body cavities hold organs that represent feelings and cognition. Inside the chest is the heart; deeper "inside" lie the "gut feelings" of stomach and intestines. Inside the skull is the "mind," an "inner world" where both men and women are ruled by unconscious "internal objects."

Thomas Laqueur (1990) demonstrated how our stories and metaphors about sexual bodies determine our perception of those bodies and how powerful notions of difference and sameness determine what one sees and reports about the body.[3] One telling psychoanalytic example of this phenomenon can be found in descriptions of female sexual anatomy by several contemporary women analysts. In these discussions female genitals are repeatedly described as hidden away, out of reach, difficult to locate. Their alleged physical inaccessibility is believed to have significant psychological consequences. For instance, Doris Bernstein (1993) lamented Freud's failure to consider the impact of the girl's own body on her psychic development. "It is," noted Bernstein, "as if she had no genital of her own" (p. 40). Bernstein insisted that the girl's body, "her experiences with it and conflicts about it, are as central to her development as the boy's body is to his" (p. 41). Bernstein described what she saw as specific developmental conflicts and anxieties of female bodies. "The girl is confronted with a different task [than the boy]—she must comprehend, integrate, and locate what is beyond sight, touch, focus, and control" (p. 48).

> The girl herself does not have ready access to her genitals, which touches on many levels of experience. She cannot see them as she and the boy can see the boy's genitals. This creates immense difficulty in forming a mental representation of parts of her body in which there are most intense physical sensations. . . .
>
> In addition to the visual difficulty, she does not have complete tactile access to her own genitals; she cannot touch and manipulate them in a desexualized way as can the boy. Hence, she does not acquire tactile, familiar, and sensual knowledge of her body that is not forbidden or tied to forbidden fantasies. Moreover, when she does touch her genitals, there is a spread of sensations to other areas . . . [p. 44].

The anxieties Bernstein believed are particular to such an anatomy are anxieties of "access, penetration, and diffusivity."

> The inaccessibility of female genitals through normal sensory modes— sight, touch, as well as specificity of sensation—creates difficulties in forming mental representations of critical parts of her body. This occurs

during the toddler phase of development when issues of differentiation and self-definition are the central developmental tasks. The phase
is also saturated with issues of control—over the body in terms of
developing musculature and anal control, with the mother in terms of
autonomy, with the world in terms of language acquisition and sym-
bol formation.

. . . Where is her genital? She must trust mother's assurance that it
is tucked away [pp. 155–156].

Bernstein believed that since "touching, seeing, controlling, manipulating
and naming (Kleeman, 1976) are the equipment with which children build
up mental representations of their own bodies, the outer world, and their
power and control over themselves, people, and things" (p. 44), girls are at
a psychological disadvantage. Bernstein saw "the diffuse nature of the girl's
genital [as having] a significant impact on the nature of her development"
(pp. 44–45). Bernstein offered excellent examples of young girls who feel a
need for greater control over their "openness," but she attributed the problem to their anatomical structures.

McDougall (1986 ) has also described a girl's physical awareness and
thus mental representation of her genitals as vague and confused. "Since the
little girl cannot visually verify her genitals nor create other than a vague or
zonally condensed psychic representation of them, she has difficulty in
locating the sexual sensations of which she has been aware since early
infancy. Clitoral, vaginal, urethral, and other internal sensations tend to be
confused" (p. 216). Like Bernstein, McDougall suggests that a girl must
depend on her mother for locating and libidinalizing her genitals.

These stories about bodies stress particular differences between males
and females. First, males have ready access to their genitals: females need
outside help to find and libidinalize their sexual equipment. A young girl
needs her mother's help; the grown woman needs a *male* partner. Second,
male anatomy does a better job of organizing physical sensations and anxieties than does female anatomy. Because a female experiences sensations in
several parts of her anatomy at the same time, her experience is said to be
"diffuse" and her sensations "confused" (rather than, for example, "multi-
sited" and "complex"). The task of organizing her sensations makes it more
difficult for the girl to focus, to come to the point, so to speak, to have the
clarity and the superior psychological and intellectual ability that derives
from male sexual anatomy.

But female genitals are not out of reach or out of sight, nor are they more
zonally "confused" and "condensed" than male genitals. Nor are they more
dependent on outside agency for libidinal priming. Little girls do masturbate.

Their fingers find their way to those supposedly inaccessible areas. Female anatomy does not make women less able to organize anxiety, nor does their anatomy put women any more at risk than men for fuzzy thinking about the world and themselves. These stories maintain gender divisions anatomy and physiology do not support.

Although female genital anatomy is not vague, inaccessible, or hidden, the language available for its description is markedly scarce. This scarcity must have its own psychological consequences (Irigaray, 1974; Lerner, 1976).[4] Although Bernstein stressed the importance of naming for development, her own vocabulary for female sexual anatomy is so limited that it is difficult for a reader to sense just what she is describing. For instance, in her consideration of a girl's body, Bernstein never mentioned the clitoris, one aspect of female sexual anatomy well suited to be found by "the normal sensory mode" of touch, having as it does more nerve endings for its size than does a penis. The only function of a clitoris is to give pleasure when it is touched, stroked, rubbed. Unlike a penis, a clitoris does not eliminate urine; unlike a vagina or uterus or penis it is not related to reproduction. Perhaps precisely because pleasure is its only function, little girls are seldom given a name for this part of their bodies. Cultures thus routinely practice linguistic clitorectomies, excising from articulation one primary site of autonomous female sensual and erotic pleasure. As Katherine Dalsimer (1986) pointed out about a related aspect of female sexuality:

> There is a rich vocabulary of slang available to describe boys' masturbation. In contrast, *not one* colloquial expression exists in English to describe that of girls.
>
> The disparity, I think, is astounding, and its implications far-reaching. . . . The virtual absence of a colloquial vocabulary means that there is no easy, joking way for the girl to learn that other girls do it, too. Simply, her secret is unspeakable.
>
> And the language of psychoanalysis tends to echo this disparity [pp. 36–37].

Elizabeth Lloyd Mayer (1985) also has noted the absence from the psychoanalytic literature of descriptions of little girls' awareness of their own genitals. In Mayer's descriptions, however, female sexual anatomy is visible and full of lively sensations. Her descriptions also demonstrate how many parts of a female body still bear Latin rather than colloquial names.

> Certainly the vagina is not easily seen or explored by the young girl, and this has significant implications for the extent to which she can mentally represent such an organ at an early age.

But the little girl's *external* genitals include a vulva as well as a clitoris. While the concentration of the girl's genital excitement may be focused in her clitoris, those clitoral sensations are embedded in a vulva that has definite and readily discerned perceptual and sensory attributes. While the extent of infantile vaginal awareness and sensation remains controversial, the girl's genitals have several externally observable and touchable aspects in which reside pleasurable sensation: the mons, the labia, the parting between the labia, and the introitus. Particularly relevant . . . is the fact that mental representation of these external aspects may constitute early precursors to conceptualization of the vagina insofar as they lead the little girl to experience her genitals *as having an opening and potential inside space*. Specifically, the parting between the labia can be recognized as an opening and associated with genital pleasure long before the vagina *per se* is likely to be imagined. . . . In sum . . . the girl, like the boy, is engaged in a process of gradual discovery, cathexis, and mental representation of her own genitals [pp. 333–334].

Irigaray (1977) has offered perhaps the most articulate psychoanalytic account of female sexual anatomy, a veritable new atlas for a dark continent. In her sexual narratives, adult female bodies are highly sexually responsive.

So woman does not have a sex organ? She has at least two of them, but they are not identifiable as ones. Indeed she has many more. Her sexuality, always at least double, goes even further: it is *plural*. Is this the way culture is seeking to characterize now? . . . Indeed, woman's pleasure does not have to choose between clitoral activity and vaginal passivity, for example. The pleasure of the vaginal caress does not have to be substituted for that of the clitoral caress. They each contribute irreplaceably to woman's pleasure. Among other caresses [are] fondling the breasts, touching the vulva, spreading the lips, stroking the posterior wall of the vagina, brushing against the mouth of the cervix, and so on. To evoke only a few of the most specifically female pleasures. Pleasures which are somewhat misunderstood in sexual difference as it is currently imagined, or not imagined. . . .

But *woman has sex organs more or less everywhere*. She finds pleasure almost everywhere. . . . The geography of her pleasure is much more diversified, more multiple in its differences, more complex, more subtle, than is commonly imagined . . . [p. 28].

In the French feminist's turning away from the dominant discourse of her psychoanalytic culture we hear echoes of Rich's (1978) call in "Transcendental Etude" for the need for a new language and a new imagery where pleasures associated with mother–child relationships are neither censored nor devalued. Irigaray (1977) cautions: "If we keep on speaking the same language together, we're going to reproduce the same history. Begin the same old stories all over again" (p. 205).[5] Irigaray examined how the symbolic becomes seen as law, how certain stories come to be seen as descriptions of reality.

> The symbolic order is an imaginary order which becomes law. Therefore it is very important to question again the foundation of our symbolic order in mythology and in tragedy, because they deal with a landscape which installs itself in the imagination and then, all of a sudden, becomes law. But that only means that it is an imaginary system that wins out over another one. This victorious imaginary system is what we call the symbolic order [quoted in Baruch and Serrano, 1988, pp. 159–160].

As her contribution to enlarging the imaginary, Irigaray (1977) offered the synecdoche of two lips. The image represents, at once and variously, the lips of the mouth and the labial lips of the vulva, women's autoerotic desire and women's homoerotic pleasure, as well as women's speaking to themselves and to each other about their bodies and their various desires. "Between our lips, yours and mine, several voices, several ways of speaking, resound endlessly back and forth" (p. 209).

Unlike Irigaray, however, Paula Bennett (1993 ) has argued that women are in fact not "invisible within our system of representation nor are their genitals definitionally without signifying power" (p. 256) and that specific female imagery already exists in women's art and poetry. She related her own difficulties opening the doors of perception. When she first saw clitoral imagery in Emily Dickinson's poems, she was threatened by her own vision: "On the one hand, I believed what I said; on the other, I could not believe it. It seemed too bizarre, too impossible to be true. For ten years, I let the paper lie" (p. 236). Bennett noted that when "my knowledge of Dickinson had deepened and so had my comfort with my own sexuality" she could see that the kind of images she had found in several poems were not isolated phenomena. "Clitoral imagery—peas, pebbles, beads, berries, nuts, buds, crumbs, pearls, pellets, dews, gems, jewels, drops, and . . . bees—was central to Dickinson's writing" (p. 236). Bennett found hundreds of "these small, round, and frequently hard objects, objects whose insignificance Dickinson stresses even when attributing inestimable value to them" (p. 236). Bennett maintained that "feminist psychoanalytic theory has had nothing to say concerning the clitoris's possible significance for treatments of women's sexuality in art, let alone in life. Instead—largely, I believe, as a result of the influence of Sigmund Freud and Jacques Lacan—feminist theorists have maintained a singular silence regarding this little organ" (p. 237).

## Lesbian Sexuality: A Preoedipal "Play with a Double Cast"

If female sexuality has been a territory difficult for psychoanalysis to explore, the sexuality of two women together has been an even darker continent, and one often imagined to be a primitive, underdeveloped region of infantile desires, autoeroticism, narcissism, and preoedipal object relations. Psychoanalytic formulations about lesbian sexuality repeat the phallocentric assumption that something is lacking or underdeveloped in female anatomy. The anatomy-based cognitive and psychological diffusivity supposedly characteristic of women becomes intensified in descriptions of lesbian patients, who in numerous clinical discussions are said to suffer from failed separation, loose boundaries, and weak and undeveloped ego states.[6] And, finally, in the kind of splitting so common in thinking about homosexuality, the emotional regression often espoused as a goal of heterosexual orgasmic experience in which boundaries between self and other can safely collapse, leading to expanded senses of self and well-being, becomes, when it occurs between two women, evidence of primitive, infantile, or pathological arrangements.

Sexual narratives that see the two sexes as "opposite," and thus complementary, insist that something must be lacking in the sexual experience of two women. "How is it possible," wondered McDougall (1980) "to maintain the illusion of being the true sexual partner to another woman?" (p. 88) For McDougall, who believes that female homosexuals unconsciously deny sexual difference, sex without a penis is an illusion. Siegel (1991) has repeated her earlier description of her lesbian patients' lack of internalized representations of their vaginas and their "ambivalent relationships" to their clitorises.[7] Illusory sex and missing vaginas. We wonder whether therapists who find these dynamics in *all* their homosexual patients might be projecting onto their patients their own difficulties with "mentally representing" certain sexual realities, such as the vaginas and clitorises and breasts and mouths and hands of two women together and the erotic pleasures they make possible. Joan Riviere (1924) once described a woman analysand's disgust and puzzlement about female homosexuality: "I mean it seems such a pointless idea, so utterly meaningless—like trying to play tennis without balls" (p. 52)! Riviere noted the "phallic symbolism" in the patient's comment but did not acknowledge its defensiveness, namely, its denial that anything about female sexual anatomy could have any sexual attraction to a woman. David Reuben (1969) evidenced similar denial in *Everything You Always Wanted to Know About Sex*. Reuben asked the question many ask who find it difficult to mentally represent two female bodies together sexually: "What do female homosexuals do with each other?" He answers: "Like their male counterparts, lesbians are handicapped by having only half the pieces in the anatomical jigsaw puzzle. Just as one penis plus one penis equals nothing, one vagina plus another vagina still equals zero." (Quoted in Klaich, 1974, p. 43). Reuben wanted "to know everything" about sex between men and women, but "nothing" about same-sex relations. So he insisted there was "nothing" there to know about.

The most common psychoanalytic defense against seeing such erotic possibilities is to equate them with the behaviors of mother and infant, thus defining them as "preoedipal" and "pregenital." Deutsch (1932) described the sexual relationship between an ex-patient and another woman.

> The patient, who was intelligent and conversant with analysis, informed me that their homosexual relationship was quite consciously acted out as if it were a mother–child situation, in which sometimes one, sometimes the other played the mother—a play with a doubt cast, so to speak. Moreover, the satisfactions sought in this homosexual love play involved chiefly the mouth and the external genitalia. No "male–female" contrast appeared in this relationship. . . . The impression gained was that the feeling of happiness lay in the possibility of being able to play *both* roles [p. 214].

Deutsch described other homosexual patients, all of whom were "more or less consciously recognized mother–child relationship with their love object." Deutsch's descriptions of their sexual practices are that of a ethnographer describing the exotic behavior of a foreign species: "Sexual satisfaction was obtained in all those cases from the following practices: close embrace, mutual sucking at the nipples, genital (and more prominently) anal masturbatory stimulation, and intense mutual cunnilingus. Of special interest is the prominence given to the double role in these cases also" (p. 215).

McDougall's (1980) five patients apparently described similar practices, and she also interpreted their relationships as preoedipal defenses against oedipal level development:

"The wishful fantasy of all these patients might be summed up as a desire for total elimination of the father and the creation of an exclusive and enduring mother-daughter relationship. This fantasy is lived out in the sexual relationship with women partners, who thus become mother substitutes, frequently with alternating roles, each being at times the mother, at times the child" [p. 108].[8]

But psychoanalysis knows that early dependency relationships contribute both vitality and anguish to adult love relationships, whether heterosexual or homosexual. We have only to listen to the lyrics of popular love songs, in which generation after generation of lovers call each other "Baby." Men sing the blues because their "Mama" is gone; women sing the blues because their "Daddy" has left them.

## Words and Images

The language available to describe sexual practices between women suffers from the same impoverishment as the language for female sexual anatomy. Many terms for female homosexuality deprive lesbian women of their female sex and code them as males: "bull dyke," "bull dagger," "butch." Other names hint at the sexual pleasures possible between women, while at the same time disgracing or effacing those pleasures. "Fricatice" derives from the Latin "to rub," suggesting pleasures other than passive receptivity, but its meaning—"an unchaste woman"—names those pleasures immoral. "Tribade" also derives from "to rub." The *O.E.D.* defines tribade as "a lesbian method of intercourse in which one partner lies on top of the other and simulates the movements of the male in heterosexual intercourse." Two women together are defined as poor imitations of heterosexuality: a woman may make the movements of sex, but she lacks the equipment to make pleasure with another woman. Alicia Gaspar de Alba (1996), who describes herself as a "Chicana lesbian/butche/torillera feminist from the border," has discussed the meaning of "tortillera," a name from her culture, pointing out that although "tortillera" was "originally a derogatory term . . . [now] we take it in our mouths, taste the truth of it, and change the meaning. In this way, we begin to own our own names" (p. 220). She compared two women making love to the slow, sensual, daily domestic rhythms of making bread.

*Making Tortillas*

My body remembers
what it means to love slowly,

what it means to start from scratch:
to soak the maíz,
scatter bonedust in the limewater,
and let the seeds soften
overnight.

Sunrise is the best time
for grinding maíz. . . .
Tortilleras, we are called
grinders of maíz, makers, bakers,
slow lovers of women.
The secret is starting from scratch [pp. 220–221].

In Chinese sex manuals, written expressly for men, two women together are said to practice "mojingzi" or mirror grinding. "Mirrors were ground together to make them smooth and the idea of female genitalia rubbing against the other female genitalia without any major protuberances invoked the simile" (Ruan and Bullough, 1992, p. 218).[9] What would the writers of those Chinese sex manuals make of female genitals as depicted in Judy Chicago's (1996) art installation *The Dinner Party*, a feminist sexual synecdoche extravaganza? *The Dinner Party* consists of a triangular shaped table, set on a floor of 99 tiles covered with women's names. Each of the three wings of the table holds 12 formal place settings. Each place setting represents a woman, either a mythical personage, such as Kali, or an actual historical woman, such as Eleanor of Aquitaine. Each place setting has identical silverware and goblets, while the specific historical and social contexts of each woman's life are represented by the use of different materials and designs and needlework on the place mat and table runners. Each plate has a different symbolic representation of female genitals.

On the first two wings of the dinner female genitals are indeed mirror smooth, being simply painted images on the plates' surfaces. But by the third table wing, which represents the period "From the American Revolution to the Women's Revolution," mirror-smooth surfaces have vanished. Female genitals now are three dimensional sculptures rising upward from their plates surfaces and from the surrounding table runners. "The plates become increasingly dimensional and unique as a metaphor for the increased freedom and individualization available as a result of what was a profound transformation in Western women's historical circumstances" (p. 105). Emily Dickinson's plate, at first glance, looks prim and virginal, a girlish valentine of starched pink lace. Dickinson never married and published few of her poems while alive. Her sexual reclusivity, however, was precisely what allowed her the freedom to develop her poetry. We might compare her plate with that of another famous virgin spinster, Elizabeth I of England, another marriage resister who managed, in that way, to maintain her independence and power. However elaborate the royal purples of the Virgin Queen's plate, its image remains a painted surface, while row upon luxurious row of lace labia stand up to surround, and to protect, the delicate vital center of the virgin poet. Then we might compare these two plates with that of Margaret Sanger. There the vibrant red sculptured tissues of vulva, labia and clitoris seem to throb with life and fullness. By the 20th century, more women were free economically and politically and, owing to Sanger and women like her, many had access to contraception, allowing them greater protection when they exercised their sexuality in or outside of marriage. Using "women's crafts," such as embroidery, china painting, lace making, and weaving, Judy Chicago and her artist colleagues sought to demonstrate that a woman's sexual anatomy is neither hidden nor inaccessible. Given proper social, political, and economic supports, a women's sexual anatomy offers her, by herself as well as with a partner of either sex, a many-sited desire.

But lesbian women find few images to help them represent their sexual experiences, although they are faced daily with images in art and advertisement of male–female sexuality. In the last several decades, lesbian-identified artists have sought to rectify these omissions and expand the languages of lesbian sexuality. For instance, among lesbian photographer Tee Corinne's (1991) images we find sensual pictures of "hands, those indefatigable lesbian sex organs" (p. 214). And women sometimes find satisfying images in seemingly unlikely places. Veronica, an analytic patient, had been complaining that while she had an abundance of heterosexual plots in her sexual fantasies, stocked up from her love of Hollywood movies, she lacked images that reminded her of the pleasures of her lesbian relationship.

"You must see the film *Microcosms!* I found my image." she announced excitedly at the beginning of her Monday session.

"That film about insects?" I (MM) asked, dubiously.

"Yes, it's about insects and bugs, but it is beautiful. I finally found an image that really speaks to my experience with Evelyn. It's the snails. Two snails make love, have sex, whatever you want to call it, in the film. It is wonderful, it goes on and on, and on and on, in slow motion, and deeper and fuller. Everything is soft and moist and it goes on and on. See the movie and watch the snails."

We went to see the French naturalists' film depiction of the hidden life of a meadow, and we watched those passionate snails. To naive observers, whatever sexual differences exist between those snails is not apparent. The amorous snails make none of the movements that Hollywood codes as male–female sexual behavior: one snail is not bigger or stronger than the other; neither snail sexually "takes" the other. Seemingly matched in size and shape, each moves toward the other to meet in an amazing moist abandon. Their bodies dissolve into each another, at multiple points of fluid contact. One could imagine those sexy snails speaking to one another at the height of their passion in language straight out of Irigaray (1977):

> We are luminous. Neither one nor two. I've never known how to count. Up to you. In their calculations, we make two. Really, two? Doesn't that make you laugh? An odd sort of two. And yet not one. Especially not one. Let's leave *one* to them: their oneness, with its prerogatives, its dominations, its solipsism: like the sun's. And the strange way they divide up their couples, with the other as the image of the one . . . [p. 207].

## Erotic Signatures

Ethel Person (1980 ), writing about female sexuality, calls for "a healthy respect for eroticism as it is experienced" (p. 629), certainly a fitting and appropriate focus for clinical psychoanalysis, as long as we remember that for humans what is erotic is never unmediated. How we understand our body's messages depends on what our culture tells us about those bodies. How we experience their sexual possibilities depends on what our culture tells us about how our bodies are constructed and how they function. Witness the phenomenon of several decades of American women valiantly trying to distinguish "vaginal" from "clitoral" orgasms. Following Money and Stoller, Person suggests that we think in terms of the individual "sex-print," the "erotic signature" of the individual, an "individual script that elicits erotic desire" (p.620), the result of complex factors, including experiences in early object relations. Person stresses that individuals will vary both in the *specifics* of their erotic signature and in its relative *importance* to their sense of identity: "To the degree that an individual utilizes sexuality (for pleasure, for adaptation, as the resolution of unconscious conflict) and to the degree that sexuality is valued, one's sexual 'nature' will be experienced as more or less central to personality" (p. 620).

We prefer the term "erotic signature" to "sex-print." "Sex-print" calls up associations to "fingerprints" and suggests a fixed and indelible desire. "Signatures," however, can and usually do change over time and through experience, just as what is erotic may change depending on relational and situational and temporal contexts. Certain erotic signatures or scripts may become more intense, more insistent, more terrifying or more satisfying in some relationships than in others and at some times in a person's life than at other times. Erotic signatures are the complex products of dynamic interactions between the conflicts and object relations of our "inner worlds" and the kinds of sexual possibilities currently imagined and prescribed by the sex/class/ethnic/political/religious attitudes and practices of our culture.

One of the fullest contemporary elucidations of this perspective is that of literary and cultural critic Eve Sedgwick. Sedgwick (1990) offers a list of axioms that "most of us know," for instance that "people are different from each other." Sedgwick marvels at "how few respectable conceptual tools we have for dealing with this self-evident fact" (p. 22). We use several of Sedgwick's descriptions of the dimensions of sexual difference to organize some thoughts about lesbian sexuality. Many people, including many psychoanalysts, might say in response to Sedgwick's axioms and our observations, "Of course, I know all this. These statements are just obvious observations about human sexuality." But what makes Sedgwick's list of the obvious significant is how rarely such knowledge is evidenced in psychoanalytic discussions of lesbian sexuality. And, as Sedgwick pointed out about these obvious axioms, "Each . . . , if taken seriously as pure *difference*, retains the unaccounted-for potential to disrupt many forms of the available thinking about sexuality" (p. 25).

- *Even identical genital acts mean very different things to different people [p. 25].*

Any act, genital or otherwise, has multiple possibilities of meaning to different people and to the same person at different times. Although most psychoanalysts know that you can not tell by looking at any behavior what is being subjectively experienced, or what that experience means to the subjects, many seem to forget this when they think and write about homosexuality, as we have seen in the descriptions by Khan, McDougall, and Qunindoz.

- *To some people, the nimbus of 'the sexual' seems scarcely to extend beyond the boundaries of discrete genital acts; to others, it enfolds them loosely or floats virtually free of them.*
- *Sexuality makes up a large share of the self-perceived identity of some people, a small share of others.*

- *Some people spend a lot of time thinking about sex, others little.*
- *Some people like to have a lot of sex, others little or none [p.25].*

"Nimbus" means the halo or aura around a saint's head in a religious paint-ing. Sedgwick here reminds us of an obvious, too often ignored fact: that which is considered sexual differs from person to person. Reducing sexual experience to certain specific genital behaviors, and then counting their fre-quency, is a violent theoretical act.

Lesbian therapists (Lindenbaum, 1985; Burch, 1986, 1987; Nichols, 1987; Vargo, 1987; Loulan, 1990) and other researchers (Blumstein and Schwartz, 1983) have reported diminished frequency of genital sex among long-term lesbian couples. Some women leave their lesbian relationships when genital sex diminishes; other lesbian couples have no complaints about "low" frequency, although they sometimes worry that something is wrong with them if they don't have "more" sex. Some lesbian therapists have used Nancy Chodorow's (1978) idea that girls have difficulties with bound-ary diffusion and differentiation to suggest that "merger" and "fusion" (intense intimacy, lack of psychological separation, overidentification) account for the diminishing of genital sex in established lesbian couples. Stone Center theorist Julie Mencher (1990) has attempted to rescue female-female sexual relationships from such categorical attributions of patholog-ical failed separation. In place of the assumption that fusion is "inherently pathological, maladaptive, or dysfunctional" (p. 3), Mencher suggests instead that "fusion is a relational pattern which particularly characterizes an intimate dyad composed of two women" (p. 4). Mencher argues that, if psychological life does not begin, as has been theorized, in states of merged symbiosis, then psychological development need not consist of a "series of progressive disengagements" from such symbiosis. Mencher maintains that the psychoanalytic "dichotomizing of 'oneness' and 'separation'" has been based on distorted values about autonomy and independence. "If we view the mother–infant relationship within an intersubjective frame, we remove it from the symbiotic matrix of oneness, total dependency, and total self-lessness (of both infant and mother); it is no longer a relationship to be for-saken, either through separation or through internalization" (pp. 6–7).

Although Mencher trenchantly addresses a foundational binary of much contemporary developmental theory, unfortunately in the process she con-tributes to another dichotomy: "the lesbian pattern" versus "the heterosex-ual pattern" of intimacy in relationships. She suggests that lesbian relationships may reflect the "specific intimacy patterns preferred by most women, but not often achieved in heterosexual relationships" (p. 1). But such categorical assumptions, however appealing, may be deceptively simplistic. Laqueur (1990) reminds us of the history of this particular assumption: "The commonplace of much contemporary psychology—that men want sex while women want relationships—is the precise inversion of pre-Enlightenment notions that, extending back to antiquity, equated friendship with men and fleshliness with women" (pp. 3–4).

Other lesbian theorists have suggested that the low frequency of genital orgasmic sex in many long-term lesbian relationships reflects women's socialization to be passive objects, rather than active subjects of sexual desire. After the initial excitement of sexuality at the beginning of the relationship, each woman returns to her pattern of waiting for the other to take the sexual initiative. In the process, lustful behavior diminishes. McDougall (1980, 1985) and Eisenbud (1982) have suggested that the low frequency of genital sex is a consequence of various unresolved preoedipal issues, including aggression.[10] Adria Schwartz (1996) suggests that "what contributes most to the diminishment [is] the avoidance of intense desire and sexual passion out of a fear of ruthlessness on the part of oneself or one's lover" (p. 170).

But lesbian writer Marilyn Frye (1988) decried the "violence" lesbians can do to their experience by being concerned about how often they "have sex." Frye noted that the "sex" act counted in sex survey questionnaires means the act of genital orgasm. Using this measure, most of the acts that lesbians spend a great deal of time doing with one other physically and sexually don't count. Frye also suspected that, if we use only that measure, "heterosexual women don't have sex [so often] either; . . . what they report is the frequency with which their partners have sex" (p. 4). Frye also noted most women's "inarticulateness" about describing their sexual desires. She called for women "to begin creating a vocabulary that elaborates and expands our meanings." She saw the necessity of adopting "a very wide and general concept of 'doing it.' Let it be an open, generous, commodious concept encompassing all the acts and activities by which we generate with each other pleasures and thrills, tenderness and ecstasy, passages of passionate carnality of whatever duration or profundity" (p. 8).[11]

Person (1980) has suggested that genital sexual activity is less significant for women than for men and that, whatever the causes, "there is a relative 'muting of female erotic impulsivity' in this culture" (p. 625).

> Genital sexual activity is a prominent feature in the maintenance of masculine gender while it is a variable feature in feminine gender. Thus an impotent man always feels that his masculinity, and not just his

sexuality, is threatened. . . . In contrast, whether or not a woman is orgasmic has few implications for personality organization. Put another way, there is a difference in the primacy of sexuality between men and women, at least in this culture. In women, gender identity and self-worth can be consolidated by other means [p. 619].

Recently there has been increased conceptual support for recognizing the significance of other than genital sexual pleasures. Lichtenberg (1989) describes the "sensual-sexual motivational system" and summarizes various child observation studies showing the effect of caretaker and infant interactions on its development.

> By distinguishing between sensual enjoyment-seeking and sexual excitement- seeking, we are able to regard more accurately many manifestations at every stage of development than if we presume a unitary goal of seeking "discharge" analogous to orgastic states. The evidence suggests that sensual enjoyment is a more powerful motive force throughout the life cycle than has been previously recognized, whereas sexual excitement seeking is more periodic and episodic [p. 219].

Jessica Benjamin (1988) has suggested that "psychoanalytic valorization of genital sexuality has obscured the equal importance to erotic pleasure of early attunement and mutual play of infancy" (p. 130). And, for Flax (1996), psychoanalytic theory can contribute to an actual "impoverishment" of desire when it reduces desire to genital sexuality and to relationship. Flax has revived other dimensions of pleasure and passion that such privilegings have rendered all but invisible: "music, food, conversation, friendship, aesthetic or athletic deployment of one's own body, love of wisdom, painting, movement, and pleasure in beauty of all kinds" as well as the pleasures of solitude (p. 583).

And, finally, perhaps some women in long-term committed relationships whose genital sexual exchanges have diminished, but whose love continues to grow, might be interested to know that Freud repeatedly pointed out that sex often diminishes after the first few years of marriage: "It is also very usual for directly sexual impulses, short-lived in themselves, to be transformed into a lasting and purely affectionate tie; and the consolidation of a passionate love marriage rests to a large extent upon this process (Freud, 1921, p. 130).

- *Many people have their richest mental/emotional involvement with sexual acts that they don't do, or even don't want to do [Sedgwick, 1990, p. 25].*

"Am I lesbian if I fantazise or dream about men?" some patients wonder. "Maybe I'm a closet heterosexual." Some patients try to inveigle from their therapists a diagnosis of sexual orientation based on the evidence of their sexual dreams and fantasies. But sexual fantasies and sexual behaviors are not the psychological litmus tests or psychic read-outs of "orientation" that some gay male therapists and some psychoanalysts would have us believe (Isay, 1989; Friedman and Downey, 1993). Our sexual fantasies and dreams are no more literal scripts than are our other dreams. The unconscious does not function like the oil gauge of a car engine. We can't just insert a dip stick, pull out a fantasy or a dream, and read out sexual orientation levels. Our fantasy objects are creatively edited amalgamations of loved and feared objects of both sexes, from various periods of psychological development. The sex of our partner, in reality and in fantasy, has meaning and significance, but it is not a psychic shorthand or synecdochical representation of some essential and dichotomous sexual orientation or "gender identity."

## Masochistic Fantasies and Lesbian S & M

Many women find their sexual fantasies disturbing. Many patients find it difficult to reveal their fantasies because they have made frightening self-interpretations about their fantasies and fear receiving equally frightening interpretations from their analysts, especially when the fantasies are sadomasochistic. During the 1980s feminist debates (Vance, 1984), sometimes known as "the sex wars," one prominent battlefield was over lesbian sadomasochism. Lesbian writers and activists, such as Pat Califia (1988), insisted that lesbian sadomasochism was empowering. Kitty Tsui's (1996) "The Cutting" might be used as a textbook illustration of certain masochistic fantasies and sexual practices.

> When Brooke first came out into the scene almost a decade ago, there were many things she thought were plain revolting: piercing—temporary and permanent—branding, canes, water sports, scat, and cutting.
> She had a friend who very much enjoyed being cut. Her friend sported the scars proudly all over her body. One day she held a cutting party. Brook politely declined. But when the night came Brooke was alone. Her date for the evening had canceled, so she went to the party for food, drink, and the company [p. 65].

Having once seen cutting, Brooke is "hooked," and searches for a proper partner for her own cutting. She finds Adrian, who asks her why she wants a cutting.

> "I've wanted it for a long time, . . . but I've never met the right person. I feel connected to you. I want to know what it feels like. I want to be with you but I can't explain why. . . . I have a fascination with sharp edges. Swords, switchblades, straight razors. And I love the taste of blood."
>
> "Just remember to keep breathing," Adrian tells Brooke. "Remember I'm right here with you" [pp. 66–67].

She cuts the Chinese character for love on Brooke's left breast. "In blood. Four strokes that she recut four times. Then she brought out a switchblade, scraped up the blood and placed the edge of it on Brooke's tongue" (p. 67). Brooke is pleased that the mark will be "permanent." "I want to keep something from you" (p. 68).

"The Cutting" is from Tsui's (1996) *Breathless*, the title taken from Tsui's poem of the same name.

> i was born
> a tough girl
> survived a childhood
> of abuse and
> abandonment
> found myself
> through struggle
> and years of
> free-falling
> through pain. . . .
> i am
> a tough girl.
> not many things
> make me gasp
> for air.
> to tell you
> the truth
> your kisses
> make me
> breathless [p. 7].

Lisa cut herself with knives and razors and burned herself with heated metal. She was frightened and ashamed of her sexual fantasies, scripts in which "things had to hurt." When she brought "The Cutting" for me (MM) to read, I noticed, as she had not, the circumstances in which Brooke had her first engagement with cutting: when she was alone, her date having "canceled." "I am jealous of Brooke," said Lisa. "She has someone to be with her while she does the cutting. It would make it so different."

Lisa wanted to understand the motivations and circumstances of her own cutting, which she experienced as simultaneously self-punishing and relieving. "I feel like when I do it I am getting control over something. When there's nothing else I can do, that at least will revoke a response. I say, 'Thank God, I can breathe again.' A wave comes over my *whole* body, my whole body from head to feet. All my muscles seem to let down and relax then. There's something with the blood. If it doesn't bleed enough it doesn't give me the same sensation. It doesn't so much hurt as make me know I am alive and healthy when I see the blood run. But it is hard to get it to run enough. And I am so angry with myself for not being able to stop doing it."

Lisa's history was marked by the early mother–infant deficiencies that Louise Kaplan (1991) sees as frequently characteristic of women who cut their skin.[12] Alone, with massive, disorganizing fear, "I-can't-breathe" terror, Lisa had sought relief and reorganization through exhausting physical activity, food deprivation, and, in what the psychiatric literature calls "delicate cutting," of her arms, legs, vagina, breast, and stomach. She also pierced her nipples and her eyebrow, had numerous car accidents, and reported various death-inviting/death-defying activities. Intense annihilation fears and destructive rages repeatedly pitched our psychoanalytic voyage into sadomasochistic straits, as Lisa provoked me to sharp, impatient confrontations or tried to bind me close to keep her from destruction. Slowly, she learned to cry instead of cut. In time Lisa became able to bear the once intolerable feelings of being "canceled" without feeling utterly abandoned and a "piece of shit." Gradually, she became able to need another without fearing being controlled or destroyed and to manage her moods alone without the need for pain.

Masochistic fantasies and behaviors such as Lisa's are not, of course, peculiar to lesbian women. And, in spite of much analytic equating of masochism with female homosexuality (Socarides, 1978; McDougall, 1980), there is no evidence that such dynamics occur any more frequently, or any more intensely, in lesbian patients than in other women.

Masochistic sexual fantasies may also have psychic roots other than traumatic early mother–child relationships. Chapter 7's discussion of clinical work with Kate and Richard relies heavily on Benjamin's (1991) explication of another source of masochism, namely, a rapprochement child's response to the loss of a mutually desired identificatory relationship with an idealized father. At this point we will discuss briefly a third common psychosocial contributor to some women's sexual fantasies, namely, gender training.

Stoller (1985) believed all sexual fantasies were at least partially founded in early humiliating trauma. He described, for instance, the sexual scripts of adult men who as boys had been sadistically forced to cross dress. Their sexual fantasies provided emotional replication of those early experiences of humiliation. "How can humiliation excite?" asked Stoller (p. 24). He understood the linking of orgasm with fantasized scenes of humiliation and submission to be evidence that sexual fantasies function as psychic survival strategies. When orgasm can take place in spite of humiliation, the fantasizer knows he or she has once more psychically and physically survived. Brooke becomes sexually aroused when she is cut by Adrian. Adrian makes her beg for permission to come to orgasm, another pairing of humiliation and submission with sexual arousal, with possible reparative intent. Tsui (1996) says, "I found myself through struggle and years of free-falling through pain" (p. 7).

We do not need, however, to posit unusual traumatic early childhoods to appreciate the physical and emotional sources that contribute to many women's sexual fantasies and sexual arousal. Early and persistent gender training makes long-lasting contributions to how female bodies are made feminine and how certain sexual fantasies come to be developed. Such gender training begins at birth. Female infants are spoken to, dressed, carried, and handled differently than are male infants. As they grow, girls are neither helped nor encouraged to have the kind and degree of physical and verbal assertion that our culture encourages in boys. These early engenderings become part of our unconscious "body egos," into which later gender trainings, of which we are more conscious, are subsumed. However active growing girls may be on the playgrounds and now on the sports fields with one another, off those fields girls are still taught to lower their voices and restrain their bodies. A proper girl keeps her legs together and her skirts down. Even in jeans or pants a woman arranges her body in more restricted postures than does a man. There are only two kinds of women who move their bodies through social space with the degree of assertion that men are gender-trained to exhibit: 1) the sexually provocative woman, the siren, the slut, the woman who is "asking for it, " and 2) the bull-dyke, the butch, the queer woman thought to have a "gender identity disorder."

It should not be too surprising, then, that in sexual fantasies many women envision themselves variously bound and enslaved. They do not move actively and eagerly toward pleasure; they must be "taken" and overtaken, usually by a man, sometimes by a woman, or by both. It is not surprising that in sexual scripts where they *are* eager and active, women often cast themselves as loose and wanton women, whores and prostitutes, nymphomaniacs. Freud (1905b, 1933a) thought that a little girl becomes a woman by renouncing the clitoris and adopting the vagina as her principal sexual zone. In this way she gives up her active masculine sexuality and replaces it with the feminine desire for a child. We believe that many women's sexual dilemmas involve managing another kind of renunciation, another kind of movement between two zones of existence. A woman must be able to renounce, in the arms of her partner, male or female, a lifetime of body-based gender training. Somehow she must become sexually assertive and expressive, without feeling that such behaviors render her sexual identity either "masculine" or immoral.

Marie Bonaparte was interested in anthropological research on female sexuality. She financially supported some of Malinowski's work and entertained one of Malinowski's graduate students, Jomo Kenyatta, who was later to become an African liberation leader and President of Kenya. Kenyatta described for Bonaparte various tribal female initiation rites that included excision of the clitoris. Bonaparte once visited a hospital in Cairo where clitorectomies were performed. Later she would write: "I believe that the ritual mutilations imposed on African women since time immemorial . . . constitute the exact physical counterpart of the psychical intimidations imposed in childhood on the sexuality of European little girls. I also think that, as regards the later sexuality of the woman, they involve the same results" (Bonaparte, 1951, p. 203).

Bonaparte was a mentally and physically energetic woman. Married to Prince George of Greece, she fulfilled her duties as a member of the royal family while practicing psychoanalysis. She used her social position and financial assets to rescue Freud and other analysts from fascist Europe. She used her analytic influence to fight Lacan within the French psychoanalytic movement. At age 77 she traveled to California to visit the condemned Caryl Chessman on death row and petitioned the governor of California and the President of the United States for clemency for Chessman (see Bertin, 1987). This powerful and dynamic woman also underwent several genital surgeries to move her clitoris closer to her vagina so that she might have proper orgasms, thus demonstrating through her own sexual struggles an instructive example of the power of theories to influence feelings and perception and to shape female bodies into accepted feminine behaviors.

- *For some people, the preference for a certain sexual object, act, role, zone, or scenario is so immemorial and durable that it can only be experienced as innate; for others, it appears to come late or to feel aleatory or discretionary [Sedgwick, 1990, p. 25].*

Hence many futile arguments about the "nature" of homosexuality between persons who have "always known" they were homosexual and persons who haven't. And the confusion and excitement when sometimes what has been previously believed to be innate suddenly "becomes" discretionary. Witness the many women who develop lesbian relationships and identity after first having been heterosexually married.

- *For some people, sexuality provides a needed space of heightened discovery and cognitive hyperstimulation. For others, sexuality provides a needed space of routinized habituation and cognitive hiatus [p. 25].*

Some people use certain sexual acts to release tension, to fill emptiness, to feel alive, whole, real, loved. Sometimes a woman for whom sex functions in any of these ways is in a relationship with a woman for whom the same sexual acts increase tension and diminish her sense of being whole, real, alive, and desirable. In such a mixed marriage, the woman who "doesn't want sex" is usually the one identified as having a sexual problem. Other lesbian partners have discovered that, although one always "initiates sex" and the other always refuses, when they can talk together about specific behaviors they differ very little in how much "sex" or what kind of "sex" each wants. They may have become stuck in a sexual dance whose movements was not reflective of either woman's desire.

Many patients (men, women, straight or gay) don't often talk directly about sex unless they have newly fallen in love or are dissatisfied with their sexual relationships. Perhaps that we hear relatively little about everyday sexual behavior is itself a function of certain analytic interventions we make or fail to make. Our patients probably learn fairly quickly that we are not interested, unless they are, in the frequency of sexual contacts or in what part of their body does what with their partner's body. More disturbed patients tend to relate sexual fantasies and behaviors more than other patients do. Sex is often felt to be a life-sustaining commodity to which they feel entitled but that others are selfishly failing to provide in the amounts and forms they require.

- *Some people, homo-, hetero-, and bisexual, experience their sexuality as deeply embedded in a matrix of gender meanings and gender differentials. Others of each sexuality do not [p. 26].*

Lesbian critic Theresa de Lauretis (1994), in a tour de force of theory reading and theory writing, offers an explanation of lesbian-specific psychodynamics. Reading the lesbian novel *Well of Loneliness* against Lacan and Freud as well, de Lauretis suggests that "lesbian desire," particularly the desire of the "mannish" lesbian, serves the function of a fetish. A fetish tries to hide or deny a loss or a lack while at the same time paradoxically pointing forever to that lack or loss. What the mannish lesbian such as the novel's heroine, the masculine-named and masculine-attired Stephen Gordon, hungers for and lacks is a mother's desire. She longs for the lost female body. She hates her own body, a body she felt her mother could not narcissistically identify with and desire. Stephen's wound and her facial scar represent this particular lesbian narcissistic injury. Stephen's masculine clothing and name function as fetish. They cover the lack at the same time as they point forever to the absence of the feminine.

De Lauretis's reading fits well the fictional Stephen Gordon, but it should not be taken as a blueprint for understanding all women who wear "masculine" clothing. Even identical gender acts mean very different things to different people. For some women, the exciting power and fit of certain gender paraphernalia—for example, motorcycles, leather pants, or short hair—derive precisely from their association with masculinity. A woman may wish to appropriate in this way certain powers usually gendered male, such as strength, swagger, freedom, sexual power. "Look at what a woman I am. My sexuality is so powerful, it can only be enhanced, even by supposedly "masculine" gender acts." Some women who make that statement are sexually attracted to men. Some women who make that statement are sexually attracted to women. For some women, wearing stereotypical male-gender paraphernalia may be a bravado performance, a leather or denim covering that masks bodyego insecurity, just as, for some women, wearing stereotypical female-gender paraphernalia is an act of bravado, a lace or silk covering masking sexual uncertainty and insecurity. You can't tell, by looking, what any woman's Levi's or any woman's lipstick may mean. Joan Nestle (1987) has pointed out the discomfort many contemporary lesbians feel seeing working-class butch–femme relationships. She insists that such relationships must be understood within the specifics of their social and historical circumstances. She describes the meanings of certain gender acts in the 1950s.

> Butch–femme relationships, as I experienced them, were complex erotic statements, not phony heterosexual replicas. They were filled with a deeply Lesbian language of stance, dress, gesture, loving, courage, and autonomy. None of the butch women I was with, and this

included a passing woman, ever presented themselves to me as men; they did announce themselves as tabooed women who were willing to identify their passion for other women by wearing clothes that symbolized the taking of responsibility. Part of this responsibility was sexual expertise. In the 1950s this courage to feel comfortable with arousing another woman became a political act [pp. 100–101].

Nestle emphasizes that butch women were not presenting as men, nor trying to pass as men; on the contrary, they were specifically announcing themselves to women as women, using the gender codes of their time. The attribution of masculinity or failed or lost femininity haunts many lesbian women. A patient described her fears in the late 70s when she began her first lesbian relationship. She was terrified that she would lose her identity as a woman. Finally she forced herself to write the sentence, "I am a lesbian." She remembered how she had laughed with relief when she wrote it. "I suddenly realized how totally female that sentence was. *Only* a woman could write it and have it be authentic."

- *Some people's sexual orientation is intensely marked by autoerotic pleasures and histories—sometimes more so than by any aspect of alloerotic object choice. For others the autoerotic possibility seems secondary or fragile, if it exists at all [pp. 25–26].*

Only the most concrete-thinking permits the assertion that if two lovers have the same kind of genitals their relationship is narcissistic. Humans establish and relish difference through a variety of measures, not simply through genital distinctions. Nor, of course, is heterosexuality synonymous with an object-related drive. A man having sexual intercourse with a woman (or a man) may be having an entirely autoerotic experience. A woman who has little access to her own autoerotism may diminish the erotic pleasures of her partner, male or female. A woman's attraction to another woman's body (or mind or behavior) may demonstrate a wish to find in that woman what she feels she herself lacks and longs for, just as a woman's attraction to a particular man may signal a similar wish. A woman may want a female lover because men represent feared objects with envied power, or because she projects onto men her own disowned capacities and feelings. A woman may want a man for the same reasons. Some patients have reported that they had assumed a lesbian relationship would be free of the sexual conflicts and relational problems they had experienced in heterosexual relationships, only to find that such problems remain regardless of the genitals of their partners.

Finally, for many women, attraction to another has less to do with perceived lacks or deficiencies than with finding in the partner satisfying similarities as well as stimulating differences. Many women long for a relationship in which they may find recognition of their desires, in all their dimensions. Benjamin (1995) saw what she calls the "erotics of intersubjective space" as characterized by "the freedom from internal and external constraint of the object, floating in the reflection of the other's knowledge, which need not be distinguished from self's knowledge." Such an experience of being known and recognized "generates a profound sense of love" (p. 172). Such erotic pleasures, *not exclusive to or necessarily characteristic of* lesbian relationships, contribute to many lesbian relationships' satisfactions as much as and often longer than the sexual passions of the first years. Poets have always searched for images to describe such passion, and lamented the limitations of language to convey the experience. Joan Larkin (1975) said it this way:

### Some Unsaid Things

I was not going to say
how you lay with me

nor where your hands went
& left their light impressions

nor whose face was white
as a splash of moonlight

nor who spilled the wine
nor whose blood stained the sheet

nor which of us wept
to set the dark bed rocking

nor what you took me for
nor what I took you for

nor how your fingertips
in me were roots

light roots torn leaves put down—
nor what you tore from me

> nor what confusion came
> of our twin names
>
> nor will I say whose body
> opened, sucked, whispered
>
> like the ocean, unbalancing
> what had seemed a safe position [p. 46]

Some things can be left unsaid because they don't need to be put into words; the speaker understands that what she knows is recognized by the other. Some things are left unsaid because they are not important enough to say; the speaker does not dwell on the unimportant differences between self and lover, on who spilled the wine or the blood or the tears. Some things are left unsaid because they are private between the lovers and will not be revealed to others, even if the passion ends. In spite of such intimacy, there are differences between any two persons. Same-sex does not equal identical; twin names can sometimes causes confusion. Some things are unsaid because no person's experience is fully sayable to another, no matter how close they are.

It is neither accurate nor clinically useful to assume that because a woman is lesbian she has categorically different sexual desires from those of other women. Judith Katz (1980) playfully spoofed that anxious and alienated assumption in "This Is How Lesbians Capture Straight Women and Have Their Way with Them." She also provided a "Dyke Check List" to help a woman determine if she is lesbian.

> Do you like to be held?
> Do you like to kiss?
> When someone bites your finger, where do you feel it?. . . .
> Do you look at the face of the person you have just made love to,
> are making love to?. . .
> Do you like to make jokes in bed? [p. 175]

Katz emphasized the common erotic ground in women's sexual desires, regardless of the sex of their partners. When psychoanalysts no longer designate female homosexual patients as a psychological group "of a special character," we might learn from their treatment something more about the development and variety of erotic signatures, and the various shapes and forms of desire.

There are, however, certain specific developmental issues that do distinguish lesbian women from other women. These are no more matters of early object relations than they are of prenatal hormones. The developmental issues specific to female homosexuality are the effects on psychic and sexual development of stigma, hatred, and social oppression. The psychological dilemmas specific to lesbian women are how to establish and maintain a satisfying sense of self, sexual desires, and relationships in the face of persistent, distorting, and harassing theories. In the next chapter we examine these developmental issues by discussing coming out, the never-ending intrapsychic and interpersonal process of identifying to self and to others as a woman who has or desires sexual experience and an intimate relationship with another woman.

# 5

# COMING OUT

## THE NECESSITY OF BECOMING A BEE-CHARMER

We are thus most aware of our identity when we are just about to gain it, and when we . . . are somewhat surprised to make its acquaintance or, again, when we are just about to enter a crisis . . .

An optimal sense of identity . . . is experienced merely as a sense of psychosocial well-being. Its most obvious concomitants are a feeling of being at home in one's body, a sense of "knowing where one is going," and an inner assuredness of anticipated recognition from those who count.

*[Erik Erikson, 1968, p. 165]*

When a woman says to herself and to others that she wants, or has, a primary relationship with another woman, she is faced with the immediate acquisition and management of a new and devalued social and psychological identity. "Coming out," identifying as homosexual to self and others, is an intrapsychic and interpersonal process through which identity is both created and revealed. Coming out is not, as is sometimes thought, a declaration or announcement through which one's essential sexual nature or orientation is disclosed. Rather, it is a never-ending psychosocial process in which a woman must continually position herself within, or outside of, or in ambivalent conflict with, her culture's definitions of, and names for, same-sex attraction and relationships. *Wherever* the woman positions herself, *whatever* names she calls herself, coming out is always accompanied by anxiety and by wishes and impulses both to hide and to reveal. Although coming out has been a primary subject of gay and lesbian literature (e.g., Weeks, 1977; Bell and Weinberg, 1978; Stanley and Wolfe 1980; Hart and Richardson, 1981; de Monteflores, 1986; Herdt, 1989a), and gay and lesbian therapists have addressed the psychological dimensions, developmental tasks, and stages of the acquisition of gay or lesbian identity (Cass, 1979, 1984; Coleman, 1982; Stein and Cohen, 1984; Hanley-Hackenbruck, 1988; Garnets and Kimmel, 1991, 1993; Cabaj and Stein, 1996), psychoanalysis has directed very little attention to coming out (Gershman, 1983; Friedman, 1988; Morgenthaler, 1988; Isay, 1989, 1996).[1] This chapter discusses coming out for women by examining papers by Freud (1920), Khan (1964), Fannie Flagg's (1967) novel *Fried Green Tomatoes at the Whistle Stop Cafe*, and the 1991 film made from that novel.

Freud (1920) reflected on the universal human tendency to keep hidden from ourselves our own desires:

> I cannot neglect this opportunity of expressing for once my astonishment that human beings can go through such great and important moments of their erotic life without noticing them much, sometimes even, indeed, without having the faintest suspicion of their existence, or else, having become aware of those moments, deceive themselves so thoroughly in their judgment of them. This happens not only under neurotic conditions, where we are familiar with the phenomenon, but seems also to be common enough in ordinary life. . . . It would seem that the information received by our consciousness about our erotic life is especially liable to be incomplete, full of gaps, or falsified [pp. 166–167].

Impressed as Freud was by the forces of repression, as well as by the amazing energies produced by loosening such "counter-cathexes," he might have appreciated Adrienne Rich's (1980) description of the moment she "came-out" to herself and in this way filled in a "gap" in consciousness about her erotic life.

> I keep thinking about power. The intuitive flash of power that "coming-out" can give: I have an indestructible memory of walking along a particular block in New York City, the hour after I had acknowledged to myself that I loved a woman, feeling invincible. For the first time in my life I experienced sexuality as clarifying my mind instead of hazing it over; that passion, once named, flung a long, imperative beam of light into my future. I knew my life was decisively and forever different; and that change felt to me like power [p. xii].

Rich uses a simple, powerful word for the nature of her attraction: "to name our love for women as love." Psychoanalysis has no concept of psychologically mature, healthy, primary love between two women. As we have seen, it has historically used names other than "love" to describe such attraction: a deviation or regression of libidinal energies arising as a defense against oedipal or psychotic anxieties; an identification with the father; a reflection of masochistic preoedipal or narcissistic object relations. From these perspectives, coming out is seen as an impulsive *acting out* of internal conflicts or deficits or as a *resistance* to working out these conflicts or deficits in the transference, or as both. Representative of this view is Siegel (1988), who described her psychoanalytic treatment of 12 women patients exploring homosexual feelings or relationships. Although Siegel (1990) later suggested that inclinations to come out may arise as a way of combating "the homophobic attitude of much of our society and many mental health professionals," she saw no necessity for personal coming out statements.

> One's sexual orientation is hardly something to be proud of; rather, it is a given that one does not much think about if one's adaptation is, indeed, healthy. Clearly, it is difficult for homosexuals to maintain their equilibrium in a hostile surrounding. But "coming out" hardly helps matters. One can, for instance, make it clear that slurs against any one group are not to be tolerated without stating one's own sexual orientation [p. 449].

Others argue that, since sexuality is a "private" matter, one's homosexuality should be kept private.

But coming out is not simply a statement made to combat discrimination nor is it usually a description of private sexual experiences. Most frequently, coming out involves choices about how to handle moments of *ordinary, daily* conversation. Even less than other social markers such as gender or "race" (whose supposedly "identifying characteristics" are thought to be discernible), that which is currently called "sexual orientation" is not self-evident. The invisibility of homosexuality forces choices about secrecy or disclosure in all social interactions that go beyond the superficial: a woman must decide whether to reveal; when and how to reveal; how to weigh the consequences of the disclosure; how much time and energy to allocate to deal with the responses in self and other set off by the disclosure; or, if deciding not to disclose, how to manage relationships with family members, friends, and work colleagues while keeping such significant information hidden. Unless an unmarried woman specifically reveals her lesbian relationship, she is assumed to be a single, heterosexual woman. This heterosexual assumption leads to interpersonal confusions and deceptions. But revealing lesbian identity or relationship can turn an ordinary conversational moment into something extraordinary.

Consider, for example, such a simple matter as two women, perhaps casual work acquaintances, discussing vacations at lunch. A woman in a lesbian relationship may avoid having lunch with her colleagues because even in such a simple conversation she must face the issue of *whether or not to come-out.* If she attempts to hide her relationship by suggesting that she vacations alone, rather than achieving any protection of her privacy, she may in fact draw more attention to herself and her situation. Her lunch companion may offer invitations for sharing vacation trips or may offer to fix her up with someone. If she identifies her lesbian partner who accompanies her on vacations as a "friend," she hides her primary significant relationship and is still assumed, therefore, to be a single, available, heterosexual woman. She must decide in these moments how much she wishes to establish an authentic friendship with this lunch acquaintance. How much does she wish to give the acquaintance honest information about her life or at least limit how much she deceives her? In myriad, daily, casual conversational moments such as these, for a woman in a lesbian relationship, keeping silent is more than remaining private. At the very least, it is keeping a secret; often it involves telling a lie.[2]

A married woman may chose not to socialize with work colleagues, and she certainly has private matters, sexual and otherwise, she does not discuss even with close friends. But a married woman does not attempt to hide from family, friends, and colleagues all signs and hints of having a primary marital relationship, and she does not identify her husband as her "friend." The anxieties and conflicts resulting from such *ordinary, daily* consequences of living in a lesbian relationship are what distinguish lesbian patients from heterosexual women patients (Eisenbud, 1982), not any special quota or variety of preoedipal disturbance, narcissistic developmental arrest, or oedipal anxieties—all of which may *also* be present in any woman. Therefore, for a lesbian woman, it is not possible, as Siegel (1990) would suggest, that sexual orientation is "a given that one does not much think about if one's adaptation is, indeed, healthy." Such "not-thinking" is a psychological luxury unavailable to lesbian women.[3]

It may be understandable, then, why so many women find that openly acknowledging their lesbian relationship casts Rich's (1980) "beam of light into the future" and why their willingness to face the challenges of such acknowledgment releases in many the sense of power that Rich experienced. But, at the same time, enormous damage to family ties, friendships, employment, professional advancement, and group membership can result from such disclosure. Such rejections are more difficult for those already psychologically vulnerable, including adolescents.

A woman's psychological capacity to manage the disclosure of her lesbian identity or relationship and to manage the consequences of such disclosure—capacities that in other circumstances would be called "ego strengths"—can lead to increasingly strengthened experiences of self; the lack of such ego strengths can lead to increasing social isolation. A woman's responses to the lifelong, never-once-and-for-all-completed process are shaped by her age, race, class, economic circumstances, and historical context, as well as by the conscious and unconscious dimensions of her individual psychodynamics.

Personal coming out announcements and family introductions of lesbian relationships frequently involve much preparation on the part of the woman and take time for family and friends to assimilate. Kleinberg (1986) sees a woman's coming out to her parents as "a critical event in a lesbian woman's life, one that is remembered forever and which is perhaps analogous to a rite of passage such as marriage" (p. 7). Kleinberg's analogy emphasizes the significance of a woman's decision to reveal to important others feelings of erotic desire and emotional attachment that may have been insistently present, confusing, and frightening since childhood and adolescence and that no social institutions or ceremonies have helped her organize or affirm, and that, in fact, most social institutions and ceremonies either ignore or repudiate.

The timing and manner of a woman's coming out reveals much about her internal world. Like marriage, coming out may be done as a way of unconsciously inviting attack and rejection by a woman in the throes of punitive internal object representations (Friedman, 1988). Like marriage, coming out may be done with defensive bravado by a woman internally conflicted and frightened of making a choice. Like marriage, coming out can be done as a way of filling inner emptiness or finding a container for overwhelming anxieties. Freud (1920) suggested that hostile revenge for failed oedipal longings may motivate homosexual object choices and such announcements to parents and others. Certainly these motives contribute to many marriages. In the most favorable of psychic circumstances, coming out, like marriage, is undertaken as a way of sharing powerful personal feelings with important others. And for some women, such as Carter Heyward (1989), coming out is an action and statement addressed to a world beyond family and friends: "To come out, then, is not merely a step in personal authenticity. It is a step also into a posture of social and political deviance and resistance. In both senses, as movement in authenticity and as act of political dissidence, coming out can become a remarkable process of relational empowerment" (p. 4). Lesbian texts are filled with the testimony of such women. But for women whose sense of self does not include the energizing status of being a rebel or a social and political pioneer, revealing one's love for women is particularly frightening.

## Coming Out in Adolescence

Erik Erikson (1963) examined identity, its development, variety, and crises, and studied the processes through which youth in various cultures come to maturity. He described the psychological situation of adolescence: "The growing and developing youths, faced with this physiological revolution within them, and with tangible adult tasks ahead of them are now primarily concerned with what they appear to be in the eyes of others as compared with what they feel they are . . ." (p. 261).

Erikson's language emphasizes the conflicting pulls of adolescence, a developmental passage between childhood and adulthood marked by dramatic physiological and psychological changes. The tasks of adolescence include the management of the physical and emotional changes, the integration of parental identifications and values with new identifications forged in groups of like minded peers, and progressive movement toward establishing primary, intimate *heterosexual* relationships outside the family.

> To be of lasting social significance, the utopia of genitality should include:
>
> 1. mutuality of orgasm
> 2. with a loved partner
> 3. of the other sex
> 4. with whom one is able and willing to share a mutual trust
> 5. and with whom one is able and willing to regulate the cycles of
>    a. work
>    b. procreation
>    c. recreation
> 6. so as to secure to the offspring, too, all the stages of a satisfactory development [p. 266].

In Erikson's stage model, as in other psychoanalytic models of psychosocial development, homosexual feelings, behavior, or relationships that are other than transitory are indicators of developmental disturbance. Laufer and Laufer (1984), for instance, have described adolescent homosexuality as a "a breakdown in the process of integrating the physically mature body image into the representation of oneself" (p. 22).[4] Peter Blos (1979) saw homosexuality as a failure properly to resolve feelings of "the negative oedipal" relationship: "The dread, horror, and ego-dystonic nature of homosexuality or perversion is often voiced quite directly by the adolescent girl or boy and constitutes in many cases the first productive approach to the problem of sexual identity" (p. 479). Erikson (1968) grouped homosexual youths with delinquents, drug addicts, and "social cynics," all being youths whose "negative identities" develop "where conditions of economic, ethnic and religious marginality provide poor bases for any kind of positive identity" (p .88). For Kaplan (1984), "the central dynamic issues . . . are not whether the adolescent makes a homosexual or a heterosexual adjustment, but how she arrives at that adjustment and the delicate balance between self-love and a capacity to love others" (p. 164). But the value-laden polarization of homosexuality–heterosexuality and the old equation "homosexuality = narcissistic object relations" surface a few pages later in Kaplan's discussion.

> The major problem that arises with homosexual love choice is that it always entails some relinquishment of genital vitality. The homosexual love act necessarily encourages the ascendancy of infantile sexuality and therefore a certain degree of surrender to the past. Thus for the homosexual the temptations to linger in the never-never land of genital ambiguity, to play at life rather than live it, are apt to be extremely difficult to resist. Nevertheless, surrender is not inevitable [p. 165].

If psychoanalysts do not consider homosexuality, by definition, as evidence of psychological or social disturbance, they must consider the developmental challenges that face an adolescent passionately attracted to those of her own sex. Faced with the "physiological revolution within" and the "tangible adult tasks ahead," how does she negotiate this developmental passage? Erikson (1963) described the adolescent mind as an "ideological mind . . . eager to be affirmed by . . . peers, and . . . ready to be confirmed by rituals, creeds, and programs which at the same time define what is evil, uncanny, and inimical" (p. 263). In addition to enduring the usual adolescence heightened and often painful self-awareness, a young woman attracted to other women finds intense cognitive and emotional dissonances. Her body's longings are deemed by numerous "rituals, creeds and programs" as weird, sick, perverse, queer, unnatural, sinful. She will find little peer or adult affirmation and is likely to find herself the object of pervasive social rejection and shunned by those who are anxious about their own sexual feelings and gender performances. If she denies her feelings, she suffers the psychological consequences of fearing, hating, and hiding her own erotic capacities. If she hides her feelings from others, she continually feels the disparity Erikson (1963) noted between how she "appear[s] to be in the eyes of others as compared with what" she feels herself to be. But if she affirms her own feelings and reveals them to others, she may face additional challenges. Socarides (1996) maintains that "whenever an adolescent confides that 'I know I'm a homosexual, I just feel it,' having thereby acquired his identity 'through inner knowledge,' this verbalization constitutes an immediate indicator for therapy" (p. 15).

Winnicott (1961) felt that there needed to be "time for adolescence" where the process of moving from childhood through pubertal changes into mature identity can unfold. In describing the experiences of youth "struggling through the doldrums" of adolescence, Winnicott insisted on the importance of the environment and its response to the adolescent. He also made a striking and unusual observation: "the boy or girl does not yet know whether he or she will be homosexual, heterosexual, or simply narcissistic" (p. 81), a statement that appears to acknowledge homosexuality as distinct from narcissism and as one expectable developmental outcome:

> Young people . . . search for a form of identification which does not let them down in their struggle, *the struggle to feel real*, the struggle to establish a personal identity, not to fit into an assigned role, but to go through whatever has to be gone through. . . .
>
> The big challenge from the adolescent is to the bit of ourselves that has not really had its adolescence. This bit of ourselves makes us resent these people being able to have their phase of the doldrums, and makes us *want to find a solution* for them. There are hundreds of false solutions [pp. 84, 87].

How and where can a lesbian adolescent acquire sufficient healthy narcissism to support pride and pleasure in her female identity and her sexuality, find her solutions to feeling real? Where can she find support for taking the necessary steps in healthy individuation from her family? If she cannot bring same-sex partners to the dances, parties, and gatherings of her classmates and peers, how can a lesbian-identifying adolescent learn to "date," that ritualized search for a permanent partner that is a primary preoccupation of adolescence and young adulthood in our culture? What religious, cultural, and legal models or images or texts or rituals help her affirm the possibility of making a satisfying and psychologically sound lesbian relationship? These psychosocial challenges affect and interact with a developing adolescent's intrapsychic conflicts and object relations issues. Their potent combinations contribute to adolescent depression, suicide attempts, drug use, alienation, and the "negative identity" ascribed to and too often realized by homosexual adolescents (see Maylon, 1981; Remafedi, 1987; Martin and Hetrick, 1988; Herdt, 1989b; Gonsiorek, 1993; Remafadi, Farrow, and Deisher, 1993; D'Augelli and Hershberger, 1993; Hartstein, 1996).

## Bee-Charming

In Fannie Flagg's (1987) novel *Fried Green Tomatoes at the Whistle Stop Cafe*, Idgie Threadgoode is a "bee-charmer," a young woman able to get honey from the hive without being stung by the bees. "Bee-charmer" is an apt name for a woman able to manage the anxieties of the never-ending process of identifying as homosexual. Such a woman must move amidst her culture's stinging names for same-sex desire. She must affirm in herself feelings and behaviors that legal, religious, and psychological institutions define as evidence of socially disruptive behavior, sinful character, disturbed or arrested development, perverse sexuality, and disordered femininity.

Flagg describes the scene in which Idgie gets her name and in which Ruth must face her own feelings.

> Idgie, who was barefoot, started walking over to the big oak tree and about halfway there, turned to see if Ruth was watching. When she got about ten feet from the tree, she made sure again that Ruth was still watching. Then she did the most amazing thing. She very slowly tiptoed up to it, humming very softly, and stuck her hand with the jar in it, right in the hole in the middle of the oak.
>
> All of a sudden, Ruth heard a sound like a buzz saw, and the sky went black as hordes of angry bees swarmed out of the hole.
>
> In seconds, Idgie was covered from head to foot with thousands of bees. Idgie just stood there, and in a minute, carefully pulled her hand out of the tree and started walking slowly back toward Ruth, still humming. By the time she had gotten back, almost all the bees had flown away and . . . Idgie [was] standing there, grinning from ear to ear, with a jar of wild honey. . . . She held it up, offering the jar to Ruth. "Here you are, Madame, this is for you."
>
> . . . [Ruth bursts into tears. Idgie apologizes and tries to cheer Ruth up.] "Just think, Ruth, I never did it for anybody else before. Now

nobody in the whole world knows I can do that but you. I just wanted for us to have a secret together, that's all."

. . . Ruth took her hand and smiled down at her. "My Idgie's a bee charmer."

"Is that what I am?"

"That's what you are. I've heard there were people who could do it, but I'd never seen one before today."

"Is it bad?"

"Nooo. It's wonderful. Don't you know that?"

"Naw, I thought it was crazy or something?"

"No,—it's a wonderful thing to be."

Ruth leaned down and whispered in her ear, "You're an old bee charmer, Idgie Threadgoode, that's what you are. . . ."

Idgie smiled back at her and looked up into the clear blue sky that reflected in her eyes, and she was as happy as anybody who is in love in the summertime can be [pp. 85–87].

Idgie's courageously sticking her hand right into the hole in the middle of the oak and coming out with honey she offers to Ruth is a powerful image of the sexual, psychological, and social situation that must be mastered by a woman who reaches for sexual love or intimate relationship with another woman. To find sweetness, she must find her way through a swarm of confusing, dangerous, and frightening identifications. Idgie has somehow learned this mastery; she can charm the bees so they don't sting her as she takes the honey. And, like many women who discover that they are attracted to other women, Idgie thinks she is the "only one." Ruth has heard of such people but has never seen one before. Ruth herself bursts into tears of relief and self-recognition when she sees Idgie emerge unstung from the swarm of angry bees, which finally disappear as Idgie offers her the honey.

It's funny, most people can be around someone and then gradually begin to love them and never know exactly when it happened; but Ruth knew the very second it happened to her. When Idgie had grinned at her and tried to hand her that jar of honey, all these feelings that she had been trying to hold back came flooding through her, and it was at that second in time that she knew she loved Idgie with all her heart. That's why she had been crying, that day. She had never felt that way before and she knew she probably would never feel that way again. . . .

She had no idea why she wanted to be with Idgie more than anybody else on this earth, but she did. She had prayed about it, she had cried about it; but there was no answer except to go back home and marry Frank Bennett, the young man she was engaged to marry, and to try to be a good wife and mother. Ruth was sure that no matter what

> Idgie said, she would get over her crush and get on with her life. Ruth was doing the only thing she could do [pp. 88–89].

Although Ruth can assure Idgie that her gift for getting honey in the midst of bees was neither "bad" nor "crazy" but, in fact, "wonderful," Ruth cannot, at this point in her life, find a way through her own anxieties to support her own desire. Instead she decides to marry and hopes that she and Idgie will get over their feelings.

Flagg sets her novel in the American South of the 1920s and 30s, a context in which it is easy to imagine social prejudice and religious intolerance against female homosexuality. But the 1991 film made from Flagg's novel reveals the difficulty contemporary America has in portraying a woman who is "normal" and "feminine" and yet wants to make her life with another woman. The film clearly shows that "tomboy" Idgie has a crush on "feminine" Ruth. But, unlike readers of the novel, viewers of the film never understand that Ruth's love is as early, total, and absorbing as Idgie's. Ruth's early love has been censored in the movie version. What names should be given to the relationship of Idgie and Ruth? Are they lesbians? Neither the book nor the film portrays Ruth and Idgie as sexual partners. The closest we come to a "sex scene" is the sensual flirtation of the food-throwing escapade. Ruth and Idgie are more than good "friends" who care for one another deeply. Both have loved Buddy and mourned his death. They raise Ruth's son together. They care for, and are taken care of by, their black workers and the tramps and homeless families of the Great American Depression. Idgie and Ruth, apparently economically independent operators of the cafe, provide the nurturing center for the Whistle Stop community. These independent women become female role models for Evelyn Couch as she deals with menopause and marriage to Ed in the 1980s. But because they do not explicitly state that the women are lesbians, both book and film leave unchallenged the many images of disordered femininity associated with women in lesbian relationships. At most, viewers of the film are prompted to consider that trouser-wearing, card-playing Idgie's love is "latent" lesbianism, but nothing prompts viewers to consider that in the "normal," "feminine," pretty, soft-spoken, *maternal* Ruth they also see a lesbian woman. The film illustrates the conflict inherent in the coming-out process. Unless Ruth and Idgie are explicitly named lesbians, a heterosexual assumption is possible. But if the relationship were explicitly named lesbian, many heterosexual viewers and readers would no longer comfortably identify with Ruth and Idgie. The film leaves Idgie and Ruth partially closeted, thus allowing them to keep their position as admirable objects of identification.[5]

A capacity for "bee-charming" is also essential in those who offer psychoanalytic treatment to lesbian patients. Analysts must be able to accompany their patients on their explorations of homosexual attractions and relationships. On these explorations, conscious and unconscious anxieties, the stinging names and conceptual confusions about homosexuality, will arise within the treatment, mix within the swarm of other anxieties, and threaten to confound and frighten the movements of both analyst and patient. Following are examples from two analytic attempts at clarifying the mind and desire.

## Coming Out in Vienna in 1920

Freud (1920) has provided a vivid description of a real-life contemporary of the fictional Idgie and Ruth, an adolescent "coming out" in middle-class Vienna in 1920.[6] He described scenes and situations still common in American families 70 years later. Throughout Freud's paper his language demonstrates how central to coming out are conflicts about openness versus guardedness and honesty versus deception.

> There were two details of her behavior, in apparent contrast with each other, that most especially vexed her parents. On the one hand, she did not scruple to appear in the most frequented streets in the company of her undesirable friend, being thus quite neglectful of her own reputation; while, on the other hand, she disdained no means of deception, no excuses and no lies that would make meetings with her possible and cover them. She thus showed herself too open in one respect and full of deceitfulness in the other [p. 148].

The 18-year-old patient tells her parents that she is in love with an older woman, a woman from a family of high social standing, but who lives outside the social conventions and has sexual relations with both men and women. At first the girl's mother becomes her daughter's confidante in the love affair. Her father is vehemently opposed to his daughter's interest in the woman.

The girl precipitates a crisis. She walks in a park with the woman at a time and in a place where she knows her father will see them. When the father sees his daughter with the woman, he turns angrily away. The woman, on learning the identity of the man who has just passed them in anger, tells the girl that they can no longer be together. Rejected by both her father and her beloved, the girl throws herself into the approach of an oncoming tram. After this suicide attempt, she is depressed for six months and stays home in bed. Her parents do not bring her for treatment during this time. It is only later, when she has recovered from her depression and resumed her public courtship of the woman, that her parents, concerned about the family's social disgrace, take action. The father brings his daughter to Freud for treatment.

Freud describes the girl's presentation: "She did not try to deceive me by saying that she felt any urgent need to be freed from her homosexuality. On the contrary, she said she could not conceive of any other way of being in love, but she added that for her parents' sake she would honestly help in the therapeutic attempt, for it pained her very much to be the cause of so much grief to them . . ." (p. 153).

Such a story would be familiar to contemporary therapists: a homosexual attraction to an older or unsuitable person; impulsive behaviors including suicide attempts; depression, family crisis, and disruption. How is a therapist to understand the girl and her feelings? Why, with friends her own age of both sexes available, does she pursue an older, unavailable woman? What is the meaning of her forcing a crisis with her father? Does she want his approval for her love, or is she unconsciously provoking his help to end the relationship? Does she provoke a crisis because she is too insecure to withstand her father's disapproval? Is she an insecure adolescent uncertain about her own choices and unable to trust her own desires and feelings? Is she in anxious flight from heterosexual relationships, in anxious flight from sexuality? Is she so frightened and confused by her attraction to a woman that she creates a confusing, dangerous, and dramatic muddle? These are the "bee-charming" issues facing an analytic therapist of such a patient.

Shortly after treatment begins, the patient brings a series of dreams. Curiously, Freud does not give us the content of any of these dreams nor any of the patient's associations. One might even suggest that he *hides* the dreams. He simply asserts that they "could be easily translated with certainty. . . . They anticipated the cure of the inversion through the treatment, expressed her joy over the prospects in life that would then be opened before her, confessed her longing for a man's love and for children . . ." (p. 165). But Freud sees a "contradiction between [these dreams] and the girl's utterances in waking life." He decides the contradiction is so great that the dreams are "false and hypocritical, and that she intended to deceive me just as she habitually deceived her father. I was right; after I had made this clear, this kind of dream ceased" (p. 165). Convinced of the patient's desire to deceive him, Freud breaks off the treatment and advises her parents that if they wanted to continue treatment, it should be undertaken with a woman analyst.[7]

What happened in this aborted therapeutic exchange? The patient tells first her parents and then her analyst that she is in love with a woman. Her analyst first reports that "she did not try to deceive me by saying she felt any urgent need to be freed from her homosexuality. On the contrary she could not conceive of any other way of being in love" (p. 153). Yet she brings her analyst dreams about "her longing for a man's love and the love of children." Are such dreams contradictions, hypocritical, and false? If a woman dreams of a man's love and the love of children, is she therefore either deceiving her analyst or not homosexual?

Compare Freud's approach to the sexuality of this 18-year-old patient with his thinking about sexuality in the case of Dora. In Dora Freud (1905a) also discovered a complexity of desire. But, on finding what he called "two currents" in Dora's emotional life, instead of seeing this as deception and hypocritical, he used the contradictory currents in Dora to illustrate his belief that "thoughts in the unconscious live very comfortably side by side, and even contraries get on together without disputes—a state of things which persists often enough even in the conscious" (p. 61).

Freud saw Dora, as he did the 18-year-old patient of 1920, as a woman motivated by revenge against men:

> In this way the transference took me unawares, and, because of the unknown quantity in me which reminded Dora of Herr K, she took her revenge on me as she wanted to take her revenge on him and deserted me as she believed herself to have been deceived and deserted by him. Thus she acted out an essential part of her recollections and phantasies instead of reproducing it in the treatment [p. 119].

But in a later footnote he added new thoughts about Dora's revenge:

> The longer the interval of time that separates me from the end of this analysis, the more probable it seems to me that the fault in my technique lay in this omission: I failed to discover in time and to inform the patient that her homosexual (gynaecophilic) love for Frau K was the strongest unconscious current in her mental life. . . . Before I had learnt the importance of the homosexual current of feeling in psychoneurotics, I was often brought to a standstill in the treatment of my cases or found myself in complete complexity [p. 120].

But in 1920, in spite of Freud's having learned the importance of the "homosexual current of feeling," treatment again came to a standstill. Although feminists and others (Bernheimer and Kahane, 1985) have critically discussed transference and countertransference issues in the case of

Dora and have questioned whether penis envy and revenge are sufficient to explain Dora's responses to Freud, less analytic attention has been given to the motivations of the nameless 1920 patient or to the transference and countertransference issues effecting that treatment. Silva (1975) criticized Freud for telling the patient that she was *homosexual*. For Silva, the patient's dreams (which we do not know) and the absence of genital sexual behavior indicated that she is not homosexual but "an adolescent who finds herself in that transitory stage so common to young people of both sexes, who feel a conscious repulsion to everything sexual, due to a repression of their natural sexual longings" (p. 359). Harris (1991) uses the case to illustrate Freud's "radical" model of sexuality and gender in which "the unconscious and symbolic meaning of bodies and genders, rather than the biological sex of the lover and beloved, carries the interpretive weight" (p. 197). Harris sees the patient's love relationship as a "heterosexual object choice in which a 'fictive' boy chooses a mother to idealize and save from an oedipal father" (p. 208). Magid (1993) focuses on "the [therapeutic] misalliance," the most "egregious" example of which is Freud's accusing the patient of lying to him in her dream. Magid criticizes Freud's interest in etiology at the expense of the patient and stresses that "the only appropriate avenue for psychoanalytic investigation is the subjective experiences of our patients . . ." (pp. 431–432).

Freud was sure that his patient was homosexual; Silva is sure that she was a confused, heterosexual adolescent. Harris sees that the young woman's apparent homosexual object choice was unconsciously a heterosexual oedipal drama in which a "fictive" boy wants "his" mother. What did Freud's patient want?

To appreciate Freud's patient's desire, one needs to understand the patient's unconscious motivations and her intrapsychic developmental history. One must also understand the particulars of the culture in which she lived, which shaped her ideas about love and sexuality and which gave her—and her analyst—names for her behavior. The young woman patient of 1920 fell in love at almost precisely the same time that Bryher met H.D. These women fell in love the midst of new definitions of women's sexuality. Although today feminists, psychoanalysts, and biologists debate about the influences (biological, social, or psychological) that motivate women who make primary relationships with one another instead of with men, for most of history, as we have seen, primary relationships between women were impossible. Historically, women's relationships with one another have always been, of necessity, secondary to, or preliminary to, their relationships with men. As long as women were socially and economically dependent on their fathers, husbands, or other male relatives, their feelings toward one another might be publicly expressed in writing, in public gesture, in tokens of loving exchange. This was expected feminine behavior in what were variously called "sentimental" or romantic friendships. Independent women, like Idgie and Ruth, began to establish partnerships whose emphasis was not on sex, but on support and "cottage and competency." Faderman (1981) has argued that the work of sexologists such as Westphal, Krafft-Ebing, and Havelock Ellis, and the work of Freud, was instrumental in changing how women understand their passionate feelings for one another. Freud's patient lived in what Faderman calls the "last breath of innocence." Faderman describes the coming change:

> Openly expressed love between women for the most part ceased to be possible after World War I. Women's changed status and the new "medical knowledge" cast such affection in a new light. I discovered abundant evidence of female same-sex love, of course, but it was almost invariably accompanied by a new outlaw status. I was then led to investigate how that outlaw status affected the women who continued to love women despite twentieth century societal taboos. I found that not only did twentieth century lesbian literature by heterosexuals usually show love between women to be a disease, but that women who were professedly lesbian generally internalized those views. This was reflected in their own literature, which was full of self-doubts and self-loathing until the 1960's [p. 20].

Freud and his young patient fought over the nature of her passion and its proper name. She called it love; he called it sexual attraction, a difference of perspective that still befuddles psychoanalytic and cultural discussions of female same-sex relationships. That difference in perspective is related to the second important factor in the cultural backdrop of the 1920 treatment: the therapeutic exchange took place in the midst of Germany's flourishing, and predominantly male, homosexual civil rights movement. Freud's therapeutic zealousness in the 1920 case arose from his belief that in this young woman he had a case that would prove the psychoanalytic theory of homosexuality—and disprove the theories of both sexologists and of homosexual activists who insisted that homosexuals were a "third sex" and that homosexuality had a constitutional, congenital etiology. To this end, therefore, he stressed that his patient was a "beautiful and clever girl, of a family of good standing," in other words, a patient in whom there was no hint of congenital family disturbance, physical masculinity, nor "third-sex" hermaphroditism.

Certainly there was no obvious deviation from the feminine physical type, nor any menstrual disturbance. The beautiful and well-made girl had, it is true, her father's tall figure, and her facial features were sharp rather than soft and girlish, traits which might be regarded as indicating a physical masculinity. Some of her intellectual attributes also could be connected with masculinity: for instance, her acuteness of comprehension and her lucid objectivity, in so far as she was not dominated by her passion. But these distinctions are conventional rather than scientific. What is certainly of greater importance is that in her behaviour towards her love-object she had throughout assumed the masculine part: that is to say, she displayed the humility and the sublime overvaluation of the sexual object so characteristic of the male lover, the renunciation of all narcissistic satisfaction, and the preference for being the lover rather than the beloved. She had thus not only chosen a feminine love-object, but had also developed a masculine attitude towards that object [Freud, 1920, p. 154].

The 18-year-old fell in love in a time of changing definitions of sexuality and femininity. Male sexologists such as Havelock Ellis and male homosexual activists such as Magnus Hirschfeld saw behavior once thought characteristic of a feminine "sentimental friendship" as evidence of "latent" or "congenital" "homosexuality." Freud saw "masculine" behavior in that which just previously would have been seen as quintessentially feminine. As further evidence of her "masculinity complex," he pointed out that she "was in fact a feminist; she felt it to be unjust that girls should not enjoy the same freedom as boys, and rebelled against the lot of woman in general" (p. 169). The object of her attentions was, significantly, an older woman who apparently enjoyed a considerable degree of economic and social independence, although that independence also earned her the outlaw reputation Faderman describes.

These societal changes, new social options for women, and new theories about sexuality may have contributed to the parents' preoccupations with the girl's openness. Ten years before they might not have minded their daughter's public display of affection toward another woman, behavior that at that time would not have been coded as sexual and certainly not as unnatural. The Oberlin College yearbook of 1920 contains a photograph of 32 young women, each identified by name, members of a group called "Lesbians," a club for writers of poetry. By 1925 those poetry lovers had another name for their organization (MacKay, 1992; see also Vicinus, 1984).

Psychoanalytic and sexologist theories of female same-sex relationships and intimacy produced strange paradoxes and contradictions as they entered the general culture and conflicted with existing ideas about female sexuality. Showalter (1990) has described the situation in England: "In 1920 Vita Sackville-West described herself as a 'Dr. Jekyll and Mr. Hyde personality,' torn between her love for her husband and her 'perverted lesbian' attachment to women; but in 1921 English legislators refused to include women in the Labouchère Amendment [which made homosexuality a criminal act] because lesbianism was too deeply disturbing even to forbid." (p. 119). Having read the sexologists and Freud, as well, the literate Bloomsbury writer Vita Sackville-West had new names for her desire. Ironically, while conservative male lawmakers in England were trying to keep the corrupt notion of sexual relations between women away from the innocent pure minds of proper women, in Vienna Freud was frustrated and impatient with what he saw as his patient's guardedness about revealing the sexual nature of her attraction. Freud saw as willfully deceptive her refusal to acknowledge to him, or to herself, what he knew must motivate her: *sexual* attraction to women based on revenge against men. Freud described what he called the patient's "Russian tactics," a military metaphor for the particular kind of silent resistance he felt the patient demonstrated:

> The analysis went forward almost without any signs of resistance, the patient participating actively with her intellect, though absolutely tranquil emotionally. Once when I expounded to her a specially important part of the theory, one touching her nearly, she replied in an inimitable tone, "How very interesting," as though she were a *grande dame* being taken over a museum and glancing through her lorgnon at objects to which she was completely indifferent [p. 163].

Freud experienced the patient's resistance to his interpretations. He interpreted the resistance as a transferential desire to defeat his treatment, as her homosexuality was motivated by her desire to take revenge upon and defeat her father. He referred the patient away.

The developing transference Freud felt so acutely was perhaps more complicated than a vengeful deception. The patient may have been testing Freud in both the maternal and paternal transferences: can you listen to me and help me see myself, find names for myself that fit my experience; or are you, like my parents, more interested in my being whom you want me to be and in my accepting your names for my desires? Freud's acknowledged interest in this case was not in clinical treatment but in the opportunity to present a case of homosexuality in women "in which it was possible to trace its origin and development in the mind with complete certainty and almost without a gap" (p. 147). Freud filled any "gap" of uncertainty by declaring that a woman attracted to a woman has "forsw[orn] her womanhood and sought another goal for her libido. . . . She changed into a man and took her mother in place of her father as the object of her love" (pp. 157, 158). Although he summarized various factors contributing to the patient's homosexuality, including an original infantile fixation to mother and the advantages for the girl of "retiring" from heterosexual pursuits in favor of her envious mother, Freud emphasized her deception of, and revenge against, men. For Freud, the patient's homosexuality was the product of her turning against the love of men when she could not have her real desire—her father's penis or his baby. The patient's dreams, therefore, "of a man's love and the love of children" were indeed contradictions, not perhaps of the patient's complex desires, but of Freud's ideas about homosexuality in women. Freud gave no indication that he was aware that any anxieties might attend the acceptance of an identity of "forsworn womanhood."

Sometimes we try to imagine the life of Freud's 1920 patient. The later life and identity of some of Freud's case studies are known. Much has been written about the Wolf Man (Freud, 1918). We know that Anna O was Bertha Pappenheim (Breuer and Freud, 1893–1895). Pappenheim became a feminist and translated Mary Wollstonecraft's *A Vindication of the Rights of Women*; she was also a social worker who organized against sexual exploitation of women and children (see e.g., Freeman, 1972; Rosenbaum and Muroff, 1984; Herman, 1992; Swenson, 1994). Kurt Eissler did interview Freud's 1920 patient, but that interview remains in the restricted section of the Freud Archives.[8] Having no access to the identity of "the beautiful and clever girl" of 1920, we are left to imagine her later life. When analysis failed, did her father put into effect his second line of defense?—"a speedy marriage was to awaken the natural instincts of the girl and stifle her unnatural tendencies" (Freud, 1920, p. 149). Did she, like Idgie's Ruth, marry and try to get over her love? Did she, like Bryher, marry as camouflage for her love? What words did she use to describe her love for the older woman? What did she read to try to understand her feelings and to find stories to live by? Did she read *The Scorpion*, Anna Weirauch's (1919–1921) three-volume novel of a lesbian relationship? Its heroine, 20-year-old Mette, is in love with the ten years older Olga. The first volume ends with Mette's forced engagement to a man and Olga's suicide (cited in Faderman and Eriksson, 1989).

Or was she fortunate enough to find Groddeck's The (1923) *Book of the It* in which, in the persona of Patrick Troll, he writes a series of letters to a woman friend about the workings of the world of the unconscious.

> Yes, I hold the view that all people are homosexual, hold it so firmly that it is difficult for me to realize how anyone can think differently.

Man loves himself first and foremost, with every sort of passionate emotion, and seeks to procure for himself every conceivable pleasure, and since he himself must be either male or female, is subject from the beginning to a passion for his own sex. . . . The question, therefore, is not whether homosexuality is exceptional, perverse—that does not come under discussion;—what we have to ask is, why it is so difficult to consider this phenomenon of passion between people of the same sex, to judge it and discuss it, without prejudice . . . [p. 195].

Freud called his patient a feminist. Was she interested, as were the German feminists of her day, in women's education, employment, and suffrage? Did she read *The Girlfriend: Weekly for the Ideal Friendship?*

We wonder what, if anything, the 18-year-old "beautiful and clever girl of a family of good standing" knew of another of Freud's patients at the time, his daughter Anna, who was 25 in 1920. Anna's own analysis with her father began in 1918 and continued until 1921. In 1919, Freud wrote "A child is being beaten," based on six cases (two men and four women). In 1922, Anna presented "Beating Fantasies and Daydream," her paper for membership in the Vienna Psychoanalytic Society, six months before she had seen her first patient, "[making] it almost certain," notes Young-Bruehl (1988) "that the patient whose case is discussed was herself—the one patient she knew intimately" (p. 104). In 1925, Dorothy Tiffany Burlingham, 34, granddaughter of Charles Lewis Tiffany and daughter of painter, decorator, glass-designer, Louis Comfort Tiffany, left her manic-depressive husband, Robert, and came to Vienna with her four children. She began analysis with Freud and moved into the floor above the Freud's at Berggasee 19. Beginning in 1927, Anna and Dorothy vacationed together; they bought a cottage together in 1930. Anna was analyst for Dorothy's children. Anna and Dorothy established a school for Dorothy's children and those of their friends. Two of its first teachers were Peter Blos and Erik H. Erikson, later to become major psychoanalytic writers on adolescence and childhood. Anna, Dorothy, and Freud fled Vienna in 1938 for England, where Dorothy and Anna established the Hampstead War Nurseries, and later the Hampstead Child Therapy Clinic for child treatment and for research and training in child analysis. For 54 years, until Dorothy's death in 1979, Dorothy and Anna had a primary and generative relationship. Anna and Dorothy no more saw their relationship as based on "sexual attraction" than did Freud's 18-year-old. And perhaps they might have shared Freud's beautiful and clever young girl's assertion that she had no wish to be "cured" of this way of loving. Dorothy wrote to Anna, "I know life without you would be quite without sense—just to live out and nothing more—I am quite sure there would be no more development" (letter of February 11, 1940, in Young-Bruehl, 1988, p. 245).

In 1928 Freud's ex-patient would have been 26 years old. What would she have made of Virginia Woolf's *Orlando* or of the just-published *The Well of Loneliness*, Radcliffe Hall's novel of "congenital" lesbianism for which sexologist Havelock Ellis wrote the preface? Its heroine, Stephen Gordon, depressed, masculine in name, clothing, and identity, self-hating, and lonely, gave up the woman she loved, the feminine Mary, so that Mary could make a normal life with a man. Stephen Gordon read Kraft-Ebbing to try to understand her feelings, and for decades lesbian women read *The Well of Loneliness* as the definitive fictional description of homosexual women.

In 1938, when Freud left Vienna, Freud's ex-patient would have been 36. Was she Jewish? Did she survive the Nazis? Did she emigrate?

In 1980 Freud's ex-patient, if alive, would have been 78. What might she have made of Adrienne Rich, poet, teacher, and mother describing that "moment when for the first time in my life I experienced sexuality as clarifying my mind instead of hazing it over"? Perhaps by 78 that once beautiful and clever girl might have appreciated Susan Leigh Star's (1980) response to medical, psychiatric, and psychoanalytic attempts to determine what makes a "real" homosexual.

> Does it count when you're seven?
> Does it count when you're eleven?
> Does it count when you're just "messing around?"
> Does it count when your "practicing for the boys when you grow up so you'll know what to do and won't be embarrassed (giggle)?
> Does it count at Girl Scout Camp and there aren't any boys around?
> Does it count in high school and you don't care about the boys anyway?
> Does it count before one reaches the hormonal stage of puberty, before latency, before the onset, ahem, of genital sexuality?
> Does it count before you have pubic hair?
> Does it count if you have one pubic hair?
> Two?
> Three?
> At what point does pubic hair constitute genuine Lesbianism?
> Does it count if one of you pretends to be a boy?
> If both of you accidentally pretend to be boys at once, does that

make you both faggots?
Does it count if you stay outside?
Does it count if you never even kiss?
Does it count if a boy watches?
Does it count if you're drunk?
   Stoned?
   Unhappy?
   Never got enough mothering?
   Got too much mothering?
   Can't have children?
   Have children already?
   Like men?
   Hate men?
Does it count if you're best friends anyway?
   If you don't have an orgasm?
   If it's a schoolgirl crush?
   If it's not reciprocated?
   If you close your eyes? [ pp. 229–230]

Star is mocking various behavioral measures and etiologic explanations for female same-sex attraction, but the questions are those of many lesbian women as they try to understand their own history and development, much of which has had to take place in secret and in confusion amidst their culture's stinging names.

## Lesbian Relationships in the Psychoanalytic Literature

Did Freud's patient ever find her way to other, more available women? She certainly received no help in understanding why she was attracted to that particular woman. In published clinical material, with a few significant exceptions (Deutsch, 1932; Lachmann, 1975; Mitchell, 1978; Eisenbud, 1986; Sanville, l991), patients do not improve their existing lesbian relationships or establish new and more satisfying lesbian relationships as a result of analytic treatment. For some analysts these outcomes need no explanation. For others who have in their practices women patients who wish to find or improve relationships with women, this absence in the literature presents more of a problem. Some would explain the absence of descriptions of improved lesbian relations as due to the level of disturbance characteristic of homosexual women. Since we do not see women who have lesbian identity or relationships as having clinical disturbances that distinguish them from heterosexual women, we explain the absence of improved lesbian relationships in analytic treatment by other factors.

The first is the analyst's personal comfort with, and theoretical support for, homosexual relationships. Eisenbud (1986) has described her own "transference to theory" and her changing conceptualizations of what she calls "Lesbian choice." Analysts must have theoretical perspectives that enable them to be at ease with the possibility that a lesbian relationship may be one possible productive outcome of the patient's treatment. When the analyst does not have such theoretical support, certain clinical results may follow. First, the anxieties and defenses in the patient which prevent the establishment of sound lesbian relationships will not be analyzed. They will simply be assumed to be manifestations of the pathology thought characteristic of homosexuality or of the disturbances which assumably make homosexual relations defensively necessary. The analyst will assume that, when the narcissistic deficits or separation anxiety or oedipal conflicts are better resolved, the patient will be freer to have relationships with men, rather than assuming that, when such issues are better resolved, the patient becomes psychically freer to follow her attraction and find more satisfying objects, which *may* remain women. Deutsch (1932) described treatment with a woman who "knew that her erotic potentialities and fantasies were directed towards members of her own sex. . . . The women were not in any instance of a masculine type, and she herself was blond and feminine. She felt no hostility toward, men. . . . and had married a man of outspoken masculine appearance, and had several children by him to whom she gave a maternal, even if not excessively warm, response" (p. 209). The patient had been aware of her attraction toward women since puberty. She came to treatment for her depressions, which had led to a number of serious suicide attempts, and for her timidity toward her women servants. The analysis focused on the patient's "aggressive, murderous hate against the mother" (p. 211). After a period of successful treatment, Deutsch referred her patient to a "fatherly male analyst" in the hope that "the patient's libidinal future would shape up more satisfactorily with a revival of the father relationship" (p. 213). By accident, about a year later she met her patient on the street and discovered that "she had become a vivid, radiant person. She told me that her depressions had entirely disappeared. The wish to die which had been almost continuously present . . . had apparently receded completely. At last she had found happiness in a particularly congenial and uninhibited sexual relationship with a woman" (p. 214). Deutsch noted that "the result of her analysis [with Deutsch] was evident. Everything that had come to the surface so clearly in the analytic transference was now detached from the person of the analyst and transferred to other women" (p. 214). When the disturbance in internal early object relationships was relieved, the patient was freed to seek new relationships. To the surprise of her analyst, she left her husband and established a relationship with a woman.[9]

Unless the analyst is theoretically comfortable with homosexual relationships, he or she may have difficulty seeing any lesbian relationship, no matter of what quality, as evidence of therapeutic progress or positive change and will not in clinical reports describe such relationships in positive terms. Some patients have painfully discovered at the end of their analyses that their analysts, who had throughout the analysis seemed to be accepting of their homosexuality, expressed disappointment when the treatment ends "prematurely," that is, without the woman's establishing a relationship with a man.

Psychoanalysis has understood that homosexuality may serve to avoid the anxieties of heterosexual relationships. What has not been understood is how marriage often serves as a defense against homosexual attraction. Deutsch's patient tried marriage although she had never really been in love with a man. Freud noted that his patient's father saw marriage as a second line of defense for his daughter, if psychoanalysis was not successful: "If this way failed he still had in reserve his strongest counter-measure: a speedy marriage was to awaken the natural instincts of the girl and stifle her unnatural tendencies" (p.149). Fannie Flagg (1987) gives a fictional description of this strategy. Bryher, a wealthy heiress, married twice, on her own terms, to maintain her financial and social independence and provide support for her relationship with H.D

## Coming Out of Psychoanalytic Closets

The second reason for the lack of descriptions of improvement in the relationships of lesbian patients in analytic treatment is that, as we have suggested, many analytic therapists whose patients' lesbian relationships do improve have kept silent about their work and have not published such cases. We find it difficult to believe that analysts have escaped the anxiety-based reactions to homosexuality so prevalent in the general culture. We do not think that those analysts whose patients' lesbian relationships improve neglect to report this development because they find it such an unremarkable occurrence. On the contrary, we believe that such analysts are in the same position as their lesbian patients—ambivalent about whether to reveal or to hide, fearing that if they do come out, their work will, at best, not be appreciated and, at worst, be attacked.

We believe that a closet has existed for analysts who treat lesbian women. "Coming out" always has risks, but some periods in the history of psychoanalysis have been more accepting of homosexuality than others (Lewes, 1988) and more tolerant of analytic work with those in "overt" homosexual relationships. Freud (1920) and Deutsch (1932) published their cases in an analytic climate more tolerant than that in which Khan (1964) described his work with a college student. Freud was impatient with his 18-year-old because she was disinterested in exploring the sexual aspects of her attraction. Deutsch's patient felt comfortable enough when she met her ex-analyst on the street to tell her she has found uninhibited sexual pleasure with a woman, and Deutsch felt comfortable enough to report this development. But, in 1964, Khan worried about how he and his patient would be seen if he described his patient's excited sexual pleasure. Khan began to describe the patient's sexual relationship, which he called "the homosexual episode" and the "focal symbiosis," and then he stopped. Khan interrupted his description of the sexual relationship with *an eight-page report of his attempts to prevent the homosexual sexual behavior through interpretation* and with a description of his anxiety as the patient, in spite of interpretations, pursued her course.

> I have already stated that the homosexual relationship had materialized in a specific state of inner emotionality [which had] been building up in her for many months. . . . It was a very unstable mood of quick oscillations and general depressive agitatedness. No amount of interpretation of the content of her material and dreams afforded her any release from it. . . . I was rather afraid she would have a breakdown or break off treatment. I even considered advising her to change to an analyst of a different sex. But recalling the experiences of Freud (1920) and Deutsch (1932), where such a measure had not been fruitful at all, I decided to continue and let her work her own way out. . . . I was fully aware that the analytic work done so far had loosened her characterresistances and manic defence and this had led to a serious threat to her ego from the resurgence of the repressed sexual and aggressive impulses [pp. 247–248].

Khan reported that the patient had avoided homosexual experience previously because she feared "being trapped" (p. 256). He stressed his concern about her sexual "acting out" and repeatedly declared that he knew the "ego-enhancing" effects of the lesbian relationship could be achieved only because *the patient was in analysis during that relationship with a male analyst*. Under these conditions he decided to "let her work her way out" in the analysis. He described what occurs after the beginning of the sexual relationship.

> A new feature now emerged. She felt very uneasy and in physical pain whenever her friend tried to penetrate her genitals with the finger. She would reflexively turn cold and aloof and shut up completely. Alongside, there was material which hinted at episodes of petty thieving in childhood. When I indicated to her that the excessive idealization of their play with the body-surface functioned as a denial of what was hidden inside, she was deeply perturbed and only gradually confessed to a shameful theft in her life. For years she had tortured herself about it. In her early college days she borrowed Marion Milner's book *A Life of One's Own* and she has never returned it. Its title had seduced her, and she was even more embarrassed by the fact that she had never succeeded in reading it through. Every attempt had to be given up because she would get too excited, hot and bothered. She could nibble at it endlessly. . . .
>
> It would be difficult to ignore the patient's point of view that her relation to her friend had been a very vital way of correcting and elaborating [a] deficient relation to her mother. . . . In this patient the negativism and the fear of emotional surrender emerged in the relation of the patient to her own excited body as the object, and was rooted in her mother's depressive and anxious relation to her in early childhood. Hence the acting out into homosexual episode on the one hand to defend herself against these anxieties and on the other to find a milieu through which she could get at a life of her own with someone who was lively and equally desirous of such mutuality [pp. 259–260].

Would Khan have been able to "let" his patient work her own way out to more permanent homosexual relationships if she had desired them? Could he have helped her identify these desires? Although his work in this case shows his concern and liking for his young patient, it also reveals his anxious "transference to theory." Khan interpreted his patient's anxiety about vaginal penetration by her woman partner as evidence that she was "not a true homosexual pervert but passed through a phase of homosexual perversion en route to health and a true integration of her femininity" (p. 256). If a woman patient had reported anxiety about vaginal penetration with a man, would Khan have interpreted her feelings as evidence that she was not a "true" heterosexual, or would he have suggested that she examine her fears or conflicts about penetration? The patient's fears of being "trapped" in a homosexual relationship also could not be explored since to Khan, apparently, such fears were "realistic" and needed no examination.

But Khan's report is unique in psychoanalytic literature because it dramatically conveys the anxiety that emerges in both patient and analyst when inhibitions against homosexuality are lifted. Every lesbian patient's anxieties about her homosexual attraction will have become interwoven with her other conflicts and fears; and, as in any analytic treatment, these overdetermined longings, fears, and defenses will be consciously conveyed as well as unconsciously projected to the analyst, who must be familiar enough with his or her own anxieties about homosexuality to help the patient untangle her issues. If this process is defensively aborted by analysts unable to tolerate the projections, they may conclude that "psychotic" or "primitive" processes, "fragile" psychic structure (McDougall, 1980), or "negative therapeutic reactions" (Quinodoz, 1989) are characteristic of lesbian patients. Khan feared that his patient would have "a breakdown." It is to his credit that he could tolerate the anxiety raised in him by his patient's one homosexual "episode," her one homosexual "affair." But if her longing to have "a life of one's own" included a permanent lesbian relationship with an available woman, her anxieties about such longings must have gone unexamined.

Khan's concern that his "permitting" the lesbian relationship would be criticized by analytic colleagues may seem idiosyncratic, excessive, or dated. But 30 years later Limentani's (1992) comments on the case in Khan's obituary suggest that Khan's fears had foundation: "Her acting out of homosexual impulses with a friend (a novel experience) was precipitated by the patient's incapacity to tolerate frustration, and on reading the report it is easy to form the impression that the analyst did little to prevent it" (p. 158). Limentani displays the discomfort and disapproval some therapists feel toward analytic work in which "homosexual impulses" are not "prevented" from seeking expression. As an analyst, he would apparently have found some way to "prevent" such impulses. Because anxieties about homosexuality are so great, patients may consciously and unconsciously provoke policing or superego responses and prohibitions from their analysts (Mitchell, 1981). Limentani's comments suggest that he would be at risk for making such countertransference-based policing responses.[10]

Like their patients, analysts of lesbian patients must be "bee-charmers," able to tolerate the anxieties attending their patients' explorations of homosexual attractions and relationships.[11] When analysts appreciate the motives for, and the consequences of *hiding* homosexual feelings, they can appreciate the power some women experience in the act of *coming out*. Under these conditions, then, analysis can provide a treatment experience, can become a "beam of light" for a lesbian patient, a way of "clarifying" her mind and her desires.

# 6

# MORATORIUMS
# AND SECRETS

## SEARCHING FOR THE LOVE
## OF ONE'S LIFE

The truth is that homosexuality is no more a perversion deliberately
indulged in than it is a curse of fate. It is an attitude *chosen in a certain
situation*—that is, at once motivated and freely adopted. . . . Like all
human behavior, homosexuality leads to make-believe, disequilibrium,
frustration, lies, or, on the contrary, it becomes the source of rewarding experiences, in accordance with its manner of expression in actual
living—whether in bad faith, laziness, and falsity, or in lucidity, gen-
erosity, and freedom.

*[Simone de Beauvoir, 1952][1]*

Cultures have various ways of explaining development that goes against the
social grain. In cultures that believe human behavior is spiritually determined, the rites of passage toward adulthood sometimes include vision or
dream quests. Youths learn the direction of their future directly from the
Spirits. A young Sioux male, for instance, might dream of a woman's burden strap instead of a warrior's bow. The dream message reveals his spiritually sanctioned adult role and identity:

If such a boy does not prefer to commit suicide, [remarked Erikson
(1963), revealing his culture's perspective], he must give up the career
of warrior and hunter and become a *berdache*, a man-woman who

dresses like a woman and does woman's work. . . . In this way, primitive cultures accept the power of the unconscious. If the deviant can only claim to have dreamed convincingly, his deviation is considered based on supernatural visitation rather than on individual motivation [p. 153].[2]

Erikson (1958) described another variety of divinely sanctioned social deviation in his biography *Young Man Luther* (1958). The 17-year-old Luther, to all appearances ready to fulfill his father's expectations, the study of law and an early and financially prosperous marriage, returned home for a few months before continuing his studies. On his way back to school, Luther was caught in a sudden violent thunderstorm. As lightning struck around him, a frightened Luther cried, "Help me, St. Anne . . . I want to become a monk." Although Luther himself fought against the implications of his own outcry and his family protested strongly, finally he did enter a monastery, the beginning of a life in which he would demand reforms that would forever change the church. Thus, for the adolescent Luther, in conflict within himself and with his father's wishes, a way was suddenly and dramatically arranged to a course that would enable him to develop an identity and a career uniquely his own. "God acted in a miraculous way and drove me on, innocent as I was; and He alone, then, can be said to have come a long way [in bringing about] that there can be no dealing between the Pope and me" (p. 97).

Erikson suggested that some creative individuals like Luther, whose identities are not consolidated during adolescence and whose lives do not develop in a straightforward manner, establish a moratorium or a time-out "after they have ceased being children, but before their deeds and works count toward a future identity" (p. 43). The monastery provided such a moratorium for Luther. George Bernard Shaw found his way to literature by literally "dropping out" of success. At age 20, Shaw left family, friends, business success, and Ireland to "avoid the danger of success without identity" (p. 44).

Most young persons who are confused or conflicted or frightened by their same-sex attractions receive neither dramatic spiritual messages nor divinely arranged moratoriums. Many live double lives, their apparent social conformity covering and at odds with their secret desires, behaviors and relationships. Keeping erotic and affectionate longings secret stifles expression, limits relational possibilities, and constricts development. But keeping same-sex desire hidden can also be an adaptive strategy, particularly for a person who is not ready to face the challenges of a stigmatized identity. Identifying as lesbian at 18 can be a very different psychological and social experience than coming out as an adult woman, a woman who is no longer emotionally and economically dependent on her family and who has established a work identity, achieved some measure of economic independence, and explored sexual, emotional, and relational experience, often including marriage and motherhood. Khan (1983) suggested that, paradoxically, sometimes a secret can serve as "potential space." The construction of the secret becomes a container to hide significant aspects of ourselves until we find safe contexts in which to disclose them. "The secret carries a hope that one day the person will be able to emerge out of it, be found and met, and thus become a whole person, sharing life with others" (p. 105).

For patients with psychic secrets, including same-sex desire, analytic treatment may provide a new kind of "potential space" in which to explore frightening feelings and confusing issues. Some patients will attempt to foreclose that self-exploration by pushing for answers from the analyst. "What do my feelings mean? What do my dreams and fantasies mean? Am I lesbian? Am I straight?" One analytic task with such a patient is to discover why it has been so difficult for the patient to find her own answers. Why does the patient need to keep her desires a secret from herself? What intrapsychic conflicts and difficulties have contributed to her moratorium? For some patients their long hidden secrets have all but lost any ability to become "potential space," and they function only as blocks to further psychological development. Some sessions of work with Hannah illustrate a not uncommon clinical presentation. A moratorium has gone on too long. Intricate psychic knots have been created, as characterlogical issues have become entangled with matters of same sex desire.

## Hannah

When Hannah, a depressed writer in her 30s, started treatment, a recent love affair with a male colleague was on the rocks, and her attempts to persuade a woman friend to transform their friendship into a sexual relationship were meeting with little success. Her major writing project had been stalled for some time, and several other projects were in disarray. She had disorienting anxiety attacks whenever she traveled and uncontrollable gagging episodes before important work or social events. "Something is wrong with me," Hannah insisted, "something deep and core."

Hannah responded to narcissistic injury and separation anxieties by a depressive and disorienting emotional collapse she called "going down a rabbit hole" and by becoming lost in confusing sexual attractions to both men and women. What Hannah wished to portray as expressions of spontaneous, uninhibited sexuality were usually attempts to regain her emotional balance through sexual conquest. In a similar manner, she repeatedly avoided difficult and stressful passages in her work by being swept up in new, distracting projects. She was left with the nagging sense that she was always "farming others' fields," that she had never quite found her own field, in either work or love.

In the first year of treatment Hannah became pregnant and had a child, an impulsive strategy unconsciously designed to situate her own vulnerability and dependency in another. Over the next five years of treatment, her child's feelings and behavior provided ample opportunity to explore Hannah's own early development and to rework her fears of dependency. The child's responsiveness also gave her great narcissistic satisfaction. Through the treatment and through the relationship with her child, she more and more became able to regain her narcissistic equilibrium when it was disturbed by events in her busy social and professional life. She completed several writing projects. She learned to date, an experience that healed early adolescent wounds and that further increased her supply of healthy feminine narcissism. Even when a challenging, year-long heterosexual relationship came to a dramatic and painful end, Hannah held on to what she had learned about herself during the relationship instead of devaluing either herself or the man. After she had tentatively set a termination date, Hannah began to explore again and more thoroughly her thoughts and feelings about relationships with women. The following sessions are from the sixth year of Hannah's analysis.

She begins the session: "I met the love of my life in my dreams last night." Hannah pauses, for dramatic emphasis. She knows I (MM) will recognize the significance of her beginning with a dream. She has usually left any mention of dreams to the last few minutes of a session. Fearful of what "core and deep" and disturbed meanings her dreams might reveal, Hannah has hidden her dreams, as she has hidden or delayed the presentation of other creative productions, trying in this way to protect them from feared critical assessment or envious attack.

Hannah knows I will also appreciate the significance of her particular choice of words, "the love of my life." Hannah has been trying for much of her life and throughout her analysis to solve a particular puzzle. Is she "straight"? Is she "lesbian"? Is she "bisexual"? And how, she has frequently worried, will she ever be able to find out what she is, while in treatment with me? Recently Hannah has been worrying that I am influencing her attraction to women. "Maybe this is all coming from you," she feared. Could I, whom she knew to be in a lesbian relationship, help her if she wanted to be heterosexual? Several years earlier, when Hannah had been exploring relationships with men, she had wondered if, somehow, I had been influencing her in that direction, namely, toward men. "Maybe this all is coming from you," she had suspiciously wondered at that time also. In the transference, I have been experienced as a narcissistic mother whose daughter could not have any desires of her own but must be just like mother: in this case, lesbian. At other times I have been experienced as an enviously attacking, narcissistic, heterosexual mother whose daughter, Hannah, was not allowed to be as "good" as mother, that, is heterosexual; or as an equally envious, narcissistic, lesbian mother whose daughter was not allowed to be "better" than mother, that is, heterosexual. When things were going well in the year-long heterosexual relationship, I was experienced as a competent mother who could encourage and help her daughter to marry. But when that relationship became difficult, I became a sexually damaged and useless mother unable to help Hannah to find a man of her own. "How can I ever identify with you?" she complained. But today, in this session, Hannah is excited. She believes she has dreamed an answer to that vexing question: Is the love of her life a man or a woman?

Hannah continues: "*She* wasn't someone I had noticed really before. She was just there. She was somehow behind me, like a couch or something." Hannah's hand waves in my direction, and she notices her own gesture. "The feeling about this experience predates you. She was putting something around me, a collar or something. Something she had made. It was playful."

I silently note the presence of the collar, however "playful." For Hannah, relationships in work or in love have often felt confining and inhibiting. Being "with someone" was like being collared, a loss of power and autonomy. But, on the other hand, being "single" was lonely, and to Hannah it was humiliating evidence of her unlovableness.

"At one point in the dream I was interested in these Ivy League people. I was all interested in them. And then I wanted to connect with her, the woman. She didn't come." There have been many examples in and out of the transference of Hannah's interest in Ivy League people, the Best and the Brightest. She could not stand to be anything but what she sometimes called "Double A Plus," and she envied those whom she saw as First Class. If designated First Class people did become interested in Hannah, they usually lost their status and value in her mind. In the dream, a woman will not come to her while Hannah is caught up in "Ivy League" attractions.

"I had to do with her what I've been doing lately. I had to take responsibility for naming something that had happened, for something I had done." Hannah now associates to several recent experiences, one with a friend and one with me, in which she had had to acknowledge her responsibility for her envious attacks. "And when I did that, then she came to me, and we were able to connect. Her ability to hold back and keep her boundary. She wasn't so needy of connecting that stuff got blurred. She was younger than me. I feared I would feel competitive. I wished for a feeling of peace in that connection. This woman was an equal. I had this feeling I would have passed over this woman. I didn't really see her. She wasn't someone I would have been drawn to. Not particularly striking. Nice and OK. She just stayed where she was, she didn't change her position. She could hold her own. She had a sense of herself. She wasn't so needy. But the more I saw and felt this dimension of mutuality between us, the more I was interested in her. I realized her breasts looked nice under her shirt. I was attracted to her.

"At one point in the dream I was making my move toward her, I was turning to her and saying I loved her. It was a risk. Was it precipitous? I saw a man observing it all, me and her. It was interesting that the man was as neutral as he was. I was less uncomfortable than I thought I would be. I wasn't going to be attacked or ashamed. That man represents someone who would have been critical of same-sex experience. But he wasn't. I'm aware as I'm telling this that I'm really damping down my feelings as I tell this. I really *loved* being in that dream. I want to say, 'I met the love of my life! Now where is she?' I wanted to go back to that dream!"

Hannah is representing her conflict about wanting or needing another. The man symbolizes her own self-critical feelings, which at least at this moment have been defused. She is aware that she is constricting feelings in the dream and in this moment's telling of the dream.

Hannah noted, "It is an unmistakable part of the dream that she, the woman, made the first move. Then I can be sure that someone wants me. The scene in the dream, it was not a lesbian conference, nobody was wearing triangles [the pink triangle that homosexuals were forced to wear in Nazi concentration camps is now a gay and lesbian pride symbol], no particular sign of 'political' affiliation. Yet this certain quality comes through. I make a move, risky. I guess even more though I wouldn't want to be in her position and discovering that the other is unavailable. That's like my experience with Grace [a friend] recently. I don't like that. I guess I can now conceive of myself as being able to be chosen, so I can dream that, but I don't like being in her position."

The image of lesbian relationships is also more benign, but frightening images of being rigidly collared if she expresses an interest in another make their presence known through negation: "not" a lesbian conference, "not" a concentration camp with pink triangles. I suggest to Hannah that she is noting that, like "the other woman," she does not so quickly lose her footing when the other person isn't available. She recently demonstrated this capacity when she was attracted to Grace but realized Grace wasn't attracted to her in the same way. Like the "other woman" in her dream, Hannah has been currently less driven to take action (envious attack, sexual acting out) to restore herself after feeling rejected. She has been less likely to get things all "blurred," to become confused about her own worth and the worth of the other person.

"I'm experimenting with letting myself not hold back so much about my feelings. Maybe I have to be more clear with people that I do love them, that I do care for them, that I need them." Here Hannah identifies in herself the capacity she gave in the dream to the "other woman," the courage to tell others of her love.

Hannah goes on to report a recent outing with a married woman friend and their children. Complicated scheduling arrangements had been necessary, but Hannah had persisted and the plans had finally worked out . "But as soon as I got it, I didn't want it. I pushed it away. I wanted so much to bolt. It was all wrong, the wrong event, the wrong person to be going with."

"You pushed it away, but you are also trying to hold on to it."

"*For dear life.* And it was actually relieving to realize that the impulse to bolt came as much with this event, with this woman, as it had with Robert [a friend]. But I get so confused about the gender issue. About what I want. Why, I keep asking myself, would I want to open up again the issue of being with a woman, a choice that would introduce marginality into my life?"

In the next several sessions, Hannah complains that there is no possible way she could meet a compatible woman. Her fears now are the same fears she had had when she was dating men: "I'll never find anyone; I'm too picky. There is no one out there like me, for me." At that time our work had helped her acknowledge first to herself and then to others, without shame, that she wanted and needed a relationship and that she was interested in meeting men. During treatment she had examined her past relationships with men as well as her feelings and experiences with the men she began to date. Although she hadn't found a husband, she had been pleased with other outcomes, including a heightened awareness of and pleasure in her sexual attractiveness, and increased comfort in social situations. Now when Hannah makes the old complaint, "I'll never find anyone; I'm too picky," I suggest that she examine the particulars of her relationships with women because feelings about those past experiences may be organizing her present expectations.

## Bars and Back Alley Feelings

The next day Hannah reports that after the previous session she had "stomach flu" and stayed at home on her couch all afternoon and evening. Although we are in the midst of a heat wave, Hannah covers herself with the blanket. She describes the "back-alley negative feelings" she associates with lesbian relationships.

"In college I had the name of the local gay bar and knew which night was women's night, in case I got so lonely or so desperate that I would try to go there. I never did. My mother took a course in 'homosexuality' at a local community college. She studied the subject. And she brought home a lesbian. She invited me to the house that day without telling either of us the agenda. 'So, Hannah, Agnes here is a homosexual. What do you think of that?' I, of course, denied any knowledge of anything. All my life I have had to go about getting what I want in surreptitious ways or getting it in small pieces, a little here, a little there. I'll never find anyone. I'll have to settle for left-overs."

Hannah's fears of women's nights at back-alley gay bars would be familiar to many women her age and class. Faderman (1991) describes the class differences and conflicts in the lesbian bars in the 1950s and 1960s. Police raids were common on gay bars until Saturday, June 28, 1969, when, at the Stonewall Inn in Greenwich Village, bar patrons, including lesbians, fought back against the police. Today annual Stonewall Marches are held in many cities to celebrate this moment in the gay liberation movement in the United States. Today, remembering those shameful back-alley feelings gives Hannah "stomach flu," makes her feel cold in the middle of a heat wave and impels her to reach for a blanket for comfort and to cover her shame. For many women, those bar visits in search of a partner were alienating and frightening. For women whose self-worth was already precariously balanced, such experiences could be devastating. Lesbian identity is certainly not Ivy League sexuality.

## Untangling Anxiety from Desire

Hannah's conviction that she had to "get what I want in surreptitious ways" has been a focus of analytic attention in several areas. What does Hannah want? It would be simpler if we assumed a drive theory of "sexual orientation." In these models, if Hannah is sexually attracted to men and has sexual fantasies about men, then she is heterosexual. If she has fantasies about and sexual attraction toward women, she is lesbian. If she is attracted to and has fantasies about both men and women, then, obviously, she is bisexual. The term bisexual, however, adds little; it simply acknowledges that the two polarized categories, homosexual and heterosexual, are insufficient and unsatisfying descriptions of the feelings and lives of many persons. To conclude that Hannah is bisexual might also imply, erroneously, that women who have not had, or do not want, relationships with men are the "real" lesbians. But the greatest conceptual limitation of these taxonomies, for Hannah or for any woman, is that they do not clarify desires. They do not help us understand what women want. They do not help distinguish, for instance, between one experience of "drive" and another. They do not appreciate how frequently the urgent visceral rush that is anxiety about intense and frightening needs comes dressed up as sexual arousal.

What does Hannah want? And why does she want it? Does Hannah want a relationship with a man? Has she anxiously, surreptitiously hidden that sexual desire by having relationships with women or by remaining single? Does she go down the lesbian "back alley" because she is too narcissistically vulnerable or too burdened by oedipal anxiety to pursue what she considers the main street, relationships with men? Were Hannah's lesbian relationships ways to avoid as well as to prepare for heterosexual marriage?

Or does Hannah want a relationship with a woman, and has she been hiding that desire because of anxieties about the social stigma she has been too vulnerable to handle? Has she needed experiences of satisfying heterosexual relationships to replenish her supplies of feminine narcissism and reduce her anxiety so that she could feel strong enough to find a satisfying lesbian relationship? Were relationships with men a preparation for, and an avoidance of, Hannah's main street, a relationship with a woman? Why has she left to the last months of her analysis this particular exploration of her feelings for women? Is she simply revisiting old issues in a termination review, or has she procrastinated getting to the "deep and core" heart of the matter? The persistence of such confusion and Hannah's ability to keep these issues "blurred" have effectively established a moratorium, a procrastinating protection against the dangers of making *any* choice that might be criticized, or of being "collared" by a partner of either sex.

## First Love

In this session, as I listen again to her hopelessness about the possibility of ever finding a satisfying lesbian relationship, I think about Isay's (1989) way of understanding the development of some of his gay male patients. Isay believes that homosexuality is innate, constitutional. He suggests that a boy who is homosexual may be experienced by his father as somehow "different." This felt difference, together with signs of the boy's oedipal love for his father, make the father uncomfortable and anxious. Out of his anxiety and discomfort, the father emotionally and physically distances from his young son. Feeling his father's distancing, the boy concludes that his feelings must be disgusting and shameful. An adult gay man with such a childhood history may report having had a "distant father." Both his early love for his father and the subsequent feeling of rejection have been repressed. The adult man with such a history may avoid committed relationships with other men for fear of reexperiencing that early, now repressed, rejection.

Although I do not share Isay's certainty about the innate constitutionality of homosexuality, as I listen to Hannah's material, I wonder if some of the persistent, seemingly impossible-to-repair, painful disconnections Hannah has described with her mother may have been in part due to Hannah's mother's unconscious, anxious distancing from her daughter's love. Hannah's mother had taken a class on homosexuality, as if love between women were a strange and foreign culture she had to go to school to understand. She then brought home Agnes, a "native" of that foreign culture, for Hannah to meet. What does a daughter feel if her own mother finds her love incomprehensible and alien?

I make a version of Isay's interpretation to Hannah. I suggest that perhaps as a child she had interpreted various experiences with her mother, the first "love of her life," to mean that she herself was unlovable, that something "core and deep" was wrong with her. Perhaps her heart had been broken early. Since she could not have her first love, perhaps she had concluded that there would never be anyone for her.

Hannah lies silent and quite still. When I ask if she has any reaction to what I have said, she says, "I'm trying to let you be my high school guidance counselor, the one I never had. Actually, right now it is terribly hard to stay here and listen to *anything*. I am furious because I have to be one thing or another. I resent it when I have to think of myself as a lesbian. Basically I felt neutered. I couldn't see Harold [a boy who liked her in high school] because my mother thought he wasn't right; I couldn't see Vivian [her first lesbian relationship] because she wasn't right. I loved my brother, and he treated me like an animal. And everybody tuned out. They turned the radio up loud and tuned out. Is it any wonder why I attack and distance?"

I note that she is saying that she had felt that *none* of the first loves of her life, mother, father, or brother, had returned her love.

"My father didn't know how to love. My mother didn't know how to love. For you to say I loved my mother and my heart was broken, . . . I don't know. No, let me be fair. My mother did come around with Connie [one of her girlfriends]. My mother is a liberal. She really believes in civil rights and fairness. I always admired that in her; I'm identified with that part in her."

## A First Date

Now Hannah describes, as she had earlier in treatment but now with more detail and a new emphasis, her first lesbian relationship with a high school friend, Vivian.

"Why was I with Vivian? She was disturbed. Why did I choose her? She was ferociously bright, but not healthy. But she was right there, and she was warm and funny. Later I found out that our friends were being called into the principal's office and asked, 'What's going on with Hannah and Vivian? What do they do together? Do they sleep over at one another's houses?' One day we cut school together. My parents were going to be gone for the day. I should have known! My parents never went anywhere together. Do you know what Vivian and I did? We went to the library, the public library, and spent the day! Then we went back to my house and crawled into bed and just held one another. My parents came home, opened the bedroom door, and that was it. Their going away, it had all been a trap, a setup, to see what we would do. They called the school and Vivian's parents. I was almost expelled. Vivian, because she was seen as the more disturbed, was sent away to another school. I was forbidden to see her or call her. She was in a psychiatric hospital for a time. She tried to commit suicide. Years later, after college, I made a point of finding her again. I found her. She was obese, looked masculine, very militant, a professional victim, provoking attack from all who saw her. I didn't like it at all, and I didn't like it when she grabbed my thigh, laid her hand on me." Hannah spoke with rage, defensiveness, guilt, and confusion.

Hannah has described the consequences of a high school lesbian "date." Two bright students who share an interest in books, skip school, and spend the day in the library. When they go home to hold each other, the sting operation set up by parents, friends, and school personnel goes into action. Vivian is expelled, attempts suicide, is hospitalized, and develops a raging, provocative, antisocial, self-hating lesbian identity. Hannah had previously described Vivian's repeated confrontations with her policeman father. We can imagine some of the characterlogical and family issues influencing Vivian's way of being lesbian.

## Separation Anxieties of the Second Individuation

The sessions just described took place during the week before Hannah was to go away for a long holiday weekend. Perhaps, Hannah had mentioned vaguely several times, she would also miss some additional sessions in the week following the long holiday. She did not mention or discuss these upcoming absences during sessions, but between sessions she left phone messages about the weekend. Perhaps—she isn't certain—she will want to reschedule the missed sessions. I was also finding it difficult to focus on these dates or on the scheduling confusion. Things were getting "blurred" again. Between Hannah's sessions I noticed that my appointment book had question marks on each day at her appointment times for the next week, but I would for some reason forget to bring these scheduling questions up during her sessions.

On Friday before the long weekend, Hannah writes her check as she walks into her session. "I wonder if it would be possible for you to hold this for me and not cash it until some time later? Would that be a problem for you?" She is walking awkwardly and looks physically off balance. She gives a confusing, irritated, and impatient explanation about being in a rush and not wanting to go to another bank for cash to cover the check, a muddled description about rushed arrangements before departure, and uncertainty about account balances.

Will I hold the check? My "holding" things for her has been a recurring request in the analysis, usually an unconscious need for me to "hold" certain feelings that she feared she could not name or contain for herself. Today she seems to be telling me, in effect, "Here is something that belongs to you, but don't use it. Just hold it; it's not really yours, yet, to use. And is this situation a problem?"

I say, "I don't have a financial problem with that, but I wonder if we might think about any significance other than financial to your feeling short of resources right now. You are going away on a vacation. Going away sometimes makes you anxious."

Hannah bristles. She says that she has delayed scheduling her vacation this summer. She has put off making a choice about where to go and when. Then she finally decided to take the vacation the following week and has made plans to do so. She is angry because she feels deprived of her vacation because she has discovered that she has work meetings with Rita next Tuesday, Wednesday, and Thursday. Hannah says that she had put these meeting dates in her calendar, but she did not look at them when she arranged her vacation dates. Now she is angry because she has reservations out of town for Tuesday night and doesn't want to lose the hotel deposit. She thinks perhaps she will get up at 5:30 on Tuesday morning and drive back to town for the work meetings.

I now understand my confusion over dates and times around Hannah's sessions in my calendar and my own "forgetting" to bring up the problem. Mentally shaking myself free of these projected identifications, I can also see that Hannah is underestimating the amount of time needed to travel back to town and be on time for the meetings with Rita. We have had many occasions in the past to examine Hannah's lateness and her underestimating the time needed to accomplish an action or to get from one place to another. Rather than point out this obvious example of that old problem, which I suspect would sound like the kind of parental criticism I am trying to avoid feeling, I make another, equally obvious point, namely, that she has been having a lot of difficulty *thinking* about taking a vacation.

"I am angry even having to think about it. If I had a partner, I wouldn't *have* to think about it. If Rita weren't so controlling, I wouldn't *have* to think about any of this." Hannah is irritable, provocative, rebelling against what she experiences as external restrictions. "I'm wasting my time talking about all of this. This is not what's important. I want to talk more about what we've been talking about, me and women, and who I should be with. Talking about this is all a waste of time, and meanwhile the session time is going by."

I suggest that, even as we speak, whatever processes that created the vacation confusion are still at work. Something needs to be looked at, and yet she says it is a waste of her time to examine it. Hannah is further annoyed by my comment.

"I have been thinking about my constant fear that I am farming other people's fields, that I can't choose what I want. I think of my father's resignation: 'Make the best of it.' Both parents, I guess, were resigned. When my mother was young she fell in love with a boy of another religion. I've told you. Her brothers took turns beating her. Her nice brother, the one she adored, he didn't beat her, he reasoned with her. She renounced the boy. *The degree of unempathic listening—whether it was the right choice or not—keeps one from moving from her center.*" Each word is said slowly, firmly, with angry emphasis. "It's not surprising I've had difficulty finding my center. I've had systematic opposition, overwhelming opposition. No one helped me, but there was a lot of holding me back. And when I think of this vacation, I think of my recent experiences on vacation." On one vacation she had become attached to a family and was quite uncomfortable with her attraction to the father; on her most recent trip, she had felt seriously suicidal again.

I say, "Maybe now we can think about your opening statement to me: hold this for me; don't cash it. You are suffering from difficulties similar to those we have in adolescence when we must "move from our centers," make choices, and accept and support our own choices. Sometimes we don't feel ready or able to take these steps. Today with the check you placed me in the position you have felt: having, but not having, unable to cash in your choices.

"Cash the check," Hannah says stonily.

"That's not my point, you know."

"Cash the check. I will figure out the arrangements." And then, angrily, she adds, "Oh, I guess you're going to say that since Vivian and I left a trail we must have wanted to be caught."

I am startled, although I have often pointed out in the past how Hannah unconsciously provokes criticism and antagonism. Frequently she has unconsciously invited/provoked me into "busting" her with critical interpretations. Only a few moments before I had to restrain myself from making a critical comment about her ridiculous time arrangements.

I say, "Well, let's think about that idea. You and Vivian didn't get 'busted' when you were in the library. Maybe you didn't have problems with *that* choice of what to do together. But somehow you and Vivian managed to signal enough people so that your parents did lay a trap, and bust you, when you were in bed together. You have said that you do not want to be like Vivian, that, in fact, she was troubled, always angry at her father, the cop, and that later she seemed a 'professional victim,' arranging to be busted by everyone. If we are frightened to go into the adult world and make our choices—for instance, to go on vacation, leaving the familiar routines of work for unknown, unstructured situations where we may act spontaneously—we may make it difficult for ourselves to arrange vacations, or we may arrange to be "busted" when we do. Your mother, as you note, chose a boy unacceptable to her family and then told herself and everyone else that she renounced him because her brothers beat her. If we fear our feelings and our ability to make choices, sometimes we arrange to be busted."

She is silent. I am afraid that, in my zeal to catch up with her, I have rather overdone my comments.

"I am thinking about my vacation plans and what I can do about them. If I do it the way I have been thinking of, getting up at 5:30 a.m., I will be late, and there will be a confrontation with Rita when I do get there. It is very hard for me not to see all this as Rita controlling me. What you say is accurate, but I certainly wish you could have *said* it differently! You have pinned my wings like a specimen."

"I have pinned your wings?" I say with astonishment, since I think I have been simply following her lead.

"Yes, as if I were a specimen, and now it's the end of the session and I can do nothing about all of this."

"You still can do whatever you want about it," I declare crisply. Anxious, provocative child and frustrated parent transference–countertransference enactments fill the air at the moment of this separation.

Hannah is annoyed as she leaves the session but says good-bye instead of storming off as she has sometimes done in the past. She calls three hours later. She says she didn't want to leave for the weekend this way. She reports that she has rescheduled her plans and has called Rita and worked out arrangements with her, thus averting the crisis. "I know it must have been hard for you today not to be irritated with me. I want to thank you for not being. I think we both did pretty well today. It was funny when there was no longer any feeling of *having* to be at the work meetings, I realized I wanted to be there. And when I suddenly had the freedom to choose the longer time away, I thought, 'Oh, dear, what am I going to do with all that freedom?' I think that is what you were trying to say to me."

When Hannah returned from the long weekend, I learned that part of her anxiety about going away this time had been that she might, while out of town, attend a gay and lesbian gathering. As Hannah had explored once again her attraction to women, she had almost brought about crises (in and out of the transference relationship) and almost got herself "busted."

A few weeks later Hannah wears a flowered dress to a lesbian discussion group. She is pleased that she is seen as feminine and is accepted at the group and that she herself isn't put off by the appearance of the women in the group. "I didn't go 'eek,'" she reports.

A few days later she describes another gay and lesbian event. "I didn't feel out of place. And I didn't feel that the others were out of place. I was observing two couples, a man and his partner and his parents. I liked the way he looked with his lover. I liked his parents. His mother reminded me in some way of mine. Then there were these women. Lee and Lillian. I kept seeing you in Lillian. Somehow it was significant, I guess, that I was looking for you in a couple. Some regret that I couldn't have you. But also trying to see you in that situation. Anyway, I saw an admirable couple, appealing. I'm comforted now in 19—, in whatever year this is, [she leaves the year uncertain, an unconscious indication that we are exploring various psychic times] to see same-sex couples who are married. I'm trying to see if this is something I could be comfortable with. I had a mixed experience of that."

Hannah now proceeds to illustrate various conflicts among these feelings. "I've had images of two men with erections. I wonder whether my ability to see two men means that to see two women is too threatening. But also some element of sexuality about men that appeals to me. I realize I'm being intellectual now." Hannah is oversexualizing a same-sex relationship, reducing it to an issue of similar body parts. "And I may not want to be in 'the lesbian community.' I may not need to pledge allegiance." She continues to need to defend against feared external and internal pressures to conform. "I'm trying to move in a way that won't be uncomfortable for me or anyone else. To see what I like. I can relate to men, too."

## Dreaming New Openings

"I had two dreams, or one dream in two parts. I was in a house, sharing it, like a co-op or something. Or like in an office where there are those partitioned areas. The sleeping areas were like those partitions, like a maze. I had one. It was really only wide enough for one bed. I had had to move from a bigger place. I did have a closet. But it was a narrow place with only one place to put things. It was not a good feeling. It reminds me of Sarah, who has just broken up with her partner. She has only a small place. I wanted to make a door between me and the one behind me. [Her hand gestures toward me.] Oh, hello! I wanted to build a narrow door, but it would be intruding on the other person's sleeping space. Then I thought of the open door there [pointing in front of her]. There were curtains on the main area and privacy most of the time, but if I wanted to masturbate how can I do that with privacy?

"This is very hard to talk about and this morning when I remembered my dream I was very upset, but I have been trying to think what you say about dreams and see if I can see my dreams differently. Then this morning when I thought about that, I remembered there was a second part of the dream.

"There was a partition door between me and those on the other side. It was like a dormitory. They had a bed and a table. I had a plant, a flowering plant, but dry with no water. I asked a woman, 'Could I use your table for my plant?' The woman was like an ex-nun, in black. It makes me think of my friend who had a relationship with an ex-nun who had died. She said the woman had touched her in her heart where it hadn't been touched before, and that stayed there even though the woman had died. I used to have an old fantasy—that to have that heart touching, even once, helps. (laughs) Now I know you need it more than once though. [Hannah is acknowledging that she accepts that what she has with me, although helpful, and that she feels will survive our separation, is not a substitute for the erotic primary relationship she needs in her life.] Anyway, I asked if I could put my plant on her table. The water perked the plant up. But a big flower fell over, dead. The plant wasn't dead. I guess that piece couldn't bear the water after so long. But I said, 'Look, there's a seed pod, green, hard, firm, like a nice pea pod.' And other pieces of the plant stalk were strong.

"In the dream, suddenly the barrier isn't there. It's not like I'm alone and single. There is someone there. As much as I hate hope, it's a hopeful dream. (laughs) I do feel that. I think it is true, that I wanted you, but that, in fact, I couldn't have you—maybe that's why the flower died, that hope of having you. I know that I can't invade your space that way. That would have been invasion, but the space I was left with was too narrow."

I say, "But another opening appears."

"It felt good to be at that gay and lesbian event and at the discussion group. It felt good to be in a space where I didn't have to be . . ., maybe 'closeted' is too strong a word for me, but guarded. You know I didn't talk about myself with the women or anything, but I didn't *have* to be guarded. It does seem to make a difference when I don't have to feel so confined, so guarded."

"Closeted," Hannah suggests, is not quite the word for her condition. Although at some periods in her life Hannah had lived openly in lesbian relationships, she had nevertheless felt confined, guarded, squeezed into too small a space. Hannah's feelings of guarded confinement have been overdetermined. They were partly fears of sexual invasion, fears that had been strengthened by actual events in her childhood when she was not physically or emotionally able to "hold her own." Her sense of constriction was also in part the product of her need to build confining restraints on her impulses and in this way try to strengthen her diminished capacities to pause, to hold back and not act when threatened. Her guardedness was a complex product of the external social structures that stigmatize lesbian relationships and the rigid, internal, psychic structures that criticized and devalued any relationship she might choose. Hannah's dream reveals the development of new internal object configurations. Now there are partitions instead of the previous exposing and out-of-control lack of privacy. Although she still wrestles with fears of restriction, Hannah notes that in the dream she is careful not to invade the analyst's space. Then, in that way that can be so clear in dream experience and so difficult to describe in words, from "the other side," a way opens. And, although there are boundaries, "the barrier isn't there." Although Hannah now has privacy, she is not "alone and single" because "someone is there."[3]

There are still puzzles and problems. In her dream Hannah set her plant on the ex-nun's table; the ex-nun/analyst "touched" her heart. But a flower nevertheless dies. Hannah suggests that that represents the death of the wish to have the analyst as partner, the death of the wish to not have to move on and find new relationships. But why does the water kill the flower? Maybe, thinks Hannah, it was too much water after such a dry spell. What happens to a parched flower? Does it dry up like a raisin in the sun? Or is crying still felt to be in conflict with blooming? Why is the analyst portrayed as an ex-nun, a sexually celibate woman? Is it still too difficult to acknowledge that the analyst has her own sexual life? Or is the representation of the celibacy in the past an acknowledgment of the analyst's (and patient's) no longer closeted, convented sexuality? Hannah's plant in the dream is strong and has new, green growth, the result, at least in part, of the analytic work. Most importantly, as the usually pessimistic Hannah notes, "although I hate to admit it," the dream is "hopeful." Hannah's dream depicts relationships in which boundaries and separations do not seem like confining collars or barriers are but more like relieving containers where action and growth can take place.

In the following weeks Hannah gave a party with a heterosexual couple with whom she had a friendly relationship. To be able to allow others to help with the party was a new accomplishment for Hannah. She has always been able to give help much more easily than to receive it. She could work with the couple rather than be so beset by envy at their relationship that she must try to disrupt their relationship or avoid them. Hannah dreamt of candidates in an election, her identification now with people who are "out there" and "going for it," not afraid to compete and show their ambition. She adjusted her termination date and started an intimate relationship with a woman. That relationship, which began full of excitement and sexual energy, did not go well, but Hannah used the opportunity to explore "coming out" with work colleagues and friends. She ended the relationship but noted that she now felt more comfortable about being seen socially as a woman in a lesbian relationship.

Just as Hannah was beginning to feel comfortable personally and socially with this identity, she met an interesting, attentive, available man. "What is this?! Did I have to go through all this, come out with a woman *again*, in order to find a suitable man?" We both wondered if these turns are still more examples of Hannah's belief that she must use surreptitious ways to gain her heart's desire.

Did this man turn out to be "the love of my life" for Hannah? Hannah's focus on the "gender issue" (that is, on the sex of her love object) often served as a diversion from difficult, object relations issues. Hannah's treatment addressed her difficulty revealing secrets, in particular what she experienced as an overwhelming and shameful need for others. "The gender issue" attempted to reduce long-standing relational issues to a concrete sexual question: "Am I gay or straight or bisexual?"[4] Although a primary source of Hannah's separation anxieties, dependency fears, and difficulty maintaining narcissistic equilibrium had been her early relationship with her mother, it is too facile to conclude that these issues "caused" her lesbian attractions. Hannah herself had been all too ready to make this simplistic interpretation. Not all women with narcissistic inadequacies and separation anxieties are attracted to women, and there were no particular clinical indications that Hannah's early history was any more troubled in these areas than is the history of patients who do not seek lesbian relations. What was necessary in the treatment was to examine the ways Hannah's separation anxieties and narcissistic difficulties had become entangled with homosexual *and* heterosexual desires and how they prevented Hannah's further exploration of attraction to any partner.

Hannah is similar in some ways to one of Helene Deutsch's (1932) patients. Both women knew that they were attracted both to women and to men from adolescence; both suffered paralyzing depressions and had difficulty holding their own in relationships. When Deutsch met her patient on the street after the analysis had ended, she was surprised to discover that the patient had left her marriage and had begun a relationship with a woman. Some might conclude then that Deutsch's patient was "really" lesbian and that her analysis had freed her fears about and defenses against her essential, or "real," lesbian sexual orientation. Others might conclude that her analytic treatment had stimulated but failed to resolve "negative oedipal longings" or that an inadequately addressed and treated narcissistic disturbance or self-disorder was now being acted out in her homosexual relationship. What might Deutsch have discovered if she had met her patient again 10 years later? Would the patient have still been happy in that relationship? Perhaps she might have been with another woman, or living alone, or with a man. What would we find if we were to meet Hannah in the future? Would she be depressed, happily married to a man, happily partnered with a woman, or happily living a satisfying single life raising her child? Wherever Hannah's attractions lead her in the future, we can hope that her analytic treatment has helped her to be more comfortable with her strengths and limitations, more accepting of her own and others' vulnerabilities, less driven by urgencies, better able to make her own choices, and to enjoy and to bear the consequences of those choices whatever they may be.

## Social Influences and Institutions

> We cannot even begin to encompass a human being without indicating for each of the stages of his life cycle the framework of social influences and of traditional institutions which determine his perspectives on his more infantile past and on his more adult future.
> [Erikson, 1958, p. 20]

Let us try to compare "the framework of social influences and traditional institutions" that helped determine the perspectives of Hannah, who was 18 years old in 1965 in the United States, with frameworks and institutions that determined the perspectives of Freud' patient, 18 years old in 1920 in Vienna. In Chapter 5 we described the debates about homosexuality among sexologists, psychoanalysts, and male homosexual activists that formed the backdrop for the analytic encounter between Freud and his patient. We described fictional depictions of lesbian relationships that were popular in the 1920s and probably contributed to Freud's patient's understanding of her love. Forty-five years later, what might 18-year-old Hannah and Vivian have found if they had looked for books about their feelings that fateful day they went together to the library? Grahn (1984) describes her own search at about that time.

> In 1961, when I was twenty-one, I went to a library in Washington, D.C., to read about homosexuals and Lesbians, to investigate, explore, compare opinions, learn who I might be, what others thought of me, who my peers were and had been. The books on such a subject, I was told by indignant, terrified librarians unable to say aloud the word *homosexual*, were locked away. They showed me a wire cage where the "special" books were kept in a jail for books. Only professors, doctors, psychiatrists, and lawyers for the criminally insane could see them, check them out, hold them in their hands. The books I wanted to check out were by "experts" on the subject of homosexuality as it was understood at that time [p. xi].

If Hannah and Vivian on their library date had looked for books about women in love with women, they might have found the work of psychoanalysts such as Edmund Bergler (1951), Frank Caprio (1954), Richard C. Robertiello (1959), and May Romm (1965). Caprio obtained some of the case illustrations for his *Female Homosexuality: A Psychodynamic Study of Lesbianism* from magazines such as *Life Romances* and *My Confession* (see Katz, 1976, pp. 184–185). Bergler (1951) claimed: "In every case of lesbianism, we find the typical personality which is characteristic for all orally regressed people: the 'injustice collector'. . . . masochistically self-provoked and self-enjoyed, warded off with pseudo-aggression" (p. 337).[5] May Romm (1965) discussed the "depreciation of the woman's sexual role by men," but her protests against sexual bias applied only to heterosexual women. She saw female homosexuality as arrested development. While warning that psychoanalysts should not set personal goals for their patients, Romm stressed the importance of heterosexual intercourse and procreation as developmental tasks, apparently unaware that many lesbians "accomplish" both.

If Hannah or Vivian had been sent for psychoanalytic treatment, would their experience have resembled that of the young college woman treated at about the same time by Khan (1964)? Or would Hannah or Vivian's experience more resemble that of Kay Lahusen's with psychoanalyst Richard Robertiello (see Marcus, 1992). Lahusen went to see Robertiello after reading his *Voyage from Lesbos: The Psychoanalysis of a Female Homosexual* (Robertrello, 1959). She told him that she did not want treatment; she wanted to meet other lesbian women. Robertiello opened his desk drawer and gave her a copy of *The Ladder*, a newspaper put out by the lesbian organization, The Daughters of Bilitis. This unusual intervention was to prove quite helpful to Lahusen as she searched for the love of her life. She found her partner, Barbara Gittings, through *The Ladder*, and subsequently both Gittings and Lahusen became activists for gay civil rights.[6]

What images of lesbian relationships could Hannah and Vivian have found in literature? Would their library have had a copy of Foster's (1956) *Sex Variant Women in Literature*? Researching works from Sappho through 1954, librarian Foster wrote the book as a remedy for her own college student ignorance about homosexuality. Hannah and Vivian might have read Lillian Hellman's (1934) *The Children's Hour* or seen William Wyler's 1961 film version, in which Shirley MacLaine and Audrey Hepburn play the boarding school teachers destroyed by slander and gossip. When Martha becomes aware that she loves Karen in the very way that she has been accused, she commits suicide.[7] Would Hannah and Vivian have found Violette Leduc's (1965) *La Bastarde,* a somber narrative of a woman whose relationship with her disturbed mother shapes her life and sexual identity?

Would Hannah and Vivian have found lesbian writer Jane Rule's (1964) *Desert of the Heart*? Evelyn, an English professor, in Reno for a divorce from her husband, is 15 years older than Ann, an artist who makes her living as a casino worker. "Hello, is what a mirror says," remarks Evelyn when she sees Ann for the first time, struck by how much Ann looks like herself. In order to see one another, Ann and Evelyn must examine the distorted images they have internalized about women such as themselves, reflections of emotional immaturity, narcissism, and unnatural mother/daughter love.

> [Ann] wanted to be with Evelyn. She wanted to know Evelyn. She wanted to be able to love Evelyn, whatever that meant. Half a dozen vague clichés came into Ann's mind, jumblings of prayer book and movie magazines that had to do with fidelity, procreation, and healthy sexual attitudes. . . . If she was to love Evelyn, she would have to fight her whole damned world, and some of it she could not live without [p. 166].

Neither Ann nor Evelyn commits suicide, and, unlike earlier fictional lesbian couples, Ann and Evelyn are together as the narrative ends, although their future is uncertain. "For the while then," Evelyn says. "For an indefinite period of time."

Now compare the images and texts available to Freud's patient and to Hannah and Vivian with those available to an 18-year-old today. Although library searches will produce newly released psychoanalytic texts documenting the pathological nature of homosexuality, today other resources await the young woman who wants, in Grahn's (1984) words, "to investigate, explore, compare opinions, learn who I might be." In 1928 *The Well of Loneliness* (Hall, 1928) was ruled obscene and was banned in England, its copies confiscated from the publisher and burned in the furnaces of Scotland Yard. Today mainstream, feminist, and gay presses publish psychology, fiction, biography, poetry, historical and cultural criticism by gay and lesbian authors (e.g., Maggiore, 1988; Boston Women's Health Collective, 1992; Bechdel, 1992; Weiss, 1992; McClure and Vespry, 1994). Adolescents can find books of lesbian erotic literature. They can read lesbian comic strips, lesbian travel guides. They can hear music by lesbian identified musicians and see films by lesbian identified film directors. A woman reader has many fictional choices. Bonnie Zimmerman (1990) cites 200 titles,[8] and the last 10 years have increased that number greatly. Instead of beginning her fictional research with Radclyffe Hall's (1928), *The Well of Loneliness*, today's adolescent might begin with Rita Mae Brown's (1973) *Ruby Fruit Jungle*. Brown's heroine Molly Bolt has a sense of humor, a sturdy sense of self-worth, and a sexual appetite. Like Leduc's (1965) Violette, Molly learns early that she is a "bastard." Like both Violette and Radcliffe Hall's Stephen Gordon, Molly has a troubled relationship with a troubled mother, but she responds differently to her circumstances. Although by the book's end Molly has not found a lasting love of her life, she has known love and friendship, as well as betrayal and loss, and she never even considers suicide.

## Bars versus School Clubs and Professional Organizations

Did Freud's patient ever find a woman partner? And where would she have met her? Where did Deutsch's patient meet the woman who made her so radiant? In Paris and Berlin of the 1920s, lesbian clubs were subject to police raids similar to those American police made on the bars Hannah avoided in the 1960s. "While later generations romanticized the life of lesbians in the 1920s in capitals like Paris and Berlin, those who moved in those circles stressed the limits. 'In spite of the freedom, or illusion of freedom, in the Weimar republic,' wrote the lesbian doctor Charlotte Wolff of her life in Berlin in the twenties, 'lesbians were watched by the police, and from time to time lesbian clubs were raided. . . . It was an ambiguous situation all around'" (Wolff, 1980, p. 76, quoted in Anderson and Zinsser, 1988, p. 222).

As we have seen, in the 1920s and 1930s only a small minority of women had the opportunity to become one of "the new women," economically capable of choosing to live independently of men. Many of those who made lesbian relationships, were, like Bryher, daughters of wealthy families, whose inheritances allowed them economic independence and escape from many of the gender restrictions oppressing other women. Today more women have opportunities for economic independence than in either 1920 or 1960, making primary relationships between women economically possible for more women. Today some women find partners through the "lesbian community," not a geographical location but a network of social relationships, organizations, newsletters from college alumni groups, professional organizations, conferences, and on-line computer forums.[9] Today in large urban areas of the United States, the diversity of age, class, race, ethnicity, religious, and political affiliations of lesbian women makes it inaccurate to speak of "the" lesbian community. There are overlapping, sometimes even class and politically antagonistic, lesbian networks. There are still lesbian bars, some still very "back alley," but there are also lesbian dating services, gay and lesbian social service organizations, sports, professional, and political affiliations. Today lesbian high school students even might attend a special gay and lesbian prom, go together to a fund-raising Walk for AIDS, or to a Gay and Lesbian film festival (Quintanilla, 1994; Signorile, 1994).[10] These opportunities exist, however, only in the larger metropolitan areas, and even in the cities it is still difficult for women to find compatible partners. Lesbian communities are unstable niches, fragilely established on the margins of a culture whose rituals, organizations, and programs still primarily support heterosexual relationships.

## Forsworn Womanhood versus Lesbian Mothers

Freud (1920) saw his lesbian patient as having psychologically forsworn her womanhood, including her desire for children. Although Freud's patient denied the characterization and although Deutsch's patient, previously married with children, was not an atypical lesbian woman, the stereotype of a lesbian as a man-rejecting and childless woman is still alive and flourishing. In actuality, lesbian women alone and together raise children born from previous heterosexual relationships and marriages. Many divorced mothers live in closeted fear of being legally declared unfit mothers and losing custody of their children if their relationship is discovered to be lesbian.[11] At the same time, increasing numbers of lesbian couples are raising adopted children or children born through alternative insemination. In 1994 The Gay and Lesbian Parents Coalition International had 60 chapters (Associated Press wire, January 23, 1994, see Appendix; Child Custody; see also Hanscombe and Forster, 1981; Martin, 1993). In 1961 Grahn had to search in banned books for images of women who loved women. In November 1996, *Newsweek* put lesbian singer Melissa Ethridge and her pregnant partner, Julie Cypher, on its cover. Such radical shifts in the "framework of social influences and of traditional institutions" will clearly have effects on "determining the perspectives" of lesbian adolescents about the possibilities available in their adult futures.

## Marriage versus Commitment Ceremonies

Freud's patient's parents feared the social disgrace their daughter's public display of affection for another woman would bring to the family. The patient's father had only two avenues of response to this threat. Either his daughter must be cured by psychoanalysis, or she must marry. Deutsch's patient knew that she was attracted to women, but she married because she could not at that time support her desire. Bryher married twice, each marriage a way to support her relationship with H.D., the love of her life. Parents still pressure their children to marry, and they send their gay and lesbian adolescents to therapy. But today some of those therapists might be gay or lesbian. Today parents trying to understand their daughter's homosexuality can find resources that were unavailable to Hannah's mother. Today that college course on homosexuality would probably be taught by gay and lesbian instructors. But if lesbian adolescents are fortunate to find the love of their life and decide to share their adult lives with lesbian partners, their parents may still face the social disgrace that prompted the father of Freud's patient to bring her to Freud to be cured. Some parents seek a therapist's help to handle their own confusion that their child is homosexual. Some find relief from shame and guilt at meetings of Parents and Friends of Gays and Lesbians. Some, such as Robb Forman Dew (1994), write their own coming-out stories. Dew describes how she is shocked by her own reactions as well as those of her family and friends when her son reveals his homosexuality. Some parents will be asked to participate in and give their support to their daughter's commitment ceremony, a ritual that proclaims to the community beyond the immediate family that two women have chosen one another for life partners.

## Tracy

Tracy and Joyce, her partner of many years, were working their ways up their respective career ladders. Close friends and a few family members knew of their relationship, but each woman was totally closeted at work and kept her social and work lives entirely separate. When Joyce's employer transferred her to another state, they commuted back and forth on weekends for one year until Tracy could join her. They bought a home together and, confident of their relationship, which had survived a difficult period of separation and transition, they decided to celebrate with a commitment ceremony. For over a year they planned the three-day gathering of friends and relatives. Tracy called me from time to time to report on continuing developments in her life after therapy.

"My new boss is terrific. When I decided to tell her what I really was doing on my 'vacation,' she took me to lunch. I had just simply got used to keeping my life to myself at my last job." Actually, it turned out that Tracy had not told her employer about the commitment ceremony until just two days before she was to leave for what she had been saying was a "vacation," and, although she then did go out to lunch with her boss, she told none of her co-workers. "When I came back and people asked, 'What did you do on your vacation,' I told them about the ceremony. That was more than some wanted to know, I'm sure."

"We crossed over another line, too. Joyce came out at work." Joyce, who had a significant position at a major corporation, had always been scrupulously careful to pass as single and heterosexual. She had taken male friends to business social events and hidden all trace of her life with Tracy. When Joyce told her own boss about her relationship, he advised her to take "the bull by the horns and take the wind out of the sails of malicious gossip." He suggested she give a party so that everyone could meet Tracy and see their home life once and for all. Joyce thus became the only "out" lesbian or gay person in that national corporation of thousands of employees, a situation that set her new challenges. She understood that closeted gay and lesbian employees would now be more likely to avoid contact with her for fear of being identified, but that they would also be watching carefully what happened to her career advancement now that she was out.

Tracy sent pictures of the commitment ceremony. She reported with some surprise that "our families actually did come. That is, our sisters came, but none of our sisters' husbands. One brother brought his wife, and one didn't. Our families hadn't met before and found they got on well together. Even friends from high school came. There were 75 for the ceremony. There were no major misbehaviors. Some family members toasted us at dinner. That was terrific. Both sets of parents seemed OK with it all, but Joyce's parents did wonder, 'What will I tell people at home?'" Joyce's parents now are faced with their own issues of coming out. They must identify themselves in their social world as the parents of a lesbian daughter, a successful woman who has found "the love of her life."

Tracy's and Joyce's parents are certainly not alone in their preoccupation with what Hannah liked to call "the gender issue." In the general culture, and in much psychoanalytic theory, homosexuality is equated with gender imbalance, gender reversals, or gender deficiency. In the next chapter we discuss various contradictions and paradoxes in contemporary psychoanalytic concepts of gender and their effects on psychoanalytic treatment.

# 7

# WHAT SEX IS AN AMARYLLIS?
# WHAT GENDER IS LESBIAN?

## LOOKING FOR SOMETHING
## TO HOLD IT ALL[1]

> What the human nature of males and females really consists of, then, is a capacity to learn and to provide and to read depictions of masculinity and feminity and a willingness to adhere to a schedule for presenting these pictures, and this capacity they have by virtue of being persons, not females or males.
>
> *[Erving Goffman, 1976, p. 8]*

At the United Nations Women's Conference in Beijing in 1995, a quarrel broke out over including the word gender in the conference document. Some delegates insisted that "gender" covered a wide range of meanings, including homosexuality and other permissive life styles (Leopold, 1995). In many psychoanalytic discussions homosexuality is the prima facie example of gender identity disturbance. Gay men are thought to have too much identification with their mothers, too little identification with their fathers, or both. Lesbian women are thought to have too much identification with their fathers, too little identification with their mothers, or both. One can either be a woman or desire a woman.

Gender, unlike anatomy, is not a permanent property of a person. Gender must be learned, and gender knowledge must repeatedly be revised and updated. One's gender is maintained by repeated, careful behavioral presentations, including complex and subtle, sexually segregated styles of occupying verbal and physical space (Goffman, 1976). Gender is maintained also on the careful avoidance of certain other presentations. Failures or refusals to make expected gender presentations disturb the social landscape, upset the social order. In the 1960s, when young men let their hair grow, some adults in the presence of such long-haired men in hippie beads, wondered aloud, "How can you tell if they're girls or boys?" Although those questioners, of course, knew quite well whether the person with long hair was a boy or a girl, their questions expressed their discomfort at some men's refusal to keep the previously agreed upon gender distinction in hair length. Why would a man wear his hair like a woman? What was the matter with that man? Was he a boy or a girl? What was happening to the social order? When Diana boogie-boarded onto a Santa Monica beach in the mid-1980s, an excited 8-year-old girl ran over with an eager question: "Are you a girl?" Since the child had previously seen only boys and men ride boogie-boards, the sight of a woman in the waves momentarily threw her, and she sought affirmation that the person on the board was, in fact, female. The sight of the grown woman doing something that previously the girl had seen only boys doing excited the child. If *that* is a girl and *I* am a girl, I can boogie too.

Even toddlers may understand that, although genital differences may be obvious, the foundations for gender divisions are less apparent. De Marneffe (1995) found that by 18–24 months, both girls and boys could tell which "anatomically correct" doll was the "boy doll" and which one was the "girl doll." Boys and girls understood the question, "What about the doll makes it a girl doll (or a boy doll)?" To answer that question, the children pointed to or touched the doll's genitals. And the toddlers understood the nature of their own genitals and could correctly answer, "Which doll looks like you?" But many children faltered when asked, "Are you a girl or a boy?" They gave incorrect or evasive answers; some even refused to answer.

How do we understand the toddlers' uncertainty and hesitation? Do their responses demonstrate conflicts or uncertainty about sexual identity? Perhaps the toddlers' hesitation and evasion demonstrated their realization that they were being questioned about more than anatomy. They were taking one of their first tests on gender and its properties. Although gender is often equated with the genital differences between the sexes, its function is to enforce sexual divisions that anatomy alone does not determine and cannot support. Before feminists insisted on degendering language, girls wondered why *everyone* was a masculine pronoun and if and how they, as girls, could be included in such notions as "All men are created equal." Do French children wonder what it is about the sea that makes it feminine and what it is about some ships, but not others, that makes them masculine? And why are all English ships feminine? Knowledge of nautical anatomy sheds no light on such genderings.

Critics of various theoretical persuasions and disciplines increasingly challenge notions about gender that split desires from identifications as well as inextricably link certain desires and identities (Schafer, 1974; Keller, 1985; Butler, 1990,1993; Sedgwick, 1990,1993; Flax, 1990, 1996; Laqueur, 1990; Longino, 1990; Garber, 1992; Hubbard and Wald, 1993; Fausto-Sterling, 1994). Benjamin (1988, 1991, 1995), Goldner (1991), Dimen (1982, 1986, 1991, 1995), and Harris (1991) have variously attempted to rescue gender discussions from concrete sexual polarities. They suggest that we understand that "the consciously experienced totality of being a male or female person," is a, sometimes, necessary fiction. It is this fiction, perhaps, that those toddlers hesitated to express. Perhaps they sensed its impressive effects on the perception of, and exercise of, individual capacities. Psychoanalytic theories about gender, transference, and homosexual object choice are riddled with the effects of such reductions.

Many psychoanalytic discussions of gender and transference seem to assume that our unconscious is constructed like an ideal nuclear family picture album, filled with portrait images of clearly defined family relationships, taken at clearly defined moments in psychological time: baby and mother; child and mother; child and father; mother and father and child. Siblings, grandparents, and other child-care persons, although acknowledged, appear rarely in such developmental photographs. In the day-by-day unfolding of analytic treatment, however, most internal representations bear little resemblance to the family photographs of developmental theory. Self- and object representations are more like multiple exposures than like freeze-frame portraits. Images are superimposed on images, the product of fantasy's shaping of memory's distortions of multiple experiences, over various times, through various relationships, with persons who themselves differ at various times and in different relationships. Genital anatomy is not solely, or perhaps even principally, the organizer of such amalgams. The varying intensity and clarity of these psychic registrations are determined by relational experiences both satisfying and frustrating, by acute traumatic exposures, by affects and intrapsychic conflicts. Our psyches probably contain multiple and expandable sets of amalgams, various aspects of which are called to conscious and unconscious awareness by contextual cues and associated affective states.[2]

Psychoanalytic gender theories do not as yet do justice to such textured and contextual experience. In most discussions there are still only a few plates on the psyche/waiter's arm: masculinity or femininity or, at best, that tired old mixed grille, bisexuality. These theories do not help us to appreciate, for instance, how often subjective experience is gender free. Our theories do not help us to appreciate the many moments when desires conflict with gender maintenance. If I, a boy, find pleasure in a green room with green curtains, am I still a boy? Can I, a girl, boogie-board? Will I lose my femininity? Instead of capturing those shifting attachments and sympathies that Woolf (1928) suggested each had "little constitutions and rights of their own," gender and transference discussions tend to reduce such possibilities to predictable sets of dramas taking place among archetypal imagos, in discrete developmental periods.

One problematic foundational psychoanalytic dichotomy is the division of psychological development into a preoedipal period, dominated by the power and presence of a mother, and an oedipal period, organized around the power of and desire for a father. Although there is disagreement about the timing of the first mental representations of father and of the onset of oedipal conflict (Klein 1926, 1928; Gaddini, 1976; Chasseguet-Smirgel, 1985) and there are increasing attempts to include fathers in early developmental schemas (Gaddini, 1976; Cath et al, 1982 and 1989; Diamond, 1986; Pruitt, 1983; Lanksy, 1989; Tessman, 1982; Benjamin, 1991), the essential structure of that developmental narrative still has general acceptance. Its deeply embedded sexual polarities support and reinforce the sexual polarities in psychoanalytic gender and transference discussions.

## Contradictions in Psychoanalytic Gender Identity Models

Stoller (1968) challenged Freudian models of gender development by asserting that sex assignment at birth, combined with conscious and unconscious parental attitudes, led to an unchangeable "core gender identity" established before the child's discovery of the anatomical genital differences. Most psychoanalytic models of sexual development and child observation studies, however, continue to stress the psychological impact of that discovery, which takes place during the same period a child is thought to negotiate the process of psychological separation. Contradictory, or at least paradoxical, perspectives exist within current gender theories about the optimal consequences of the discovery. One perspective is expressed in Fast's (1984) differentiation model of gender identity development, itself a formidable challenge to and revision of Freudian theory. Fast sees boys and girls alike as "overinclusive in their early experiences, not aware of limitations inherent in being of a particular sex" (p. 19). The developmental task for both boys and girls is the management of the sometimes painful awareness of each sex's limitations. Although Fast does not explicitly address homosexuality, her model can easily be used to support the assumption that "mature gender identity" (heterosexuality) involves choosing an "object" who has achieved an equally monosexual, and "opposite," gender identity. McDougall (1989), for instance, describes what happens following the discovery of the anatomical genital difference: "the genital suddenly becomes an object that can be pointed out and named, and that marks you as belonging ineluctably to one clan only and excluded for ever from the other. . . . Much psychic work is required in order to carry out the task of mourning that will eventually allow the child to accept the narcissistically unacceptable difference and assume its monosexual destiny" (p. 205).

Coexisting (sometimes in the same theorist) alongside the assumption that psychological maturity results in the attainment of a monosexual identity is a contradictory psychoanalytic perspective in which optimal gender development (at least for a heterosexual person) derives from the achievement of an internal *mix* of sexual identifications, an achievement believed essential for mature object relationships as well as for creativity. From this position, McDougall (1989) stresses the "importance of different identifications with *both* parents that essentially structure the sense of sexual identity for all children" (p. 206). Ogden (1987) believes that a monosexual choice can lead to rigid inauthenticity: "Healthy gender identity . . . occurs when one does not have to choose between loving (and identifying with) one's mother and loving (and identifying with) one's father. . . . Disorder of gender identity can be understood as disturbance of the intrapsychic dialectical relationship of masculinity and femininity" (p. 496).

Those who define the characteristics of the creative work ego of a psychoanalytic therapist usually see the need for more than monosexual identity. Some try to undo the sexualized split by describing the ideal analytic gender in metaphors of bisexuality and of heterosexual intercourse. For instance, Chasseguet-Smirgel (1984) suggests that "the analyst's bisexuality must be well integrated to enable the development of the baby made by the analysand in their work together, the baby which represents the analysand himself, recreated" (p. 175). Noting that "the two sexes are marked at the psychic level by the integration of their identifications with their two parents" (p. 169), she believes a "maternal aptitude . . . plays an essential role in establishing the analysand in the analytic situation. . . . The analytic relationship itself . . . [is] a repetition of the mother-infant relationship in its most primitive and immediate aspects . . ." (p.170). Male as well as female analysts are thus usually expected to manifest identifications and functions similar to what Winnicott (1958, 1965, 1971) termed maternal preoccupation, the ability to maintain a holding environment for the patient/infant.

Chasseguet-Smirgel (1984) suggests that maternal aptitude "must also have its limits. Are they not to be found in the analyst's masculinity, in identification with the father, whether the analyst is a man or a woman, which enables the child to cut his tie to his mother and to turn towards reality?" (p. 175). Chasseguet-Smirgel's polarizing associations here are common to much psychoanalytic theory: mother-based identifications, which pull toward connection, "symbiosis," or "merger" are contrasted with father-stimulated identifications, which pull toward "reality." But Chasseguet-Smirgel is herself dissatisfied with her association of "reality" with father and masculinity, and like Freud (1905a, 1925, 1931, 1933a), she tries to qualify the implications of these sexual polarities. For instance, she links the "capacity *to wait* and watch a relationship develop, . . . the slow, patient daily labor which is our task" with the "femininity" of the analyst, which she sees as "more closely linked with the reality principle, in certain respects, then masculinity" (pp. 173–174).

Chasseguet-Smirgel struggles to free herself from the brambles of a bisexual metaphor where qualities and capacities and functions are divided *between* the supposedly opposite sexes rather than being understood as properties shared by both sexes. Other examiners also get caught in these tangles. Bernstein's (1991) description of an "integrated analytic identity" in a female analyst reveals both the sexual polarities of her model and her awareness that such sexual splits must be somehow reunited.

> The daughter, now analyst, must extricate herself from the regressive and sexual aspects of her relationship with her mother. She must integrate the different, body-alien, ordering aspects of her father into her psyche and into her professional work. This requires the female, most particularly as analyst, to be able to move back and forth with safety and flexibility between regressive, erotic, intuitive modes, and intellectual, curious, truly analytic modes, often within a single hour [p. 47].

In Bernstein's description, the supposedly sex-linked attributes are highly visible: sensitivity to the body and to its erotics and the capacity to regress and to demonstrate "intuition" are associated with the relationship with and identifications with mother, while the "body-alien" "ordering" mind, the "intellectual, curious, truly analytic modes" are seen as capacities achieved through identification with an oedipal father.

Sexually polarized developmental models make it difficult to realize that both boys and girls identify with both mothers and fathers, as well as with sisters, brothers, aunts and uncles, and grandparents. Actually, the sexual polarities have been so pervasive that it is only recently that fathers have been included in descriptions of early development. (Winnicott, 1965; Burlingham, 1973; Cath et al. 1982, 1989). Many analytic observers who acknowledge a father's psychological presence in early development see his primary function as helping to establish difference, a process usually assumed to consist of distinguishing between dichotomous possibilities. Mahler, Pine, and Bergman (1975), in their influential model of separation-individuation, emphasized a father's importance as the first object outside the supposedly "symbiotic" maternal–infant orbit. Actually, Mahler did not include fathers in her observations; and Abelin (1980) based his conclusions on the observation of one little boy and his younger sister. Those observations "confirmed my previous hunch that around 18 months gender identity emerges more readily in boys, generational identity in girls. . . . Before rapprochement, the father remains a peripheral, if exciting, object for the girl, tinged with eroticized stranger anxiety. By contrast, he has become the primary attachment object for the boy" (p. 158). Abelin had hypothesized that early triangulation (child–mother–father) set in motion the rapprochement phase: "In this respect, however, I found more than I had bargained for. Although the father emerged so clearly as an object of deep and specific attachment during the first two years of life, so did siblings and other children, grandparents, and various other familiar adults" (p. 155).

But Abelin did not include the significance of this observation in his conclusions of how differences are established and how identifications are made. In place of the variety and complexity of object relationships and identifications he had observed, he returned to the developmental schematic of mother–father–child triangulation and maintained that it reflected "an inner blueprint for epigenetic development. . ." ( p. 165).

Developmental and gender theories hold fast to polarities, or, at best, to triangularities. These models are uncomfortable with much cross sex identification. Freud (1921), Greenson (1968), Stoller (1968), Tyson (1986, 1989), and Green (1987) stress the importance of a father for "gender identity development" in a boy, helping him "disidentify" with his mother, a process deemed essential in the child for healthy gender identity, that is, the prevention of homosexuality. In women, identification with father, particularly in women who love women, has most frequently been seen as a defensive regression from a love relationship to identification in order to avoid oedipal anxieties or to avoid psychotic merger with mother (or both) (Freud, 1920; Jones, 1927; McDougall, 1980, 1989.) Freud did not mention a father in relation to a girl until she discovers anatomical sexual difference and, as a consequence, immediately enters her oedipal phase. Leonard's (1966) discussion of the important identification a daughter may make with her father considered only oedipal fathers. Spieler (1984), using attachment theory to review the developmental and clinical literature, came to the conclusion the fathers were neither "first strangers" nor "first others," but were, from the beginning, significant objects of attachment for girls as well as boys. But she did not suggest that identification might result from this relationship. Ogden (1987) describes a transitional relationship essential for a girl's successful entry into the oedipal period: "the little girl falls in love with the (not fully external) mother who is engaged in an unconscious identification with her own father in her internal set of oedipal object relations" (pp. 488–489). But Ogden's developmental schema still lacks one love relationship that itself might also provide a transition to oedipal relationships and make those relationships either more or less traumatic, namely, an early relationship with a father. Although Tessman (1982) believes that a girl's early relationship with her father does have developmental significance, she did not suggest that a young daughter identifies with her father. On the contrary, according to Tessman, the girl uses her father to represent difference from self and mother. Tessman does, however, see fathers as the focus of more than oedipal erotic excitement for daughters. Fathers are also the object of girls' "endeavor excitement, which begins during the period of individuation. . . . Unlike erotic excitement, it is not gender linked, but has to do with the anlage for autonomy, with growing freedom to experiment with one's skills" (pp. 236–237).

According to Benjamin (1991), however, *both* boys and girls want to identify with father. In the developing mind of the rapprochement child, a father "represents a different kind of object—a subject—who is not so much the source of goodness as the mirror of desire. He represents a subject who can want and can act . . . to fill those wants. The child gains from him not merely direct recognition through approval or confirmation, but recognition through symbolic identification with this powerful subject who is his or her ideal" (p. 283). Benjamin maintains that a girl's ability to identify with her father in this capacity to want, and to act, depends to a great extent on the father's ability to identify with his daughter, on his ability to feel and to convey, to his daughter as well as to his son, "This little person is like me."

Benjamin's concept of agency is not sex linked. And the presence of a parent who is male is not necessary for its development. But Benjamin does suggest that various problems may result when a girl has a male parent who is present enough to serve for the child as idealized subject of desire, but who is emotionally unavailable or unable to help the girl establish this identification within herself. Benjamin (1988) has described masochistic surrender as an attempt to gain the recognition of an idealized subject of desire. For Benjamin, a girl's "a child is being beaten" fantasies are not depictions of regressed oedipal wishes, but straightforward descriptions of a girl's dashed desires for her father's recognition and the humiliation associated with this loss.

## Sexual Polarities in the Transference Literature: Neglected Transference Relationships

A review of the literature on transference reveals the sex and gender polarities and the prohibitions against certain identifications it has inherited from developmental narratives. Significant transference possibilities have, as a result, been neglected. Cross-sex sibling identifications and transferences, rarely discussed, are usually considered substitutes or stand-ins for maternal and paternal identifications. So powerful is the effect of the developmental dichotomy between (maternal) preoedipal and (paternal) oedipal that discussions of transferences to early fathers do not exist in the literature. Even analysts who specifically focus on paternal transferences discuss only transferences to oedipal fathers (Fenichel, 1945; Blum, 1971; Chasseguet-Smirgel, 1984; Kulish,1984). Karme (1979) believed that male patients found it difficult to establish such a paternal transference with a female analyst because they feared attack by a "phallic" woman. Goldberger and Evans (1985) suggested that relying on the concept of a phallic woman revealed a "limitation" in the "imaginative repertoire" (p. 307) of a woman analyst. But neither Karme nor Goldberger and Evans included a boy's early relationship with his father in their "imaginative repertoire" of transference possibilities. Several of their male patients reported longing to identify with the analyst, the analyst's work, and the analyst's abilities. Both Karme and Goldberger and Evans, interpreting such longings as evidence of a boy's identification with his mother, failed to imagine that their patients' longings might also be those Freud (1921) saw as characteristic of a boy's (but apparently not a girl's) loving identification with father.

> Identification is known to psychoanalysis as the earliest expression of an emotional tie with another person. It plays a part in the early history

of the Oedipus complex. A little boy will exhibit a special interest in his father; he would like to grow like him and be like him, and take his place everywhere. We may say simply that he takes his father as his ideal. This behavior has nothing to do with a passive or feminine attitude toward the father (and toward males in general); it is on the contrary typically masculine. It fits very well with the Oedipus complex, for which it helps to prepare the way [ p.105].

Karme (1993) and Goldberger and Evans (1993) revisit paternal transference with female analysts and male patients, but neither reexamination mentions the possibility of early father–son transferences. Diamond (1993) describes a male patient who, at the close of his work, told her, "You are my mirror image—I looked at you and saw myself reflected." Diamond believes that "the transference imagos that this patient so eloquently articulated may be conceptualized as a movement from the preoedipal maternal through the oedipal paternal to the erotic maternal transference" (p. 206). Diamond does not identify herself in the transference as an early father, another self-reflecting mirror.

Transference discussions of women patients and female therapists generally focus on mother–daughter relationships. Early maternal transference and transferences to an envied oedipal mother are examined. Pregenital erotic maternal transference and countertransference are explored (Wrye and Welles, 1994). Paternal transferences are assumed to be toward an oedipal father (Fenichel, 1945; Kulish, 1984; Person, 1985; Blum and Blum, 1986; Meyers, 1986; Lester, 1990; Bernstein, 1991). For instance, Ogden (1987) describes a particular countertransference impediment in the treatment of female patients by female analysts. "Arising from the inadequacy of the transitional oedipal relationship is an inability on the part of the female therapist to engage in a relatively unconflicted identification with her own father in her unconscious set of oedipal object relationships . . ." ( p. 494). But Ogden does not suggest that a female therapist must also engage in a relatively unconflicted identification with an other than oedipal father.

Bernstein (1991) attributes women's difficulties recognizing paternal transferences to the problem women therapists have in seeing themselves as "penetrating," another oedipal catchword. Meyers (1986) also sees women therapists at risk for missing paternal transference.

> All significant early object relationships are reexperienced in a new version in the transference; all unconscious fantasies are transferred onto the analyst, so that at one time or another the analyst is reacted to as a father, mother, brother or sister, regardless of the actual gender of the

analyst. A frequent problem indeed is that this is overlooked. The oedipal father image behind the maternal figure is often missed in the transference with the female analyst [p. 165].

But Meyers's list of "all significant early object relationships" does not include an early father–daughter relationship or any transference manifestations of such a relationship. Similarly, Person (1985), who described how a woman's erotic oedipal transference could mask an early maternal transference, does not mention the possibility of an early paternal transference in her women patients. Even Lester (1990), who has specifically pointed out the difficulty women analysts have experiencing paternal identifications, discusses only the complexities of the maternal transferences and of the transferences toward oedipal fathers.

Although Benjamin's (1991) descriptions of both girls' and boys' desires for an identificatory love relationship with a father early in development may help us find missing aspects of development and may enlarge our imaginative repertoire of transferences, we must avoid creating yet another portrait for the family album: *the preoedipal father.* We are not interested in adding yet another static archetype to existing developmental dramas. We are interested in examining how polarized sex and gender paradigms in development and transference theories, and their attendant prohibitions against and anxieties about certain cross sex identifications, affect clinical treatment. In the following clinical illustrations two patients, in their parting gifts and dreams, demonstrate how important cross-sex identifications contributed to their gender and sexual insecurities and to their analyst's clinical confusions.

## Richard

Richard was bringing to a close nine years of intensive psychotherapy. He had originally been brought to treatment by his wife, who complained that Richard was "just like a man, emotionally closed and inaccessible." She beat her fists on Richard's body, in session and out, in frustrated attempts to gain access to his "insides." Richard responded by secreting himself behind walls of guilty compliance. Conjoint sessions were stalemated dramas of her escalating frustration and his guilty, passive resignation. When I (MM) attempted to refer Richard to another therapist for individual treatment, he surprised me by bursting into tears: "*You* are my therapist," he protested, revealing under the duress of forced separation the attachment he had hidden in the previous sessions.

Over the slow years of analytic treatment, we created our reconstructed understandings of the origins of Richard's highly developed capacities to disappear emotionally, even when he appeared to be present. The son of socially prominent and narcissistic parents, Richard kept as low a profile as possible. He saw himself as a "worker bee" who toiled for the good of the family. An intellectually gifted and wealthy man, Richard appeared to the world, as he had to the referring physician, as "a shy graduate student who works somehow in his father's business." During treatment Richard moved from existing in a state that he termed "semi-suicide" to a life in which he could more fully claim his feelings, assets, and his relationships. He divorced and made a second marriage with a more compatible partner. Prompted by the insistent messages of his dreams, Richard reclaimed his relationships with his children, which he had surrendered in the marital wars.

We explored Richard's various conscious and unconscious identifications with nurturing figures. Sometimes I was the grandmother who had cared for him from early infancy. Richard believed that she had become estranged from the family, when he was nine, because he had been too attached to her and because she had tangled too much, on his behalf, with his dominating father. Sometimes I was Richard's mother, who managed her anxieties through compulsive neatness. In the transference, my carpets or couch might get stained with Richard's spills of messy neediness.

Richard worried about his extraordinarily highly developed ability and need for attending to others. He identified with a title on my bookshelf, *Dutiful Daughter*. "Am I gay?" he wondered, caught in that gender thicket where nurturing care and attentiveness to feelings = feminine = homosexual male. Richard was initially elated and relieved by his strong sexual desire in his second marriage. But that potency was soon threatened by Richard's preoccupation with his wife's menstrual periods and by his fear, during sexual intercourse, that she had forgotten to use her diaphragm. He kept a mental calendar of her cycle and was surprised at my comment that all men did not know the exact state of their wife's menstrual cycle. Finally it became clear that it was not his wife's protection that worried Richard. It was his own. At the height of male potency, and in the intimacy of sexual intercourse, he thought about diaphragms because he was afraid of losing control and "opening" himself.

As Richard became more comfortable with sexual potency and emotional vulnerability, he began to explore new creative enterprises in his business and social worlds. These movements would, in turn, bring new anxieties. And at every step he took away from being an asexual worker bee, he reworked his fears that I, in the transference his narcissistic and oedipal father, would disapprove and threaten: "Don't get too big for your britches."

In the last year of treatment Richard became interested in Robert Bly and the men's movement. Although fearful of hurting me, both mother and father in the transference, if he wanted to explore experiences with others, he organized a group for fathers and sons at his children's school and an adult drama group in which he could revive some talents given up in his first marriage. He was aware of his positive transference to the leader of his men's group and realized that he was consciously redoing some steps in his development, namely, forming male friendships, developing his physical potential through sports, and enjoying the admiring attention of women. Although his father had died without Richard's experiencing any significant change in their relationship, he cherished his few memories of their closeness.

Richard, never able to give presents to loved ones at Christmas or other occasions, left this task to his secretary. He feared both that he had nothing to give and that what he might offer would arouse the receiver's envious attack. In the last month of treatment, he spoke several times of having a parting gift for me. He said he had known for some time what he wanted to give to me. "I just hope I have the courage to do it." In one of his last sessions, he brought the gift, a painting of a Native American shaman alone against a night sky. The shaman stands, his blanket gathered around him, a medicine wand in his hand, a buffalo skull at his feet. His head is uplifted, eyes closed, envisioning other realities. "This figure moves me. He is me. He is you. I hope you aren't upset that it is a man, or that I think of you this way. He is all of us who take this way, who make this journey, this search. This painting was my father's. I knew when he died that I might want to give it to you. It represents for me, us, you and me, and what we have been doing together."

Through his gift, Richard enabled me to see one of his most vital internal object relationships, identifications, and transferences. Ogden might see the shaman as a transitional or paradoxical figure, the father-in-the-mother, a bridge of identification for a boy as he makes his journey of development. Another image in this symbolic multiple exposure may be Richard's grandmother, whom he lost at nine years, the same number of years he has spent with me. Richard identifies the shaman with his father, a longed-for and idealized figure with whom he also wished to identify, a relationship he had also needed in order to find his way and make his journey. The needs and desires for this relationship, which Richard worried that I, like his father, could not see and accept, had provided much of the positive motivation in Richard's treatment. I had recognized and explored his identifications with his mother and grandmother; I had interpreted his expectation of his father's attack for his desires and abilities. I had also reflected to myself frequently about my own puzzling lack of envy of this wealthy and powerful man. Instead of envy, I felt a deeply satisfying pleasure in his assets. Sometimes I had assumed that my lack of envy must result from his low profile defense against envious attack, and I made this interpretation. Sometimes I had assumed that my pleasure in his abilities reflected his wish for an admiring mother, and I made that interpretation. But like Karme (1979), Goldberger and Evans (1985), and Diamond (1993), I had not been able to imagine myself *also* as the longed-for admiring *father* of a splendid and admiring son. I had had problems identifying this transference, not because of concerns about seeing myself as penetrating, castrating, or phallic, but because of inexperience and discomfort identifying with this idealized Subject and because of the limited transference possibilities in my clinical imagination.

## Kate's Case

Kate's analysis was a reparative exploration of frustrating narcissistic vulnerabilities. Although Kate felt that her parents loved her, she complained that she had never felt able "to fit in" with her family. Of her ever-busy, constantly-in-motion mother, Kate said, "I follow her around like a puppy even now to get her attention." Kate, who seemed indeed often like an out-of-bounds puppy, high spirited, but "bouncing off the walls," used the analytic relationship to internalize the experience of being "grounded" by a containing object. Kate rarely spoke of her father. She described a kind but emotionally inaccessible, somewhat vague figure, usually asleep in front of the TV. Early in treatment she brought her father a piece of her work and was disappointed and frustrated by his inability to identify with it. Kate saw her brother as "a successful family man," but she believed that she and her sister had problems. "My brother just walked in my father's footsteps. My family didn't know what to do with girls." She described the contents of what she called "my case," an overnight bag, train case, or woman's make-up case. She reported that her maternal grandmother had had such a case and had filled it with the medicines for her somatic disorders. Her mother had such a case and filled it with the tools of a profession she had been too frightened or conflicted to pursue. "My case has only the odds and ends I've been able to pick up in my few travels" Kate said.

One particular memory of Kate's illustrates the shattering narcissistic and rapprochement issues that were the focus of much of the analysis.

Young Kate had seen someone eating a soft-boiled egg in its shell. When her mother asked one morning how she wanted her eggs, Kate said she wanted a "raw" egg. Although her mother told her she would not want to eat a "raw" egg, Kate, remembering the egg in the shell and not understanding that the egg had been cooked, insisted she did want a raw egg. After several such exchanges, her mother grew impatient: "All right! *Here's* your raw egg!" She shattered the egg shell and dropped its contents onto Kate's plate.

Kate's interpretation of this experience was that it happened "because I didn't know the right answer." To protect herself against painful, humiliating shatterings, Kate tried to avoid all moments in which she didn't know "the right answer." She searched for gurus, both men and women, who could provide that answer. Kate's fears of making her own choices and expressing her own desires resulted in unsatisfying masochistic passivity and in sometimes explosive fury at feeling controlled. Kate had had a seven-year long, stormy relationship with Joyce, characterized by many fights, breakups, and reconciliations, and she had had a series of shorter relationships with unavailable women. Her relationship with Margo, begun in the third year of treatment, provided Kate many opportunities to explore her fear of making choices. Kate had difficulties with what she called "holding my own," rather than surrendering her desires and choices to Margo. To Kate, Margo represented the ability to take pleasure in choosing clothing, makeup, and jewelry, capacities that Kate coded as feminine, and the ability to take pleasure in power and competition, a quality that Kate gendered as masculine and also wished to make more her own.

In the middle of our fifth year of work, Kate and I (MM) were once again reworking in the transference anxieties about choice. Kate worked for several months on a project that she was certain I would not like and would not have chosen to do. She feared that I would "hate" her, that Margo would hate her, that all "feminists" would hate her. She dropped hints about the work which hooked my attention and concern, but then she refused to discuss her thoughts or feelings further. She had the "ambitendency" (Mahler et al., 1975) of a rapprochement child, the "rapidly alternating desire to push mother away and to cling to her" and "the standing on the threshold" indecision characteristic of the period (p. 96).

Finally Kate and I reached our rapprochement crisis. She brought me a sample of her work but denied that it was "really" her creation; she insisted that she had done it only to satisfy her male employer. She insisted that she felt like a "prostitute" having to do such work for his profit. "Your name is on it. You wanted to do this," I challenged, confused by her ambitendency and frustrated by her disowning her creation.

Instantly I became in the transference the shattering mother who insisted, "You wanted *this* egg. This is what you chose." Feeling misunderstood, hurt, and angry, Kate raged or lay silent in several weeks of sessions. She was sure now that I had never understood her. She threatened to leave. I interpreted her disappointment that I was not the longed-for guru who could show her how to make a choice that no one would ever disagree with. I interpreted her reluctance to acknowledge that her mind and its productions could be different from mine. The crisis resolved, and Kate announced, "I actually feel better now." Shortly after these sessions, she set a date for termination.

Although throughout most of the analysis I addressed aspects of what I considered maternal transferences, sometimes I would briefly but intensely feel that I was a man in the transference. These moments were puzzling because I could not point to anything in the clinical material that accounted for my feeling. For instance, after a series of sessions in which she focused on difficulties holding her own with a co-worker, Kate brought me a bouquet of home-grown roses. "These are for you, for the past sessions. You'd be great in business!" Although somehow I sensed that I was a *male figure* to whom Kate was giving roses, I could not understand why Kate gave a gift of roses to a man at the moment she felt success in business. What kind of "gender identity confusion" was this? And was the confusion hers, mine, or ours?

There were other passages in the work in which I could more easily understand my sense of being the recipient of male transference projections. For instance, for some weeks during which both Kate and her father were undergoing medical treatments, psychic surgery and the myth of the Minotaur in the Labyrinth became interwoven metaphors for the analysis. Kate feared that she, like her father, suffered from a "sexual disease." Was she too masculine if she liked to feel powerful at work and she loved women? Would "cure" mean she must lose Margo? Kate hated herself for these confusing thoughts and hated and feared exploring them. I was cast as the doctor/analyst/hero/ Theseus, equipped with a sword with which I would enter the confusing maze. I had the power to destroy the monstrous male malignancy inside. Kate was the raging half-bull, half-human Minotaur trapped inside defensive word mazes and, at the same time, the monster's sister, Ariadne, who in the myth gave Theseus the clues to the labyrinth, even though it destroyed her own life. "She did it for love," Kate said of Ariadne's aid to Theseus.

During these weeks as we explored Kate's concerns about her physical health and her sexuality, I gradually realized that Kate was no longer coming to sessions in the oversized "unisex" (in other words, men's) clothing that had previously been her style. On my couch now lay a woman whose shapely body had previously been hidden by that camouflage. Kate brought a dream, "I dreamt you gave me a gift. Flute nuts. In a bag. And then you disappeared." Kate felt happy about the dream, but had little interest in the flute nuts except to say, "They are something you don't usually see in that form. Like cashews in their shells." Although the dream seemed to confirm my countertransference experience of being male, one whose gifts are a phallic flute and nuts in a bag, I realized that I did not understand her pleasure in her dream. At the very moment that Kate was wishing/fearing psychic surgery to *remove* some unwanted male identifications, she seemed to also be rejoicing in a gift of male genitals. How does a gift of what seems to be male genitals make a woman more comfortable showing off the body she had previously kept hidden? How does a gift of male genitals make a woman feel more comfortable with her sexuality and her sexual choices? Was she wishing/dreaming her way out of penis-envy? Should we see the flute nuts/cashews in shells as seeds in husks or eggs in ovaries?

These puzzling moments of receiving flowers and of giving flute nuts were not accompanied by any triangular conflicts in or out of the transference. I never saw Kate's difficulties as being primarily about oedipal conflicts. Oedipal anxieties were there intertwined with narcissistic fears. But Kate's desire did not seem to be to take mother from father, or father from mother, nor did she seem to be complaining that they had one another. And it did not seem that Kate's anxieties about the undeveloped state of her "case" or the "diseased" state of her genitals arose from fears of punishment for oedipal wishes. I could not see her as motivated by a desire *for*, or envy of, those with a penis; I saw her as more worried that she might *have* an internal penis, which she *didn't* want. Her wishes for me to help fill her traveling case and her fears of the gynecological/analytic procedures necessary to cure her disease and remove something "abnormal" which had gotten inside suggested fears similar to what Mayer (1985) calls *female castration anxiety*: the fantasied loss of *female* genitals.

Nevertheless, in a corner of my mind remained the memory of Kate's transformation from unisex/youth to woman and the memories of feeling myself a pleased and admiring and admired man in the transference. What did these feelings mean? Did my countertransference feelings demonstrate Ogden's (1987) idea that the oedipal father as love object is first introduced by the transitional figure of the mother-as-father and by the mother's ability to identify with her own oedipal father? Should I understand Kate's lesbian relationship with Margo as a preoedipal defense against heterosexual desires? Did my not making an oedipal paternal transference interpretation collude with such repressed wishes in Kate? Did these interpretations fit Kate's case?

Kate had set her termination date for March 1. Before she left for a two-week break at Christmas, Kate gave me a gift she had given me at the beginning of her treatment: an amaryllis bulb. "This is always the perfect gift," she had said on both occasions, expressing an uncharacteristic certainty about her choice. During that Christmas break Kate contracted hepatitis and was away from sessions for three more weeks. Just as she was about to return, her father died. We were left suddenly with one month of sessions remaining, the bittersweet culmination of our work. The amaryllis bulb sent up tall green shoots and lovely coral blossoms. In our final weeks together, we both watched these graceful symbols of the changes that had taken place in Kate. Watching the transformations of the amaryllis, I found myself musing about the flower, as I had about the dream of the flute nuts/cashew seeds. I found I could not settle on the sex of that amaryllis. Out of the round brown bulb, a phallic green stem had grown dramatically erect. The amaryllis reminded me of Dylan Thomas's (1957) famous identification with flowers: "The force that through the green fuse drives the flower/ drives my blood" (p. 10). The force within the brown bulb had driven through the green phallic fuse of stem, only to transform into vaginal flowers whose petals were spread open, whose erect stamens were pollen filled. The sexual reproductive anatomy of the amaryllis was vibrantly visible, but even bisexuality seemed a poor description of its arrangements.

On Friday of the week before the last week of the analysis Kate brought a dream: "Two men. One older or bigger. I don't know where they are exactly. There is a frameline at the bottom. Things I can't see. Like I was watching a film. Maybe it is a car or a convertible with the door closed. I couldn't see below the waist. The men are sweaty. There is a leather harness. One says to the other to do something, like 'Hit me.' The other says, 'OK' But I realize, although I thought at first when I looked it was an atmosphere of violence, he wasn't hitting him. He was caressing him. What an odd dream! Usually you say something about a dream like this that it's about you and me," Kate prompted. But I was unable to put myself and Kate into the scene as a way of understanding its significance. Kate was asking for a transference interpretation I didn't know how to make.

That weekend, in one of those serendipitous opportunities for analytic learning, still resonating with Kate's dream images, I heard Jessica Benjamin present "Father and Daughter: Identification with Difference—A Contribution

to Gender Heterodoxy," her discussion of the importance of a girl's identification with her father. Using Benjamin's (1991) perspective, I thought
again about various passages in Kate's analysis. I remembered the difficult
weeks before and after Kate had brought me her work. Kate had trouble
claiming her own agency and her own choices because of fears about psychological separation. She had not been able to internalize a sense of herself as a person, a subject, who could want and chose. She and I had
explored these disturbances and identifications arising from her relationships with her mother, grandmother, and sisters.

At the same time, however, there were also difficulties associated with
her relationship with her father. When she had brought her father her work,
she felt he could not understand or identify with it. Now I realized how I
had also been this father in transference. Since Kate could not feel that she
*shared* agency with her father, she and I had fought over which one of us
was the subject of desire. She *"knew"* I did not like such work. Therefore,
she experienced my attempts *to return* agency to her—"This is what *you*
wanted. It has *your* name on it"—as her father's rejection. At the same time,
she experienced her employer as a father who demanded that she prostitute herself in such work for his pleasure and profit, not hers. My dislike of
the work meant that, as her feminist mother, I did not understand or
approve of her desire to be loved by the idealized and powerful father; I
wanted to keep her from father and his recognition. We had survived the
intensities of these overdetermined, impacted splits and transferences,
although I did not interpret this transference. And Kate was still trying, in
the last days of her analysis, to bring to our awareness this important relationship. One of her attempts had been her Friday dream.

From Benjamin's (1991) perspective, Kate's dream of two male figures,
one older, one smaller could be seen as "A Child Is Being Beaten, Revised
Edition." Since we can't see "below the waist," at first look it seems as if one
younger or smaller male is requesting to be "hit" by an older bigger man.
There is "an atmosphere of violence." But, it turns out, said Kate, that "he
is caressing him." Something has happened to change the "atmosphere of
violence" to one of "caress." Kate's wishes to be like her father no longer
require harness and punishment. What has happened?

In Benjamin's terms, a loving recognition from a rapprochement father
has repaired the humiliation of the wish for mutual identification and
removed any need for masochistic ("hit me") solutions to this desire. Kate
had attempted to merge herself with idealized gurus because she felt forever other than the Ideal. Merging with an omnipotent object had been necessary because her own capacities to contain anxieties, to calm, and

self-stabilize were incomplete. Merging was also necessary because her own capacities to want and to choose were conflicted and incomplete. Over the years, Kate had made many comparisons between our ways of working. I had always understood these comparisons as arising from maternal identifications. I thought that her increasing comfort with these identifications had contributed to her growing confidence about the contents of her "case," that overnight container she needed for her sexual journeys. But Benjamin's (1991) concept of an identificatory love relationship with a rapprochement father added another dimension of possibilities. It also helped explain the puzzling countertransference experiences of being an admired and admiring male object. It helped explain the dream in which I gave her a gift of flute nuts at the time of her most dramatic transformation. "You gave me the gift and then you disappeared," she had said. A girl makes a *symbolic identification* with her idealized father, if he is able to enjoy and encourage that identification. Comfortable with having internalized this aspect of the ego Ideal, instead of a defensive monstrously phallic Minotaur, and no longer worried about exposing either an aberrant monstrosity or fragmented "odds and ends," she can more comfortably display her female body.

I had recognized Kate's longing for firm containment and for room to make her own choices, and I interpreted these as longings for a mother more attuned, a mother who, able to allow and support separation and individuation and love for a father, could sit still and pay attention. These were accurate, but not sufficient, transference interpretations. She and I had also changed "the atmosphere of violence" to one of "caress" by living out together in transference a longed-for identification with her father.

To the next session, Monday of the last week of her analysis, Kate brought the following dream:

"I dreamt I was on a bike, racing a car. My mother and my little sister were in the car. I thought it was interesting that I felt I could go pretty far. Then my bike got hard to pedal. I had no first gear. First gear is for starting up. I came to a stop. There was an old man in long underwear. I think of my father. We went inside. It was warm inside, poor but cozy. I was there for some time. I guess some stuff happened. Some movement or something. Then I was in this office. I saw my father. I was so happy when I saw him. I said, 'Oh, look, here's my father.' When I said that, he covered up his face, and pulled away. He said, 'Don't do that. Don't say I'm here.' Because I had pointed him out he was going to disappear. I woke up so depressed. I don't know if I have ever felt so depressed. I felt so alone. Bereft. I guess it's about my father's death. I think he's there and he's not."

The dream narrative contains Kate's depiction of her need for treatment (her vehicle of individuation lacked a gear), what had been helpful in that treatment (a poor but cozy father inside allows movement to happen), and a description of a recent new edition of an old injury (father fearfully denies his presence). This dream was Kate's response to my failure to understand her previous dream of the two men, one smaller, one bigger. She had invited me to make a transference interpretation. My inability to do so replicated for Kate the difficulties she had felt with her father. My response must have felt to her as if I were covering my face and forbidding her to suggest that I was the older man to her younger smaller one. Although she had come to think that her father was indeed "inside," she had lost him again.

Kate had recently been describing her father's last days. On his deathbed her father had told her brother, "You were always the perfect son." Kate had been surprised to hear from her brother that this was the first and only time their father had ever said this, since Kate had always imagined that her brother and father had had "a perfect father–son relationship." "But," said Kate, "my father was a family man. Beyond what he could say. You felt that." As her transference father I had also lacked words, but Kate had nevertheless "felt" our mutual pleasure of identification. And we were now perfect son and father, at my "deathbed," the last week of the analysis. I told Kate that, although we had talked much about her feelings toward me as her mother, we had not noted enough how she had seen and experienced me as like her father. Kate wept deeply. "That seems so generous of you to say you could be like my father." Her tears expressed her longstanding wish for the recognition from her father that she had always believed her brother, by virtue of his sex, had felt, and her relief with my finally becoming aware of this identification.

Over the next several sessions, she eagerly explored the ways I resembled her father for her. "One reason," she said, "that perhaps you as my father have been so in the background here is because, you know, he always was. In the background. It wasn't until he died that I really knew how much he was the anchor, the center around which the family moved. He was still, silent." Kate's anchor metaphor associates a "holding environment" with her father, a vague yet stable background object in the midst of movement and change.

Then Kate told me about the flowers. "I did tell you about the flowers, didn't I? My father was a gardener; that is, he grew flowers. He had 200 rose bushes. He was always moving them around in the yard. He had all the flower bushes we gave him as children. He planted them in the ground. He had camellias, azaleas, gladioli." She named all her father's flowers. I remembered the romantic roses brought to me when she succeeded in "business," her confidence about giving the amaryllis, always "the perfect gift." Kate had hidden well this love for her father. Even had I been more experienced in looking for paternal transference, I would not have thought, without such prompting, to look for a father among the gifts of flowers. The amaryllis had indeed been the perfect gift. Kate "knew" that gift would please because such gifts had always pleased her father, who must have enjoyed and encouraged this aspect of loving identification with him. In her transference gifts of flowers, Kate had conveyed unconflicted pleasure in being able to choose. In the countertransference, I had enjoyed her gifts as well as shared her confusions about gender.

On Wednesday Kate said, "You know we have never talked much of babies. You tried once or twice, but I didn't want to. Since my father died, I have wanted to have a baby. I probably won't have one, but the feelings are back. He was such a family man. He loved children, especially babies. When I was 32, I wanted very much to have a baby. [She had never said any of this before.] I had a good job, lots of money, but I had no relationship. When I decided to move, I felt I was making a decision not to have a baby. I knew if I wanted to really succeed in my work, it would be a long time before I had money again, and besides I wanted to be in a relationship. Margo's wanting a baby is stirring all this up again."

Kate's "feelings are back." Now more secure in her own sexuality, partly because, more comfortable about her identification with her father—the parent who loved children especially babies—the gardener who nurtured flowers, Kate could feel again her generative desires.

Kay continued: "I had a dream. It had to do with that pin you wore yesterday. The silver pin with the three Indians. You know, silver is not the only precious substance. There is also chocolate. I am in a building. Many floors. There is a party, festive. The woman I had the crush on is there. [This is a reference to a recent dream in which she has a crush on a woman who reminded her of her brother and of me.] The woman says, 'I really have to go.' She goes downstairs. Should I talk to her? Was she upset or something? I was unsure. There are many steps down, many people. I look for her on all the floors. I never did find her. Some people know where she went; some don't. Some holiday has just passed. There are tables with many chocolate figures, like your pin. Wrapped in silver paper. There's some of civil war figures. Big ones, small ones, a series in a necklace, cowboys and Indians. The people there say, 'You can have as many as you want.' It seems they're not charging for them now. They don't seem to mind that I gather so many up. I still feel almost guilty, semisneaking. There are these brass letters K and M. M is for you I guess and also for Margo. I take them. And there were other letters. I took a whole bunch. I thought, 'Maybe I can spell something out later.' I was looking for a box to put this all in. That was the main thing I was doing. For so long it seemed. Looking for something to hold it all."

She was crying deeply as she finished telling the dream. I recalled to myself one of her previous dreams in which she had opened a closet door and was embarrassed to have me see that the closet was filled with chocolate rabbits wrapped in silver foil. Now she was again anxious, feeling "semi-sneaking" as she stashed away all the sweet possibilities. In contrast to the "odds and ends" of her initial overnight case, now she seemed to experience a plenitude of internal contents. I said, "There is one very good place to put chocolate." She laughed. "You mean I have to eat them all." I suggested that her dream indicated that she had found, after a long time looking, something to hold it all. She hoped that she herself could now hold inside various precious objects and that she was aware she was taking away some letters to spell out, in the future, new projects unknown at this time.

## Benedicte

A third example of a patient whose gender anxieties and conflicts around creativity had roots in her relationship with her early father is McDougall's (1989) Benedicte, a homosexual woman writer who came to treatment because of a writing block. At 15 months, had Benedicte suffered a traumatic loss of her father, whose loving care had been more nurturing than that her mother could provide. Benedicte used a different strategy than Kate for managing the anxiety of carrying within a necessary but disowned identification with a beloved man. Whereas Kate hid her body in oversized clothing, Benedicte's solution was to wear tight pants and sweaters that outlined her body, thus making clear that she was physically female. Material from the first interview suggests that transference desires for her father, lost during the period of rapprochement, may have influenced Benedicte's choice of analyst..

> J: I asked her what kind of help she had in mind.
> B: Perhaps you could collaborate with . . . er . . . me . . . that is . . . er
> . . . I don't think it's a real analysis that . . . er . . . I need . . . but someone like . . . er . . .you . . . who writes as well.
> J: But I'm an analyst rather than a writer [p. 206].

But McDougall is both an analyst and a writer. Was her reluctance to acknowledge *the shared identity* with Benedicte in the first interview in part an unconscious countertransference response to the unconscious transference wish: "I need someone like . . . er . . . you . . . who writes as well," a wish for recognition *by the early father* of shared agency? McDougall may have missed this paternal transference because of her oedipal interpretations of Benedicte's blocked creativity. In a dramatic moment in the analysis, Benedicte also recovered her lost connections to her early father and gained a surer sense of her own physical dimensions. Perhaps McDougall as a woman analyst shared our difficulty imagining herself the beloved father of a rapprochement child who longed for a homoerotic identificatory relationship. Benedicte's unconscious desires for this relationship may have been satisfied by her identifications with McDougall, although they must have been left unnamed.

## Looking for Something to Hold It All

One reader of an earlier version of this chapter, pointing to Kate's dream in which she is in "a convertible" and "can't see below the waist," commented that Kate's gender identity was "still unsettled" at the end of the analysis. We agree, but we don't find this "unsettledness" disturbing, nor do we see it as evidence of Kate's refusal to acknowledge sexual difference, as did that reader. Another reader suggested that Kate's father was "really" the mother in the family and that the "reversed" parental arrangements had led to Kate's gender disturbance. That reading seems to accept the gender-split functions we see as problematic. Men as well as women hold, and women as well as men mirror agency, however little our gender rules or gender theories may acknowledge these capacities and actualities. The various self- and object representations of Kate and Richard, visible at moments in their analytic work, do not necessarily reveal special gender identity disturbances in them or in their parents. Instead they illustrate the richness and variety of all self- and object representations, complexities that the concrete sexual dichotomies of development, gender, or transference theories have limited usefulness for appreciating.

At the same time, we believe that clinical psychoanalysis has a singular capacity, as Sedgwick (1990) once hoped, "to introduce a certain becoming amplitude into discussions of what different people are like" (p. 24). Harris (1991) reminds us that "unlinking aim from object and allowing the play of sexual forms and symbolic meanings for bodies, selves, and acts are the radical core of Freud's theory of desire and gender" (p. 201). Musing on the dream of the flute nuts, "something you don't usually see in that form, like cashews in their shells" and watching the "perfect gift" of the amaryllis, we see that the analyst was not able to settle on a monosexual gender identity for either. But the analyst lacked paradigms to support her mental associations. Richard's gift was to be able to envision himself and his analyst and their work together in that shaman. He feared that his analyst would be uncomfortable with his vision and with cross-sex identifications, as he had been. As we undo the gender splits of much developmental theory, we may realize that an aptitude for loving mutual identification in every parent is indeed a developmental gift to the child: a shaman's gift of inner vision that helps a boy feel that he can grow into a subject of desire instead of an asexual worker, a gift of flute nuts that gives a girl confidence that she, too, is a person equipped with agency. As we undo the concrete equating of anatomical sex (of self and of object) with specific psychic functions, we can understand that a homosexual relationship does not by definition indicate distinguishing oedipal dynamics.

Assumptions of sexually split capacities, desires, and objects restrict men as well as women. These genderings make it difficult for sons to identify comfortably with mothers and other women, for fathers to identify comfortably with daughters, and for girls, women, and those in gay and lesbian relationships to see themselves as legitimate subjects of desire. We are all still looking for something better to hold it all.

# 8

# WHEN THE PSYCHOANALYST IS LESBIAN

## "A CERTAIN IDEALIZATION OF HETEROSEXUALITY"

In clinical literature, the analyst's heterosexuality has always been an unmarked, not-necessary-even-to-mention, given. Until recently, if one person in an analytic dyad was homosexual, it was the patient, never the analyst. And as McDougall (1991) has pointed out, even as analysand the patient who is homosexual sometimes is seen as illegitimate:

> Two experienced colleagues, one from Europe, the other from North America, related an almost identical incident. Each had prepared a paper dealing with aspects of homosexuality and illustrated with a clinical case. Both were asked publicly how they justified having taken such people into treatment and why they referred to their work as "analysis" since "homosexuals are not analyzable." Of course, some homosexuals are unanalyzable—and some heterosexuals, too [p. 190].

McDougall suggests that such questions "may be due to a certain idealization of heterosexuality" (p. 190). She cautions analysts to be mindful of their tendency to project onto others their "unanalyzed" parts. "What of our disavowed homosexual, narcissistic, criminal, and megalomanic tendencies?" (p. 178) she asks. McDougall's series, in which "homosexual" is included with narcissistic, criminal, and megalomanic, itself suggests a certain idealization of heterosexuality, and her use of "our" in addressing other analysts assumes that the class of analysts includes only heterosexuals. Her omission of homosexual therapists from the class of analysts is probably understandable, however, given how few gay and lesbian therapists have actually become members of that class.

## Transference Development When the Analyst Is Homosexual

Some analysts will argue that homosexual patients are indeed analyzable, that homosexual therapists can be trained as analysts, and that the whole issue of the therapist's homosexuality is irrelevant. Given the well-elaborated analytic practice of limiting personal disclosures by the therapist, patients need never even know that their analyst is lesbian. Patients would simply assume the analyst to be heterosexual, and transference fantasies and projections could develop and be analyzed.

That position ignores several significant factors. Most analysands know a great deal about their analysts, anonymity notwithstanding. The frequency, regularity, and intimacy of the analytic relationship contribute to the formation of fantasies and to the transference, but they also provide for an accumulation of knowledge about the actual analyst. Day after day, season after season, year after year, patients consciously and unconsciously register the changes in their analyst's office, clothing, moods, levels of attentiveness, qualities of silences. Since every analytic interpretation is also, at some level, a disclosure, patients become finely attuned to what and how their analysts hear, as well as to what and how their analysts avoid hearing (see Frommer, 1994; Renik, 1994; Spezzano, 1994). Freud knew that feelings and knowledge can, and regularly do, pass from the unconscious of one person to the unconscious of the second without entering the consciousness of either. Only denial allows us to take for granted that heterosexual identity or relationship is not only assumed but in many ways disclosed by heterosexual analysts. To give only the most obvious example, personal anonymity would require that analysts who wore wedding rings would remove them during analytic hours and thus avoid disclosing this piece of biographical information. Removing wedding rings is hardly standard psychoanalytic practice. On the contrary, some analysts would be likely to wonder about the feelings of patients who never allowed themselves to look for the presence or absence of a ring on the third finger of their analyst's left hand.

Some lesbian and gay therapists suspect that homosexually identified therapists may use the principle of therapeutic anonymity to defend against their own anxieties about coming out to their patients. They argue that therapists who do not acknowledge their homosexuality can be of little help to their gay and lesbian patients.[1] They argue that homosexual therapists should serve as role models for their homosexual patients and demonstrate by the acknowledgment of their homosexuality their comfort and pride in being gay. But gay and lesbian patients have persons other than their therapist to use as "role models" for self-acceptance. In fact, a patient who reported difficulty finding any valued figures among gay and lesbian persons would be signaling an issue ripe for examination in the treatment.

The issues surrounding therapist disclosure are many and complex and have concerned analytic therapists in a variety of circumstances from pregnancy to terminal illness (Weiss, 1975; Abend, 1982; Dewald, 1982; Fenster, Phillips, and Rapaport, 1986; Alexander et al., 1989; Morrison, 1990, 1997; Schwartz and Silver, 1990; Etchegoyen, 1993; Goldstein, 1994, 1997; Greenberg, 1995; Renik, 1995; Uyehara et al., 1995; Crastnopol, 1997; Chused, 1997). Any disclosure by a therapist—including that of homosexual identification—may function, but does not necessarily function, to short-circuit a fuller exploration of the patient's thoughts and feelings. Any disclosure can be, but does not necessarily have to be, a self-serving enactment in the service of a therapist's anxieties, need for admiration, attention, sympathy, and so on.

Patients may learn from sources other than their analysts about their analysts' homosexuality. Some analysts believe that such a discovery should be seen in the same way as a patient's discovery of other information about the analyst's life—such as that the analyst is or is not married, is divorced, has or does not have children, is or is not a Democrat, is or is not Jewish, likes opera, or goes sailing on vacation. We wish that homosexuality *could* be added to such a list of discoveries, but, unfortunately, in this climate of prejudice and confused thinking about homosexuality, we do not believe that the discovery—by either a lesbian or a heterosexual patient—that the therapist is lesbian is the same as most other discoveries. This discovery will raise greater anxieties and confusions about the analyst's integrity, psychological soundness, competence, and neutrality. It is even more important, therefore, that the particular meanings and significances this information has for the patient be explored and analyzed. We agree in principle with Goldstein (1997) that "therapists should feel free not to self-disclose to patients. . . . [and therapists] have rights to their privacy . . . and limitations about what they can deal with in the therapeutic process at certain times"

(p. 56). Yet, we suspect that in the case of homosexuality the ground rules are different. To help a patient explore her feelings about the knowledge or discovery that her analyst is lesbian, the gay or lesbian analyst must be comfortable confirming the accuracy of the patient's intuition or knowledge. An analyst is not, of course, required to disclose on demand, but if a patient has been willing to disclose feelings, fears, and fantasies about the analyst's homosexuality, a lesbian or gay analyst's refusal to confirm amounts to a denial and will create a breach in the analytic fabric of trust and authenticity, creating an unanalyzable secret sink hole into which all manner of unrelated phenomenon can and probably will fall.

We have never initiated any disclosure about the existence of our relationship to our patients. Neither, however, have we ever denied it. We have tried to understand the feelings and reasons motivating the wish to know and the timing of the questioning, as well as what answer the patient fears/hopes/dreads she will receive to her query. It is usually difficult, of course, to understand the various and ambivalent feelings patients have about their wishes, fears, intuitions, suspicions, or knowledge. We may hear in patients' material what seems to be an awareness of our lesbian identification as well as a reluctance to speak about this awareness. Therapists who have been pregnant (Fenster, Phillips, Rapaport, 1986; Uyehara et al., 1995) have described similar clinical dilemmas—how to respond to those who can perceive and speak of the pregnancy, how to respond to those who reveal in their comments that unconsciously they know their therapist is pregnant but aren't willing or ready yet to acknowledge what they know. We try to use the discovery of our lesbian identity or relationship as analysts try to use all material in analytic treatment. We try to explore with each patient its particular significance and meanings.

### Beth

"I can't talk," was Beth's initial complaint. She was to demonstrate her difficulty repeatedly over the course of the analysis. Although Beth had many good friends, both men and women, she felt hopeless about ever "being able to be with someone." Beth was deeply troubled by her inability to feel connected to her parents, particularly to her mother. She felt somewhat closer to her father but could talk to him only about what she considered superficial subjects. She felt that neither of her parents understood her feelings or her interests. And she admitted that she told them very little. "They feel like strangers to me," she confessed guiltily.

Referred to me (MM) by a gay and lesbian agency, Beth indicated that she wanted to know nothing about my personal life. She had had depressing and unsatisfying lesbian relationships, but, she said, "I don't know for sure what I am." After about six months of treatment, a friend of Beth's, believing that disclosure would please Beth and make it easier for her to talk to me, told her that I was in a lesbian relationship. "You and your therapist are the same. You're lesbians," the friend informed Beth. Although Beth had come to me through a referral from a gay and lesbian agency, she was shocked and disturbed by this information. She did not tell me of her friend's disclosure for many months.

When Beth finally began to discuss her reactions, she said she had felt relieved that I had a relationship. It made her feel hopeful to know I "had someone." She could not bear to think of me as being as lonely and alone as she felt. But at the same time she was also disappointed to learn that I was with a woman, although she was ashamed of these feelings and worried about telling me. Discovering my relationship also made certain feelings more frightening. If she felt strongly attached to me and if I was lesbian, did that mean she was lesbian? Although she longed to feel "connected" to a woman with whom she could identify, Beth was not sure she wanted to feel attached to or identify with a lesbian woman. Moreover, she worried whether she would be able to explore her own sexual feelings with me, if they did not involve women. Would I be angry and reject her for such thoughts and fears? Would she still feel close to me?

Beth, who found it agonizingly difficult to speak to me about anything, could not speak about these complicated feelings. She told me so little and hid so much that I did not notice her further withdrawal after her friend's disclosure. My not noticing frightened her, giving her as it did more evidence of my limitations. I was a "stranger" parent who would not understand her. Far from relieving this patient, as her friend had hoped, the disclosure set in motion complicated and disturbing transference responses, which had to be carefully untangled. On the other hand, the unsought disclosure did precipitate Beth's bringing directly into the analytic relationship some early experiences of self and object loss.

It took Beth a long time to be able to use the couch, and, even after lying down, for many months she kept one foot on the floor, a visible brake against a frightening regression. Beth feared that if she talked to me and told me of her feelings, if she took off the brakes and let herself go in the analytic relationship, she would be devastated. She *knew* I would become angry and send her away, and she kept trying to avoid that moment she was certain would come.

Beth began to establish in many sessions a frustrating kind of connection. Apparently awake and alert, Beth would lay motionless and silent. She could maintain this position through several sessions. She insisted at these times that she could not talk or that she had no thoughts or feelings to talk about. Sometimes I tried simply to sit quietly and wait for Beth to move or to speak, a position I found comfortable with other patients and with Beth herself at other times. In these particular sessions, however, in spite of consultation and continued self-supervision, I frequently could not remain comfortably still and silent. I felt Beth's controlled stillness, her refusal to speak, her mental alertness coupled with her refusal to acknowledge thoughts and feelings as provocative. I felt a pressure to insist that, in spite of what she maintained, a silent, motionless body and a mind with no feelings and thoughts were problems. If I spoke about these things, Beth only deepened her silence and somehow managed to increase her uncanny physical stillness, and I would then feel even more frustration. When I did manage to keep to my resolve to remain silent until she spoke, I felt the punitive withholding of my own silence. On the few occasions when I managed to remain quiet and comfortable because I lost myself in my own thoughts, Beth suddenly got up from the couch and left. She seemed to prefer, or need, the sessions in which I could not contain my frustration and in which my comments amounted to verbal jabs at her mute inertness. Those sessions left her apparently unscathed, and she sometimes even reported feeling energized and "more alive" because of them.

What was happening in this intensely enacted transference–countertransference? Did Beth's mindless, wordless, feelingless presentation demonstrate a determination or wish to fuse with an early maternal object? I did not feel that sleepy, hypnotized state I usually equated with pressures for fusion, nor did Beth's alertness suggest that she had regressed to being at one with her object. Why couldn't I let her be? Why did I have so many urges to poke at her and find out what was going on? Was she projecting her own desires to get inside me? Had Beth's regression in the analysis brought us to the "basic fault" of her developmental history, the pathological preoedipal, sadomasochistic object relations that Jones, Deutsch, Socarides, McDougall, and others, have discussed as influential in female homosexuality?

I would wonder aloud to Beth, when we experienced one of these recurrent episodes, why she needed such a sharp, attacking object. Beth finally told about the slivers of glass she sometimes used to cut herself with and to bring herself out of what she called her "zombie state." Gradually she revealed other behaviors that she feared were life threatening or at least self-destructive. She watched movies with sadistic images and got high on cocaine, all the time fearing she would have a heart attack. In various other ways she recklessly endangered her body. Her behavior frightened her, and yet she could not stop. She had hoped never to have to tell me about these things. Although I still hated the sessions in which I struggled against becoming the sharp object that "would bring Beth to her senses" and to her feelings, now at least I had some way of understanding my sadistic countertransference urges. Sharp objects, the risk of death and pain, although frightening, brought Beth back to her senses when she felt like a "zombie," when she had lost her feelings. What appeared to be masochism was a strategy for restoring and focusing feeling. It was better to be alive and frightened than a numbed zombie. But what set off the dissociated states in the first place? Beth could say nothing about this matter.

One day near the office Beth had a panic attack when she saw Diana and me in a car together. On another occasion, when she met Diana on the stairs of the office building, Beth ran out of the building and down the street in fright. Beth was ashamed of the intensity of her own reactions at these moments and was confused about their meanings. I too was confused, since Beth spoke so little about her feelings about me. Was Beth's panicked response to meeting Diana evidence of "negative oedipal" feelings in the transference? The negative oedipus complex was one psychoanalytic formulation of female homosexual development. But was I even allowed to consider that Beth was using Diana and me as a transferential parental couple? Could a same-sex relationship be used in this way for transference creation? Nothing in my reading or training had suggested such possibilities, but something was happening in the transference that seemed to concern Beth's unconscious fantasies in response to seeing me and my partner.

Beth had been openly resistant to describing her history, her family, her dreams. As our analytic relationship became increasingly intense, confusing, and disturbing, Beth became more motivated to understand what was happening between us and what, if anything, of her early history and object relations she might be unconsciously reenacting with me. We discovered, when she was ready and able to look, some hints about one set of object relationships that were being replicated in the transference.

Beth's first experience of attachment had been shaped by two caretakers. Her maternal grandmother had lived with Beth's parents for the first seven months of Beth's life. Beth had been told that her grandmother had undertaken most of her early care and had been the only one able to calm and comfort her through colic and early sleep difficulties. When her grandmother moved out of the family home, the loss of an experienced maternal object, the calming grandmother, may have been traumatic for the seven-month-old child. Beth may have felt left with a "stranger" mother with whom she did not feel connected and who herself could not feel well-enough connected to her child.

Trying to understand her childhood, Beth searched the family photo albums for clues. In early photographs, Beth is staring at the camera, a depressed and anxious child, sometimes alone, sometimes awkwardly holding a younger sibling. In one photograph Beth's smiling mother is arm and arm with Beth's older cousin. Three-year-old Beth stands at a distance from that easy twosome. She is frowning, and her whole body is stiff and tense. Beth had no memory of these moments in the photographs, but she said that the first thing she can ever remember is "feeling that I was going to die." She had had panic attacks in childhood and had been terrified of funeral homes and cemeteries.

During her latency years, Beth frequently spent weekends at her maternal grandmother's home. Nights were always terrifying. She could not sleep without the pillow that she quite consciously identified with her grandmother. When the pillow started to lose its feathers, Beth felt the terror and anguish she had felt as an adolescent when her grandmother moved again, this time out of state.

Beth's grandmother had died the summer before Beth entered treatment, but I did not know this important piece of Beth's history and therefore could not understand its role in her seeking treatment until after the analysis had ended. When Beth read this case description, she corrected my misconception that her grandmother had died when she was a teenager. Perhaps my confusion was related to Beth's own confusion about the timing of the loss, an early traumatic separation that had repeated, each weekend, and again in adolescence, and that she feared would repeat again if she ever allowed herself to feel so connected and dependent on another person.

We were able to relieve some of Beth's overdetermined fear of dying, some of her night terrors, her terror and depressions at separations, her profoundly melancholy identification with her grandmother, her longing to be reunited with her, and her fears that she would be so united through death. Beth dissociated to protect herself against the fear of overwhelming longing for an object lost too early and the equally strong fear of abandonment that felt like death. As treatment progressed, we became able to predict when we would have one of our "terrible sessions." Every step Beth took toward attachment to objects, human or otherwise, would set off the zombie states, states that, as the analysis developed, might prompt Beth to turn me into a sharp, alerting object. As we worked and reworked our understandings, Beth stopped cutting herself and stopped her destructive, risky behavior. Gradually our "terrible sessions" decreased and finally ended.

So let us turn again to Beth's panic upon seeing Diana and me in a car and her startled flight after meeting Diana on the stairs. We might imagine that Beth's anxiety in that moment is similar to the "stranger anxiety" a six- or seven-month-old child may display suddenly toward a person other than the mother, sometimes even toward her father. Gaddini (1976) has described some of the dynamics of early stranger anxiety and the establishment of the first external object. He emphasizes the importance of the child's early illusion of self-omnipotence and the child's ability to imitate that experience in fantasy. This self-assuring ability allows the child to withdraw from instinctual external stimuli when they become too painful. "When he withdraws, he is able to hallucinate a bodily experience which satisfies him and which, although created omnipotently in fantasy by himself to compensate for an unsatisfactory one, is an imitative attempt to repeat a kind of satisfaction which he in fact has previously experienced" (p. 398). But a new stage follows that, for a variety of reasons, can be experienced traumatically:

> Dependence on the external object exposes the child to the loss of self omnipotence. It is the object, then, that acquires the most powerful and threatening omnipotence. This anxiety is mainly self-centered, and seems mainly concerned with self-loss. . . . Object dependencies exposes the child to the fear that the object is not stable enough, that it can be lost, and that the self will not survive [pp. 398].

Analyzing Beth's responses to those meetings helped us reconstruct a jarring premature presence of a first "external object," which in Beth's case was probably not her father, but her mother. Beth had had an early traumatic experience "that the object is not stable enough, that it can be lost, and that the self will not survive." She had lost her grandmother, the calming object. She had barely survived, was in a zombie state. One of the reasons Beth had been pleased to hear that I had a partner was that she did not want me to feel as without an object as she felt. But at the same time she did not want to know I was with a woman because, in one aspect of the transference I was her grandmother. If another woman appeared, I would go away. And, if she lost me, she feared she herself might die.

Later in treatment Beth reported that she had also sometimes felt excited by seeing Diana and me together. She imagined Diana was more physically active than I was and that Diana enjoyed some of the athletic pastimes that Beth herself liked. She sometimes imagined us together in various circumstances, including imagining us as sexual partners. Beth had had similar fantasies when she lived for a time with her cousin and his wife. Although she felt calmer and "better" when she could create these imaginary scenes, she was frightened by such fantasies and ashamed for thinking about me "that way." Beth's unexpected meetings with a transferential parental couple may have made her feel as though she was being suddenly surprised in the midst of secret sexual fantasies.

Beth's fantasies set me a task that would be commonplace for a heterosexual analyst. To interpret Beth's fantasies, I had to see myself functioning in the transference fantasies as a beloved and admired member of a loving and sexual parental couple. Nothing in the analytic literature offered me any theoretical support to make this interpretation, and much in the analytic literature would have found such a transference interpretation impossibly repugnant. Can a lesbian relationship serve as the object of heterosexual parental transference? The question is similar to the one Hollywood film-makers began to ask in 1997 when TV star Ellen DeGeneres came out as lesbian and her girlfriend, Anne Heche, also came out. Would Heche continue to be able to play the lead in heterosexual love stories? Would audiences "believe" her in the role? Rock Hudson had been able to have a career as a heterosexual romantic lead throughout his lifetime because his homosexuality remained hidden. The question goes to the heart of the intensity of feelings about homosexuality. Male analysts are expected to be able to serve as objects of early maternal transference, female analysts as objects of paternal transference, although, as we discussed in Chapter 7, psychoanalytic literature is silent about a female analyst's serving as the object of early paternal transference.

In spite of the lack of theoretical support for my interpretation, I suggested to Beth that she was using her fantasy of my relationship, as she had her fantasy of her cousin's marriage, to imagine two persons loving each other and living together. I said that she sometimes imagined herself as a child of these parental couples and that through these fantasies she could identify with these figures and could imagine that someday she too would share her life with another. When Beth found this interpretation relieving, I could then interpret her longing for parents she could talk to, who could identify with her and welcome her identification with them. But where was the envy supposedly so much a consequence of the child's awareness of a parental relationship from which the child was forever excluded? Was Beth's homosexuality serving as a defense against that envy? Or did I need to understand other oedipal arrangements? For a child who felt her parents as strangers, the sense of feeling connected in fantasy and in identification to parental figures who had their own loving relationship was not disturbing but comforting.

The termination phase was a time of much integration for Beth. She realized that, although she felt great sadness at our parting, she would not die from this separation and, in fact, felt hopeful that someday she would be able to find someone to love and to "be with." Months after the analysis had ended we met to discuss this case description. Beth described her new lesbian relationship. "Sometimes I get with her like I was with you, not talking, going away, but we get through it. It's slow, but it's getting better and better."

As the work with Beth illustrates, neither analyst disclosure nor nondisclosure determines what is therapeutic. The establishment of an analytic relationship and the maintenance of a secure and reliable analytic frame *that fits and works for the two persons engaged in the analysis* allow the development and analysis of transference of unconscious but influential object relations.

To allow for the creative construction of transferences, we attempt to allow patients to choose their own ways to use us in their transference projects. Each patient makes different choices about how to use us and how to respond to what she discovers or imagines about us. As analytic therapists we have shifting functions in an asymmetrical and intersubjective encounter. We reflect and observe, but never "objectively," outside the encounter. We try to serve as "containers" and namers of feelings that patients find difficult to hold and represent. We are "objects" that patients use in various ways to create the arrangements of their internal world, so that both patient and therapist, as subjects, can observe, experience, and understand more fully these arrangements. Patients find what they need and use what they find to construct their dilemmas in the analytic playground.

## Narcissistic Issues When the Analyst Is Lesbian

Beth had not wanted to bring into the analysis her discovery of her analyst's lesbian relationship. As well as being consciously disappointed by this information and worried about its effect on her own identity, Beth had also avoided acknowledging her discovery as a way of defending against the establishment of a particular early transference relationship and its terrors. Some patients will have information about their therapists even before treatment begins. That information has played its part in the patient's choice of therapist, although those motivations may not be conscious. Married analysts whose patients know they are married will explore the wishes and fears connected with such knowledge and observe any reluctance their patients may have to acknowledge what they know about the therapist's life and how they feel about their knowledge. Similar clinical issues arise in treatment when the analyst is lesbian. When it is clear that the patient has this information from the beginning, its meanings to the patient must be examined.

## Rita

Rita knew of my relationship and had even read some of my publications before coming to me (DCM) for analysis. Since she had not been specifically referred to me and did not identify as being interested in issues of homosexuality, why, I asked, when she could have chosen many analysts, did she choose me? Why did she specifically go to an analyst she knew to be lesbian? Rita claimed that my lesbian identity was an issue of no significance in her choice. Although I knew it must have significance, I had no choice but to await developments. When the treatment came to a sudden, premature, and unsatisfying end, at least one of Rita's motivations for choosing me became clearer: As a way of protecting her own narcissistic vulnerabilities, Rita had picked a woman therapist toward whom she felt superior. In her mind, my homosexuality devalued me as a person and as a therapist. Since I was lesbian, I could never be a person of enough value to threaten her worth, nor of enough importance that it would cost her to lose me. Unfortunately, in the same way, I could not be or become an object of enough value to help her.

## Paula

Paula's treatment illustrates another patient's ability to use her therapist's homosexuality to address and repair narcissistic issues. Paula's perfect marriage of several decades had been brought to an unexpected end by her husband's sudden death. For several years we had been examining her difficulty mourning, her worries about her children, as well as her pleasure in discovering abilities in herself that her marriage had never afforded opportunities to experience. When she became interested in dating again, she discovered that she was critical and ashamed of a man she was seeing. Disturbed by her own criticalness, she kept projecting it onto her friends' opinions of the man, although the projections would not hold. They all liked him.

One day Paula came to session extremely anxious. She was so nervous that she was barely able to speak, but finally she said, "I believe I know something about you. I must tell you. I've tried not to, but I must. I am afraid that if it is not true, and I tell you, it will hurt you terribly; and if it is true, I will not want to see you anymore." She then told me (MM) that she thought I was "with a woman," and she thought she knew who the woman was. She named my partner.

Paula was always irritated if I asked her how she felt about a given subject. She disdained such comments as "Rogerian" deflections away from her problems and as time-wasting, stalling maneuvers on my part. "I *know* what I feel!" she would point out impatiently. "What am I going to *do* about it?" Her irritated protests did not always dissuade me from offering my comments, but at this moment I knew that any comment about Paula's obvious feelings would have indeed been a deflection away from the problem before us and would have been defensive, stalling maneuvers on my part. Paula and I had arrived at a very significant moment in the treatment. She was confronting me with a piece of information that, if I confirmed its accuracy, might mean she would reject me and leave treatment. Paula watched me with intense interest and anxiety as she told me that she had by chance recently seen me waiting in a concert line with another woman. An observant and intelligent woman, Paula had allowed herself to become aware of the possible nature of the relationship she was observing. Paula watched me with dread as she confronted me with something about myself that was certainly seen as less than perfect. I said something to that effect to her and thereby acknowledged the accuracy of her observation.

Paula cried bitterly. She told me that she feared she could no longer be in treatment with me. Since I was "with a woman," she felt I would not be able to help her with her "feelings about finding a man." Even as she expressed these quite real fears, she felt their palpable irrationality, since just previously she had been feeling greatly helped by me toward this desire. My *being* homosexual had not been detrimental to her treatment; her *discovering* my relationship was the problem.

Paula did stay in treatment, but to do so she had to come to terms with her great disappointment in me. As a woman who valued her own integrity and honesty, Paula looked carefully at what a struggle it was for her to "keep" me once she had discovered my "flaw." Paula was experimenting in the transference with keeping a relationship with a person she found flawed, although otherwise sustaining. She hated acknowledging her feelings about my homosexuality and was ashamed to realize their strength.

Certainly this patient could have used many things about me to do this particular piece of her own work, but she had found, by chance and by observation, that aspect of her therapist most useful to her at that moment to explore her own dynamics and dilemmas. She experimented first by observing me as I handled the projections and the realities. Together we could use this experience to understand more fully the anxieties about some

of the "closets" she had inhabited in her life, her shame about their contents, and her sadness for the insecurities that had created a need for such
secrets. Working through the transference with me, the flawed but valued
object, helped her live in greater peace with herself, and helped her choose
to marry the man she deeply loved but who also had some human and visible imperfections.

This would not, of course, be the experience of all patients. Some might
have similar feelings but different issues about such a discovery. Some might
leave treatment or, worse, stay in treatment but with disappointments and
anxieties that went unvoiced and unexamined. Many homosexual or heterosexual patients would never knowingly choose to see a lesbian therapist,
but those who, knowingly or not, have found their ways to us have educated us in the variety of ways that transference can be created and transferential parental couples constructed. Their work provides continuing
illustrations of the human psyche's ability to use what is at hand for its own
repair. To close this chapter, we offer one more example from the case of
Ann from Chapter 2.

## Ann

As Ann became more involved with the lesbian groups in her area, she
began to do volunteer work. One day, while doing some office work for a
lesbian organization, she found my name on its mailing list. "What's going
on here?" she asked. As Ann explored her feelings about finding my name
on the list, it became apparent that Ann's question, like Paula's statement,
also prompted by a chance occurrence, was her way of trying to understand
something of her own life by constructing it in the transference. Her mother
had seemed to Ann an almost asexual person, without any intimate relationships. In the transference, I had been that mother, devoid of other relationships, existing only with Ann. Her father's sexuality and relationships
were also a mystery. What little information she had about him had been
provided by her grandmother and mother, but she knew they disliked him,
and, although she did not know why, they distrusted him sexually. She had
only one memory of ever being alone with her father, on a walk to a store.
When he died, she and her mother went to his home to pack up his furni-
ture. Left alone for a few moments by chance in his bedroom, she felt that
she had only a final few moments in which to try to understand her father.
Looking through his belongings, she saw some sex magazines by his bed.
"What's going on here?" was the question Ann came to understand she was
asking about the sexuality of both her father and her mother, and she felt
she had had to understand each of them and their brief relationship together

through bits and pieces of puzzling clues, such as sex magazines by a bed, and in the transference, my name on a lesbian organization's mailing list.

In many ways there is nothing particularly unusual or unique about these moments of analytic treatment with Ann, Beth, and Paula. This is the stuff of daily life in an analytic practice: patient and therapist exploring together the meanings and sources of the patient's thoughts and feelings about many matters, including fantasies about and actual experiences with the therapist. In the next and final chapter, descriptions of some of our experiences during psychoanalytic training and a brief history of psychoanalytic training institutes' policies about admitting homosexual candidates provide background for why it has been necessary to demonstrate that an analyst known to have a lesbian relationship can serve as a useful object for the construction of transference and its interpretation.

# 9

# HOMOSEXUALITY AND PSYCHOANALYTIC TRAINING

You can get it if you really want,
But you must try, try and try, try and try
You'll succeed at last.

[Jimmy Cliff, 1972]

In 1934 H.D. left Vienna, worried about Freud's remaining in a city in which she had seen swastikas painted on the sidewalks on her way to her analytic appointments. H.D.'s *Tribute to Freud* (Doolittle, 1956) contains some of Freud's letters to her. He wrote of his love for his dogs, his interest in her and in Bryher, and his pleasure in her gifts, including the flowers she sent him in England on his 80th birthday.

> I had imagined I had become insensitive to praise and blame. Reading your kind lines and getting aware of how I enjoyed them I first thought I had been mistaken about my firmness. Yet on second thoughts I concluded I was not. What you gave me, was not praise, was affection and I need not be ashamed of my satisfaction.
> Life at my age is not easy, but spring is beautiful and so is love.
>
> Yours affectionately
> Freud [p. 179].

This short communication from analyst to ex-patient contains what has been too often missing in psychoanalytic history and treatment: *shared identifications between heterosexual analyst and lesbian patient*. Freud shared H.D.'s love of the myths and antiquities of classical Greece. H.D. had read Freud's work; he had read hers. Freud and H.D. shared an appreciation of the world's beauty and longings for affectionate regard and respectful recognition. Bryher had been equally fortunate in her choice of analyst. She and Sachs shared a love of reading, Shakespeare, the Elizabethans, film making, and psychoanalysis.

Elisabeth Young-Bruehl, the biographer of Anna Freud, has described a biographer's need for empathy for her subject, including "empathy-to-difference." Young-Bruehl (1992) reports coming to a "screeching halt" when in one of Anna Freud's letters she read the following comment concerning a homosexual applicant for training: "I know from past experience that it is no good for any kind of course, or any kind of institution, to permit people with sexual abnormalities." Young-Bruehl writes: "I hated this sentence, for myself, and for all homosexuals who have had to endure psychoanalytic intolerance and pathologization. I continued to hate it until, many months later, I found Anna Freud's unpublished clinical reflections on male homosexuality and began to understand what that sentence meant to her, how it protected her, how it represented her" (p.10).

Anna Freud's statement also so thoroughly represented the policies and practices of psychoanalytic institutes that, more than 50 years after Bryher and Sachs and H.D. and Freud had their shared analytic adventures, Stoller (1985) could still write:

> The passing years, with their burden of more clinical knowledge, have, I fear, shown that we analysts have not done well in trying to understand homosexuality. In fact, we have been as inept as we were before correcting the matter in our theories of the development of females and femininity. . . .
>
> Is it improper to suggest that some analysts' problems in understanding homosexuality have—to put it delicately—psychodynamic roots? That would tell me, as the more rational explanations do not, why we have by-laws against accepting homosexuals as candidates, members of the faculty, or supervising and training analysts. The justification for such regulations is our "knowing" that these people must, by definition, be as alleged: fatally flawed psychoticlike creatures in states of near-annihilation of the self (covered over, of course, by normal-appearing behavior) [ pp. 181–3].[1]

## Lesbian Candidates in Psychoanalytic Training in the 1980s

When we applied for psychoanalytic training in 1984, the American Psychoanalytic Association was in the midst of being sued in U.S. Federal

Court for restraint of trade due to its policy and practice of refusing to admit nonmedical therapists.[2] As a nonmedical therapist open about her lesbian relationship, it seemed highly unlikely that Maggie would be admitted to any American Psychoanalytic Association-affiliated institute. Diana, with a medical degree and residencies in both adult and child psychiatry, considered applying to a local American-affiliated institute where her analyst was a training analyst. She was cautioned by various members of the analytic community, including her analyst, that our relationship was too well known for Diana to be admitted. "There are some who would be quite willing to admit you," he said, "but others will prevent that." Some colleagues urged her to apply. If she was rejected, her case could help establish the pattern and practice of discrimination in the American Psychoanalytic Association. Diana did not want to be a legal case statistic; she wanted to be a psychoanalyst. Fortunately, other area psychoanalytic institutes were not affiliated with the American. Diana applied to a newly established, multidisciplined institute. During her application process, Diana and that institute followed a practice later made familiar by the U. S. Department of Defense: "Don't ask; don't tell." She did not mention our relationship in her written application, and she was not asked in oral interviews about her personal relationship. Maggie applied to another, better established, multidisciplined institute. She stated in both her written application and oral interviews that she was in a longstanding lesbian relationship, which she had no intention of leaving. "Oh, well, you haven't decided yet," commented a senior training analyst interviewing her for admission. He apparently hoped and expected that Maggie, through her training analysis, would decide to leave her relationship.

During our first year of candidacy, we "came out" to our classmates. During our training, we attended social events and conferences at both institutes. We made friends among our fellow candidates and generally felt accepted on the basis of our abilities and our work by teachers and supervisors. Upon completion of our training, we both became members of our respective institutes. We owe much to many courageous analysts who chose to admit us to training and were willing to teach and supervise us and admit us to membership in their societies.[3]

During our training, however, we could not avoid noticing in published writing, in conference presentations, and in seminar discussions the anxiety and ignorance many analysts demonstrated about homosexuality and the unconscious alienation that many analysts had toward gay and lesbian persons. For example, when we attended our first major psychoanalytic conference in 1985, we heard speaker after speaker in a packed auditorium refer to their homosexual patients as "perverts." During those presentations we felt dizzy and nauseous. Were we nauseous because, being perverts, we were obviously defending against psychoanalytic understanding of our disorder? Like April Martin (1995), we often "felt ill equipped" to enter into intellectual debates about homosexuality. Like Martin, we felt ill equipped to answer such questions as, "Don't be offended, but . . . how do you know you *don't* have a disorder" (p. 258)? Was the conference too advanced for our level of our training? Was our current mental and emotional disorganization evidence of what McDougall (1980) calls:

> a nexus of character traits which affected most of my patients, and which I have also noted in clinical writings by other analysts. Unless compensated by meticulous reaction formations these patients tend to display an inability to organize their lives in even the smallest details. Some of them seemed to live in the midst of disorder and confusion to a punitive degree. The inability to work constructively, or even in some cases to arrange papers, pack a suitcase, or make a decision, exemplified the fear that independent ego activity is dangerous [p. 116].

Or were we sick with fear as we realized the cognitive and emotional distances between ourselves and others at this conference and overwhelmed at the task of bridging such distances?

Many colleagues were surprised that we were not enthusiastic about McDougall's writing. She had a reputation among feminist analysts for being "liberal" about homosexuality. McDougall (1980, 1985) criticizes psychoanalysts for having narrow definitions of perversion. "What acts do we designate as 'perverse'? Who is a 'pervert'? One might well reply that everyone knows the answer: a pervert is someone who does not make love like everyone else. . . . To concentrate uniquely on a patient's sexuality is an artificial approach that ignores the rest of the personality" (1985, pp. 245–246).

But aspects of McDougall's thinking gave us, and other lesbian therapists, considerable pause. In her formulations about female homosexuality, McDougall did indeed concentrate on the patient's sexuality, and she ascribed to lesbian patients the psychological characteristics—immature superego development, ego impairment ("crippled," "paralyzed" ego functions), narcissistic preoccupation—that she and others had previously argued had been falsely defined as characteristics of normal female psychology. In spite of her own cautions to others:—"It is hardly justifiable to label the sexual deviant according to his or her sexual practice alone, even if this act is considered a symptom. (Would we say of someone unable to sleep like everybody else, 'Bah, he's an insomniac, you know'!" (p. 246)— and in spite of her own warnings to speak of "homosexualities" instead of "homosexuality," McDougall repeatedly defined what she believed to be psychological differences between "homosexuals" and "heterosexuals" and repeatedly elaborated the psychic "situation" of "the homosexual."

> In homosexual men and women, we find a family romance of a specific kind, and one which needs to be carefully analyzed if we are to understand the personality structure which results and the role of homosexual objects in the psychic economy. In addition, therefore, to corresponding factors in ego structure and in the defense mechanisms used to maintain its precarious equilibrium, there is a striking similarity in the way in which these patients present their parents. My female homosexual patients might all have been of the same family, so much did the parental portraits resemble one another. My own clinical observations have been amply confirmed by the findings of other analytic writers on this subject, in particular Deutsch (1932, 1944–45), Socarides (1968), and Rosen (1964) [McDougall, 1980, pp. 94–95].[4]

McDougall maintains that homosexual relationships contain "to a greater extent than heterosexual ones, a hidden dimension of envy," that "the homosexual situation is inevitably precarious," and that homosexuality is a "sexual identity that disavows sexual reality and masks inner feelings of deadness." She sees homosexuals as belonging to a category of persons neither neurotic nor psychotic, a group she calls "third structure" persons in which she also includes patients with addictions, antisocial symptoms, and certain psychosomatic conditions. Homosexuality is, finally, a defense against psychosis: "The homosexual pays dearly for this fragile identity, heavily weighted as it is with frustrated libidinal, sadistic, and narcissistic significance. But the alternative is the death of the ego" (p. 138). She does not confine herself to describing the problems of her four homosexual patients but repeatedly generalizes her observations to all lesbian women: "What is more specific for homosexual women is the pathological introjection of the father figure and the erotization of defenses against the depressive and persecutory anxieties that result from these distorted structures" (p. 135).

McDougall's reputation for being liberal about homosexuality was bolstered among many feminist psychoanalysts by her 1986 article, in which she described her countertransference envy of a woman patient's relationship with her mother. "Our homosexual libido serves first of all to enrich and stabilize our narcissistic self-image. . . . The homosexual investment, usually divested of its conscious sexual aim, gives warmth and richness to the affectionate and essential friendships we maintain with other women."

(pp. 221–222). But McDougall was clearly writing for heterosexual women analysts and was intentionally "leaving aside the question of manifest homosexuality, with which I have dealt extensively elsewhere" (p. 222). Homosexuality in heterosexual women could be narcissistically, intellectually, maternally, and creatively enhancing. Homosexuality in other women was another matter. In 1989 McDougall published new clinical material, the case of Benedicte, in which she offered additional clinical support for her theory that paternal identifications contributed to the formation of female homosexuality. In this article she distinguishes between transsexuals, who "disavowed and rendered meaningless their biological sex," and homosexuals; she calls homosexuality "a deviation in gender identity."

"Gender identity" became during the 1980s a hot-button psychoanalytic topic, frequently a code word for discussions of homosexuality. For instance, at a local analytic conference on "Gender Identity Disorder," the clinical material presented to illustrate the topic was the analytic treatment of an adolescent boy who was homosexual. During the treatment, the analyst had arranged a female sexual surrogate for his young patient, hoping in this way to help him become heterosexual. The analyst's willingness to acknowledge this countertransference-based departure from analytic practice was perhaps laudatory, but, when he read excerpts from a letter the patient had written several years after termination, he seemed unaware that the patient, then in his 20s, was still trying to help his analyst understand his homosexuality.

Teresa DeCrescenzo, a lesbian social worker who worked with gay street adolescents and children, questioned the conference's assumption that homosexuality was synonymous with a "gender identity disturbance." Although we agreed with her comments, we did not speak up at that conference. Many therapist/parents in the audience asked how to "prevent" homosexuality. During a coffee break, a woman colleague told us that at her son's preschool the children sometimes dressed up in costumes. Should she be worried about the effect of such play on his gender identity? We did not know how to frame responses to such a question, confounded as it was by anxious conflating of homosexuality, cross-dressing, and gender identity disturbance. In moments such as these, we were acutely aware of the enormous chasm between many heterosexual analysts and their homosexual colleagues, friends, and patients, a chasm invisible to many heterosexual persons, but painfully apparent to those homosexually identified. How were we to bring attention to the existence of this chasm without creating on all sides more anxiety and further alienation?

In a clinical seminar, a candidate described a new patient who had just called for an appointment. The patient had identified himself as gay and said he wanted to become a rabbi. He complained bitterly about the prohibitions against homosexuals' obtaining rabbinical training and about what he saw as the moral hypocrisy of some of the rabbinical elders, who refused him admission when they learned of his homosexuality. He devalued his rabbi, who had been his mentor until he disclosed his homosexuality, and complained that the rabbi, too, was corrupt.

The seminar leader, a well-known and beloved senior analyst, immediately began to describe the patient's dynamics. "Amazing! A homosexual who wants to be a rabbi!" He compared the patient to a "double agent who wants to spy for both sides." He pointed out that the patient's desire for rabbinical training demonstrated his attempt to deal with his oedipal rivalry with the father by contemptuously *becoming* the father instead of *becoming like* the father.

Maggie, a member of the seminar, was struck by the swiftness of this assessment. Where, in the material so far presented, was there evidence that the man wanted to "become" the father rather than "become like" the father? Certainly the patient sounded both irritable and irritating. But was irritable contempt a characteristic that distinguished homosexual would-be rabbis from others? Were heterosexual rabbinical candidates never contemptuous, defensively or otherwise, of their fathers and teachers?

Unlike the seminar leader, Maggie could not so easily distance from this patient. The necessity that she must mentally register one shared identification with the patient prompted her to consider another trial identification: the similarities between psychoanalytic candidates and rabbinical students. She knew the history of psychoanalytic institutes and homosexual applicants. She followed in the national press the conflicts over ordaining gay and lesbian ministers or rabbis and over allowing homosexual ministers or rabbis to perform services or head congregations. Did she herself want to become an analyst because she wanted to *become* the father (or mother?) rather than *becoming like* the father (mother)? Did the fact that she was in a lesbian relationship make her motivations for seeking training categorically different from those of the other members of the seminar? She and her fellow candidates sometimes complained about various inadequacies they perceived in some of their analytic elders. They had even wondered occasionally if analytic institutes weren't in curriculum and structure somewhat like sectarian schools of theology, headed by special priestly classes of training analysts. She and some of her fellow candidates had ruefully remarked upon their frustrated wishes for more ideal institutes and more ideal analytic teachers.

A woman candidate in the seminar suggested that the patient's irritating tone might be the result of his fear that he was unlovable and may reflect his despair about ever being found acceptable. She was suggesting that projective processes might be at work in the patient–therapist interchange. But the emotional distancing of the seminar leader from the patient had been instant, thorough, and apparently unconscious. He began to discuss female homosexuality. He jokingly assured the class that any lesbian patient who came to him for treatment would go away cured, because she would fall in love with him in the transference. He compared lesbians to Salome: just as Salome had taken revenge against John the Baptist by having his head cut off, lesbians take revenge for not having penises by wanting to castrate men.

Maggie's lesbian relationship was known to all the candidates in the seminar. Her presence during his comments created increasing tension in the seminar. Maggie suggested to the seminar leader that there did not necessarily need to be a pathological motivation behind the patient's desire to be a rabbi. With a kind of courtly grace, the senior analyst responded that it might be difficult for her, a beginning candidate, to understand the situation. He explained that homosexuals were unconsciously conflicted; their complaints about exclusion were externalizations of their own internal conflicts. Homosexuals acted out their internal pathology in various ways, such as applying for rabbinical training and then complaining when they were rejected. Sensing that she was not in full agreement with his comments, he moved to articulate a position that he felt confident she could share. "At least you will agree," he said, "that those who have not achieved heterosexuality are not psychologically mature enough to manage the requirements of such training."

Maggie's situation at that moment was not an unusual one for those in lesbian relationships. She had significant information about herself that another person did not have. She and the other seminar members understood that the seminar leader assumed her to be heterosexual; otherwise, he would not have made any of these statements in her presence. He would never have so freely associated aloud about his ideas about lesbians. Unless one is consciously and intentionally a racist, a racial slur is not knowingly made in the presence of those who might object to such remarks. Unless one is consciously and proudly anti-Semitic, an anti-Jewish statement is not made to a Jewish colleague. But when speakers are ignorant of the composition of their audience, some listeners will be faced with peculiar decisions. One must decide, and quickly, which response—silence or disclosure—will, at this moment, be more honest? Which response—silence or disclosure—will be more helpful, more hostile?

At the beginning of the discussion, Maggie had remained silent, hoping the seminar leader would change the subject or that the comments of others might shift the discussion. She could keep silent now, particularly since she had just been asked to agree that rabbinical training can be accomplished only by those who have "achieved heterosexuality." The seminar leader was the analyst of some of her colleagues, some of whom were present. Did that increase her responsibility for trying to prevent his continuing in this manner? What about her own relationship with the seminar leader? If that was ever to have any authenticity, could she knowingly allow him to continue as the only one in the room without essential information? At the same time, however, she knew there was no way to give him that information without causing him, at least momentarily, shock or embarrassment. Aware of her own rising anxiety, the mounting tension in the seminar, and the consequences both of keeping silent and of speaking, Maggie said, "I am undertaking psychoanalytic training, and I am in a lesbian relationship."

Immediately the seminar leader, who was sitting beside her, turned away and began talking to another candidate about a topic unrelated to the case or any of the issues at hand. In a few moments he suggested the group take its coffee break, during which he confided with great distress to another candidate, "I never would have said those things had I known she was a lesbian!"

The seminar leader was understandably shocked. He had never expected to have a lesbian candidate in his psychoanalytic seminar. There had never been homosexual candidates present in his seminars, or at least there had not been any present who had identified themselves. He felt comfortable, therefore, in the seminar room making statements about homosexual persons he would never have made in their presence.

Maggie knew she had been too anxious and angry to be articulate and that others had been anxious witnessing her exchange with the seminar leader. She wrote some of her thoughts about the session to the seminar members and suggested that they all read together "Problems with the Term 'Homosexuality'" and "Psychoanalytic Research on 'Homosexuality': The Rules of the Game," two chapters from Stoller (1985). The seminar leader began the next session by inviting discussion of Maggie's letter and Stoller's articles. That discussion was probably unsatisfying to everyone. Some feared that Maggie wanted to censor free speech about homosexuality, to permit only those words and those thoughts deemed acceptable by homosexuals. Such fears often develop when previously exclusive settings become more inclusive. When those who have been the excluded objects of definition and discussion (women, members of racial or ethnic groups, gay men or lesbian women) enter the discussion as active subjects and contribute to making the definitions, their presence can create anxious hyperawareness and self-censoring. That suppression may then be experienced as if it had been imposed from without, by the previously excluded other, now present. When the American Psychoanalytic Association passed a resolution of nondiscrimination against homosexuals at all levels of training and practice, Charles Socarides, a prolific writer on homosexuality, feared that his academic and civil rights to analyze homosexual patients, to speak, and publish about homosexuality were threatened. Although nothing in the resolution prevented Socarides or anyone else from analyzing, speaking, and publishing in any way he wished, the resolution's intention to open psychoanalytic training and institute advancement to homosexual analysts potentially changed the analytic climate of discussion; Socarides and others felt threatened.[5]

Maggie is a member of another clinical case conference a few years later. The seminar leader tells the class that he has been in a study group for many years on the analytic treatment of homosexual patients. His group has discovered that "every lesbian patient, if she allows herself to go deep enough in her analysis, acknowledges that she wishes to suck the vagina of her female lover because it is like sucking milk from the breast." The seminar members all look expressionlessly into some middle distance. Their faces become silent masks. The seminar leader reads the sudden change in the class as disagreement. He cordially invites discussion. "Well, if I am wrong, and someone here knows something more about lesbians, tell me. Let me know." Maggie is certainly not going to speak up this time. She doubts that he would have so confidently defined the sexual desires of all lesbian women, in her presence, had he known she was one of that group. She leaves it to his analysand, a seminar member, to tell him "from the couch" about why the class suddenly fell so silent.

The task facing psychoanalysis is how to have "manifest" (i.e., open, not closeted, not silent) homosexuals as candidates in seminar rooms, as members of institutes, as supervising and training analysts, able to contribute their thoughts and experience to psychoanalytic study without producing shock or fear of repressive censorship. Until it is safe for analysts in homosexual relationships and analysts in heterosexual relationships to talk freely together in seminars, on institute curriculum committees, on institute admission and progression committees, on journal editorial boards, it surely cannot be safe for gay or lesbian patients to speak freely in their analytic treatment.

Although we have had many opportunities to experience the visible shock and subsequent self-censoring of some who learn of our relationship, we also have had experiences in which acknowledging our relationship made discussion exciting and productive. For example, during one conference dinner, we sat at a table with other women candidates. The dinner speaker had been stimulating, and we all had had some wine. Someone asked Diana why she, a psychiatrist, was not a member of one of the local medical institutes. "Maggie, which answer shall I give them?" she asked. She was asking if she should give the actual story or the cover story she sometimes used on such occasions. "Tell them the whole story," Maggie suggested.

Diana told the history of her training. She had originally wanted to be a psychologist. Although an honors student at an excellent college, she had been rejected by the graduate school of her choice. Only then had she decided to go to medical school. Several years later, she met one of her college teachers and asked her about that puzzling and disturbing psychology graduate school rejection. "Oh, I wrecked your application," said the teacher. "I wrote you a poor letter of reference. I had gone to that graduate program, and I knew that the woman who was the head of the department was a latent lesbian. She made it hard for women graduate students." A teacher in whose class Diana had been an honor student had agreed to write her a recommendation and, without telling her, had purposely set about to keep her out of graduate school. How was Diana to understand this? She had so admired and respected that teacher that for many years she could not allow herself to realize what the teacher had done and why she must have done it. The teacher probably had suspected that Diana was lesbian. In acting out her prejudice, the teacher had even managed to convince herself that she was only trying to protect Diana. Diana was not eager to experience another rejection by applying to a medical institute for psychoanalytic training, especially when she had been warned beforehand that she would be rejected. The women at the dinner were shocked to learn that analytic institutes had unacknowledged policies against admitting openly homosexual candidates. Upon reflection, though, they realized that they could not name any analyst who openly identified as homosexual. But the absence of such analysts and the reasons for their absence had never occurred to them.

They asked other questions. Several were surprised to learn that Diana had previously been married. Some were surprised that we didn't dislike men. Some wondered if relationships between women were "easier," perhaps were even somehow "better" than heterosexual relationships. But such attributions of "natural" mutuality between two women are as erroneous as attributions of "against nature" pathology.

All of us at that conference dinner table were so excited by our discussion that we lost track of time and place. Waiters who tried to remove plates were impatiently waved away. Those at other tables had finished desert before we reluctantly surrendered our entrée plates. The conference speaker came down from her seat on the dais to ask if she could join our table. "You are the noisiest, liveliest table in the room. I was sitting up there on the podium, fascinated watching you all. What are you talking about?" Such experiences made us realize how little opportunity some analysts, many of whom were treating lesbian patients, had to talk about the lives of lesbian women. Such experiences also showed us that, when it could be felt safe enough, some would ask questions and we could find ways to answer from our experience.

## Inside and Outside the American Psychoanalytic Association

While we were analytic candidates in training, others were pressing for changes within American psychoanalysis. In 1987, Richard Isay proposed that the American Psychoanalytic Association take a position similar to the one taken 15 years earlier by the American Psychiatric Association:

> Whereas homosexuality in and of itself implies no impairment in judgment, stability, reliability, or vocational capabilities, therefore, be it resolved that the American Psychiatric Association deplores all public and private discrimination against homosexuals in such areas as employment, housing, public accommodation, and licensing, and declares that no burden of proof of such judgment, capacity, or reliability shall be placed upon homosexuals greater than that imposed on any other person. Further, the American Psychiatric Association supports and urges the enactment of civil rights legislation at local, state, and federal levels that would insure homosexual citizens the same protections now guaranteed to others. Further, the American Psychiatric Association supports and urges the repeal of all legislation making criminal offenses of sexual acts performed by consenting adults in private [Bayer, 1987, p. 137].[6]

Richard Simons, President of the American Psychoanalytic Association in 1987, referred Isay's proposal to the Executive Committee, which decided it was not appropriate to adopt the APA's statement, or to adopt a statement of its own, because the American Psychoanalytic Association did not take a formal stand on social issues that did not directly affect psychoanalysis. However, Ken Hausman (1989) pointed out that the "Association has in the past . . . released statements on issues such as the proliferation of nuclear arms, the Vietnam war, abuses committed by the military dictatorship in Argentina, and restrictions on providing birth control information to adolescents" (p. 2).

Instead of passing the resolution, the Executive Committee asked the Committee on Social Issues to discuss whether the American Psychoanalytic Association should adopt a statement deploring discrimination against individuals with AIDS. But at the Association's annual meeting in 1987, no statement against discrimination of persons with AIDS was passed. Homer Curtis, APsaA President in 1989 and an opponent of the AIDS resolution, explained that psychoanalysts "have no expertise in AIDS issues or its sociological aspects" (quoted is Hausman, 1989, p. 2). Did Dr. Curtis think that "the AIDS issue" did not affect psychoanalytic treatment or that no psychoanalysts were affected by AIDS issues?

In January 1989 Richard Isay again introduced a proposal to the American Psychoanalytic Association, this one certainly directly related to the practice of psychoanalysis, namely, that the American Psychoanalytic Association go on record as opposed to the use of homosexuality as a reason to reject applicants to its affiliated training institutes. The Executive Council decided at this point to endorse the 1973 American Psychiatric Association's position statement on discrimination, which it had refused to endorse two years previously.[7] Instead of passing Isay's proposed resolution, the Council reaffirmed the American Psychoanalytic Association's statement on principles and ethics, which held that admission and progression through affiliated institutes should be based on "careful evaluation of personal integrity, analyzability and educability, not on presumptions based on diagnosis, symptoms, or manifest behavior" (Hausman, 1991, p. 2). Isay's proposal was defeated, because, it was argued, there was no need to make *specific* mention of homosexuality in such a statement. Homer C. Curtis (1989) complained in a letter in *Psychiatric News* that an earlier article "describing Dr. Richard Isay's crusade against alleged discrimination by the American Psychoanalytic Association" had led readers to "erroneously believe that our association has such a policy."

> There is no such policy and no "official" view of homosexuality advanced by the American or by psychoanalytic theory. To claim otherwise not only misrepresents our position but also impugns the

humane intentions of psychoanalysts, the very nature of whose work
demands that they be in constant empathic touch with the suffering of
their patients. . . .

   While giving several anecdotal reports where homosexual applicants have not been accepted, Dr. Isay does not speak of those who
have been accepted and trained. I am sure he is aware of such cases,
including some, past and present, who have been important contrib-
utors to psychoanalysis.

   Curtis did not mention the names of any of those "past and present" who
had had such training and made such contributions.

   But Isay and a few others persisted, and two years later, on May 9,1991,
the Executive Council of the American Psychoanalytic Association passed
a resolution saying it "opposed and deplores public or private discrimination against male and female homosexually oriented individuals."

   It is the position of the American Psychoanalytic Association that our
   component institutes select candidates for training on the basis of their
   interest in psychoanalysis, talent, proper educational background, psychological integrity, analyzability and educability, and not on the basis
   of sexual orientation. It is expected that our component institutes will
   employ these standards for the selection of candidates for training and
   for the appointment of all grades of faculty [Bulletin of the American
   Psychoanalytic Association, 1992, p. 608].

   At the same time, however, the Association's Board on Professional
Standards deleted from its statement wording that would have specifically
barred discrimination against homosexuality in the appointment of "training and supervising analysts." The Standards Board maintained that the
statement's inclusion of "all grades of faculty" covered training and supervising analysts. George H. Allison, APA President in 1991, said that a majority of the Standards Board believed that to include the wording proposed
by Isay would make the statement a call for "affirmative action," rather than
a statement condemning discrimination (Hausman, 1991).

   On April 30, 1992 the Executive Council approved a motion by Ralph
Roughton to amend that position statement, and to now *add* the phrase
"including training and supervising analysts" (Bulletin of the American
Psychoanalytic Association, 1992, p. 608). Although the Council's action
came after it had received a letter from the ACLU (on behalf of the American
Medical Student Association and the National Lesbian and Gay Health
Foundation) protesting the exclusion of that language from the statement,
Marvin Margolis, M. D., Chair of the Board of Standards, denied that the

Council's action to include the previously rejected language had been taken in response to the ACLU letter. He maintained that the recent extension of the antidiscrimination policy only corrected an "oversight" in the previous wording and was not a response to the protest. Margolis also said that he thought the accounts of antigay bias were overblown. "'I've come across some prejudiced individuals along the way,' he said, but [he saw] no evidence that there is pervasive discrimination against homosexuals at psychoanalytic training institutes" (Hausman, 1992, p. 16).[8]

So in 1992, after five years of internal debate and a long history of denial and rationalizations, the American Psychoanalytic Association finally endorsed the position taken 20 years earlier by the American Psychiatric Association. Isay commented on the struggle to have the antidiscrimination clause extended to all aspects of admission and institute advancement. "The words are relatively easy. Putting them into action to ensure that gay men and lesbians learn and work in an environment that respects their sexual orientation is the next hurdle. . . . The next important step is to get the educational curricula at the analytic institutes to include information from the growing number of studies about the development of lesbians and gays, and to stop teaching that homosexuality is caused by conflicts that result in deep pathology" (Hausman, 1992, pp. 13, 16).

Today there are signs that, to a greater extent than ever before, institutional American psychoanalysis is changing its practices about homosexual therapists. The American Psychoanalytic Association now has a Board and Council-supported Committee on Issues of Homosexuality, chaired by Ralph Roughton, a longstanding critic of antihomosexual bias within the American. The committee's "purpose is to become aware of persisting bias and discrimination and to facilitate changes in attitude and policy through consultation and education" (Roughton, 1996).[9] The 1997 Annual Meetings of the American included a discussion group entitled "New Perspectives on Homosexuality: A Gay Analyst Presents A Gay Patient." Following this presentation the Committee on Issues of Homosexuality sponsored a reception "to welcome gays and lesbians to the meetings and to celebrate diversity and inclusivity in the American."[10] The Committee has also sponsored workshops on Homosexuality and Psychoanalytic Education. In 1996 Roughton joined the membership of the Association of Gay and Lesbian Psychiatrists, and at the AGLP meeting in May 1997 Roughton informed us, "The American now has its first two gay and lesbian training analysts. I am one of them."

More changes have taken place in institutes outside the jurisdiction of the American. Gay and lesbian analysts, such as April Martin, David Schwartz, Mark Blechner, Jack Drescher, Kenneth Corbett, and Chris Sekaer, all trained in non-American institutes, such as the William Alanson White.

To put such changes in perspective, compare American psychoanalytic institutes on the issue of training homosexual therapists with those in other countries. Describing the situation in the British psychoanalytic world, O'Connor and Ryan (1993) point out that "not until 1991 did a review article critical of prevailing psychoanalytic views and practices appear in a professional journal. Even then the author [Cunningham, 1991] felt constrained to write under a pseudonym rather than identify herself publicly" (p. 203). O'Connor and Ryan (1993) also described Mary Lynne Ellis's frustrated attempts to obtain information about the admissions policies of four psychoanalytic training organizations (p. 205).

Even in countries such as Holland, Germany, France, and Finland, which have active gay and lesbian movements, we have not been able to locate homosexually identified psychoanalysts.[11]

## Homosexuality and Psychoanalytic Training in the 21st Century

In order to integrate gay and lesbian analysts into institutional psychoanalysis, training curriculums will need additions and revisions. On this matter psychoanalytic institutes have the advantage of being latecomers to change, thus having the benefit of learning from the considerable experience of other educational institutions—from elementary schools to medical schools—which have already set in motion such curriculum changes (Chasnoff and Cohen, 1996; Stein and Burg, 1996). Publications by analytically oriented gay and lesbian therapists (Glassgold and Insenza, 1995; Burch, 1997) and by gay and lesbian analysts from a variety of analytic orientations offer curriculum committees and faculty a range of perspectives from which to explore the various issues (Schwartz, 1993a, b, 1995, 1996; Corbett, 1993, 1996; Lesser, 1993,1995; Blechner, 1993, 1995; Frommer, 1994, 1995; Martin, 1994, 1995; Domenici, 1995; Drescher, 1995,1996a, b, c, 1997). We expect publications by these and other gay and lesbian analytic therapists to increase in the future (Blum, in press).

Psychoanalysis must also revise some of the narratives about its own family's history. Analysts have not been very forthcoming about acknowledging their gay and lesbian children. When analysts do begin to acknowledge that they have gay and lesbian children, some of their colleagues may be more personally motivated to examine the psychoanalytic tradition of linking pathological family dynamics with homosexuality. When the children (and grandchildren) of heterosexual analysts are the schoolmates of the children (and grandchildren) of lesbian and gay analytic colleagues, families of all configurations will have more personal reasons for redressing social stigmas.

The integration of homosexual persons into psychoanalysis will not take place any more smoothly than comparable attempts to integrate openly gay men and lesbian women into religious, military, and educational institutions. When the issues are ignorance and lack of exposure to homosexual persons, then information and personal contact with gay and lesbian persons can help bring about change. But we have only to remember the history of lay analysts within the psychoanalytic movement to appreciate that, in matters of prejudice and discrimination, ignorance and lack of exposure to the devalued other are rarely the prime movers. In the opening decades of the movement, prominent nonmedical analysts made major contributions to theory and practice, and, like Sachs, were the training analysts of medical analysts. To those determined, because of financial and other fears, to exclude lay analysts, Sachs and Anna Freud were not seen as representative lay analysts; they were, on the contrary, seen as exceptions to the rule of lay incompetency. Some will see the inclusion of homosexual therapists as the erroneous and dangerous outcome of forced political correctness, rather than the product of clear thinking and simple decency. We expect the same kinds of practices to occur in psychoanalytic institutes that continue to take place in other institutions around racial and sexual integration. Some institutes will admit homosexual applicants only if their qualifications far surpass those of heterosexual applicants, in effect keeping the barrier in place under the guise of keeping the standards up. Some institutes will not take seriously the necessity of providing institute-wide discussion and support for the inclusion process. Some institutes will admit unqualified lesbian and gay candidates, whose difficult or failed training experiences will reinforce the belief that homosexual therapists are not suited to become psychoanalysts. Some institutes will stop asking themselves, "Will we take any homosexual applicants?" and begin to worry about, "How many can we take without fear of being seen as 'a gay institute'?" The route from candidate to member to training analyst is lengthy and often arduous. When the analyst is lesbian or gay, the politically sensitive aspects of that process will certainly become intensified in some institutes. Heterosexual candidates may not feel comfortable choosing homosexually identified training analysts for fear that their analysis and psychoanalytic genealogy will be tainted. The International Psycho-Analytical Association will have to undergo lengthy internal debates among its members and its affiliated societies over institutional policies and practices. Some societies may choose to resign from the International rather than incorporate the kinds of changes taking place at the moment within some American institutes.

## An Analytic Experiment in Trial Identification: Ferenczi and O.S.

Nevertheless, institutions and people can and do change, given the necessary conditions. Exceptional people sometimes overcome exceptional external constraints. The most fortunate persons are those whom fate provides opportunities for change. Psychoanalysis is one such fateful encounter that offers new learning to both patient and analyst. Little (1960) believed that whatever else analysis is, it is also "an interaction between two people. Without such interaction, though the patient might grow, the analyst would not, and only work that promotes growth and ego development in both is worth what analysis costs both to do" (p. 31). Some analysts have been moved to change their minds about their theories and beliefs about homosexuality because of their relationships with their homosexual patients. Eisenbud (1986) recounted her experience when she heard her patient's reactions to her article on homosexuality. The Sachs-Bryher correspondence certainly suggests that Sachs revised his thinking about homosexuality, at least about homosexual persons as analysts, owing to his personal relationship with Bryher.

While Bryher and Sachs were exploring psychic reality and experimental filmmaking in Berlin, in Budapest Sándor Ferenczi (1932) was engaged in his own research with patients, experiments that he recorded in his *Clinical Diary*.Vida (1991) discussed the changes that took place in Ferenczi's thoughts about female sexuality during the period covered by the *Diary*, January to October 1932. She noted that he "spared no effort to listen to patients of both sexes, to take their complaints seriously as a confirmation of psychic reality" (p. 280). She credited Ferenczi with being among those who have helped "represent more accurately a woman's subjective reality in the theory of her sexuality" (p. 280). The *Diary* also suggests that

Ferenczi may have been in the process of rethinking his ideas about homosexuality. Rachman (1993) believes that Ferenczi tried, in *Female Sexuality*, to avoid theories of degeneracy and "to bring a new perspective" to the study and treatment of homosexuality (p. 83). Ferenczi had asked Rosa K, a female homosexual who dressed as a man, to write her autobiography, an early example, notes Rachman, of considering the perspective of the other in the treatment process.

*The Clinical Diary* records numerous examples of Ferenczi's observing the effect of the attitudes of an analyst on a patient. For instance, to a woman patient (later identified as Clara Thompson) who had apparently described having had homosexual feelings, Ferenczi made "the disclosure of my never-before-expressed dislike of a homosexual relationship." After this disclosure, which Ferenczi called his "psychoanalytic confession," his patient had "a feeling of colossal triumph and self-assurance never experienced before." She exclaimed, "So I was right after all!" Ferenczi's acknowledgment of what had been apparent all along to the patient confirmed her sense that she could tell the real from the duplicitous. When that particular "confusion of tongues" was undone, Ferenczi reported that the patient was able to "know" (remember) more about her own childhood sexual traumas (p. 103).

In notes scattered throughout *The Clinical Diary*, Ferenczi recorded his work with O.S., an independently wealthy American woman. O.S. arrived in Budapest accompanied by her lesbian lover, "two monkeys, three dogs, and several cats . . . and a . . . talented girl, who had been in real danger of becoming depraved [whom O.S. had adopted] in order to allow her to develop into a distinguished artist" (pp. 140–141). O.S.'s mother, grandmother, and great-grandmother "all went mad after giving birth to a child." The patient's father was an alcoholic. Her governess had an affair with O.S.'s hypochondriacal uncle. Her mother divorced her father and married a famous doctor who wanted her money. By the time O.S. came to Budapest, her mother was in a mental institution and her stepfather had committed suicide by jumping out a window of his own hospital. Ferenczi clearly felt that the O.S.'s family had been quite disturbed.

> Evidently everything was done (1) to protect the patient from any excitement, (2) to keep the ideal of insanity away from her. But this unusually intelligent little girl, who felt perfectly healthy, nevertheless appears to have seen through everything; but she was stricken by the fear of going mad herself and consciously accepted the attitude of her environment: (1) she shielded herself from emotions (which she identified with insanity; (2) she fled from conscious anxiety by resorting to phobic protective measures [p. 100].

O. S. had fallen in love with girls in college. In Europe she had become pregnant during a brief heterosexual affair. Returning home, she had married a rich admirer at her stepfather's urging, "for the sake of appearances," believing that she would be able to divorce after the child was born. Her stepfather and husband hoped she would become reconciled to marriage. She felt sorry and guilty for not loving her husband.

> The patient enters analysis with an American doctor, who helps her to some extent but ends up moralizing and trying to persuade the patient that she should adjust to the marriage. She tried for years to come to me, but I could accept her only after a three-year waiting period . . . [p. 101].

> The tragedy of this case is that even after the patient had grown up, and obtained possession of her fortune and the right to dispose of it, she still does not really have the courage to enjoy this freedom herself. She continues to feel the compulsion to sacrifice herself for others, just as she in fact had to sacrifice her whole childhood and youth, and even a part of her intelligence, to her insane—crazy—environment. She is moved to tears and immediately to charitable intervention [p. 149].

O.S. came to Ferenczi "so terrified of physical pain that she had acquired from Paris two hundred dollars worth of her own anesthetic equipment, which she wants to be used even for the most minor dental intervention" (p. 138). Ferenczi also recorded that O.S. "suffers from a helpless compulsion of being unable to watch any suffering without somehow alleviating it, lets almost everyone enjoy some of her great wealth except herself" (p. 148). Ferenczi, however, made a different interpretation than did O.S.'s previous analyst about her difficulty with her own pain and the pain of others: "Was analyzed for years on the basis of the principle of repressed sadism, without the slightest success and also without giving her the feeling that anyone had ever understood her. In the end, I had to decide, having placed myself entirely in her position, to accept it as probable that in her case the original reaction is no defense but a need to help" (p. 148).

Ferenczi set aside his theory when it did not prove helpful and made a trial identification with his patient. He decided to try to see things from her point of view. "I had to decide, having placed myself entirely in her position, to accept" her way of understanding her feelings. Ferenczi believed that O.S. had suffered trauma at six weeks old when she had been left alone in a hotel room for several days with her mentally ill mother and was "subjected to no one knows what treatment—until at last they were discovered." Ferenczi's diary ended before he and O.S. could have had the opportunity to treat "the twin sister, let us say six weeks old, [who] lies buried in her in the same state of rigidity that she fell into in the course of the trauma" (pp. 197–198).

Regarding the patient's homosexuality, Ferenczi made the following arrangement:

> The analysis began according to a plan worked out in advance; to leave the homosexuality alone, in the vague hope that it would resolve itself in the course of the analysis, and led by the idea that the analysis cannot begin with a refusal. Complication: her feminine partner she has brought with her wishes to be analyzed; in view of some external problems and at the urgent request of O. S., I agree to devote half of the sessions to the partner. She is a case of sensitivity slightly tainted with paranoia: alternate attacks of excessive goodness and outbursts of hate [p.100].

Since the patient was unable to bear having treatment for her pain while N.D., her lesbian partner suffered, Ferenczi split the sessions between them. "Patient [O.S.] struggles with complete lack of affect, without any visible success, but her woman partner, who makes more rapid progress, starts to help me in the analysis" (pp. 101–102).

On May 8, 1932, Ferenczi recorded that O.S., having lost her defensive hyperactivity, came to session with "a feeling of absolute inner emptiness." Ferenczi noted that a change had also occurred in him: "At this critical moment my 'having (or having been) woken up' then appears to have intervened." In his new state of clarity and heightened perception, Ferenczi saw that what looked like "apparent deterioration" in the patient was actually "an uncovering of the actual state of affairs, and thus . . . progress" (p. 102). That evening the patient masturbated in her sleep. She asked her partner, who had noticed her behavior, not to tell Ferenczi. "Naturally, however, she did not promise this. Perhaps under the influence of the sympathy she expected from me, she now found the courage—overcoming all her infantile timidity and inhibitions—to admit to a passion. It will perhaps be less difficult task now to reunite the split-off part of the person, affectivity, with the rest of her personality" (p. 102).

In the privacy of his clinical journal, Ferenczi described his determination to make trial identifications with his patient, to momentarily "place myself entirely in her position." He used simple language to record his thoughts, even as he struggled to push the boundaries of theory and technique. We don't know the outcome of O.S.'s treatment or how Ferenczi's theories about homosexuality might have been changed as a result of his experience with this patient. Ferenczi died of pernicious anemia on May

22, 1933, leaving behind in his diary various contradictory thoughts about female homosexuality. "It has been too little noted that female homosexuality is in fact a very normal thing, just as normal as male heterosexuality" (p. 78). At the same time he described homosexuality as arising as a sexual defense due to trauma: "Homosexuality . . . is forbidden, yet not so 'impossible,' 'unmentionable,' 'unthinkable' as *heterosexual union*" (p. 172). He thought female homosexuality was "a *replacement* of maternal feelings by orgasmic ones" (p. 172), although his own notes about O.S. suggest that she had replaced orgasmic feelings with maternal or affectionate ones.

> Every analysis of a woman must end with homosexuality, that of a man with heterosexuality. The most profound submergence means the mother or the womb situation; obviously for a woman this is a relationship with someone of the same sex, for a man with someone of the opposite sex. "On revient toujours." One might say that homosexuality is the next-to-last word in the analysis of a woman. The (let us say male) analyst must let all the maternal qualities prevail and inhibit all aggressive, male instincts (the unconscious ones as well). This will lead to a manifestation in the female analysand of *spontaneous* (that is, not forcibly imposed) tendencies toward passivity and toward being loved in a quite penetrating manner, as corresponds to anatomy. The ultimate phase of a woman's analysis would thus be, without exception, the spontaneous development of the desire to be passive and to be a mother [p. 75].

But a few paragraphs later Ferenczi is wondering "what is 'normality?'" and he is turning over once again the meaning of female homosexuality in a woman's life.

Ferenczi died before he could fully assess the results of his various experiments intended to help "to place myself entirely in the patient's position." Ferenczi knew and acknowledged his dislike of female homosexual relationships and that his dislike was mixed with some male and medical jealously. Concerned about the effect of parental sexuality on children, Ferenczi also was beginning to realize the power that analysts held to impose their beliefs on patients who, like vulnerable children, might comply with such impositions from their analysts. Perhaps, had Ferenczi lived longer, O.S. might have helped him understand that some of his ideas about homosexuality were also distortions that analysts imposed on patients. "O.S. is right when she says, 'I know very well (as indeed all children know) when what I want is something bad, when I am afraid of something, when I have feelings of guilt and shame. But I refuse to take on myself the exaggerated accusations of the adults, and I also refuse to declare certain things shameful that to me are absolutely not so" (p. 165).

We are impressed that O.S., in spite of her disturbed family, her own crippling anxieties, and her own fear of going crazy, still could resist the "exaggerated accusations" of others about what is shameful. And so we end our discussion of female homosexuality with a different question than the one we had when we began psychoanalytic training. Then we thought that psychoanalysis would help us understand what *causes* homosexuality. Now, for us, the more interesting question is what *enables* some women, such as O.S., Bryher, Freud's 18-year-old patient, Deutsch's patient, Ann, and Kate, and Beth—in spite of crazy families or angry parents, in spite of internal conflicts and insecurities, in the face of societal stigma and discrimination— to preserve their own psychic and sexual reality? Without positive images or language to support their subjective experience, what enables some women to search for partners and to make productive lesbian relationships? The narratives we have gathered will, we hope, stimulate other psychoanalysts to become as interested in these questions as in questions of etiology. The narratives will, we hope, enable analysts to make trial identifications with their lesbian patients as these patients make of their lives a study and learn to support their own desires.

# APPENDIX

## Introduction

The following information is excerpted from major online news services during the years 1993 to 1997. It highlights issues that lesbian women might be aware of and, in many cases, concerned about. It demonstrates contemporary social, cultural, and legal tensions around homosexuality. It is the climate in which lesbian patients live, work, and love.

The information is presented in chronological order within the following topics:

> Education
> Religion
> Child Custody
> Adoption
> Reproductive Rights
> Domestic Partnerships and Same-Sex Legal Rights
> Same-Sex Marriage

*Note:* Most items are direct quotes from newswire articles. Often the first sentence or two of the article is used.

## EDUCATION

| | | |
|---|---|---|
| 12-10-93 | Massachusetts | Without debate the Massachusetts House and Senate passed a bill, the first state to do so, saying no one shall be discriminated against in a public school or have his or her studies interfered with on account of sexual orientation. Governor Weld signed the measure. He credited the bill's success to the young people who rallied, marched, and held vigils at the State house to press the lawmakers to act. The director of the Catholic League for Religious and Civil Rights complained that the law is "unnecessary legislation over a contrived issue." [AP] [UPI] |
| 1-2-94 | New Jersey | Rutgers, the state university of New Jersey, is among hundreds of schools—public and private, secular and religious—that are introducing homosexuality into academic discourse and making their campuses gay friendly. Even the language has changed. It is "lesbian, gay and bisexual" or "lesbian-gay-bi" or "LGB." And "queer theory" is a bona fide scholarly area of study that investigates the meaning of sexual desire and gender in society. [AP - Arlene Levinson] |
| 1-10-94 | California | Gay Rights Fight Moves on Campus. Activists on both sides have targeted high schools in battles over curriculum and support groups. Some celebrate a new boldness, others say values are best taught at home. |

Los Angeles has been a leader. In 1984 Virginia Uribe started Project 10 in the Los Angeles School system. The program, which offers counseling and support groups for gay teenagers, has been widely praised by educators and vilified by critics.

In 1992 the Los Angeles school district proclaimed June as Gay and Lesbian Pride Month.

In 1992 state educators proposed health education and textbook content guidelines that included scattered references to gays and families headed by same-sex couples. The guidelines were adopted with some changes, but the mention of homosexuality was retained.
[Los Angeles Times - Tammerlin Drummond & Bettina Boxall]

| | | |
|---|---|---|
| 1-13-94 | California | About 300 people listened to hours of spirited debate before the Trustees of the Huntington Beach Union High School District voted 4 to 1 to allow a gay student support group to continue meeting in a local high school. [LA Times - Debra Cano & Doreen Carvajal] |
| 1-19-94 | New York | A leading Episcopal divinity school announced a new policy. Committed same-sex couples will be eligible for seminary housing apartments. The church policy continues to hold that sex is appropriate within marriage only. [AP - David Briggs] |
| 2-15-94 | New York | New York City public schools have a revised multicultural teaching guide. Nearly all references to gay and lesbian parents have been dropped. The revision is part of the backlash to the considerably more liberal teaching guide of two years ago, which noted that teachers should be aware of alternative families, including gay and lesbian parents, and that "children should be taught to acknowledge the positive aspects of each type of household." [UPI] |
| 2-22-94 | Illinois | A textbook on human sexuality used in a |

| | | |
|---|---|---|
| | | local high school has been banned following complaints by some parents who objected to sections in the book about homosexuality, masturbation, and abortion because they were not explicitly labeled as wrong.<br>[UPI] |
| 3-1-94 | New Hampshire | The faculty at Dartmouth College voted to kick ROTC off campus, saying the military still discriminates against homosexuals and that this contradicted the college's nondiscrimination policy. The Student Assembly voted overwhelmingly to retain ROTC.<br>[AP] |
| 3-15-94 | New York | The State University of New York moved to ban military recruiters from 29 of its campuses because of the Pentagon's anti-gay employment policies.<br>[UPI] |
| 4-18-94 | New Hampshire | Dartmouth College's Board of Trustees voted to keep Army ROTC on campus, but they added that they would work to change the federal government's "don't ask, don't tell" policy on gays in the military.<br>[AP] |
| 4-19-94 | Ohio | The newly elected president of the American Association of University Professors listed nine goals for his two-year tenure. One of them was "ensure that gay, lesbian, and bisexual faculty members are given full access to equal and fair treatment in the profession."<br>[UPI] |
| 5-20-94 | Michigan | The University of Michigan accepted a recommendation from a task force to grant same-sex partners of UM employees and students the same benefits as heterosexuals |

—health and life insurance benefits and housing benefits.
[UPI]

| | | |
|---|---|---|
| 5-22-94 | California | Los Angeles hosted the first gay and lesbian prom ever sanctioned by a public school district in the United States. Teenagers from 30 LA high schools danced at the prom, billed as "Live to Tell."
The event, which had not been widely publicized outside the schools, drew a handful of protesters from One Lord, One Faith, One Baptism Christian Church in Long Beach.
[LA Times - Michael Quintanilla] |
| 6-7-94 | New York | Over a 100 people demonstrated in front of the New York Board of Education's Brooklyn headquarters, protesting multicultural education they contend contains sex education for 6- and 7-year-old children and advocates homosexuality.
[UPI] |
| 6-10-94 | Pennsylvania | Student wins lawsuit. A Carnegie Mellon student claimed his First Amendment rights had not been protected when he was fired as a resident assistant in April 1991 because he refused to wear a button espousing homosexual rights during a sensitivity training session on gay, lesbian, and bisexual issues.
[UPI] |
| 6-18-94 | California | A gay Los Angeles high school teacher, teaching in a district that had an official policy of nondiscrimination, was verbally derided with antigay invective by students for many months; he finally left. Quotes from some of the students: "It's not a dislike [of being gay]. It's a hate of gays." "I feel that being gay is not normal. . . . I feel threatened by gays." And a quote from one of the teachers: "This problem has not |

been resolved. Nobody has educated [the students]. Nobody has said, 'This is not the way it should be.'"

Despite all the gay-friendly resolutions adopted by the Los Angeles school district, gay teachers said they remain mostly in the closet.
[LA Times - Bettina Boxall]

| | | |
|---|---|---|
| 6-20-94 | United States | A study by the Carnegie Foundation for the Advancement of Teaching reported that in the United States, nearly one in three university professors indicated that they felt there were political or ideological restrictions on what they published. Faculty members interested in tenure or grant money steered away from controversial topics, including gay studies. [Washington Post - Mary Jordan] |
| 6-22-94 | New York | Elders attack religious right, praise gay groups. Surgeon General Joycelyn Elders . . . opened a national conference on gay and lesbian health issues. She praised gay and lesbian groups for their work on AIDS awareness. . . . She attacked what she called the "un-Christian religious right" for its opposition to education programs in such areas as sex and AIDS. She said that health education does not mean teaching young people how to have sex. "Nobody has to teach us how to have sex. God taught us how to have sex. We've got to teach them responsibility." [Reuters, UPI] |
| 6-26-94 | Massachusetts | Northeastern University has a new policy to recruit openly homosexual faculty members. A professor who is lesbian says, "In many instances, when gays and lesbians apply for jobs, they may hide things in their background—like their work with a gay or lesbian student group—out of fear |

it may hurt them. I think this will allow them to identify themselves."

Stanford University and the University of Iowa make similar recruiting efforts but homosexuals are not listed in the schools' formal affirmative action statements.
[AP - Glen Johnson]

| | | |
|---|---|---|
| 6-28-94 | Washington, DC | Steven Spielberg testifies at a hearing of the Senate Judiciary Subcommittee on the Constitution on hate crime; he urged high school courses on intolerance be required by the states. "Hatred exists not because people have never seen or heard of a Jew, or a Latino, or an African-American, or an Asian, or a Native American or a homosexual. . . . It exists because people learn to hate from parents, peers, culture and negative experiences."<br>[UPI] |
| 6-29-94 | California | A San Diego second grade teacher invited her gay son to speak to her class. This event caused such controversy that the teacher was formally reprimanded for the "unauthorized visit."<br>[LA Times - Tony Perry] |
| 7-19-94 | Connecticut | A Superior Court judge ruled that military recruiters were permanently banned from the University of Connecticut Law School because the Pentagon's new "don't ask, don't tell" policy discriminates against homosexuals and Connecticut law bars state agencies and institutions from helping any employer that discriminates against homosexuals.<br>[AP] |
| 8-2-94 | Washington, DC | The US Senate voted 63-36 to deny federal funds to public schools that teach acceptance of homosexuality. Specifically mentioned were distribution of instructional materials, counseling, and referral of |

students to gay organizations. Sens. Jesse
Helms and Bob Smith authored the
proposal.
[AP - Robert Naylor Jr.]

| 8-2-94 | Washington, DC | Helms's bill's language softened. Senate votes 91-9 on an amendment providing no federal education dollars may be used in support of sexual activity, "whether homosexual or heterosexual." [UPI] |
|---|---|---|
| 8-22-94 | Washington | The president of the Lake Washington Education Association in Washington state said curriculum challenges by religious conservatives have a chilling effect on teachers. "People from the far right will do things like print up flyers that say, 'Do you know you have a pervert teaching around your child?' and they'll pass it around neighborhoods." Several teachers talked about books that were banned from their schools or sections of books being blacked out. A Shreveport, Louisiana fifth grade teacher and president of the local NEA chapter said texts were censored if homosexuality was in any way said to be an alternative lifestyle. She said teachers were told, "We do not want you to talk about this unless you say it's a deviant lifestyle." [AP - Carole Feldman] |
| 9-29-94 | Pittsburgh | The publisher of a University of Pittsburgh newspaper pulled a story about the first wedding of two homosexual men at Heinz Memorial Chapel on the school campus. |
| 10-02-94 | Ohio | Kent State University offers a new course, Sociology of Gays and Lesbians. 75 students are enrolled in this controversial class. Last year the University of Akron offered a course on gay and lesbian literature. Last spring Ohio State University offered a course on gay and lesbian |

cultural theory.
[UPI]

| | | |
|---|---|---|
| 11-1-94 | Texas | The student government at Stephen F. Austin State University voted 30-26 to stop funding the school's Gay and Lesbian Student Association, which had received $106 this year. Students who argued for the funding cut said, "We didn't want to have a group on campus that might in some way champion violation of Texas law." The reference was to Texas's century-old sodomy law, which is not enforced. [AP] |
| 11-10-94 | Texas | The President of Stephen F. Austin State University countered the Student Association's defunding of the Gay and Lesbian Student group. He said the ban would violate the group's First Amendment rights. [UPI] |
| 11-15-94 | Massachusetts | Massachusetts becomes first state to require its training programs for future public school teachers and administrators to provide instruction about problems confronting gay and lesbian students and how to address them. Sixty Massachusetts colleges and universities will be affected. [UPI] |
| 11-15-94 | California | UCLA students are protesting the campus ROTC program, asking that homosexuals be accepted unconditionally into the program. |
| 11-17-94 | California | ROTC Still Draws Protests, But Issue Now Is Bias Against Gay Students. Nearly three decades after students picketed Reserve Officers Training Corps buildings to protest the Vietnam War, demonstrators are again challenging ROTC on the tree-lined paths at UCLA. But unlike protesters of the late 1960s |

who wanted to shut down the corps,
today's demonstrators want to open its
doors wider so homosexuals can be
accepted unconditionally into the
program.
[WP - Kathryn Wexler]

12-12-94          Virginia     Despite the fact that 97.7% of parents of
                               public school children in Fairfax County
                               support the sex education courses that had
                               been state mandated, Gov. George Allen
                               introduced a plan to make sex education
                               optional for local students. He and the
                               conservative groups opposing mandatory
                               sex education feel that the current pro-
                               gram imposes too many questionable val-
                               ues on students, especially when it seems
                               to approve of homosexuality or the use of
                               condoms.
                               [WP - Robert O'Harrow Jr. & Steve
                               Twomey]]

1-21-95           Missouri     A history high school teacher in St. Louis
                               showed a film about the Holocaust and
                               then held up a poster showing emblems
                               used to identify people in concentration
                               camps. He said, "If I had been in Europe
                               during World War II, they would have put
                               this pink triangle on me and gassed me to
                               death, because I am gay." Parents' reactions
                               to his disclosure were varied. One said, "I
                               really do feel he has the right to say he's
                               gay." Another parent, who said she had
                               nothing against Wilson being gay, added
                               "We just don't want him to teach it to our
                               kids."
                               [AP US & World - Connie Farrow]

2-18-95           California   The Gay, Lesbian and Bisexual Resource
                               Center is set to open at the University of
                               California at Irvine on April 3. There are
                               about 20 other similar centers in the U.S.
                               [LA Times]

| 6-28-95 | California | UC Berkeley Extension announced a new course in its award-winning program on children and the Changing Family—Children and Youth in Gay and Lesbian Families.<br>[PR Newswire] |
|---|---|---|
| 7-1-95 | California | About 100 attended a prom for gay and lesbian youths in Northern California. One young woman said, "I could have gone [to the regular school prom], but there were so many threats made to me like, 'Dyke go to prom and we'll kill you.'"<br>[AP US & World] |
| 8-30-95 | England | Students at London's Brunel University banned Army recruitment at the annual fair where new students are invited to join clubs and societies. They said the action was taken to protest the Army's policy of not allowing lesbians and gays into the armed forces.<br>[PA News] |
| 8-31-95 | Washington, DC | The Rev. Lou Sheldon, who directs the Anaheim, California based Traditional Values Coalition, claimed to have been providing research and documents to a House subcommittee that is preparing for a hearing on what he called "promoting homosexuality" in public schools.<br>[AP US & World - Kim I. Mills] |
| 9-6-95 | Ohio | Columbus, Ohio Board of Education members voted against adopting discrimination protection for gay, lesbian and bisexual employees, saying they were afraid of inflaming the community. The board also refused to place the resolution adding sexual orientation to its antidiscrimination policy.<br><br>Former school board candidate Glenn Elder spoke: "God made whites, blacks, women and men. He did not make |

homosexuals. We don't give special privilege to someone just because they do
something wrong. It doesn't mean we hate
that person. We just hate what they're
doing."
[UPI Mid-Atlantic US]

9-18-95      Washington, DC    At its annual convention in July, the
                               National Education Association (NEA)
                               passed a resolution proclaiming a
                               "Gay/Lesbian History Month." Concerned
                               Women for America (CWA), the largest
                               women's organization in the country, is
                               outraged by this action. On behalf of
                               600,000 pro-family members, Dr. Beverly
                               LeHaye, CWA's president and founder,
                               pledges to mobilize parents in all school
                               districts to stop this attempt to "indoctri-
                               nate our children. We are calling on
                               Congress to act on behalf of the true
                               majority of Americans and cut all funding
                               for the NEA."
                               [PR Newswire]

9-26-95      New Hampshire     A New Hampshire high school English
                               teacher said she will appeal her dismissal
                               for assigning her students books with
                               homosexual themes. She was fired in May
                               after officials learned she had had her
                               classes read four works by May Sarton,
                               Bette Greene, and E.M.Forester.
                                 The high school officials said she was
                               fired for insubordination, not prejudice
                               against homosexuals, and claimed she
                               defied orders to hold off using the works
                               until parents had been notified.
                               [UPI]

10-17-95     Michigan          Wayne State University joined the
                               University of Michigan in extending health
                               insurance and other benefits to partners of
                               its gay employees.
                               [UPI]

| | | |
|---|---|---|
| 10-26-95 | Pennsylvania | Philip Cohen, president of Chelsea House Publishers spearheaded two projects targeted for the 14- to 19- year-old reader. "Lives of Notable Gay Men and Lesbians" and "Issues in Lesbian and Gay Life." On the whole, school librarians, perhaps fearing controversy, have held back from ordering the books. The titles released include: *James Baldwin* by Randal Kenan, *Willa Cather* by Sharon O'Brien and *Lesbians and Gays and Sports* by Perry Deane Young. |
| | | One school librarian fumed "After all, you wouldn't publish 'Great Alcoholics' or 'Famous Fat People.'" |
| 2-14-96 | Alabama | Critics of a University of Alabama gay conference, including Alabama's attorney general, lost their bid to block the conference when a federal judge rejected state claims that the meeting is illegal. The two-day Lesbian, Gay, and Bisexual College Conference of the Southeastern United States will begin with the theme; "Voices of Diversity: Living Out in the South." |
| | | Cathy Wessell, who organized the conference exclaimed, "I never anticipated any of this. I have just been amazed." [AP US & World - Jay Reeves] |
| 2-15-96 | New Hampshire | A group of parents and teachers in Merrimack, NH filed a federal court suit that challenged a new school board policy against teaching anything "positive" about homosexuality. The suit argued that the policy is harmful to students and violates the First Amendment right to free speech of both teachers and pupils. "The policy harms Merrimack students who need the freedom to think, the freedom to learn, and the freedom to investigate and discuss ideas," said Susan Ruggeri, the president of the town's Teachers Association. [UPI] |

| | | |
|---|---|---|
| 3-13-96 | Massachusetts | When a high school social studies teacher told her class she had a wonderful relationship with her lesbian partner, she crossed a line: beyond what her students needed to know, a teen-ager's parents claim. The Jeneis said that their daughter Johanna was so upset by the revelation she was forced to transfer to a parochial school. In a so-called demand letter that often precedes a lawsuit, the parents claim Johanna was denied her right to a public education and are seeking $359,571 from the suburb of Brookline, $300,000 of it for emotional distress.<br>[AP US & World - Katharine Webster] |
| 3-20-96 | Connecticut | Military recruiters are no longer welcome on the campuses of state-supported schools in Connecticut because of a state Supreme Court ruling that the military discriminates against gay men and lesbians. "Gay men and lesbians have a right to be free from the discriminations and degrading homophobia that is prevalent in our society," wrote Justice Berdon in siding with the 3-2 majority.<br>[Reuters World Report - Mike Clancy] |
| 3-21-96 | Michigan | State lawmakers and two universities are on a collision course over the issue of extending benefits to the gay partners of staff members. The Senate Appropriations Committee has attached an amendment to the higher education budget that would cut state funds to any community college or university giving benefits to the unmarried, domestic partners of staffers. The amendment, which was approved 7-5 and sent with the budget to the full Senate, clashes with policies already in place at the University of Michigan and Wayne State University.<br>[UPI Central US] |

| 4-6-96 | California | The UCLA gaybruin Internet forum offered information about The Gay, Lesbian, and Straight Teachers Network (GLSTN). It is the only organization of gay and straight teachers and community members working to end homophobia in elementary and secondary schools. Founded in the Boston area in 1990, GLSTN today has over thirty local chapters and has sponsored programming in twenty- nine states in the past year. Chapters exist in: Atlanta, Austin, Boston, Chicago, Cincinnati, Cleveland, Colorado, Columbus, Connecticut, District of Columbia, Detroit, Los Angeles, Maine, Minneapolis/St. Paul, New Hampshire, New Mexico, New York, Philadelphia, St. Louis, San Diego, San Joaquin, Tampa Bay, Washington State. http://www.glstn.org/freedom/ [gaybruins@UCLA.EDU] |
|--------|------------|------|
| 4-19-96 | Utah | The state Legislature voted to ban gay student clubs in high schools to prevent homosexuals from "recruiting" others into "a lifestyle that can kill them." The bill cleared the Senate, 21 to 7, and the House, 47 to 21. Gov. Mike Leavitt is expected to sign it. The issue of gay clubs in Utah schools erupted last year when students at a Salt Lake City school formed a Gay-Straight Alliance. The school board reacted by banning all school-sponsored extracurricular organizations. [LA Times] |

Utah Governor Mike Leavitt is expected to sign into law a bill that would effectively ban gay and lesbian clubs from local schools. In January, the Salt Lake City School Board voted to ban all non-curricular clubs from campuses after students tried to form gay and lesbian clubs at three

local high schools.
[Reuters World Report]

5-15-96    Massachusetts    A federal judge refused to remove a controversial photo exhibit of gay and lesbian
families from elementary schools in the
town of Amherst, saying it does not violate
the rights of parents who object to it. The
20 black and white pictures, titled "Love
Makes a Family: Living In Gay and Lesbian
Families," depict children in various family
settings with their gay or lesbian parents.
The organizers of the show said the photos
were designed to "address issues of family
diversity and homophobia." But the lawsuit filed by a group of parents against the
Amherst School Committee charged the
exhibit encouraged "sodomy and fornica-
tion," and said it was not "age-appropriate"
for viewing by elementary school pupils.
[UPI]

5-16-96    California    UC Berkeley is considering a new "theme
floor" in a residence hall for gay and bisex-
ual students. If approved, the floor would
feature programs and speakers on gay
issues such as coming out on campus.
Activities would be tied in to a new gay
and lesbian studies minor offered on campus this year. All students—straight and
gay—would be welcome to apply.
[Oakland Tribune via gaybruin]

5-24-96    California    A lesbian girl who had threatened to sue
her high school if she could not take her
girlfriend to the prom will be allowed to
bring her to the dance, her attorney said.
The Hacienda Heights/La Puente School
District reversed its decision less than 15
minutes after receiving a letter threatening
a lawsuit if Venessa Alcazar was not
allowed to attend the prom with her lesbian date. Alcazar said she hoped it would
give other students the courage to attend

|          |            | proms and other high school events with same-sex partners. [UPI] |
|----------|------------|---|
| 5-29-96  | California | U C Riverside's Academic Senate will vote on an interdisciplinary program in Lesbian, Gay & Bisexual Studies. The minor would offer courses focusing on gender and sexuality from such varied departments as literature, dance, sociology, history, women studies and ethnic studies. Several area politicians, however, have come out against the minor characterizing it as unacademic and immoral. Assemblyman Brett Granlund said: "Do you want to have a degree in child molesting just because people who don't happen to be child molesters might want to know more about what they're missing?" [gaybruins@ASUCLA.UCLA.EDU] |
| 6-18-96  | California | fr. gaybruins@ASUCLA.UCLA.EDU<br>    State of the UCLA LGB Community by Emmanuel A. Sanchez . . . But now there is just so much available to every queer person at UCLA—from the above mentioned [GALA, Ten Percent, the Lesbian & Gay Greek Chapters, the Faculty & Staff Network] to the LGB networks in the professional schools and groups like MAHU, La Familia, SHOUT, Gaybruins, Grad Student Network. . . . |
| 6-30-96  | Australia  | Two ninth grade students from Canterbury Boys High School in Sydney were suspended for calling their gym teacher, Mr. D'Arcy, a "faggot" and a "poofter." Mr. D'Arcy is heterosexual but said he was offended by the taunts and horrified at the treatment many gays have to endure. [AAP Australian Associated Press] |
| 7-10-96  | Australia  | A Catholic college principal's description of homosexuals as "an unfortunate aberra- |

tion" would increase intimidation and harassment of gay and lesbian students in Catholic schools, "Jeffrey," a Catholic teacher at the school, claimed. He also said he would be dismissed if his homosexuality became public knowledge.
[AAP]

7-10-96          Washington          Professors at Western Washington University now can post stickers declaring their offices safe zones for gay, lesbian, and bisexual students. One of the deans who supports the sticker program said that the stickers are a response to surveys showing that gay, lesbian, and bisexual students felt invisible on campus or felt hostility from others. "When you create a diverse campus, you need to create a climate in which those diverse students feel comfortable," she said.
[The Bellingham Herald - Lisa Gaumnitz as quoted on gaybruins@ASUCLA.UCLA.EDU]

7-31-96          Illinois          The 7th U.S. Circuit Court of Appeals ruled that 20-year- old Jamie Nobozny may sue his former high school for allegedly failing to protect him from anti-gay assaults and harassment while he was a student. While attending middle and high school in Ashland, Wisconsin, Nobozny and his parents asked the schools to safeguard him from his attackers, but school officials allegedly told them that Nobozny had to learn to expect such abuse because he is gay.

A friend-of-the-court brief was filed in support of Nabozny's appeal by the National Association of School Psychologists, the National Association of Social Workers, the national organization of Parents, Families, and Friends of Lesbians and Gays, and the Chicago

lesbian and gay social services agency, Horizons.
[UPI]

| | | |
|---|---|---|
| 7-31-96 | Michigan | A gay teacher said he quit his job at a suburban school recently because he could no longer take the harassment felt from co-workers, students and the public. Gerry Crane taught music for three years at the 450-student school. He was publicly humiliated at a December school board meeting in which the board issued a statement directed at him, which condemned homosexuality and said homosexuals were not proper role models for students. Weeks earlier Crane had been "outed" by a disgruntled student who learned Crane and another man had "married."<br>[UPI] |
| 8-27-96 | Washington, DC | Results of the annual Phi Delta Kappa/Gallup poll reported on a broad range of education issues. 63% did not think schools should teach about gay and lesbian lifestyles and 58% said gay and lesbian clubs should not be allowed in public schools.<br>[AP - Deb Riechmann] |
| 9-18-96 | California | "IT'S ELEMENTARY, Talking About Gay Issues in School," a new film that challenges the censorship of mere discussions of gay issues in schools is being screened to help California legislators make important educational policy decisions for the State of California. The film, by an academy award winning film maker, kicks off its official 30+ city premiere in Salt Lake City, where the City school board banned all extracurricular clubs from district high schools, just to prevent students from forming a lesbian and gay interest club. At the heart of the film is inspiring footage of how children, ages five through 13, |

respond when teachers find appropriate creative ways to confront anti-gay prejudice and counter gay invisibility.
[PR Newswire]

10-8-96     Pennsylvania     Defying warnings from school officials, more than 250 middle- and high school students in Elizabethtown marched out of classes to protest their school board's new "profamily" resolution. The resolution, passed September 17, says "pro-homosexual concepts on sex and family will never be tolerated or accepted in this school." Students also objected to its description of the two-parent family as "the norm."

The board's resolution matches one sent to districts by the Concerned Women for America, a conservative Christian group, in response to a National Education Association resolution on diversity, racism, sexism, and sexual orientation.
[AP]

11-13-96     Kuwait     Some 500 Kuwait University students staged a sit-in strike to protest against a published report alleging lesbian activity on campus. Professor Shuaib was quoted in the November issue of al-Hadath magazine as saying that lesbianism was common among women in Kuwait, especially at Kuwait University. She has come under much attack by fellow professors and students since then. Gay rights and sexual issues in general are taboo in the Moslem conservative Gulf Arab states. The editor of the magazine said the Information Ministry had referred him to the administrative prosecutor for offending the Kuwaiti public by publishing such claims, adding that his monthly received an official "final warning" of closure if it repeated the offense.
[Reuters]

| 11-20-96 | Wisconsin | A Wisconsin school district agreed to pay nearly $1 million to a former high school student for failing to protect him from harassment and abuse because he was gay. Jamie Nabozny, now 21 years old, said the abuse by other students ranged from name-calling to being shoved, beaten, spat upon and even having his head pushed in a urinal. He said he was kicked in the stomach so many times he later required surgery.<br>[Reuters, AP] |
| --- | --- | --- |
| 11-21-96 | Virginia | George Mason University, concerned that a gay student center would flout the state's anti-sodomy law, abandoned the $15,000 project. Supporters of the center, who say hate crimes are increasing on campus, envisioned a room where gays would be safe from harassment and have access to resource material with homosexual themes. Although Virginia's antisodomy law is on the books, it is rarely enforced. And another state university, Virginia Tech, already has a gay center.<br>[AP] |
| 11-26-96 | Los Angeles, California | The Faculty Executive Committee of the Academic Senate of UCLA unanimously approved a proposal for a Program in Lesbian, Gay, and Bisexual Studies at UCLA.<br>[gaybruins@ASUCLA] |
| 12-26-96 | Israel | Using a mincing, high-pitched voice, Israeli President Ezer Weizman denounced and made fun of gays during an address to high-school students in Haifa. "[Homosexuality] is abnormal from a social point of view," Weizman said. "I don't like it. . .I like a man who wants to be a man and a woman who wants to be a woman, but not a man who wants to be a |

woman."
[USA-Bob LaFont]

| | | |
|---|---|---|
| 1-22-97 | United States | "School Shouldn't Hurt: Lifting the Burden from Gay, Lesbian, Bisexual and Transgendered Youth," a report of the RI Task Force on Gay, Lesbian, Bisexual and Transgendered Youth, is now available on the world wide web. The address is: http://www.members.tripod.com/~twood/safeschools.html [gaybruin@ASUCLA] |
| 1-23-97 | Thailand | A furor has broken out in Thailand over a government ban on homosexuals becoming teachers. The ban bars homosexuals from teacher training colleges on the grounds that they do not make good role models. Education Minister Rangsitphol said, "The ministry has not violated human rights. The ruling is only aimed at banning people with improper personalities from being models for youngsters." Critics asked how Rajabhat Institute can accurately tell who is homosexual and who is not. Prof. Prangsri admitted that the screening process would not be easy, but promised that it would be successful. Institute officials maintain that they can detect signs of homosexuality during interviews with candidates. Homosexuality is accepted in generally conservative Thailand. Homosexuals are free to join most professions and some are even popular television stars. [Reuters, IPS] |
| 1-28-97 | Alabama | The state of Alabama asked the 11th Circuit Court of Appeals to uphold a 1992 Alabama law banning public funds for any campus group "that fosters or promotes a lifestyle or actions prohibited by the (state's) sodomy and sexual misconduct laws." Specifically, the state of Alabama |

asked to be allowed to block college and university groups that promote homosexuality from obtaining state funds.

There was no indication when the appeals court would rule on the case. [Reuters]

| | | |
|---|---|---|
| 1-28-97 | Arizona | A veteran Tucson lawmaker will sponsor legislation by an anti-gay group banning support groups for homosexual students from public school and college and university campuses. Rep. Schottel, a third-term legislator, said he agreed to sponsor the legislation on behalf of Frank Meliti, head of the Traditional Values Coalition. The measure, according to Meliti, will be patterned after similar legislation approved last year in Utah. That law, approved in a special session, allows school districts to deny access to clubs that "materially or substantially encourage criminal or delinquent conduct, promote bigotry or involve human sexuality." [Arizona Daily Star - Howard Fischer] |
| 2-1-97 | California | California State University, Sacramento, surrendered to the U.S. military, retreating from an order that banned ROTC on campus because the Pentagon discriminates against gays and lesbians. CSUS Pres. Gerth said he felt obligated to reverse course after federal officials threatened to withhold $50 million in student aid and research funds if Reserve Officers' Training Corps were not allowed on campus. [Sacramento Bee - Robert D. Davila] |
| 2-97 | California | Assemblymember Sheila Kuehl introduced "The Dignity for All Students Act - AB 101." This bill simply adds "sexual orientation" to the existing non-discrimination language of the California Education Code. This bill would apply to all public school districts, community college districts, and |

|          |              | to the California State University system. It would also apply to the University of California, given the approval of the university Regents. This bill requires the administration of each school and campus to ensure that programs and activities are free from discrimination based on sexual orientation, as they now must on the bases of race, ethnicity, religion, age, sex, color, and physical and mental disability. [gaybruin@ASUCLA] |
|----------|--------------|----------|
| 2-18-97  | California   | Felix Rocha Jr, Member of the Orange County Board of Education writes in opposition to Assembly member Sheila Kuehl's calling AB101 "The Dignity for All Students Act." He said: "In my opinion, homosexuality has no dignity!. Sexual orientation is just a fancy phrase by Kuehl to give some sort of legitimacy to her distorted beliefs toward homosexual rights. Sexual orientation has no claim to civil rights nor individual rights, for that matter, in the education of our children. To enact a law that specifically bars discrimination based on sexual orientation in public education, including employment, athletics, financial aid, curricula and student activities, is wrong." [LA Times] |
| 2-19-97  | Pennsylvania | A Pennsylvania State University student says the university infringed on his freedom of speech this week, when a student panel refused to extend official recognition to his anti-gay group. [Academe Today] |
| 3-7-97   | Pennsylvania | An anti-gay student group won recognition at Penn State University, after an appeals board decided it would not break the institution's discrimination codes.   The group, called STRAIGHT, which stands for Students Reinforcing Adherence |

In General Heterosexual Tradition, may now use Penn State letterhead and meet in university buildings—and will have to admit lesbians and gays as members.
[AP]

| | | |
|---|---|---|
| 3-12-97 | Massachusetts | Harvard University's John F. Kennedy School of Government was investigating a series of letters sent to several students containing anti-gay threats and ethnic and racial slurs. The letter's authors claimed to be members of the faculty as well as the student body who "feel that affirmative action is wrong. We are against any 'politically correct' diversity measures at this school."<br>[Reuters] |
| 3-21-97 | Massachusetts | The Massachusetts Institute of Technology will guarantee financial aid packages to its ROTC students whose military funding is cut because of their sexual orientation, the school said.<br>[Reuters - Leslie Gevirtz] |

## RELIGION

| | | |
|---|---|---|
| 12-4-93 | Lutheran | The first draft of a 21-page Lutheran statement on sexuality says that churches should re-examine their traditional disapproval of gay and lesbian couples. The report suggested that faithful gay relationships or even the blessing of committed same-sex unions is "strongly supported by responsible biblical interpretation." The Evangelical Lutheran Church in America (ELCA) has 5.2 million members and has been studying issues of sexuality since 1989.<br>[LA Times - John Dart] |
| 12-9-93 | Lutheran | Negative reaction to the release of the |

21-page draft "The Church and Human Sexuality: A Lutheran Perspective" led to the removal of the director of the study. An official statement from the Church Council said no statement would be recommended to a Churchwide Assembly unless it would stand on biblical foundations and merit widespread support within the church.

The United Church of Christ is the only major Protestant denomination to permit the ordination of homosexuals. In the last two years, the Episcopal Church, the United Methodist Church, and the Presbyterian Church (U.S.A.) have rejected proposals to loosen church strictures on homosexuality.
[AP - David Briggs]

| | | |
|---|---|---|
| 12-11-93 | Episcopal | Delegates to the annual convention of the Los Angeles Episcopal Diocese issued a compromise resolution which allows priests who have been "blessing" same-sex unions to continue to do so while priests who have refused to perform such ceremonies may continue to refuse. |

Last month, the Episcopal Diocese of Massachusetts voted to ask the church's national legislative body, the General Convention, to direct the preparation of rites and ceremonies celebrating gay and lesbian unions.
[LA Times - Larry B. Stammer]

| | | |
|---|---|---|
| 1-19-94 | Episcopal | A leading Episcopal divinity school is opening its seminary housing to homosexual couples despite church policy declaring sex is appropriate within marriage only. [AP - David Briggs] |
| 2-10-94 | Roman Catholic | Pope John Paul said the Roman Catholic Church would fight a European Parliament resolution passed on February 8th (159-96) which proposed that homosexual couples be allowed to marry and adopt |

children. He added that society could not
achieve authentic progress without safe-
guarding the unity of the family.

Two years ago, the Vatican issued a
document to contest moves to give homosexuals equal rights, particularly in the
United States. That document said homosexuals could legitimately be discriminated
against in employment, housing and the
adoption of children.
[Reuters - Philip Pullella]

| | | |
|---|---|---|
| 2-19-94 | Episcopal | North Carolina Episcopalians turned down a proposal (73–57) to ask the national church to create a ceremony for gay and lesbian marriages.<br>[AP] |
| 2-20-94 | Roman Catholic | The LA Times published a poll based on written responses from 2,087 Roman Catholic priests and 1,049 Roman Catholic nuns in dioceses across the United States. By a decisive 80% to 14% margin, priests would oppose any church-sanctioned marriage between homosexuals. Nuns oppose such unions 72% to 14%. Responses to whether engaging in homosexual behavior was a sin, 73% of priests and 62% of nuns said it was always or often a sin.<br>[LA Times, UPI] |
| 2-20-94 | Roman Catholic | Pope John Paul blasted the European Parliament (EU) for its resolution that homosexual couples should be allowed to marry and adopt children. "A relationship between two men or two women cannot make up a real family, and, more to the point, you cannot allow such a union the right to adopt children who do not have a family," the Pope said, raising his voice.<br><br>The author of the EU resolution said studies in the United States and elsewhere had shown that children brought up in |

homosexual families or by homosexual couples received a good education and did not necessarily become homosexuals. The Pope flatly rejected this. "These children are greatly endangered, greatly harmed, because in this so-called substitute family they will not have a father and a mother but two fathers or two mothers," he added.
[Reuters - Philip Pullella]

| | | |
|---|---|---|
| 2-25-94 | Mormon | Mormon Church leaders have called on their nearly 9 million members to actively oppose same-sex marriages. A church spokesman said the statement came in response to debate in Hawaii over efforts to legalize homosexual marriages.<br>[AP] |
| 2-27-94 | Lutheran | A half-dozen parishioners testified in support of Rev. Merkel in a church hearing to determine if he should be defrocked as pastor of St. Paul's Lutheran Church in Oakland. He was charged with violating church rules by being "a practicing homosexual."<br>[UPI] |
| 3-13-94 | Anglican | The Church of England swept away centuries of tradition when it ordained 32 women to the priesthood, authorizing them to preside over the central religious rites of the Anglican faith. But some 700 clergy have threatened to defect to Roman Catholicism rather than acknowledge the women as priests. "If we look at the Episcopal church in America we see the sorry state that they're in, gay marriages and all the rest of it," said Canon Widdecombe, whose sister Anne, a government minister, has already switched to Catholicism.<br>[Reuters - Anne Senior] |
| 3-15-94 | Roman Catholic | The Vatican attacked attempts to recognize |

homosexual marriages, saying the move could lead to the recognition of incestual relationships. The Vatican newspaper, L'Osservatore Romano, said allowing homosexual couples to marry and adopt children could be the first of a series of immoral unions. "What if incest began to spread as an instinct, would that be marriage too?" the paper asked.
[Reuters]

| | | |
|---|---|---|
| 3-22-94 | Roman Catholic | The archbishop of Washington has written President Clinton complaining that Surgeon General Joycelyn Elders is advocating acceptance of homosexuality. Cardinal Hickey condemned her support of homosexual adoptions. "It is one thing to defend the human rights of homosexual men and women; it is quite another to encourage, as she does, a life-style which puts so-called homosexual unions on a par with marriage and family and condones homosexual behavior among young people," he wrote. [AP] |
| 4-28-94 | Jewish | A report from a commission of Conservative rabbis encourages Jewish leaders to reconsider whether homosexual relations can be part of God's gift of sexuality if other moral standards are obeyed. This report is called the first modern attempt to draft a sexual ethic by any branch of Judaism.<br><br>The commission hopes to present its report to the assembly which represents 1,500 Conservative rabbis who serve 1.5 million congregational members. [AP - David Briggs] |
| 5-26-94 | Church of Scotland | The Church of Scotland ruled that gay sex and "living in sin" were against God's law.<br><br>Traditionalists won the day in a heated debate at the General Assembly of the |

| | | |
|---|---|---|
| | | Protestant church over two controversial reports calling for more tolerance for homosexual love and gay marriages. [Reuters] |
| 5-28-94 | Roman Catholic | A delegation of cardinals officially presented to Pope John Paul II the English version of the new Catechism of the Catholic Church, the first universal book of the church's teachings in 428 years. The last universal catechism was issued in 1566 after the Council of Trent. |
| | | Although its condemnation of homosexuality is tempered by a call for "respect, compassion and sensitivity" toward gay people and a rejection of "unjust discrimination" it also states: |
| | | "Basing itself on Sacred Scripture, which presents homosexual acts as acts of grave depravity, tradition has always declared that 'homosexual acts are intrinsically disorder.' . . . Under no circumstances can they be approved." [AP and Washington Post-Bill Broadway] |
| 5-29-94 | Roman Catholic | In London gay protesters disrupted a service of consecration in Westminster Cathedral for the new Roman Catholic catechism, saying it denigrated homosexual love. [Reuters] |
| 6-9-94 | Christian | People For the American Way released a report that said fundamentalist Christian groups have increased political activity in all regions of the U.S. but most strongly in the South and Midwest. Anti-homosexual movements are active in some 25 states. [Reuters - Michael Posner] |
| 6-10-94 | Roman Catholic | "Doonesbury" offended some Catholics with its series that suggested the church once sanctioned same-sex marriages. The strip mentioned a book published by Yale |

University's John Boswell, who discovered what he believes to be Catholic liturgies for a same-sex ceremony (see 6-19-94 entry).

At least two newspapers refused to run the strips.
[AP]

| | | |
|---|---|---|
| 6-11-94 | Protestant | Members of the University Congregational Church in Seattle hired a gay couple to share a ministerial job. The vote (3 to 1) marked the first time a mainstream U.S. church has called a gay couple to share a ministerial position. |

The Seattle church is part of the 1.5 million-member United Church of Christ, which often is described as one of the most liberal Protestant denominations and one of the few that sanctions homosexual ordination.
[Reuters]

| | | |
|---|---|---|
| 6-14-94 | MCC | Metropolitan Community Church was founded in 1968 by a Pentecostal minister excommunicated for announcing his homosexuality. It now has 30,000 members and branches in 16 countries. It embraces gays, lesbians and transsexuals. |

MCC has been denied membership in the National Council of Churches.
[Reuters - Laney Salisbury]

| | | |
|---|---|---|
| 6-17-94 | Presbyterian | The General Assembly of the Presbyterian Church (U.S.A.) voted to prohibit ministers from blessing same-sex unions. [Washington Post - Bill Broadway] |
| 6-19-94 | Roman Catholic | In the Middle Ages, men who loved each other were commonly united by priests in Christian ceremonies much like weddings between men and women, John Boswell of Yale University says in his new book, *Same-Sex Unions in Premodern Europe.* "In almost every age and place the ceremony |

fulfilled what most people today regard as
the essence of marriage: a permanent
romantic commitment between two people, witnessed and recognized by the community."

A Connecticut priest who has known
of Boswell's work for many years said he
has been using the liturgies to perform
marriage ceremonies for gay and lesbian
couples. He was excommunicated from
the Roman Catholic Church earlier this
year due to involvement with a denomination of lesbians and gays that calls itself the
Ecumenical Catholic Church.
[AP - Brigitte Greenberg]

6-21-94      Christian Coalition     Rep. Vic Fazio at a breakfast at the
National Press Club accused the "radical
right" of secretly taking over state parties
and financially dominating campaigns
with expenditures unreported to election
authorities. He said the "radical right"
wants "to carry views that are distinctly
religious over into government and to try
to impose those as laws." He cited reli-
gious-right views on homosexuality, censorship and public expressions of faith.
[AP - Jill Lawrence]

6-23-94      Roman Catholic         President Clinton rejected requests from
the Catholic archbishop of Washington to
disavow Surgeon General Joycelyn Elders's
comments about sexuality. Cardinal
Hickey accused the surgeon general of
encouraging "a life-style which puts so-
called homosexual unions on a par with
marriage and family and condones homosexual behavior among young people."
Clinton replied that he was "committed to
building a society that promotes tolerance
and acceptance of diversity." Issues such as
homosexual marriage "are left to the individual states and are not under the juris-

diction of the federal government."
[WP - Robert D. Novak]

| | | |
|---|---|---|
| 6-23-94 | Episcopalian | The fourth draft of the Episcopalian bishops' document on sexuality asked the church to uphold an ideal of lifelong faithful unions for both heterosexual and homosexual couples and to greet gays and lesbians with hospitality rather than hostility. At the same time, the document also related traditional church teaching that sex is reserved for heterosexual marriages and stopped short of advocating changes in church law on the issues of gay ordinations or the blessing of same-sex unions. Bishop Frey, dean of Trinity Episcopal School for Ministry, said, "In its present form, it would be the most embarrassing document the bishops have even produced." [AP - David Briggs] |
| 6-26-94 | Roman Catholic | Pope John Paul said homosexuality, "free love" and contraception were "morally unacceptable" behaviour that "distort the deep significance of sexuality." [Reuters - Philip Pullella] |
| 7-3-94 | Roman Catholic | About 10,000 gays and lesbians marched through the streets of Rome to support demands that included the right to form legally recognized couples and adopt children. The Pope, speaking the day after these demonstrations, repeated that children should only be born within monogamous, heterosexual marriages. "Children are the fruit of love of only one man and only one woman," he said. [Reuters] |
| 7-29-94 | Promise Keepers | During the spring and summer, more than 230,000 mostly white Christian men have attended Promise Keepers meetings. The organization, started four years ago, is |

aimed at helping Christian men commit themselves to God and their communities. It has been criticized for preaching hate. One example is its firm anti-homosexual stand which holds that "the Bible clearly teaches that homosexuality violates God's creative design for a husband and wife and that it is a sin."
[WP - Thomas B. Edsall and AP - Robert Unruh]

8-16-94    Moslem    Egypt's population minister tried to calm Islamic opposition to the upcoming summit conference on population to be held in Cairo. He said fears expressed by Islamic groups that the conference would encourage homosexual couples to bring up families were misplaced. He said the United Nations had already defined families as "the husband, wife, and their children. . . . We are not going to redefine principles agreed on at previous meetings."
[Reuters - Dominic Evans]

8-24-94    Roman Catholic    Argentina's top Roman Catholic cardinal apologized for calling homosexuals an ignoble stain on the face of society and suggesting they should be put in a ghetto. "It was a joke, something that just crossed my mind," Cardinal Quarracino told a TV interviewer.
[Reuters]

8-26-94    Episcopalian    An Episcopalian Convention downgraded the draft of a human sexuality statement to a less influential study document. The document had urged church members to welcome homosexuals and recognize same-sex relationships. The next day 45 bishops protested the change. "Our lives and our experience as bishops have convinced us that a wholesome example to the flock of Christ does not exclude a person of homosexual orientation," said one of the

bishops.
[AP]

| 10-14-94 | MCC | Two months ago, the Metropolitan Community Church opened a new church in Huntsville, Alabama. Many have opposed it. One Baptist minister said it "has created quite a furor among the Christian community." Another minister of a nearby congregation erected a sign saying "Homosexuality is a sin," and several neighbors scrawled derisive messages on posters across the street.<br>[AP - Jay Reeves] |
| 10-22-94 | Christian | Conservative Christians tried to put anti-gay rights measures on the ballot this year in 10 states and succeeded in only two: Idaho and Oregon.<br><br>Kelly Walton, chairman of the Idaho Citizens Alliance, is the driving force behind Idaho's Proposition 1 which would prohibit Idaho's state or local governments from giving homosexuals protection under anti-discrimination laws. It would bar public schools from suggesting homosexuality is acceptable, and would require libraries to keep books on homosexuality away from minors. Walton says that homosexuality is "everywhere. Nowhere in the country are we safe from people who want to portray a very deadly behavior as healthy and normal."<br>[AP - David Foster] |
| 2-4-95 | Presbyterian | The Presbytery, made up of representatives of 65 Presbyterian Church (U.S.A.) congregations endorsed a policy that prohibits its ministers from blessing same-sex unions.<br><br>"We think that people probably can't help the sexual orientation they have. But we think they can help and control homosexual practice. . . " said one Presbyter. |

The denomination considers homosexuality a sin, but ordains gay ministers if they are not practicing homosexuals.
[AP]

| | | |
|---|---|---|
| 3-18-95 | Church of England | The Church of England, mired in controversy over homosexuality among its clergy, now has its first acknowledged lesbian priest. The Reverend Ros Hunt revealed publicly that she is a lesbian. A national debate on the church and homosexuality has intensified since the start of this month when a 74-year- old retired Anglican bishop revealed he was gay. [Reuters] |
| 7-6-95 | Presbyterian | The Presbyterian Church filed a friend-of-the-court brief backing opponents of Amendment 2, Colorado's anti-gay rights amendment. The U.S. Supreme Court will hear the case. Amendment 2, approved by Colorado voters in 1992, prohibits governments from passing laws protecting homosexuals. A representative of the General Assembly of the Presbyterian Church said: "We are advising the U.S. Supreme Court on the Presbyterian Church's (stand) on the . . . protection of the civil and human rights of homosexuals." [AP] |
| 8-18-95 | Episcopal | Episcopal bishops voted to bring retired Bishop Righter before a formal church trial because he ordained an openly gay man in 1990. Righter has denied any wrongdoing, saying church doctrine in this case does not limit a bishop's right to ordain a "canonically qualified candidate." [AP - David Briggs] |
| 8-19-95 | Lutheran | The newly elected leader of the Evangelical Lutheran Church in America (ELCA), the nation's fifth-largest Protestant denomination, said that he is still trying to figure out |

|  |  | his own position on issues such as the ordination of homosexuals and whether same-sex relationships are part of God's plan.<br>[AP - David Briggs] |
|---|---|---|
| 8-24-95 | Lutheran | Retiring head of ECLA, Bishop Chilstrom, said his own perspective has changed from thinking homosexual acts were perverted to viewing gays and lesbians as people who "are no different from us than people who are left-handed."<br>[AP - David Briggs] |
| 9-5-95 | Christian | A CBS special on the "Christian right" reported that in Merrimack, NH, the school board's 3-2 conservative Christian majority began to impose its agenda for the schools, including the teaching of creationism and banning classroom discussion of homosexuality.<br>[AP - Scott Williams] |
| 11-9-95 | Methodist | A homosexual student group, Gays, Lesbians and Extras, won approval from the Student Government of Texas Wesleyan University but President Schrum vetoed the decision, citing a conflict with United Methodist doctrine. He said that, because the United Methodist Church does not sanction homosexuality or fund gay groups, the university "will not officially authorize, sanction or fund any campus group that avows homosexuality."<br>[AP] |
| 11-15-95 | Baptist | A powerful Florida Baptist group has asked its 1 million members to boycott Walt Disney Co.'s parks and products, saying Disney showed a lack of moral leadership by extending health insurance to partners of homosexual workers.<br>[AP - Lisa Holewa] |
| 11-15-95 | Christian Coalition | The Illinois Christian Coalition is conduct- |

ing a petition drive to keep its home town of Bloomington from adopting an ordinance guaranteeing civil rights protections to gays and lesbians.
[UPI]

| | | |
|---|---|---|
| 12-20-95 | Roman Catholic | The Vatican issued a sex education guide to help Roman Catholics save their children from sin. On homosexuality, it advised parents not to raise the issue at all before adolescence and to seek expert advice if necessary. It reiterated a Church blanket ban on homosexual sex, which it said was "against the laws of nature." [Reuters - Jude Webber] |
| 1-11-96 | Christian Churches | Keith Hartman's book, *Congregations in Conflict: The Battle over Homosexuality* will be published in February. He says that homosexuality is "the most divisive element facing the church today."<br><br>Groups such as the Quakers are leading the way toward tolerance. Hartman noted that two Quaker congregations in Durham and Chapel Hill, N.C. took several months of detailed discussion before deciding to allow same-sex marriages. [AP - Gary D. Robertson] |
| 1-11-96 | Lutheran | Two small San Francisco Lutheran congregations that defied their mother church by ordaining active gay and lesbian ministers were expelled from the denomination. The Lutherans allow ordination of gay ministers only if they take a vow to abstain from having relations with members of the same sex. [AP] |
| 2-4-96 | Anglican | Some 300 senior Anglican church leaders worldwide, including Archbishop Desmond Tutu, have backed a campaign to ordain practicing homosexuals as priests. The clerics have signed an advertisement |

praising the campaigning work of the Lesbian and Gay Christian Movement, or LGCM, which will appear in religious newspapers.

The issue of homosexual bishops potentially could split the church and some senior clerics jumped to condemn the trend. "If successful, this campaign will split the church finally and completely," said George Austin, the Archdeacon of York, northern England. "It is much more divisive than the issue of women priests, and will alienate decent Christian people who don't want to see buggery blessed." [UPI]

| | | |
|---|---|---|
| 3-13-96 | Protestant | A Protestant pastor, Rev. Rhem, was asked to step aside by Michigan Reformed Church of America leaders last month. A committee of church officials discovered that Rhem believed homosexuality was "a diversity of creation, not a sin" and that the Bible is not the literal word of God. [UPI] |
| 3-21-96 | Mormon | In his soon-to-be-published book *Same-Sex Dynamics among Nineteenth-Century Americans: A Mormon Example*, historian D. Michael Quinn suggests that the attitudes of 19th century Mormons toward the whole range of same-sex relationships were far more relaxed than what he calls the rampant "homophobic concerns" of today. It wasn't until 1968 that the church made homosexual acts grounds for excommunication. [AP - Vern Anderson] |
| 3-27-96 | Roman Catholic | The Vatican has appealed to voters not to support politicians who endorse same-sex marriages, such as the mass wedding ceremony for homosexuals in San Francisco |

this week.
[AP]

| | | |
|---|---|---|
| 3-28-96 | Jewish | A group of Reform rabbis endorsed the legalization of homosexual marriages but stopped short of recommending that rabbis perform the ceremonies.<br>[AP - Michael Raphael] |
| 4-3-96 | Episcopal | The presiding Episcopal church leader, Edmond Browning, will end his 12-year term next year. He has been in the midst of a raging battle with other church representatives. His most recent crusade to make the church more welcoming to gays and lesbians follows his criticism of racism and a continued push for women's rights.<br><br>Browning suggests that the church should see the Bible's condemnation of homosexuality the same way it sees its endorsement of slavery: an ancient stricture made untenable by modern culture and science.<br><br>As on most controversial issues, Browning has found himself at the centre of the storm. He believes the confrontation over homosexuality will harm the church. "It's not a matter that's going to be settled by a court case . . . it's a matter of the heart," he said.<br>[Reuters-Eric Frazier] |
| 4-21-96 | Methodist | Homosexuality is at the forefront of the agenda for the 8.5 million-member church's quadrennial meeting taking place in Denver.<br><br>Morris Floyd became a member of Affirmation, a Methodist homosexual-rights group, in 1978. He said at times he just feels a sense of fatigue, knowing the likelihood of substantial progress is slim. But he added: "I think it will continue to be an important issue in the church for another generation at least. The gay, |

lesbian, bisexual people in the churches are just not going to go away. . . . They are going to continue to confront the church."

And when they do, people like the Rev. James Heidinger, president of the Good News movement, will be there to oppose them. "Most of us are weary of it [but] for many people, it's a bottom-line issue. It's a go-to-the mat issue."
[AP - David Briggs]

| | | |
|---|---|---|
| 4-23-96 | Methodist | The United Methodist Council of Bishops today upheld church policy opposing the ordination of gays and declaring homosexuality incompatible with church teaching. |

Church policy upholds the civil rights of homosexuals, but says "self-avowed, practicing homosexuals" may not be ordained. The church also says the practice of homosexuality is incompatible with Christian teaching and says no denominational money may be given to promote the acceptance of homosexuality.
[AP - David Briggs]

| | | |
|---|---|---|
| 5-16-96 | Uniting Church of Australia | Australia's third largest Christian church has broken with centuries of Biblical tradition in issuing a controversial report on sexuality supporting gay clergy, same-sex marriages and relationships out of wedlock. |

Rev. Drayton said the report does not deviate from the Bible, but reflects an understanding of the Bible and contemporary society.

On the subject of homosexuality . . . the report said "there is no legitimate reason for rejecting homosexuality or homosexual relationships." The report supported gay relationships if they were right relationships. "Right relationships are characterised by agape, the love, caring and compassion embodied in Jesus Christ." On the subject of gay clergy, the

report said: "The task group has found no
evidence that a person who is a homosexual is less fit for ministry, or that a homosexual minister damages the credibility of
the ministry, any more than anyone else."
Regarding marriage, the report said: "The
key moral question is not whether we
should hold onto the institution of marriage, but the quality of the marriage relationships."
[Reuters - Michael Perry]

| | | |
|---|---|---|
| 5-28-96 | Episcopal | An Episcopal court, in its first heresy trial of an Episcopal bishop since the 1920s, dismissed heresy charges against a retired bishop who ordained a non-celibate gay man. It ruled that church doctrine does not explicitly bar the ordination of practicing homosexuals. It also declared a 1979 resolution against the ordination of non-celibate gays is nonbinding. The ruling did not say whether the church now condones the ordination of gays. |

Reacting to this decision, ten bishops
representing about 10% of all U.S.
Episcopalians hinted that they might break
away from the church.
[AP - Kevin O'Hanlon]

| | | |
|---|---|---|
| 6-25-96 | Unitarian | The Unitarian Universalist Church voted to support legal recognition of gay mar- riages, the first major religious denomina- tion in the country to do so. The Boston-based denomination has a history of support for gay rights. In 1970, it called for an end to gay discrimination, and in 1980 it said gays should be allowed to serve in the ministry. [AP] |
| 6-26-96 | Presbyterian | In a move described as unprecedented within the Presbyterian Church in the United States, a governing body has ordered an elder stripped of his ordained |

office because he is gay. The action upheld the denomination's longstanding prohibition against the ordination of homosexuals. [Reuters]

| | | |
|---|---|---|
| 6-30-96 | Presbyterian | John Buchanan of Chicago was elected as next leader of the 2.7 million-member Presbyterian Church. He said he believes gay men and women should be allowed to become practicing clergy, but will leave it up to individual congregations to decide if they want to allow it in their churches. Although each candidate stressed that the vote should not be viewed as a referendum on gay clergy, the results seemed to speak otherwise.<br>[UPI US & World] |
| 7-6-96 | Presbyterian | The governing body of the Presbyterian Church (USA) voted (313-236) to ban the ordination of practicing homosexuals, calling on gays and lesbians to stay celibate if they want to be accepted as deacons or ministers. Commissioners also decided to support the civil rights of same-sex partners. The amendment will be sent back to local leaders of the church for final approval.<br>Opponents saw the vote as a step backward. "We are asking people again: 'Don't ask. Don't tell. Let's live our lives in secrecy.'"<br>[Reuters & AP - Martha Mendoza] |
| 7-8-96 | Church of England | A survey of attitudes among the Church of England's ruling body showed that more than half the members of the General Synod still opposed the ordination of homosexual priests—but activists said it also showed growing support for greater tolerance.<br>[PA News - Jo Butler] |
| 8-3-96 | Presbyterian | In Taipei, Taiwan, a gay man is founding |

|         |                 | Taiwan's first gay church, an unauthorised but tolerated offshoot of the tradition-bound island's Presbyterian church. [Reuters - Jeffrey Parker] |
|---------|-----------------|---|
| 8-25-96 | Anglican Church | Homosexual couples should be assessed as ineligible to provide foster care to children despite new state government-backed anti-discrimination guidelines, The Anglican Church said. Anglican Home Mission, the church's welfare arm and the third largest nongovernment foster care provider in NSW, said children in foster care should have the security and role modeling of a "normative family." "My point is that we ought not to experiment with children where that degree of research has not yet been sufficiently undertaken to give any guarantees or assurances that there is the required degree of stability within same sex couples" said Rev. Dillon, Home Mission executive director. [AAP] |
| 11-9-96 | Evangelical | A survey of churchgoers linked to the Evangelical Alliance UK revealed that 96% of British congregations believe gay sex to be wrong. The same number say they would not accept Christians living in homosexual partnerships. [PA News - Padraic Flanagan] |
| 11-13-96 | Romania | Romania's Orthodox church, inherently conservative, asked parliament earlier this year to brand homosexuality as a crime. [Reuters - Roxana Dascalu] |
| 11-16-96 | Anglican | More than 2,000 gay Christians gathered for Britain's first cathedral service in celebration of homosexual worship. The service—commemorating 20 years of the Lesbian and Gay Christian Movement (LGCM)—took place at Southward Cathedral in south London. It was held |

amid an atmosphere of crisis in the Church of England unparalleled since the battles over the ordination of women priests. Kirker, LGCM general secretary, who estimated that a third of Church of England priests are gay, said today's service was a sign of the increasing acceptance of lesbians and homosexual men by the church.

Protesters gathered outside the cathedral waving banners declaring "Sodomy and lesbianism—a perversion to be repented, not an orientation to be celebrated" and "The wages of sin is death." [PA News - Andrew Woodcock]

| | | |
|---|---|---|
| 1-21-97 | Baptist | A Topeka, Kansas, church whose members regularly engage in antihomosexual picketing lost a Supreme Court appeal today and must continue to limit its demonstrations outside another church's building. The justices, without comment, let stand rulings that bar Westboro Baptist Church members from picketing outside St. David's Episcopal Church in Topeka shortly before, during or shortly after any religious service. Since 1991, Westboro Baptist's Rev. Fred Phelps and his followers began what he calls a ministry of public religious pickets with a central message of "God Hates Fags." [AP - Richard Carelli] |
| 2-9-97 | Lutheran | A Protestant church council in northern Germany has decided to give homosexual couples the right to a church blessing if their partnership resembles a marriage. A majority of the Lutheran church synod based in the town of Rendsburg also agreed to recognize any relationships that were similar to marriage in a landmark vote. But it was not clear whether the practice would go ahead because the synod's |

decision could still be vetoed by the church's bishops who had a month to decide on their position.
[Reuters]

2-11-97            Anglican          Gay couples living in a monogamous relationship received tacit approval from the spiritual head of the Anglican Church in Australia today. The Primate of the Anglican Church, Melbourne's Archbishop Keith Rayner, said the marriage between a man and a woman was the ideal form of a living relationship, and that the next ideal state was a monogamous gay couple. "This style of living, in a different degree, is closer to the pattern of life that God intends (than single promiscuity)," Archbishop Rayner said.
[AAP - Alan Gale]

2-16-97            Roman Catholic    Dissident Roman Catholics plan on standing in front of cathedrals across the country today looking for support for their proposed reforms. They are asking churchgoers to back a referendum titled "We Are Church." The referendum, among other things, calls for women's ordination, optional celibacy for the clergy and respect for the rights of gay and lesbian Catholics. The Referendum started in 1995 in Germany and Austria where more than 2 million Catholics signed it. The U.S. campaign aims to collect 1 million signatures by mid-May.
[AP]

2-97              Kerusso Ministries  Hope '97 is a year-long project in which Michael Johnston will bring his message of hope in Christ to cities across America. The tour includes rallies in 15 major U.S. cities. The tour will offer seminars on how to minister to individuals struggling with homosexuality and how to counter the

homosexual agenda in your community.
[American Family Association Journal]

| | | |
|---|---|---|
| 3-2-97 | Roman Catholic | Emotions ranged from joy to anger as the 400,000-member Rochester Roman Catholic Diocese held its first ever Mass for gays and lesbians. Police stood guard, protesters chanted prayers outside, and people filled the 1,100-seat Sacred Heart Cathedral as Bishop Matthew Clark joined a handful of bishops nationwide that have held a Mass for homosexuals. [AP] |
| 3-18-97 | Presbyterian | In a major setback to Christian gay-rights activists, the Presbyterian Church (U.S.A.) has voted to make its ban on the ordination of homosexuals part of church law. [AP - David Briggs] |

## CHILD CUSTODY

| | | |
|---|---|---|
| 12-3-93 | Virginia Bottoms Case | The American Psychological Association, jointly with the American Academy of Child and Adolescent Psychiatry, the National Association of Social Workers and the Virginia chapter of the NASW files brief with Virginia Court of Appeals in the Bottoms case. |

A judge removed 2 year old Tyler from his mother (Sharon Bottoms) and awarded custody to his grandmother, Kay Bottoms who had brought the court action. The grandmother had said the boy would grow up not knowing the difference between men and women if he lived with his mother, Sharon, and her lover, April Wade. Brief states: "Sexual orientation should not be a sole or primary factor in deciding any aspect of parental rights."
[AP - Lauran Neergaard]

6-21-94 Virginia Bottoms Case  Sharon Bottoms regained custody of her son when a state appeals court ruled that the woman's sex life—though illegal under Virginia law—does not make her an unfit parent. Boy's grandmother will appeal to Virginia Supreme Court

            "A parent's private sexual conduct, even if illegal, does not create a presumption of unfitness" Judge Sam W. Coleman wrote.

            "Lesbian custody cases are the most frequent form of discrimination against lesbians across the country" said Paula Brantner, interim legal director of the National Center for Lesbian Rights (NCLR).
            [AP - Larry O'Dell]

6-26-94 Virginia Bottoms Case  Kay Bottoms appeals case to Virginia Supreme Court. Custody of Tyler remains with grandmother, Kay Bottoms.
            [AP]

1-4-95     Sydney  Australia's Family Court chief judge calls for homosexual couples and their children to be recognized as legal families, sparking bitter debate between gay activists and conservative politicians.
            [Reuters]

2-23-95    Bottoms Case  The American Academy of Matrimonial Lawyers, representing 1,500 divorce and matrimonial law attorneys, filed a friend of the court brief in the Bottoms Case. They said homosexuality in and of itself should not prevent a parent from retaining custody.

            "Any presumption that a homosexual parent is 'unfit' for custody simply by virtue of his or her homosexuality is a doctrine based upon prejudice and stereotypes which deprives a parent of fundamental rights and privileges guaranteed under the Constitution, while simultaneously ignoring

the best interests of the child," the academy said.
[UPI]

4-21-95  Virginia Bottoms Case  The Virginia Supreme Court ruled 4-3 in overturning a lower appellate court ruling which had returned custody of Tyler to his mother, Sharon Bottoms. She lost custody of 3-year-old Tyler.

The Court cited the "moral climate" in Sharon Bottoms' home and the "social condemnation" the boy would face outside it because of his mother's sexual orientation. The court ruled that although homosexuality alone is no reason to take children from their parents, it can be considered an important factor in custody battles.

Elizabeth Birch, executive director of the Washington- based Human Rights Campaign Fund, said "Anyone who truly cares about families should be morally outraged that the government has taken a child from his own loving mother because of other people's prejudices."

According to NCLR, the highest courts in 8 states have ruled that homosexuality is not reason to automatically deny custody, and those in five states (Mississippi, Missouri, North Dakota, South Dakota and Oklahoma) have ruled that it is.
[AP - Larry O'Dell]

2-28-96  Virginia Bottoms Case  Upholding an earlier ruling, a judge denied Sharon Bottoms request to regain custody of her 4-year-old son and denounced her for plans to make a TV movie about the custody battle against her mother.
[AP - Zinie Chen]

8-13-96  Florida  A Florida appeals court is dealing with two cases in which a lesbian mother has been denied custody of her child because of her sexual preference.

In one of the cases, which the appeals court has not yet decided, a lower court judge awarded custody of a12-year-old daughter to the ex-husband, even though he once served eight years in prison for killing his first wife.

Mary Ward raised Cassey since the couple split up in 1987 and said all was fine until last year when she went to court seeking an increase in child support. Instead of dealing with her request, Circuit Judge Joseph Tarbuck of Pensacola took away her daughter, ruling the child "should be given the opportunity and the option to live in a non-lesbian world."

In the other case, the appeals court granted a new hearing for another lesbian mother who lost custody of her 4- year-old, ruling that the woman could not be denied custody solely because of her sexual orientation.
[UPI - Chris Codd]

8-21-96  Virginia Bottoms Case

A judge ruled that Sharon Bottoms, who lost custody of her 5-year-old son can visit with the boy at her home as long as her live-in lover, April Wade, is not around. Ms. Wade is not even allowed to talk to the boy.

"I don't understand how anybody can tell someone they can't speak to someone else. It breaks my heart," said Sharon Bottoms.
[AP - Bill Baskervill]

8-30-96  Florida

A Florida appeals court upheld the lower court decision to award custody of a lesbian woman's 12-year-old daughter Cassey to the girl's father, who once served eight years in prison for murder.

Cassey lived with her mother until last summer, when Judge Tarbuck revoked custody, saying he wanted to give Cassey a chance to live in "a non-lesbian world."
[AP - Jackie Hallifax]

| 10-3-96 | Illinois | An Illinois appeals court was asked to decide Thursday whether a woman's same-sex relationship is grounds enough for her to lose custody of her two children to her ex-husband. |

The ex-husband received a favorable ruling from a Tazewell County Circuit Court judge who said the woman's relationship with another woman would bring "social condemnation" on the children, a boy and girl.

Attorneys for both sides argued before the Illinois appellate court in Ottawa. That court is expected to issue its ruling later this year.
[UPI]

| 10-15-96 | Raleigh, NC | A father can keep custody of his two sons even though he lives with a homosexual lover, the North Carolina Court of Appeals ruled today. |

The unanimous appeals court ruling overturns a lower court decision that said the children were exposed to "unfit and improper influences" that could damage them emotionally and socially.
[AP - Dennis Patterson]

| 12-18-96 | Illinois | An Illinois appellate court has awarded custody of two children to their bi-sexual mother, Rebecca S., saying the father had not proven his ex-wife is an unfit parent. The court also noted that state laws treat homosexual and heterosexual parents the same in custody matters. Rebecca S. first won custody of her children in 1991 when her seven-year marriage ended. Two years later, she moved in with a woman. Ex-husband Stuart S. remarried and then filed for custody. A County judge granted custody to the father last January, citing "the burden of social condemnation" he believed the children might face. But the appeals court noted that two psychologists examined the |

children and found the arrangement was not causing emotional problems.

Stuart S. says he wants his children raised in a Christian household and says he will take the case to the Illinois Supreme Court.
[UPI & AP - Christopher Wills]

| | | |
|---|---|---|
| 1-23-97 | Florida Ward Case | Mary Ward died of a heart attack at the age of 47, suddenly ending a case that attracted national attention.<br>[UPI] |

2-26-97  Florida Packard Case  A Florida appeals court is considering a case that attorneys on both sides hope will clarify how state courts should treat gay and lesbian parents in custody cases. Julie Packard, a lesbian, is appealing an Okaloosa County court ruling giving her ex-husband custody of her two daughters. When the ruling was handed down, Brian Packard was preparing to remarry and Judge Heflin said that meant he would be able to "provide a more traditional environment for the children" than their mothers could.

An attorney for Julie Packard told the 1st District Court of Appeal that Judge Heflin considered nothing but the mother's sexual orientation in making the ruling, and seemed to have "an almost prurient interest in the sexual life and sexual conduct" of his client.
[UPI]

# ADOPTION AND FOSTER PLACEMENT

3-14-94  Illinois  Cook County Judge Yates granted a lesbian woman the right to adopt her partner's biological child in a state precedent. It is the first time an Illinois court has recognized the right of an unmarried lesbian couple to adopt. Yates initially held that only single people or married couples could adopt. The ACLU intervened.

Illinois joins Massachusetts and Vermont, whose Supreme Courts have both recognized gays and lesbians rights to adopt.

| | | |
|---|---|---|
| 6-30-94 | London | The first British lesbian couple was granted joint parental rights over the child born to one of them. "It means that in decisions involving education and health" the non-biologic mother will be a legitimate, legal parent. [Reuters] |
| 7-6-94 | Washington DC | Former U.S. drug czar and Education Secretary William Bennett, quoted from his book, The Book of Virtues: "I'm for leaving people alone but I'm not for vali-dating, I'm not for homosexual adoption." [Reuters - Alan Elsner] |
| 10-23-94 | Vatican City | The Vatican delegation at last month's pop-ulation conference in Cairo blocked lan-guage in the gathering's final document that it felt could have been construed as defending a right by homosexuals to marry and adopt children. [Reuters - Phillip Pullella] |
| 11-28-94 | Illinois | A Cook County judge ruled that two les-bian couples from Chicago have no legal standing to adopt children under Illinois law. A court-sanctioned adoption would have assured uninterrupted medical insur-ance benefits from the adopting partner's employer and custodial rights if the bio-logical mother dies.<br><br>In one case, a woman wanted to adopt a girl born to her partner through artificial insemination. In the other, a woman wanted to adopt her girlfriend's two children. [UPI] |

| | | |
|---|---|---|
| 1-11-95 | Illinois | The ACLU announced it will appeal the November 1994 Cook County judge's decision denying a lesbian couple's request to adopt children. "We believe that the circuit court decision is flawed," Geoffrey Kors, director of the ACLU's Gay & Lesbian Rights Project, said. "The statute clearly states that any person may adopt and that adoption decisions should be made in the best interest of the child." [UPI] |
| 1-26-95 | Nebraska | A directive from the director of the state Department of Social Services states that foster children won't be placed in the homes of known homosexuals, and gay people will be denied foster home licenses under a new state policy.<br><br>A bill that would prohibit foster care licenses from being issued to unmarried, unrelated adults is before state lawmakers. [AP] |
| 3-13-95 | California | Gov. Pete Wilson has reversed a new state policy allowing adoptions by gay and lesbian couples. Last December 1994 the Social Services Director issued a directive to local adoption and welfare agencies saying that "a stable and permanent home" is best for adoptive children.<br><br>Gov. Wilson ordered the Social Services Director to restore a 1987 policy that banned adoptions by any unmarried couples. [AP] |
| 5-11-95 | Canada | Four lesbian couples have been allowed to adopt children under a ground-breaking decision by a Canadian court, lawyers for the women said on Thursday. Ontario court Judge David Nevins granted adoption orders to the eight women, saying the definition of spouse under the relevant law in Ontario was discriminatory and violated |

Canada's charter of rights and freedoms.

Nevins ruled that the Child and Family Services Act, which precluded gay and lesbian couples from applying to adopt, could not be justified in a free and democratic society.

The ruling follows the defeat last year of an Ontario government bill that would have extended spousal rights to same-sex couples, including the right to apply for adoption.
[Reuters]

| | | |
|---|---|---|
| 6-16-95 | Australia | The New South Wales branch of the National Party voted to oppose the adoption of children by same-sex couples. [AAP - Margaret McDonald] |
| 6-22-95 | Australia | The British Queen's representative in Australia, the governor-general, Bill Hayden, has supported gay marriage and adoption rights for same-sex couples. The governor-general by convention only rarely speaks publicly and almost never on controversial matters. "It is difficult to see how there can be a sustainable objection to partnership contracts similar to marriage." In contrast to Hayden's perspective, the Anglican Archbishop of Brisbane suggested that adoption for same-sex couples would erode traditional family values. [AAP] |
| 7-3-95 | Washington, DC | Unmarried couples in "committed relationships"—including gay male and lesbian companions—are permitted to adopt children under District law, the DC Court of Appeals has ruled. "If children available for adoption are likely to be denied permanent, loving homes when unmarried couples are refused the opportunity to adopt . . . we would have to say it would be absurd and unjust if the adoptions were denied," |

Associate Judge John Ferren wrote in the majority opinion.
[WPOST - Nancy Lewis]

8-25-95      Illinois      Two lesbian couples seeking to adopt their children were granted their petitions by a Cook County judge. The ruling came after an Illinois Appellate Court ruling last month that held, for the first time, that unmarried couples, including gays and lesbians, have the same adoption rights as married couples in Illinois. The Illinois Appellate Court sent the petitions back to the circuit court, where the petitions were granted.

In one of the cases, "Kay" and "Deb" sought to jointly adopt their three-year-old daughter, whom Kay conceived through artificial insemination.
[UPI]

11-2-95      New York      New York state's highest court, The Court of Appeals, ruled that gay and heterosexual domestic partners can adopt each other's biological children.

"Gay parents, like non-gay parents, want the best for their children. The court's ruling will allow any parent in the state to better provide for their children's needs and interests" said Beatrice Dohrn of the Lambda Legal Defense and Education Fund, a gay rights group which represented the lesbian couple.

New York becomes the third state after Massachusetts and Vermont whose top courts have recognized the right of homosexuals to adopt their partner's child.

Mark Elovitz of the American Civil Liberties Union Gay and Lesbian Rights Project said "The impact is to provide legal and emotional stability to families with lesbian and gay parents. It means the child can have the benefit of a legal relationship

with both parents and that is important for insurance benefits or if the biological parent should pass away."
[AP - Joel Stashenko]

| | | |
|---|---|---|
| 12-21-95 | New York | Following the November 2, 1995 New York State Court of Appeals ruling, an upstate New York Family Court judge reversed his prior decision and ruled that Gail Massina could adopt the biological child of her partner, Patricia Irwin. [UPI - Sascha Brodsky] |
| 2-15-96 | Ohio | A Senate bill overhauling Ohio's adoption process is expected to be reconciled with a House version next week, after senators defeated an attempt to prohibit homosexuals from becoming adoptive or foster parents. |
| | | The controversial amendment to prohibit adoptions by anyone "who practices homosexuality or is participating in a same-gender marriage or domestic partnership" was tabled, effectively killing it. [UPI] |
| 4-16-96 | Netherlands | The Dutch parliament voted 83 to 58 calling for same-sex couples to be given adoption rights. The Dutch government is not bound to implement parliament's vote. [Reuters World Report] |
| 8-19-96 | United States | A Harris poll found that 61% of Americans disapprove of a female couple who live together adopting a child. [AP US & World] |
| 10-27-96 | New York | Nearly six in ten Americans think that gays can be just as good at parenting as heterosexuals, but almost half oppose adoption by gay couples, according to a Newsweek poll released Sunday. |
| | | Newsweek said the opposition was down from previous surveys: 65 percent opposed gay adoption rights in 1994, and |

52 percent were against it in May.
[The Associated Press]

| | | |
|---|---|---|
| 11-26-96 | Australia | Queensland Families, Youth and Community Care Minister Lingard said he was not worried by suggestions that his plans to ban single men and lesbian couples from fostering children breached the state's anti-discrimination laws. Mr. Lingard said yesterday the previous Labor government had allowed people to become foster parents "willy nilly" under the category of "approved person." Mr. Lingard said his department would now review all current approved foster parents under the Shared Family Care program. [AAP] |
| 3-21-97 | California | Assembly Bill 53 was heard in the Assembly Judiciary Committee on March 19, 1997. AB 53 would prohibit discrimination on the basis of marital status in state adoptions. |

Current law is silent on "the best interest of the child" with regard to marital status. This silence is appropriate as marriage is not necessarily an indicator of parental fitness. Recently, however, the Wilson administration put forward proposed changes to the state's adoption regulations. These regulations, though not yet adopted, will state that an adoption by an unmarried couple is not in the best interest of the child. AB 53 would provide that unmarried couple may adopt, and that a social worker may not advocate that an adoption by an unmarried couple is against the best interest of the child based solely on the couple's marital status. AB 53 will allow unmarried, loving, fit parents—of any sexual orientation—to adopt children. [Frontiers]

# REPRODUCTIVE RIGHTS

6-22-94          Vatican City    The Vatican blasted homosexual women
                                 who want to have children by artificial
                                 insemination, branding this as an aberra-
                                 tion of nature. "This condition of homo-
                                 sexuality cannot be considered 'normal' in
                                 a person. One must make every effort to
                                 eliminate or correct it," the Vatican news-
                                 paper said in an editorial.
                                     An Italian gynecologist who had
                                 admitted a lesbian woman into his artifi-
                                 cial insemination program said:
                                 "Homosexuals have as much love to give
                                 children as heterosexuals."
                                 [Reuter - Philip Pullella]

6-29-94          Italy           After a year of work, an Italian-govern-
                                 ment appointed committee published
                                 guidelines for artificial insemination amid
                                 furor over a lesbian who gave birth after
                                 artificial insemination with sperm from a
                                 donor bank. The committee recommended
                                 that artificial pregnancy programs should
                                 be restricted to "adult couples of different
                                 sex who are married or at least bound by a
                                 stable and loving relationship and . . .
                                 preferably are of a potentially fertile age."
                                     Father Concetti, the Vatican's chief
                                 moral theologian, told Italian radio that he
                                 welcomed the guidelines. He said artificial
                                 pregnancy for lesbians challenged the
                                 divine order. "It represent a challenge to
                                 reason and nature and by extension a chal-
                                 lenge to God, the creator of man and
                                 woman, of nature and the rules that gov-
                                 ern the life of the universe," he wrote in
                                 the Vatican newspaper.
                                 [Reuters - Paul Holmes]

7-8-94           London          A government spokesperson said that the
                                 British national health service may move to
                                 exclude single women and lesbians from

receiving an infertility treatment. A representative from the Gay and Lesbian Christian Movement said that "homosexuals as taxpayers had just as much right to all health treatments as heterosexuals." He also dismissed suggestions that single mothers or gay couples do not make good parents.
[Reuters - Patrica Reaney]

| | | |
|---|---|---|
| 4-3-95 | Italy | Italy's physicians . . . have banned artificial insemination for women over 50, surrogate motherhood and barred lesbians from undergoing artificial insemination.<br>[Reuters - Phillip Pullella] |
| 8-9-95 | Vancouver | A Canadian doctor who refused to provide artificial insemination to a lesbian couple has been ordered to pay the women nearly $2,480 US by a human rights panel. It found that the doctor denied the couple a service usually available to the public because of their sexual orientation.<br>[Reuters] |
| 2-3-97 | Australia | Medicare benefits may be withdrawn for lesbians seeking access to donor sperm to start a family, according to federal Health Minister Wooldridge. Deputy Prime Minister Fischer says society should tolerate gay and lesbian couples but should not have to "subsidise their child-bearing whim."<br><br>The furor arose after a Queensland Anti-Discrimination Tribunal finding last Friday that a Brisbane lesbian seeking donor sperm had been discriminated against.<br>[AAP - Doug Conway] |

## DOMESTIC PARTNERSHIPS AND SAME SEX LEGAL RIGHTS

| | | |
|---|---|---|
| 12-16-93 | Baltimore | Baltimore moved to extend health benefits to the partners of gay municipal employees. [AP] |
| 2-14-94 | Sacramento | Assemblyman Katz introduced two bills in the California Assembly to extend health benefits to unmarried couples, including homosexual couples, and allow them to register as domestic partners. [UPI] |
| 3-6-94 | United States | Increasing numbers of private companies are rewriting their benefits policies to include non-traditional couples. Some began by offering health and other benefits to the unmarried partners of heterosexual employees and then extended the benefit to the partners of gay and lesbian employees. Companies included: Apple Computer, Levi Strauss, Ben & Jerry's, Stanford University, MCA-Universal, Warner Bros., Viacom, HBO, LA Philharmonic. [LA Times - Brad Bonhall] |
| 5-5-94 | Austin, Texas | The City Council's move last September to provide insurance benefits for all "domestic partners" of city employees, including same-sex partners, was reversed by voters after a campaign organized by a religious leader. Proposition 22, which won approval with 62% of the vote, amended Austin's charter to limit benefits to the husbands, wives and other immediate relatives of city employees. [AP] |
| 5-20-94 | Michigan | The University of Michigan accepted a recommendation to grant same-sex partners of UM employees and students the same |

benefits as heterosexuals. A task force recommended extending health and life insurance benefits to homosexual spouses and to allow same-sex couples to live in university housing.
[UPI]

| 5-21-94 | California | Biotechnology concern Genetech Inc. announced plans to extend benefits to gay and lesbian employees' domestic partners. Beginning June 1, Genetech plans to offer gay and lesbian employees' live-in partners such benefits as medical-, dental- and vision-care insurance, child-care benefits and bereavement leave. [UPI] |

6-5-94      Minneapolis

The city cannot offer health care benefits to partners of its gay and lesbian employees, a judge ruled. State law does not recognize same-sex partners as dependents or spouses, and City Council acted beyond its authority when it adopted the domestic partners ordinance, Judge Hedlund said. She ruled in a lawsuit led by a taxpayer.

"It's amazing that we can struggle for seven years and it can all be undone in a couple months," said Anglin, a library employee who began the legal battle that led to the ordinance in July 1987.
[AP]

6-9-94      Portland, Oregon

Portland's city council made city health benefits available to gay and other unmarried couples when they erased legal marriage as a requirement. The council voted unanimously in favor of extending health insurance coverage to the partners of gay and other unmarried city employees. The action contrasted with moves over the past 18 months in more than 20 rural Oregon communities and counties to adopt ordinances that prohibit the recognition of gay rights, including extending city benefits to

gay couples.
[Reuters]

| | | |
|---|---|---|
| 6-12-94 | Vermont | Vermont agreed to provide health care benefits to the unmarried partners of state workers. Both heterosexual and homosexual partners will be eligible for the same health and dental benefits now offered to spouses, said state Personnel Commissioner Thomas Torti. Vermont is the first state to offer coverage for unmarried partners.<br>[AP] |
| 6-12-94 | United States | 25 years ago, lesbian and gay relationships were not recognized and the concept of "domestic partner" had yet to be heard. Today, numerous municipal governments (including Laguna Beach, W. Hollywood, Berkeley, San Francisco, Seattle, and Cambridge, MA.), dozens of private universities and colleges (including the Claremont Colleges, Stanford and the Univ. of Chicago) and many private corporations have extended various benefits to the partners of gay employees.<br>[LA Times - P. Nardi] |
| 6-22-94 | Virginia | Despite the vehement objections of Gov. George Allen, Virginia housing commissioners approved new regulations today allowing homosexual couples, unmarried heterosexuals and other unrelated people to jointly obtain state housing loans.<br>[Washington Post - Peter Baker] |
| 9-7-94 | Seattle, Washington | About 90 couples, mostly gay or lesbian, taking advantage of a new Seattle ordinance registered with the city clerk. A member of the Seattle Commission for Lesbians and Gays said: "It celebrates commitments and is a way to say publicly, 'This is the person I'm going to share my life with.'" There is no legal advantage |

offered to the couples.
[AP - Melissa Campobasso]

| | | |
|---|---|---|
| 9-11-94 | California | California Governor Pete Wilson vetoed a bill that would have made California the first state to officially recognize the rights of unmarried couples regardless of their sexual orientation. The bill would have allowed the state's estimated 500,000 unmarried couples to register with the Secretary of State. Couples would then be entitled to hospital visitation rights and broader rights in conservatorships if a partner became incapacitated. Wilson said: "We need to strengthen, not weaken, the institution of marriage. . . Government policy ought not to discount marriage by offering a substitute relationship that demands much less—and provides much less than is needed both by the children of such relationships, and ultimately much less than is needed by society." [Reuters] |
| 10-94 | South Hadley, Massachusetts | Joining Smith College and other area nonprofit employers, trustees of Mt. Holyoke College have voted to include employee same-sex domestic partners and their dependents in MHC policies and qualified benefits, including coverage under the group health insurance plans, bereavement and family leave, tuition reimbursement and waiver benefits, and use of College facilities. [The Uncommon Uncommon Women] |
| 11-1-94 | Canada | Two gay men, living together for 46 years, are asking for the spousal allowance associated with one of their federal old-age pension, the equivalent of American Social Security. Theirs is the first homosexual rights case heard by the Canadian Supreme Court. (see 12-27-94) [Reuters - Dawn Brett] |

| 12-27-94 | Canada | Public opinion polls show that a majority of Canadians support spousal benefits for homosexual couples, and 38 percent say gay couples should be allowed to adopt children; gays serve in the military here with little public objection. |
| | | In the US, 36 cities or states, including the District of Columbia, recognize "domestic partnerships" that entitle partners in gay or common-law relationships to some or all of the other's dependent benefits. So do at least 57 major companies, as well as a number of educational institutions and non-profit organizations, according to the National Gay and Lesbian Task Force Policy Institute.<br>[Washington Post Foreign Service - Anne Swardson] |
| 1-30-95 | Minneapolis, Minnesota | A state appeals court upheld a district Judge's decision last June. Minneapolis can't offer health care benefits to partners of its gay and lesbian employees.<br>[AP - Pam Schmid] |
| 3-29-95 | California | A renewed attempt to extend limited legal benefits to domestic partners—including homosexuals—was rejected Wednesday in its first state legislative test.<br>The measure, identical to one vetoed last year by Gov. Pete Wilson, would have allowed unmarried couples to register their relationships with the state and given them limited rights to will property and secure hospital visitation rights.<br>[UPI] |
| 5-14-95 | Australia | The New South Wales Industrial Commission gave same-sex couples the same family leave rights as heterosexual couples. One lobbyist, upset with this decision, warned that homosexuals wanted to redefine the meaning of "family."<br>[AAP] |

| | | |
|---|---|---|
| 6-21-95 | Australia | The British Queen's representative in Australia, the governor-general, has supported gay marriage. Gov. Hayden, who by convention only rarely speaks publicly and almost never on controversial matters, said in a speech late on Wednesday that homosexual couples should not be discriminated against. "It is difficult to see how there can be a sustainable objection to partnership contracts similar to marriage," he said. [Reuters] |
| 7-7-95 | Colorado | The Coors Brewing Co. has a two-month-old new policy that offers benefits to domestic partners of employees, including homosexual mates. [UPI] |
| 8-30-95 | North Carolina | Drug-company Glaxo Wellcome, Inc. will extend medical and dental coverage nationwide to the live-in companions of its gay and lesbian employees. "This is just one more element in our benefits package that (recognizes) diversity in the work force and will help us attract and retain quality people," said company spokeswoman Nancy Pekarek. [AP] |
| 10-6-95 | California | Walt Disney Co. has quietly extended health benefits to partners of its gay and lesbian employees, reversing course after initially resisting a trend among major entertainment companies to provide so-called "domestic partner benefits." [Wall Street Journal - Thomas R. King] |
| 10-12-95 | New York | NYNEX, a New York-based telephone company, has joined the list of companies that have extended health care and other benefits to same-sex partners of gay employees. The change is meant to accommodate "those employees involved in rela- |

tionships that can't be recognized through existing laws," said a company spokesperson, adding, "diversity in our company is a major issue and this is a way of recognizing the need. It's simply in keeping with the times."
[AP]

| | | |
|---|---|---|
| 10-17-95 | Michigan | Wayne State University has joined the University of Michigan in extending health insurance and other benefits to partners of its gay employees. The two Michigan universities are among about 5% of the nation's colleges that now offer such coverage.<br>[UPI] |
| 10-18-95 | Florida | A group of state lawmakers have denounced Walt Disney Co. for extending health insurance to partners of gay and lesbian employees and asked the entertainment giant to reconsider its decision. In a letter to Disney chairman Michael Eisner and its board of directors, 15 legislators said the move was "a big mistake both morally and financially" that would alienate their family-oriented base of customers.<br>[AP - Adam Yeomans] |
| 11-1-95 | Washington, DC | In a defeat for gay rights advocates, the House voted (249- 172) to repeal a District of Columbia law that allows city workers to register domestic partners for health benefits.<br><br>The measure's sponsor, Rep. John Hostettler, R-Ind., said the law, which also gives gay city residents the legal right to visit their partners in the hospital, contributes to the "moral and legal erosion of the traditional family."<br>[AP - Kimberly A.C. Wilson] |
| 11-15-95 | Florida | A powerful Florida Baptist group has asked its 1 million members to boycott |

Walt Disney Co.'s parks and products, saying Disney showed a lack of moral leader-
ship by extending health insurance to
partners of homosexual workers.
[AP - Lisa Holewa]

12-12-95   Palo Alto, California   Palo Alto city council passed a plan to
establish a registry of homosexual and
other unmarried couples who want to for-
malize their relationships at City Hall.
Couples who register may be able to take
advantage of reduced rates at health clubs
and transfer frequent flier mileage. In
California, only a few cities register partners, including San Francisco, Berkeley,
Los Angeles, West Hollywood, Laguna
Beach, Long Beach and Santa Monica.
[UPI]

1-18-96 Los Angeles, California   The Directors Guild-Industry Health Fund
will extend spousal benefits, including
health and dental coverage, to members'
same-sex domestic partners. It is the second entertainment union health plan to
offer same-sex benefits, after the Writers
Guild-Industry Health Fund.
[Reuters - Ted Johnson]

1-29-96        San Francisco,   Since 1991, at least 3,000 unmarried
California   heterosexual and gay couples have
obtained a benefit they couldn't find in less
liberal cities: certificates recognizing them
as domestic partners.
[AP - Dara Akiko Tom]

2-13-96        United States   Gay and lesbian employees of United
Airlines announced they are creating a new
employee group, United at United, to
advocate for domestic partner benefits
(including health, travel, family leave and
pension benefits), diversity/sensitivity
training, and AIDS awareness and
education.
[PR Newswire]

| 3-9-96 | Bogota, Colombia | Gay couples living together in Colombia have no right to the state benefits granted to heterosexual couples, a top court has ruled. The Constitutional Court rejected a lawsuit that sought to gain health, retirement, and other legal benefits for lesbian and homosexual couples. [AP] |
|--------|------------------|------|
| 3-26-96 | San Francisco, California | Mayor Willie Brown presided over a ceremony in which more than 200 gay couples tied the knot in a commitment ceremony approved by the city supervisors in January. In groups of 20, the couples marched down the aisle to say their vows on stage. "We pledge, while in this union, to be responsible for each other and to be committed to a relationship of loyalty and mutual caring." The couples kissed after the words "I hereby pronounce you lawfully recognized domestic partners."<br><br>Under the city's 1991 domestic partnership ordinance, couples already have visitation rights in hospitals, shared health plans for city employees, and bereavement leave for city workers when a partner dies. [AP US & World - Karyn Hunt] |
| 4-21-96 | Australia | Australian probate law has been revised so that unmarried partners of either gender will be eligible to share in the estate of his or her partner who dies without leaving a valid will. This is a first for homosexual couples in Australia. [AAP] |
| 5-20-96 | San Francisco, California | A proposed ordinance was introduced before the San Francisco Board of Supervisors which would force the vast majority of companies doing business with the city to offer domestic partners benefits coverage to their employees. [UPI] |

| | | |
|---|---|---|
| 5-21-96 | Hungary | Parliament members voted 207 to 73 to recognize common-law relationships between homosexuals. The new law entitled gays to inherit property from their partners and receive a deceased partner's pension. It did not allow them to adopt children.<br>[AU US & World] |
| 6-7-96 | Philadelphia, Pennsylvania | Health care and family leave benefits will be extended to the domestic partners of all non-civil-service city employees, including those in same-sex relationships, under an order the mayor signed. A total of 500 employees work in the executive and administrative branches of the city government affected by the order.<br>    A measure the City Council rejected in 1993 would have extended health care, leave and pension benefits to the partners of all the city's 25,000 employees. The measure also sought to require companies doing business with the city to enact similar policies.<br>[AP] |
| 6-22-96 | France | Tens of thousands of gays and lesbians marched in Paris and other major French cities in support of legal recognition for homosexual couples.<br>    Protesters were seeking a "contract of social union" giving gay and lesbian couples a formal legal status ensuring them equal rights with heterosexuals in such matters as housing, inheritance, and taxes.<br>    France's opposition Socialist Party said this week it would ask parliament to approve legal status for homosexual couples.<br>    French law does not now recognize gay or lesbian marriages although a handful of cities issue certificates of cohabitation to same-sex couples. The certificates |

have no legal weight but entitle gay couples to certain rights such as discounts on the national rail system.
[Reuters]

7-1-96        Boulder, Colorado        Three same-sex couples obtained "domestic partnership" certificates Monday, the first day of Boulder's registry for unmarried couples.

The registry, one of at least a dozen nationwide and the first in Colorado, is open to unmarried couples over 18—heterosexual, gay and lesbian. For $25, they can publicly register their commitment to one another.

Boulder's domestic partnership certificate includes these declarations:

—We are in a relationship of mutual support, caring and commitment and intend to stay so.

—We are each other's sole domestic partner.

—We are not related by kinship closer than would bar marriage in the State of Colorado.

—We are not married.

—We are both at least 18 years of age and competent to contract.

—We share a life and home together.
[AP]

7-4-96        Netherlands        A parliamentary majority backed the idea of civil marriage and adoption rights for same-sex couples in April 1996.

In June a committee of experts was appointed to study the national and international consequences of legalizing same-sex marriages and to report and advise on possible legislation before August 1997.

It is the adoption rights which are at the heart of the controversy surrounding the extension of civil marriage to gays.

While Sweden and Norway afford

same-sex partnerships equal rights with
regard to property ownership, taxation,
pensions, social benefits, inheritance and
divorce, they expressly exclude adoption
rights.

The Dutch government (unlike parliament) favors a similar arrangement, fearing
full legal parity could arouse international
ire and jeopardize Dutch adoptions of foreign children.

Cynics see the new committee as a
way for the government to buy time on a
sensitive issue with a view to finding a
compromise.
[Reuters]

8-10-96                 Oregon    A judge ordered the state to offer health
insurance to the partners of gay state
employees, saying failing to make the same
benefits available to gay and heterosexual
couples amounts to discrimination.

Judge Gallagher ruled that the Oregon
Employees' Benefit Board violated the state
constitution by denying spousal benefits to
three lesbian couples who have all
"enjoyed a long-term and committed
relationship identical to marriage."

Gallagher's ruling appears to be the
first of its kind in the nation. Cities such as
Philadelphia and San Francisco have
offered health benefits to partners of gay
city workers, but no court order was
involved and the benefits did not extend to
state employees.

The state has 30 days to appeal and
has not yet decided to do so.
[AP - William McCall]

9-13-96                 Canada    The Canadian Human Rights Tribunal
ruled on Friday that companies do not
have to give pension benefits to partners of
homosexual employees.

But the court urged the federal government to change the law so that pensions could be granted in the same way that other benefits such as medical plans are for homosexual spouses.

Noting that pensions are governed by federal law, it said: "We urge the federal government to act swiftly to amend the legislation that prevents employers such as Air Canada from extending pension benefits to same-sex spouses."

[Reuters]

9-14-96    Atlanta, Georgia    A conservative legal foundation has filed a lawsuit against Atlanta's new domestic partnership plan in an effort to overturn an ordinance that it says would encourage homosexuality.

Last week, the City Council passed an ordinance that will authorize insurance benefits to the unmarried, live-in partners of city employees.

[AP]

9-17-96    Denver, Colorado    The City Council voted 11-1 to extend health benefits to the partners and families of gay city employees. The ordinance would affect about 85 to 100 of the city's 8,500 workers and cost about $150,000 a year in premiums.

[AP]

9-20-96    United States    IBM on Thursday joined nearly 470 other large corporations, governments and universities in the United States that provide the same benefits to same-sex couples as to married couples. That's up from 250 a year ago, according to Common Ground.

Lotus Development Corp., which IBM acquired last year, took the step in 1990 and was among the first to do so.

In recent months, several other household names, including Walt Disney Co. and American Express Co., have also extended health benefits to partners of gay

workers. Other companies with similar
policies include Microsoft Corp., Time
Warner Inc., Levi Strauss & Co., and
Apple Computer Inc.

IBM employs about 225,000 people
worldwide and 110,000 in the United
States. In 1974, it was the first large company to include sexual orientation in its
nondiscrimination hiring policy.
[AP]

10-9-96     Cincinnati, Ohio     Cincinnati would become the first city in
Ohio to offer health benefits to the part-
ners of its gay and lesbian city workers if a
resolution introduced in city council
Wednesday is approved.
[UPI]

10-22-96     Sweden     Monica, a lesbian woman, gave birth last
winter to a daughter, conceived by artifi-
cial insemination. Attempts to transfer
some of her one-year maternity leave to
her same-sex partner, Pia—a practice
common among heterosexual couples—
were rejected.

But after a change of heart, the insurance office has declared that Monica and
Pia have "the same rights as in a
conventional marriage."
[Reuters]

11-8-96     San Francisco,     Mayor of San Francisco signed legislation
California     that was approved by the San Francisco
Board of Supervisors. The ordinance,
which takes effect within six months, bars
the city from signing contracts with companies that do not offer the same benefits
to domestic partners as married couples.

The legislation is believed to be the
first of its kind in the nation.

The legislation requires companies
wishing to do business with San Francisco
to provide benefits to the domestic partners of their employees if they provide

them to the spouses of their employees.

The legislation covers benefits such as bereavement leave, medical leave and health insurance. The legislation does not require companies to provide benefits that they do not already provide spouses.

San Francisco city and county workers already receive domestic partner benefits. More than 3,500 couples are registered as domestic partners in the city.
[AP, Reuters]

| | | |
|---|---|---|
| 12-9-96 | Los Angeles, California | The Los Angeles Unified School District, one of the largest in the nation, is considering whether to extend employee insurance benefits to domestic partners. The board held brief but emotionally charged hearings last week on the issue, which would offer health, dental and vision coverage for live-in partners of employees, whether homosexual or heterosexual. [UPI] |
| 12-10-96 | Los Angeles, California | The Los Angeles Unified School District has postponed consideration of a proposal to extend employee insurance benefits to domestic partners. [UPI] |
| 12-10-96 | Brazil | A Senate committee approved a measure that would recognize the union between gay couples. The measure would allow gay couples to sign a contract of partnership giving them the right to file joint tax returns as well as grant inheritance and pension rights to the surviving partner should one of them die. Gay couples would not, however, be allowed to adopt children nor use one or the other's surname. The bill must now be voted on in both the Chamber of Deputies and the Senate. [AP] |

| 12-14-96 | Texas | Perot Systems is now offering health insurance benefits to gay and lesbian partners of employees. This is the first major Texas-based company to make such an offer. [UPI] |
|----------|-------|----------------------------------------|
| 1-10-97 | Israel | An Israeli district court in a landmark decision ordered the army to recognize a gay man as the spouse of a deceased male colonel and extend him the same benefits a military widow. [Reuters] |
| 1-26-97 | San Francisco, California | San Francisco told United Airlines it had to obey an ordinance requiring companies doing business with the city to offer spousal benefits to their workers' unmarried and same-sex partners. The issue arose after United asked for a new 25-year lease to build kitchens and a maintenance facility at San Francisco International Airport. [AP - Martha Irvine] |
| 2-1-97 | Colorado | The University of Colorado regents will soon be asked to confront the issue of whether to extend benefits to the partners of gay and lesbian faculty and staff. If extending the benefits is approved, CU would join more than 500 public and private employers around the country in doing so. [Boulder Daily Camera] |
| 2-7-97 | San Francisco, California | The Independent Gay and Lesbian Employee Association At United Airlines and two of the airline's unions have joined forces to urge United to comply with San Francisco's new Domestic Partner Ordinance. [PR Newswire] |
| 2-7-97 | San Francisco, California | San Francisco's Roman Catholic archdiocese has struck a compromise with the city that brings the church into compliance |

with a domestic-partners benefits law without violating religious teachings. Specifically, the deal would let employees of Catholic groups—or any other organization doing business with the city—to designate someone in their household as eligible to receive "spousal- equivalent benefits."
[AP]

| | | |
|---|---|---|
| 2-10-97 | San Francisco, California | United Airlines and San Francisco's city government have reached a compromise that should end a dispute over whether the airline must offer benefits to unmarried life partners of its employees. According to Supervisor Ammiano, United has committed to complying with the domestic partners law in the future. [Reuters] |
| 3-10-97 | United States | Profamily organizations call on American Airlines to stop promoting homosexuality. Family Research Council President Gary Bauer joins the American Family Association's Donald Wildmon, Coral Ridge Ministries' D. James Kennedy and Concerned Women for America's Beverly LaHaye in signing a 7-page letter to American Airlines President Robert L. Crandall asking him to cease American's sponsorship of pro-homosexual activities. "Anything that serves to reinforce (homosexual) behavior holds back the healing process by which homosexuals achieve restored gender identity and the chance at a fuller life," the writers state. [PR Newswire] |
| 3-11-97 | California | Bank of America, the third-largest U.S. bank, said it would extend health benefits to the domestic partners of its gay or heterosexual U.S. employees starting next year. Bank of America already offers bereavement leave and family sickness |

leave to domestic partners. The bank newsletter said domestic partners applying for coverage "must be in a committed relationship that has existed for at least six months, and must be responsible for each other's welfare on a continuing basis." [Reuters - Adrian Croft]

3-12-97     Chicago, Illinois     A key Chicago City Council committee has voted to extend government employee health benefits to the gay partners of homosexual city employees. The city's Finance Committee voted 15-7 in favor of the proposal—which is backed by Chicago Mayor Richard Daley—despite loud protests and demonstrations from anti-abortion and fundamentalist religious groups. [UPI S]

3-12-97     Washington, DC     Sen. Robert Torricelli, D-N.J., has extended benefits of the family-leave law to gay members of his staff. A homosexual-rights group said other lawmakers have done it informally, but that the freshman senator is the first to write it into his office policy. [AP]

3-13-97     South Africa     Five of South Africa's leading universities, including the University of Cape Town, have taken the controversial step of recognizing gay and lesbian unions by extending full marital benefits to gay and lesbian staff members. These staff members will be allowed to register same-sex partners for pension and medical aid benefits and will be entitled to all other benefits granted to married staff. [COMTEX Newswire]

3-18-97     Illinois     The Illinois Senate supported a measure requiring municipalities that try to extend government employee health benefits to

the domestic partners of homosexual city employees to provide them to the unmarried partners of heterosexual employees as well.
[COMTEX Newswire]

3-19-97    Chicago, Illinois    The Chicago City Council has approved (33-18) an ordinance giving government employee health benefits to the gay partners of homosexual city workers.
[COMTEX Newswire]

## SAME-SEX MARRIAGE

3-6-94    United States    Lawsuits seeking to force states to recognize gay unions have become a priority among many gay-rights lawyers. Legal actions are pending in Florida, Arizona, and the District of Columbia, and last year the marriage policy in California was unsuccessfully challenged by two West Hollywood men who sued after the L.A. Co. clerk denied their application for a marriage license. Although no state recognizes gay unions, 5 CA counties and several cities do. L.A., W. Hollywood and Laguna Beach are among 8 municipalities that offer varying degrees of recognition of same-sex unions.

A pending CA Assembly bill that would allow gay couples to register their relationships is modeled after the policies of these cities. Under the measure [introduced 2-14] gays would be able to will property to their partners, participate in family-only hospital visits and gain conservatorship rights in the event one becomes incapacitated.

Although gay partners sometimes have lawyers draft contracts and agreements that attempt to duplicate marriage

benefits, it is estimated that such agreements can address only 60% of what is covered in a heterosexual marriage. For example, the agreements cannot guarantee the same protections in areas such as child custody, pension plans, health coverage and Social Security benefits.
[Los Angeles Times]

| 1-2-95 | Stockholm, Sweden | Hans Jonsson and Sven-Olov Jansson exchanged wedding vows becoming the first Swedish couple to marry under a new law allowing homosexual marriages. |

Sweden became the third Nordic country—after Denmark and Norway—to allow homosexuals to register partnerships with all the rights and obligations of marriage except adopting children or having a church wedding.

51 years ago, homosexuality was a crime in Sweden.
[AP]

| 3-15-95 | Cambodia | Two Cambodian women, one dressed as a man, married legally in a ceremony attended by hundreds of well-wishers and friends. The newspaper story said "both women love each other very much"; the event was described as a "strange story." |

There is no word for homosexuality in the Khmer language.
[Reuters]

| 7-5-95 | United States | A new poll showed that a third of the nation's voters believe that two people of the same sex should be able to get married if they love each other. |

[AP - Jeff Holyfield]

| 7-5-95 | Amsterdam | A recent poll indicated 73% of respondents backed legal marriage between same-sex couples with 44% supporting an extension of existing marriage laws to homosexuals. |

[Reuters]

| 8-14-95 | Riga, Latvia | A gay couple took their vows in an unofficial but highly publicized wedding that activists hope will help overturn a law against homosexual marriage. A 1991 law prohibits gay marriages, so the couple registered their union with an advocacy group, the Latvian Association for Sexual Equality. [AP] |
|---|---|---|
| 8-24-95 | Minneapolis, Minnesota | The United States' fifth-largest Protestant denomination, the Evangelical Lutheran Church in America, after years of emotional debate, recently decided to postpone indefinitely work on a policy statement on sexuality because it was unable to reach a consensus on issues such as the ordination of gays or the blessing of same-sex unions. [AP - David Briggs] |
| 9-18-95 | Canada | The House of Commons rejected a gay legislator's proposal to extend legal recognition to same-sex marriages. [AP] |
| 12-1-95 | Sweden | Some 49 Swedish Lutheran priests protested to their bishop about his encouragement of gay "marriages" in their churches. They protested the exchange of wedding rings and a nuptial kiss in a recent ceremony. Sweden's Lutheran church has encouraged priests for several years to bless homosexual relationships in church but the protesting priests said the Gothenburg service went one step further towards a formal marriage service for homosexuals. [Reuters] |
| 12-21-95 | Atlanta, Georgia | A federal appeals court has ordered the attorney general, Michael Bowers, to defend his decision to withdraw a job offer |

to a lesbian attorney after learning of her
plans for a commitment ceremony with
her partner.

Bowers had maintained that his office
could not employ a lawyer who openly
flouted Georgia law, which prohibits same-
sex marriages. He also maintained that
hiring Ms. Shahar would complicate
enforcement of state sodomy laws, which
he successfully defended in 1986 before
the U.S. Supreme Court.
[AP US & World]

| | | |
|---|---|---|
| 1-6-96 | Europe | Denmark, Norway and Sweden now allow homosexual partners to register with the state and to claim many (though not all) of the prerogatives of marriage. The Dutch are moving in the same direction. In France and Belgium, cities and local governments have begun recognizing gay partnerships. |

As of today, however, there is no country which gives homosexuals the full right
of marriage.
[*The Economist*, p. 13]

| | | |
|---|---|---|
| 1-18-96 | Texas | A "Friends" episode that depicts a lesbian wedding ceremony is getting a decidedly unfriendly reception from at least one television station. |

The NBC affiliate KJAC is pre-empting
the installment scheduled to air tonight,
saying it is unsuitable for traditional family
viewing. The popular program will be
replaced with a Super Bowl special.
[AP]

| | | |
|---|---|---|
| 1-18-96 | Ohio | "Friends" episode will not be aired by NBC affiliate in Lima, Ohio. |

The episode, entitled "The One With
the Lesbian Wedding," features Candace
Gringrich, a lesbian activist and sister of
House Speaker Newt Gringrich, as a lesbian minister. She officiates during an

exchange of vows between two female characters.
[UPI]

| 2-1-96 | United States | Alarmed by efforts in Hawaii to let gays wed, several states are moving closer to banning recognition of same-sex marriages.
California's Republican-controlled Assembly voted 41-31 to block the state from recognizing same-sex marriages.
A House committee in Washington state approved a bill to ban same-sex marriages.
A committee in Idaho's legislature introduced a bill that would make same-sex marriages performed in another state invalid in Idaho.
In 1993 Hawaii's Supreme Court agreed with three gay couples that they had been unconstitutionally denied marriage licenses in 1990. The justices said the state had to show a compelling interest to ban such marriages and sent the case back for trial in a lower court.
[AP] |
| --- | --- | --- |
| 2-1-96 | Des Moines, Iowa | Several Republican presidential candidates Saturday signed a pledge against giving legal acceptance to "same sex marriages" at an election meeting at a Des Moines church held with all the fervor of a revivalist meeting.
Around 3,000 conservative Christians attended the meeting organized by an organization called the National Campaign to Protect the Sanctity of Marriage at the First Federated Church in Des Moines.
[Reuters] |
| 3-1-96 | Michigan | State Senator Van Regenmorter, chair of the Michigan State Judiciary Committee, introduced a bill that would make same-sex marriages performed legally in other states illegal in Michigan. He said: "I think |

|  |  |  |
|---|---|---|
|  |  | it leads to further disintegration of the traditional family unit." [UPI] |
| 3-6-96 | Illinois | Backed by the Christian Coalition, an Illinois Senate committee endorsed a bill that would extend the state's ban on same-sex marriages to those performed out of state. [UPI - Sean Davis] |
| 3-13-96 | Colorado | State lawmakers approved a bill banning same-sex marriage in Colorado. The bill passed 33-31 in the House and 20-14 in the Senate. [AP US & World] |
| 3-23-96 | San Francisco, California | Metropolitan Community Church of San Francisco honors 25 years of gay weddings on Sunday, March 24. More than 100 ceremonies were performed just in the past year at the MCC Church, one of the largest lesbian/gay organizations in the city, as well as one of the largest churches in San Francisco. [PR Newswire] |
| 3-26-96 | Colorado | Governor Roy Romer vetoed a bill that would have banned same-sex marriages in Colorado and not honored such unions performed elsewhere, calling the measure "mean-spirited and unnecessary." [AP - Jennifer Mears] |
| 3-27-96 | Vatican City | The Vatican denounced a ceremony in San Francisco at which over 200 gay couples were symbolically married. The Vatican spokesperson cited the pope's statement that same-sex marriages create "moral disorder" and urged nonsupport to candidates who back homosexual unions. [AP] |
| 3-28-96 | United States | Idaho, South Dakota, and Utah have passed bills defining marriage as a union |

between a man and a woman.

Efforts to ban same-sex marriage have failed in 11 states—Colorado, Iowa, Maine, Maryland, Mississippi, New Mexico, Rhode Island, Virginia, Washington, West Virginia and Wyoming. [AP]

| | | |
|---|---|---|
| 3-28-96 | Philadelphia, Pennsylvania | The 1,750-member Central Conference of American Rabbis (CCAR), the U.S.'s largest group of rabbis, endorsed same-sex civil marriages. It was the first support of single-sex unions by a rabbinical group from any of the three major branches of Judaism. It cited "our Jewish commitment to the fundamental principle that we are all created in the divine image."<br><br>In 1997, CCAR will vote whether same-sex religious marriage ceremonies should be approved.<br><br>In 1990, the Central Conference voted to accept homosexual rabbis. [AP US & World & UPI Mid-Atlantic US] |
| 4-1-96 | California | Assemblyman Pete Knight introduced a bill in the California legislature. It stated: "A marriage contracted outside this state between individuals of the same gender is not valid in this state." The bill passed in the House. Assemblywoman Sheila Kuehl, the Legislature's first out lesbian, urged colleagues to vote against the bill. "Let me remind you that whenever any minority has been demonized in the past in this country or any other country, one of the strongest tools used against them has been to withhold the right to marry." [UPI US & World] |
| 4-2-96 | Sweden | A homosexual couple were barred from marrying at the Swedish embassy in Paris because French authorities do not allow marriage between people of the same sex." [COMTEX Newswire] |

| 4-16-96 | Netherlands | The Dutch parliament voted in favor of legalizing same-sex marriages; it passed a motion calling on the government to draft legislation to make it possible for gay couples to marry. The Dutch government is not bound to implement parliament's vote and has been resistant to such legislation, stating that it might affect the Netherlands' reputation abroad. [Reuters World Report] |

4-29-96       Michigan       Gerry Crane and his lover of four years, Randy Block, "married" each other in a private commitment ceremony in October '95 in Grand Rapids, Michigan. When word of his gay "marriage" leaked back to the school in rural Byron Center (pop. 6,500) where Crane has been teaching for three years, outraged parents demanded he be fired.
[*Time* Magazine 4-29-96]

5-13-96       Washington, DC       Republicans introduced the bill dubbed the "Defense of Marriage Act" into both houses of Congress. The bill said that each state may decide for itself whether to acknowledge gay marriages and defines marriage under federal law as the legal union between one man and one woman.

Reactions and statements varied.

Rep. Bob Barr: "Something needs to be done to keep gay marriage invalid under federal law to make it clear that same-sex couples are ineligible for various federal benefits, including Social Security."

Gary Bauer of the Family Research Council: "Will America move to protect marriage—the foundation of civilization—or will America become the first nation to destroy marriage? . . . At stake is nothing less than the future of the nation and the well-being of our children."

Rep. Barney Frank said the argument

that homosexual marriages threatened heterosexual marriages was "bizarre."

Elizabeth Birch, executive director of the Human Rights Campaign, said the bill before Congress discriminates against gays and lesbians, "your constituents, your sports heroes, your co-workers, your neighbors."
[Reuters]

| | | |
|---|---|---|
| 5-20-96 | South Carolina | Gov. Beasley signed a bill banning same-sex marriage in South Carolina. He said: "The state of South Carolina sends a very clear message that we support the oldest, long-living institution in the history of humanity. That is marriages between man and woman." [AP US & World] |
| 5-24-96 | United States | A poll by Newsweek reported: 58% of Americans oppose legally-sanctioned gay marriages, 84% supported equal rights for gays in jobs, 80% supported equal rights for gays in housing. [Reuters World Report] |
| 5-24-96 | llinois | The governor of Illinois signed a measure that bans the recognition of same-sex marriage in Illinois. He said: "This law will maintain the status quo by making it clear that we will not be forced to accept them here even if other states permit such marriages." A similar measure passed the Illinois Senate but failed in the House in 1993. [UPI US & World] |
| 5-28-96 | Netherlands | The Dutch government agreed to appoint an independent committee to investigate legalizing same-sex marriages. If the Dutch government approved same-sex marriages, it would become the first country in Europe to legalize same-sex marriages. Denmark, Norway, and Sweden allow |

|  |  | same-sex partnership registration that but only confers limited legal status. [Reuters World Report] |
|---|---|---|
| 6-1-96 | United States | States that have banned same-sex marriages: Alaska, Arizona, Georgia, Idaho, Illinois, Kansas, Oklahoma, South Carolina, South Dakota, Tennessee, and Utah. [AP US & World] |
| 6-27-96 | Iceland | Iceland's parliament passed a Bill on Homosexual Marriages granting gays the right to marry in a civil ceremony. The law faced no opposition from church leaders. Iceland is the fourth nation in Europe to legalize homosexual unions. |

Iceland, whose population of 265,000 is ruled by a moderate conservative government, follows in the wake of Denmark (1989), Norway (1993) and Sweden (1995) in legalizing gay marriages.

The law does not give gays the right to have church weddings, to adopt children or to have children by artificial insemination.

It does, however, go further than laws in any other country in that if one partner in a gay marriage already has a child, the other can have shared custody of that child.
[AP]

| 7-11-96 | Washington, DC | Comments on Defense of Marriage Act in House of Representatives, July 11, 1996, by Rep. John Lewis, an African-American Democrat from Georgia's 5th District. |

"Mr. Chairman, this is a mean bill. It is cruel. . . . This bill is a slap in the face of the Declaration of Independence. It denies gay men and women the right to liberty and the pursuit of happiness. Marriage is a basic human right. You cannot tell people they cannot fall in love. Dr. Martin Luther

King, Jr. used to say when people talked about interracial marriage and I quote, "Races do not fall in love and get married. Individuals fall in love and get married." Why do you not want your fellow men and women, your fellow Americans to be happy? Why do you attack them? Why do you want to destroy the love they hold in their hearts? Why do you want to crush their hopes, their dreams, their longings, their aspirations?"
[Gaybruin 7-15-96]

| | | |
|---|---|---|
| 8-30-96 | Alabama | Governor James of Alabama signed an executive order banning recognition of same-sex marriages in Alabama. This brings to 14 the number of states that have passed legislation banning same-sex marriages. Delaware and Mississippi passed similar bills in the last two months. [AP US & World] |
| 9-20-96 | Washington | President Clinton signed the "Defense of Marriage Act" |
| 10-29-96 | Honduras | Gay prisoners at one Honduran jail are being encouraged to "marry" one specific partner to prevent the spread of AIDS, authorities say. "The main cause of death in the prison is not fighting or even murder, but rather AIDS," Obdulio Rodezno, chief of the medical department at the Central Penitentiary in Tegucigalpa, told reporters. Officials said the unions are valid only inside the penitentiary because gay marriages are illegal in Honduras. [Reuters] |
| 11-10-96 | Taiwan | More than 500 guests, including officials of the Taipei city government, attended Taiwan's first public gay wedding Sunday, between a Taiwanese author and his long-time American companion. |

Wearing a traditional Chinese scholar's robe, Hsu You-sheng exchanged vows and rings with Gray Harriman at a downtown hotel.

The ceremony was praised by social reformers, but will not be legally binding because Taiwan does not recognize same-sex marriages.

[AP]

12-3-96          Hawaii     Judge Kevin Chang ruled that same-sex marriages are legal, making Hawaii the first state in America to recognize that gay and lesbian couples are entitled to the same privileges as heterosexual married couples. In his ruling, Judge Kevin Chang found that the Hawaiian state government had failed to establish a "compelling state interest" to justify the prohibition against same-sex marriages.

Robert Knight, Director of Cultural Studies for the Family Research Council, criticized Judge Chang's ruling and said Chang should be removed from office. Knight asserted that the Hawaiian Attorney General's office deliberately underargued the case by "ignoring a mountain of evidence that homosexuality is destructive to individuals, families, and society and that homosexuality is a changeable condition."

Fifteen states have passed legislation barring homosexual couples legally married in other states from receiving benefits in their states. These benefits include Social Security and Medicare, joint insurance for health, home, travel, and cars, family leave to take care of a sick partner, hospital visitation rights, the right to will property and money to a partner, and the ability to file a joint tax return, among others.

Fourteen mainland states are considering

similar legislation to that passed in Hawaii, while 17 legislatures have thrown out anti-gay marriage bills.
[Reuters - Ken Kobayaski, Andrea Shalal-Esa; PR Newswire]

| | | |
|---|---|---|
| 12-4-96 | South Africa | A new constitution guaranteeing equal rights in South Africa won approval from the Constitutional Court. It includes a Bill of Rights that protects gay rights. The new constitution prohibits discrimination on the basis of sexual orientation, meaning that, in principle, gay marriages would be allowed. Gay marriages have already taken place unofficially in South Africa, but there has yet to be a court case to determine their legal status. [AP - Duncan Guy] |
| 12-4-96 | Los Angeles | The Rev. Louis Sheldon, head of Traditional Values, a coalition of 31,000 churches nationwide, said the Hawaii ruling "marks the beginning of a national debate which will decide the central moral issue of our civilization—the fate of the institution of marriage." He said the ruling was disappointing, but added, "This is only the beginning. No reasonable American will support this extreme effort to sanctify and sanction something which is sinful and unnatural." [Reuters - Michael Miller] |
| 12-4-96 | Hawaii | Hawaii ruling that allows gay marriages was put on hold until Hawaiian Supreme Court makes a ruling. [AP] |
| 12-5-96 | Massachusetts | Gov. Weld announced that marriages which result from the Hawaiian decision will be fully honored in Massachusetts. He also said the DOMA is unconstitutional. [gaybruin] |
| 12-9-96 | Netherlands | Homosexual couples in the Netherlands |

would be permitted to register their relationship as a legally binding union under a proposed law. The proposal, which has broad backing in parliament and is expected to become law in January 1998, would give registered same-sex couples nearly identical rights as married heterosexuals, except that gay couples would not be allowed to adopt children, said a justice Ministry spokeswoman.
[AP]

| | | |
|---|---|---|
| 1-22-97 | Maine | An anti-gay rights group in Maine, Concerned Maine Families, says it has more than enough signatures to force a statewide referendum on a proposal to define marriage as the "union of one man and one woman." Concerned Maine Families is the same organization that pushed an unsuccessful referendum in 1995 to exclude homosexuals from state civil rights protection. [UPI] |
| 2-6-97 | Hawaii | Hawaii's Senate called for a constitutional amendment to ban same-sex marriages while approving a new law that would give gay and lesbian couples many of the benefits of married heterosexuals. [AP - Bruce Dunford] |
| 2-12-97 | Mississippi | Gov. Kirk Fordice denounced same-sex relationships as "perverse" Wednesday as he signed a law making Mississippi the 17th state in a year to ban homosexual marriages. |

"For too long in this freedom-loving land, cultural subversives have engaged in trench warfare on traditional family values," Fordice said. Mississippi's law also denies recognition of homosexual marriages performed in other states. And Fordice said the law would ensure that gay couples do not enjoy benefits of marriage

such as health insurance.
[AP - Gina Holland]

2-21-97     Washington, DC     At least 1,049 federal laws provide benefits, rights, and privileges based on a per-
son's marital status, according to a newly
released report by the General Accounting
Office, an arm of the U.S. Congress. The
report, commissioned to assess the possible ramifications of the anti-Gay Defense
of Marriage Act, lists all 1,049 statues by
name and U.S. code number.
[Washington Blade - Lou Chibbaro Jr.]

2-22-97     Washington     Gov. Gary Locke vetoed a bill banning
same-sex marriages, calling it "divisive and
unnecessary." The vetoed measure defined
marriage solely as a union between a man
and a woman. As in many other states,
legislative action was prompted out of concern that courts in Hawaii may legalize gay
and lesbian marriages.
[LA Times]

2-26-97     Sacramento     California state lawmakers have revived
legislation against same-sex marriage that
was killed last year. It would bar California
from recognizing gay marriages. Knight's
son, who is gay, has publicly opposed his
father's legislation, but Knight would only
say that he and his son had agreed to disagree.
[UPI, AP - Rich Harris]

3-3-97     California     Californians oppose legalizing same-sex
marriages but favor extending some of the
benefits of marriage to homosexual
couples, according to a new Field Poll.
The survey found that 56% of Californians
oppose legalizing homosexual marriages,
but that 67% support allowing couples
living together such rights as hospital
visitation, medical power of attorney and
conservatorship. A smaller majority, 59%,

|         |         | supports allowing domestic partners to receive such benefits as pensions, health coverage, family leave and death benefits. [San Diego Union-Tribune - John Marelius] |
|---------|---------|---|
| 3-6-97  | Florida | The Florida chapter of the ACLU is fighting legislation that would prohibit the recognition of same-sex marriages in the state. A state House committee unanimously passed the bill, saying it could save Florida from suffering the fate of Sodom and Gomorrah. [UPI] |
| 3-22-97 | Poland  | Poland's Parliament finally approved a new post-communism constitution for the country. On demands by the church, the new constitution outlaws homosexual marriages and guarantees the right of religion classes in schools. [AP - Monika Scislowska] |
| 4-1-97  | Maine   | Maine lawmakers passed legislature banning same-sex marriage in Maine last week. Maine Gov. Angus King refused to sign the ban into law, saying it "sows hate and division" among state residents. He said he did not veto the measure because it would have triggered a statewide referendum. [UPI US & World] |
| 4-29-97 | Hawaii  | The state Legislature voted Tuesday to grant gay couples many rights and benefits now enjoyed by married couples, while putting an issue on the ballot that is likely to bar the legalization of gay marriages. The compromise bills were intended to reverse the Hawaii Supreme Court's landmark 1993 ruling that found a ban on same-sex marriage unconstitutional. The Legislature placed a constitutional amendment on next year's general election |

ballot that would give it the power to reserve legalized marriages to heterosexual couples.
[AP - Bruce Dunford]

4-30-97      Florida     A bill to ban same-sex marriages in Florida is awaiting a decision by Gov. Lawton Childes whether to sign the measure. If it becomes law, Florida would be the 19th state to refuse to recognize homosexual unions by defining marriage a legal union between one man and one woman.
[UPI]

# NOTES

## Prologue

1. See, among others, Boetti (n. d.), Lifshin (1982), Daly (1978), and Grahn (1984).
2. See Freud (1933a, p. 132) for the much-cited explanation of the defensive function of women's invention. But Freud (1930) also noted that "psycho-analysis can supply some information which cannot be arrived at by other means, and can thus demonstrate new connecting threads in the 'weaver's masterpiece' spread between the instinctual endowments, the experiences and the works of an artist" (p. 212).

In some times and cultures women weave; in other times and other cultures men weave. Contemporary floors wear carpets woven by Kurd women or women from Tibet and Morocco. On the walls of fashionable city homes hang rugs woven by Navaho women. Navaho weavers originally learned their skills from their Pueblo neighbors, cultures in which only the men wove. Historically it has usually happened that "women's work," such as making garments or cooking food, often became "men's work" when it began to be used outside the home and became valuable in a market economy. Thus we see Penelope weaving a shroud for her father-in-law and women spinning in fairy tales. Anderson and Zinsser (1988) point out that as production shifted from "localized, subsistence production to long-distance trade and manufacturing centers" the changing technologies and economies worked to the disadvantage of women:

> From the fourteenth to the seventeenth centuries, the overwhelming majority of women in guilds in the towns of France, Germany, Italy, England, Belgium, and the Netherlands worked in the textile and clothing trade. In Paris, London, and Florence women exercised a virtual monopoly on all of the processes involved in the production of silk cloth. Yet even in these protected and privileged crafts, the traditions of women's work operated inexorably both before and after the advent of commercial capitalism. Even in the silk industries in London, the silkwomen never had the right to make the most lucrative product, "whole cloth." Male weavers took over that process [p. 408].

3. Contemporary discussions of the concept of self in psychoanalysis and the use of narratives in clinical work include Mitchell (1991, 1993) and Schafer (1992).

4. See letter from Freud to Lytton, in which Freud says he read with enjoyment all previous works by Lytton, in Meisel and Kendrick (1985, pp. 332–334).

5. "You could not have escaped Freud in the literary world of the early twenties. Freud! All literary London discovered Freud about 1920 . . . the theories were the great subject of conversation wherever one went at that date. To me Freud is literary England . . . after the first war. People did not always agree but he was always taken in the utmost seriousness" (Bryher to Susan Stanford Friedman, cited in Friedman, 1981, p. 18).

For further views of the Bloomsbury/Freud connections, see Holroyd (1971), Meisel and Kendrick (1985), and Friedman (1985).

6. For examples of gynecologists' cautions about education for women, see Smith-Rosenberg (1985a):

> The human body, Victorian male physicians insisted and male educators readily concurred, was both hierarchical and fragile, its delicate balances easily destroyed by external forces. A closed energy system, the body allocated scarce energy resources governed by rigid, biologically determined and gender-linked priorities. Within the male body, the higher organs— the brain and heart—dominated. Predictably, the reproductive organs dominated the female's body. The woman who favored her mind at the expense of her ovaries—especially the woman who spent her adolescence and early adulthood in college and graduate school—would disorder a delicate physiological balance. Her overstimulated brain would become morbidly introspective. Neurasthenia, hysteria, insanity would follow. Her ovaries, robbed of energy rightfully theirs, would shrivel, and sterility and cancer ensue.
>
> Society, late-nineteenth century physicians warned, must protect the higher good of racial health by avoiding situations in which adolescent girls taxed their intellectual faculties in academic competition. . . . Such medical admonitions, published in ever-growing numbers by America's most eminent physicians (Harvard Professor Edward Clarke, for example, or Philadelphia's elegant society physician S. Weir Mitchell), exerted a strong influence upon educators, even those connected with institutions that admitted women. Throughout the 1870s, state legislators debated the advisability of their universities' offering unrestricted educational programs to women. A number of universities that did admit women prescribed a lighter courseload, or refused to permit women's admission to regular degree programs [pp. 258–259].

Although ill informed about human physiology, the gynecologists were correct in some of their predictions. Many women who went to college in those first generations did not marry or have children. At global population conferences today, the connection is frequently made between lowered birth rates and education for women.

7. Appignanesi and Forrester (1992) suggest that Freud might have read work similar to Woolf's, but perhaps with little effect on his thinking.

> It is likely that Freud read some of H.D.'s work before her arrival. An American friend had given him *Palimpsest*, three overlayered stories trac-

ing woman's development as artist, using antiquity as a psychological trope. The burrowing in the past, the writing over of one personality with new ones which are yet determined by the old, signaled a set of interests not so dissimilar from Freud's own—though not in an idiom with which Freud, thoroughly un-modernist in his tastes, was familiar [p. 388].

Freud (1900) had earlier used the palimpsest metaphor in *The Interpretation of Dreams* (p. 135n).

# Introduction

1. See Katz (1976, pp. 23–24, p. 570, n24). Jefferson was a "liberal" on the matter of punishment for sodomy in that he opposed the then-current practice of the death penalty for this offense.

2. Crompton and Robson (1980/81) challenge the idea that lesbian women were exempt from legal prosecution. But Hart (1994) argues that "their research does not indicate that lesbians were equally subjected to legal prosecutions; rather, it shows that gay men and lesbians have not been prosecuted in the same way and for the same offenses. The historical relevance of this difference resides largely in the idea that lesbianism remained a *secret* that could be kept from 'women'—white, middle-and upper-class wives and daughters of the legislators" (pp. 5–6).

Brown (1986b) also disagrees with Crompton. She argues that "among the hundreds if not thousands of cases of homosexuality tried by lay and ecclesiastical courts in medieval and early modern Europe, only a few involved sexual relations between women" (p. 68). Hart also discusses Havelock Ellis's "Sexual Inversion in Women." Hart notes that "a large proportion of his text and footnotes are given over to reporting instances of homosexuality among women outside the circle of white, European patriarchy. Although Ellis's ostensible purpose in these citations is to point out that lesbianism is not abnormal but rather a common and frequent practice worldwide, this documentation effectively produces a racially marked image of the lesbian as distinctly nonwhite" (p. 161, n3).

3. See Brown (1986b):

> Even more than male sodomy, sodomy between females was "the sin which cannot be named." In the sixteenth century, Gregoria Lopez had called it "the silent sin," *peccatum mutum*, and earlier Jean Gerson had called it a sin against nature in which "women have each other by detestable and horrible means which should not be named or written." For this reason the famous jurist Germain Colladon (16th c.) advised the Genevan authorities, who had no prior experience with lesbian crimes, that the death sentence should be read publicly, as it normally was in case of male homosexuality, but that the customary description of the crime committed should be left out. "A crime so horrible and against nature," he wrote, "is so detestable and because of the horror of it cannot be named." The problem was not just that Colladon had a particular abhorrence for this kind of offense, but that because women were thought to have weaker natures, it was feared that they were more susceptible to suggestion [p. 75].

Brown points out that Foucault also makes almost no reference to lesbians. "[H]is argument that certain forms of sexuality only began to be denied by Western society in the seventeenth century can only be sustained by disregarding denial of lesbian sexuality in the medieval and early modern period" (p. 500, n53).

4. Or perhaps none of this is so, since Sappho's life is long lost in rumor, gossip, speculation. See Bernard (1994), Bing and Cohen (1991), and Campbell (1982).

5. Traub (1995) argues that "a vocabulary was available to Western writers with which to describe women's erotic desire for and contact with one another," namely in the pre-18th-century travel narratives describing the erotic behaviors of foreign exotic women. These, however, were not examples of women who loved women writing about their own desires.

6. See, for instance, San Francisco Lesbian and Gay History Project (1989).

Smith (1996) describes the economic double standards of industrial England. Smith shows the religious and union opposition to the "pit girls" of the Lancashire coal mines. These women workers went bare armed, wore trousers under skirts, which they rolled up to their waists to keep them out of their way as they sorted coal. The pit girls' work was dangerous, but they had more freedom and were perhaps safer than the women in the textile factories, who lumbered in heat in full skirts that caught in the heavy machinery. Since the pit girls were paid less money than men to sort coal, they threatened the male workers' income and were treated as sexual and social deviants.

7. See Smith-Rosenberg (1985a,b, 1994), Benstock (1986, 1989), Babcock and Parezo (1988), Sklar (1985), and Aptheker (1989).

Smedley (1943) describes Chinese women trying to gain cottage and competency by working in factories 10- and 14-hour days. Smedley describes her meeting in 1930 with some women silkworkers of Canton. Many such women were said to have secret "Sister Societies"; many refused to marry or, if they did marry, agreed to have only one son and to pay for their husbands to have concubines so they could work. Smedley's Chinese male guide was disgusted by such women. He said they were known as homosexual throughout China. "They're too rich—that's the root of the trouble" (p. 103).

8. Faderman (1994) describes some effects of these erasures and distortions:

> In 1956, as a teenager, I began to consider myself a lesbian. Almost as soon as I claimed that identity, being already enamored of books, of course I looked around for literary representations that would help explain me to myself. I did not have far to look, because the pulp book racks at the local drugstore exhibited a dizzying array of titles like *Odd Girl*, *Twisted Sisters*, *Twilight Lovers*, *We Walk in Shadows*, and *Whisper Their Love*. . . . I was depressed by their pathos and bathos. . . .
>
> I wanted "real literature," the kind I read in my English classes, to comment on the lifestyle I had just recently discovered with such enthusiasm, to reveal me to myself, to acknowledge the lesbian to the world. Naturally, my high school English teachers never gave me a hint about where to look for such literature. As an undergraduate in college I was an English literature major, but the only time I learned about a lesbian book was in an Abnormal Psych class, where *The Well of Loneliness* was mentioned. As a graduate student, although I read Emily Dickinson, Sara Orne Jewett, Willa

Cather, Virginia Woolf, Carson McCullers, Elizabeth Bishop, and even Sappho, I never had a professor who mentioned the word "lesbian" or acknowledged that love between women had ever been a subject of literary focus. In 1967 I received a Ph.D. in English without the slightest notion that lesbian literature had a rich history and that many of the writers I admired—in fact almost all of those few women writers who were studied in graduate school—had contributed to that history [p. vii].

Compare the words of Coletta Reid (1976), another woman looking for stories to live by: "In the spring of 1970 I went to the Washington D.C. Public Library to search the card catalogue for entries under 'lesbian.' This was a personal quest; I wanted to discover how the women who went before me had lived. There were only three listings: Sappho's Poetry, Frank Caprio's *Female Homosexuality*, and Krafft-Ebings's *Psychopathia Sexualis*" (p. 21).

Librarian Jeannette Foster, seeking a remedy for her own ignorance about homosexuality, researched works from Sappho through 1954. The result was *Sex Variant Women in Literature* (Foster, 1956).

See also Stimpson (1981) and Cook (1979a).

9. See the excellent discussion by Sautman (1996).

10. See Faderman (1981, p. 254) and Foster (1956, p. 63). The 1992 film *Basic Instinct* offers a contemporary representation of this trope. See Hart (1994).

11. For instance, Henry (1948) provides, in addition to case studies of "Bisexual Cases, Homosexual Cases, and Narcissistic Cases," "masculinity-femininity tests," and the corresponding physical correlates, detailed drawings of characteristic lesbian anatomy ("areolas," "typical sex variant vulva," "pupuce: varieties in size, form and surface"), pp. 1100–1130.

12. Jeannette Marks and Miss Woolley would certainly not have called themselves lesbian or homosexual. But they certainly saw themselves as more than friends.

When Marks spent a summer away from Woolley, Woolley unself-consciously wrote that nightly, following her prayers, she caressed the bed on which they had slept together, pretending it was Marks's body. She placed this passion within a marital context, considering Marks and herself married. Indeed Woolley experienced the church service marking Jeannette's conversion to the Episcopal Church (from the Quakerism of her parents) as a marriage sacrament during which they gave their hearts to God and to each other [Smith-Rosenberg, 1985a, p. 274].

See also Wells (1978), Faber (1980), Faderman (1981), and Young-Bruehl (1988).

Katz (1983) cites Wells's response to reading the Marks-Woolley correspondence: "It seemed to me impossible to ignore or suppress the content of the letters, impertinent to continue to read them, and quite unthinkable to publish them" (p. 5). Katz also quotes Faber's response to reading the letters of Eleanor Roosevelt and Hickock: "Why couldn't this collection be locked up again, at least for several decades?" (p. 8).

See also Cook (1979a,b), Sahli (1979), Rupp (1980), and Vicinus (1984).

For other discussions of writing biography and issues of homosexuality see O'Brien (1994). O'Brien (1988) describes Cather's silence about her lesbian relationship and

O'Brien's need to find her own voice to speak up to, and back to, Cather and Edith Lewis, with whom Cather had lived for 40 years and who wanted the word "lesbian" kept out of the book.

A more recent biography of a woman with primary relationships with women which has had the benefit of these earlier biographers' struggles is Horowitz (1994).

13. Some texts set us a particular problem. If we know the writer is lesbian but she does not made that identification clear in her writing, we do not disclose it in our writing.

14. The panel on May 6, 1989 was entitled "Psychoanalysis Re-Examines Love and Sex Among Gays and Lesbians." Its members were Bertram Schaffner, M.D., Chair, and Jack Drescher, M.D., both from the William Alanson White Institute; Karin Lofthus Carrington, a Jungian analyst; Joseph P. Merlino, M.D. from the Division of Psychoanalytic Training at New York Medical College; and Alan Kagan, M.D. from the Postgraduate Center for Mental Health in New York, The Psychoanalytic Medicine Division.

15. Dominici, Blechner, Lesser, and Schwartz all trained in institutes not affiliated with the American Psychoanalytic Association.

16. Elind (1991) provides a succinct definition of postmodern characteristics:

> Implicit, and often explicit, in the grand theories was the conviction that causality could best be dealt with by explaining phenomena at one level of observation or conceptualization by other phenomena at a different, often deeper, level of observation and conceptualization. The germ theory of disease, for example, explains a variety of observable surface phenomena, such as flu symptoms, on the basis of unobservable microscopic organism or viruses. . . . Within psychoanalysis, observable memory blocks and slips . . . are said to be the consequence of unobservable drives and defenses. . . .
>
> The post-modern emphasis is away from grand theories and from explanations in terms of levels. While the importance of grand theories and level explanations is not denied, the value of more limited theories and of greater attention to surface-level phenomena is emphasized. To illustrate, the mathematics of chaotic phenomena, such as the dispersal of cream globules in a cup of coffee, reflects the post-modern emphasis on more circumscribed and surface-level theorizing. In sociology, the work of Erving Goffman is quintessentially post-modern in its emphasis on exquisitely detailed descriptions of surface level "impression management" activities such as reading a book while dining alone [pp. 10–11].

But see also Adams and Tate (1991), who note that "fragmentation" and "uncertainty" were characteristics of reality for women writers of the modern age.

> Developments in the new areas of psychoanalysis and film, in experimental publishing, in art and music, and in modes of living all influenced modernist writing. The period encompassed a wide range of innovative literary forms and ideas, from the decadent writing of the 1890s to the various avante-garde movements (imagism, futurism, dadaism, surrealism, etc.) and beyond. Fragmentation, uncertainty and open-endedness—challeng-

ing and transforming traditional values and forms—also characterised modernism. . . .

It is often argued that modernism explored the loss of belief in a stable, "essential" self. Women, however, have been seen as the "other" to man's "one," and as mirrors to reflect the (imaginary) wholeness or unity of man. As the myth of the unified, autonomous self began to be explored and exposed *as* myth women were less likely than men to mourn its passing as they had never had the right to full participation in it in the first place" [pp. xiii–xiv].

17. Stoller (1988) wrote:

Have I sufficiently indicated that the ethical problems of getting patients' permission to publish may be insoluble? The old riddle: when someone says "yes" to a powerful figure what parts of the "yes" come from love, fear, insight, possession of the facts, the state of one's digestive tract, the season of the year, the phase of the moon? Exhibitionism, vindication, revenge, desire to help humanity, desire to help me, fear of reprisal from me, to solidify things learned during treatment? All could play a part [p. 389].

18. We informed some patients in the last months of their treatment (and some patients long after treatment had ended) that we might be writing about our work together. All those we so informed reported being anxious yet eager to read whatever we wrote. We told the patients that we would not publish anything they felt made them identifiable and that we would be available to discuss any feelings they had in response to reading our descriptions. Analyst and patient usually had one or sometimes two face-to-face office meetings together during which patients responded to what had been written, offered their views of various moments in the treatment, and reminded the analyst of events the analyst had forgotten or not mentioned in the writing. These meetings allowed some patients an opportunity to reflect on their analytic experience, to register how they felt now about the past treatment, and to inform the therapist of events that had taken place since termination of treatment and which they felt had connections to that treatment. One patient found the reading painful and disappointing. The others reported finding the experience integrating and rewarding, as we did as analysts and as writers.

# 1

# Superior Guinea-Pig: Bryher and Psychoanalysis

1. See Friedman (1981, 1985). Friedman is the foremost scholar of H.D.'s relationship to psychoanalysis. She has excellent discussions of the Bryher-H.D. relationship, as do Appignanesi and Forrester (1992).

See also Richards (1992). Richards's thesis is that Freud's gift through the analysis was "that creative work, not social or sexual gratification, was Doolittle's satisfaction in life. The bisexuality [Freud told H.D. she was "a perfect bi."] was a resolution that allowed Doolittle to bow gracefully out of the lesbian activity without rejecting Bryher, and thus biting the hand which had so generously fed her" (p. 400). We do not concur with Richards's analysis of H.D.'s treatment with Freud or her understanding of H.D.'s relationship with Bryher. Their relationship was not founded on what Richards apparently means by "lesbian activity," namely, sexual behavior, nor did H.D. "bow gracefully" out of the relationship after her sessions with Freud. Their 43-year relationship, like most enduring relationships, was sustained by a mixture of their mutual dependencies, both healthy and neurotic, by their "shared understanding about the importance of creative work," and by their other mutual interests, including the shared parenting of Perdita.

See also Arens (1995).

The definitive biography of H.D. is by Guest (1984). In her preface, Guest notes that the book also, of necessity, encapsulates the biography of Bryher.

For additional discussions of Bryher's life, see Hanscombe and Smyers (1987), Benstock (1989), Adams and Tate (1991), and Weiss (1995).

2. According to the papers at the time, Ellerman left "the biggest fortune ever dealt with at Somerset House. It does not include any of Sir John's large holdings in shipping and other interests." He left £17,223,977 in cash; the total estate was estimated at £30,000,000. John Jr. inherited the title and £600,000 absolute and £2,000,000 in trust; Bryher inherited £600,000 absolute and £600,000 in trust (Guest, 1984, p. 216).

Bryher's early novels included *Development* (1920) and *Two Selves* (1923). With Trude Weiss, Bryher wrote a German textbook, *The Light-Hearted Student* (1930). Geography books included *West* (1924) and *A Picture Geography for Little Children, Part One: Asia* (1924). Bryher's historical novels are listed elsewhere.

Among the writers Bryher supported were Dylan Thomas and his wife, Caitlin, who received the Bryher Foundation Traveling Fellowship (Guest, 1984, p. 255).

3. H.D. wrote a fictionalized account of Bryher's suicidal feelings in the unpublished "Asphodel" (1921–1922). In 1921 Bryher published a poem entitled "Extract" from which the following lines are taken:

> Is anything sweet as death? Spice, lily, peachflower? . . .
> You are the swift welcome of a body. You are the passionate Aphrodite of
> the poppies.
> It is no use pretending; I hate it all, all of it. . . .
> I—the liar—I that pretend I would fight and love—I ask at the end
> "Is anything sweet save death!"

Adams and Tate (1991), p. 230.

Bryher's memoirs and letters record other suicidal thoughts and impulses. In 1933 while Bryher was at her home in Switzerland and H.D. was in Vienna in analysis with Freud, Bryher reported that "on waking this morning it seemed to me that I was not as comfortable as I might be and I found an open penknife in bed with me. . . . It might have been most dangerous" (Bryher to H.D., March 20, 1933). Bryher passed off the penknife incident as "sheer codpiece of course," and interpreted her behavior as due to anxiety about the upcoming visit of actress Elizabeth Bergner.

She was taken with Zilboorg's paper on suicide at the 1934 IPA Congress:

> Zilboorg spoke brilliantly on suicide. Savage races believe that a natural

death means death—they call it among Eskimos "the narrow land" but suicide leads to immortality, the unused life if you get me, is lived out in par-
adise. Think he meant that horror of suicide is purely civilization, not
usually found in primitive races [to H.D., August 30, 1934].

In early 1938 in Boston a depressed Bryher almost "accidentally" killed herself. She
wrote to Schmideberg:

Maybe I shall not reach the [IPA] Congress however. I hopefully shut the
windows and turned on the gas the other morning. Evidently my unk was
in two minds, because I suddenly started sniffing and wondering what in
the world was happening and soon rectified the matter, but I have not the
faintest recollection of doing it nor of what I did in the preceding half hour.
It interests me that one can be so washed away by one's unk, as it were;
consciously I never can believe in amnesia though I have read of it, and
had it happen several times. It is a little worrying though for it has always
been the sign for one's unk to turn into a hedgehog and mistreat one worse
than usual [Bryher to Walter Schmideberg, January 26, 1938].

Bryher had recently been finding "things personally very difficult." She had been
depressed by her visit with Marianne Moore whom she described as "so mama-dominated
that to speak to her, one addresses the question to mama and is perhaps—and perhaps
not—answered by Marianne. I was served with peppermint tea and vitamin biscuits.
Given a lecture on deep breathing and they spoke a prayer" (Bryher to Schmideberg,
January 17, 1938). Moore's relationship with her mother may have revived Bryher's earlier suicidal feelings about her own stifling family. She had also complained about "such
dirt about what has been going on with regard to the family estate since my father's
death" (Bryher to Schmideberg, January 17, 1938). She had declined sessions with Sachs
and had gone to the prize fights with Macpherson instead. "I find scraps of p.a. just at
this moment rather difficult than otherwise. There have been times when it worked
excellently, but I think it is really not very wise just now" (Bryher to Schmideberg,
January 17, 1938).

Both the penknife episode and the oven incident may have been related to separations from Sachs and whatever real and transferential feelings were connected to those
separations.

4. Ellis (1938) on inversion:

In male inverts there is a frequent tendency to approximate to the feminine type and in female inverts to the masculine type; this occurs both in
physical and in psychic respects, and though it may be traced in a considerable number of respects it is by no means always obtrusive. . . . Among
female inverts, there is usually some approximation to the masculine attitude and temperament though this is by no means always conspicuous.
Various minor anomalies of structure or function may occur in inverts. The
sexual organs in both sexes are sometimes overdeveloped or, perhaps more
usually, underdeveloped, in a slight approximation to the infantile type;
gynecomasty is at times observed; in women there may be a somewhat
masculine development of the larynx, as well as some degree of hypertri-

chosis. (Marañón finds that male traits tend to appear on the right side of the body, female on the left.) Male inverts are sometimes unable to whistle. In both sexes a notable youthfulness of appearance is often preserved into adult age. The love of green (which is normally a preferred color chiefly by children and especially girls) is frequently observed [pp. 231–232].

5. Edith Lees Ellis, Havelock's wife, was a lesbian who made several speaking tours of the United States.

6. In 1918 Bryher had written *Amy Lowell: A Critical Appreciation*.

7. See McAlmon (1938). Weiss (1995) and Benstock (1986) discuss H.D.'s and Bryher's avoidance of Paris in terms of their difficulties with their estranged husbands (Richard Aldington and Robert McAlmon), who lived in Paris. But Bryher suggests an even earlier reason for her dislike of Paris in a February 24, 1937, letter to Walter Schmideberg:

> Do you really like Paris? It was a nightmare to me as a pup, and for years I have been careful to avoid it. Then I got excited about the Front Populaire and don't mind it so much, but this really is a sheer triumph of mind— and literature. It is a city in memory, of being interminably dragged round shops (how I hated them) with occasional merciful interludes when one was quite small, on the roundabouts of the Champs Elysees.

8. For discussions of such marriages of convenience, see Garber (1995), pp. 373–374.

9. *Close-up. An International Magazine Devoted to Film Art* was published in Territet, Switzerland from July 1927 to December 1933, monthly and quarterly, edited by Kenneth Macpherson and Bryher, and reprinted by Arno Press, New York, in 1971. "We expected it to last three issues and had five hundred copies printed. It was an immediate success and when we ended after the collapse of the silent film, six years later, we had five thousand readers" (Bryher, 1962, p. 245).

10. For a discussion of this film, see Weiss (1992).

11. See Wolff (1986). Hirschfeld was also a "favoured guest" at the 1911 Weimar Congress of the Psychoanalytic Association and was identified there as the Berlin authority on homosexuality. Earlier, in 1906, Hirschfeld had written, at Freud's request, to defend Freud against Fleiss's charge that Freud was aiding Dr. Swoboda to steal Fleiss's concept of bi-sexuality. Hirschfeld left the Berlin Psychoanalytical Society in 1911, after which Freud apparently no longer held him in favor. Clark quoted Freud as saying, "Magnus Hirschfeld, who has left the ranks, was no great loss, a flabby, unappetizing fellow, incapable of learning anything" (in Wolff, 1986, pp. 101–102).

12. Faderman and Eriksson (1980) reported that Berlin had 60 places "where lesbians could go to talk, dance, play, and meet other women—places for middle class lesbians as well as for working class lesbians. . . ."

> *The Girlfriend: Weekly for the Ideal Friendship,* sponsored by the Federation for Human Rights (a homosexual organization which, in the 1920s, boasted a membership of 48,000) where lesbian nightspots were openly advertised and where individual women could place their own ads about

their desires to meet other lesbians. Such freedom and openness failed
to take root anywhere else in the world again for almost half a century
[p. xxi].

The economic and class divisions among Berlin's lesbians are well illustrated by the
following comments about *The Girlfriend* by Charlotte Wolff (1980), lesbian psychiatrist. Visiting Berlin again in 1977 for the first time since forced to flee in 1933, she met
contemporary lesbian feminists, who later wrote to her.

> My correspondents wrote to me about a research project in which they
> wanted to involve me. They had searched for documents of lesbian life in
> the twenties, a period they rightly looked upon as the lesbian El Dorado.
> A magazine, *Die Freundin,* had been published in Berlin from 1924 to
> 1933, and Eva R. had discovered that the whole set was still intact and
> lodged in the Staatsbibliothek in East Germany. She had retrieved and pho-
> tocopied all its numbers. It is difficult to understand how a whole collec-
> tion of such "degenerate" literature could have survived the Nazi period,
> but soon I had thirty photocopies of *Die Freundin* in my hands. I agreed
> to write a foreword to the project which was to be published in book form.
> As I was myself a "period piece," my correspondents wanted to interview
> me during my visit. . . . I read these magazines, which are a strange part
> of German cultural history before Hitler, with amusement, disbelief and
> absorbing interest. I had never come across *Die Freundin* when it had
> appeared, a sure proof of the secrecy surrounding its publication, though
> homosexual films and plays had been in vogue in the twenties. *Die
> Freundin* had obviously been an "illegitimate child" which did not dare to
> show its face openly. The lesbian world which it depicts had little in com-
> mon with the homosexual women I knew and the places I frequented. Its
> readers must have been of a different class who loved, wined and danced
> in a different world. They came together every week in localities on the
> Alexander Platz and the surrounding district where the poorer people
> lived. The following advertisement in *Die Freundin* illustrates better than
> any second-hand description the way those lesbians enjoyed themselves:
> "Sonnabend, 30 Juli, 1927. *Nur Damen* treffen sich jeden Mittwoch und
> Sonnabend im ALEXANDER-PALAIS. 'Ein Sommernachtstraum.' (Only
> ladies meet each Wednesday and Saturday at Alexander Palace. "A Summer
> Night's Dream.") [pp. 255–256].

[13.] See Gay (1988), pp. 460–463. See also footnote, p. 771n: "For psychoanalysis in
Berlin, see. . . the extremely instructive Festschrift, Zehn Jahre Berliner Psychoanalytisches
Institut (Poliklinik und Lehranstalt), ed. Deutsche Psychoanalytische Gesellschaft (1930),
with informative short reports by Ernst Simmel, Otto Fenichel, Karen Horney, Hanns
Sachs, Gregory Zilboorg, and others on all aspects of the institution, its rules, its stu-
dents, its patients, and its program."

[14.] H.D. saw Chadwick April 13–July 15, 1931. Bryher financially arranged for this
treatment, as well as H.D.'s with Freud and after Freud, with Walter Schmideberg, and
later in Switzerland at Küsnacht Clinic with Erich Heydt.

[15.] Writing to Schmideberg on February 18,1937, Bryher recalls these days:

Róheim brings back Berlin. As a great favor, and duly on my best behaviour, I was allowed in to his lectures at the Institute there. It must have been in 1929 I think, or 1930. In those days, strange as it may seem, I too, took p.a. very seriously. I also did not know so much German. I think the first lecture was one of my most *painful* moments. Róheim apparently spoke a very strange German, and relapsed every few sentences into English, added to this he quoted us long sentences, verses, and names in Papuan. It was very interesting but I knew there would be also a day, or rather, morning, of reckoning, because I had my hour at eight then, or nine. . . . [k]nowing I would be questioned, and knowing that if I could not answer successfully, it would be discovered . . . [sic] that maybe I wasn't so sure of the fundamentals of p. a. as I had given to believe, . . . in spite of my protestations that nobody could possibly be expected to follow a lecture in Papuan. Fortunately before the second one occurred, I happened to encounter Turtle at a film, and I was with his friends, the Metzners, and he gave them a very clear summary of what the Róheim stuff was all about. . . . I took my incursions into the Institute so very solemnly then but I have got over it. As you have, no doubt, noted.

[16.] Also in Isay (1989, p. 6).

[17.] See discussion in Abelove (1985). Abelove's source for the correspondence on homosexual applicants is Spiers and Lynch (1977) and a set of letters known as the "Rundbriefe," in the Otto Rank Collection at Columbia University Library. Spiers and Lynch also use the Rundbriefe. See also Jacoby (1983).

Sachs (1923) does not make any direct mention of homosexuality in this discussion.

[18.] Bryher met Norman Douglas, author of *West Wind* in 1922–23. Mark Holloway, Douglas's biographer said Douglas was "one of the many of Bryher's 'drunks'" (Guest, *1984*, p. 156).

[19.] See Sachs (1927) on the issue of lay analysis.

[20.] Sachs had previously spent two years in Switzerland recovering from pulmonary tuberculosis that had begun in 1918 at the IPA Congress in Budapest.

[21.] Sachs wrote to Bryher:

> About your possible cooperation with Pabst allow me one piece of advice: insist on Metzner being of the cast and put your foot firmly down on that. *Not* only because he is such an excellent, artistic worker but from him you will always hear what's wrong and where you really stand. More than his intelligence it is the clearness and integrity of his character that makes him an invaluable compass in the stormy sea of film-making. You know how much I admire Pabst and this includes his character as well as his genius, but he has the "artistic temperament," is subjected to sudden changes and unforseen influences—Metzner is not [November (?) 29, 1932].

These would prove to be prophetic words since Pabst, who Bryher worried would never be able to make his films under the brown shirts, in 1939 "after first announcing his intention to move to Hollywood abruptly chose to stay in Europe and make propaganda films for the Nazis" (Dijkstra, 1996, p. 419). Dijkstra discusses Pabst's films, including *Pandora's Box*, pointing out the "self-conscious conflation of anti-feminine and anti-Semitic images."

"Though it is no doubt true that many of Pabst's film's original viewers would have missed many of his more abstruse symbolic allusions, general audiences could not help but be affected, at least on a semiconscious level, by the evil message hidden in *Pandora's Box* . . . [and] the film's blatant anti-Semitism" (p. 419).

22. See Bryher to H.D., April 29, 1933. See also Friedman (1985, pp. 339 ff) for a discussion of the gift of the puppy and its relationship to H.D.'s analysis and Freud's association of H.D. and Perdita with his favorite daughter Sophie, who died, and her son Heinerle, Freud's favorite grandson, whom he also lost.

23. Although H.D. had planned to return in the fall, she did not go back to Vienna until October 1934. Friedman (1981) described H.D.'s attitude toward her analysis:

> H.D.'s tribute to her guide reveals strikingly how misleading it would be to view H.D.'s purpose in analysis in the early days of psychoanalysis through the perspective of what psychiatry has become in the present. The commonly perceived chasm between doctor and patient, expert and "mentally ill" person, was easily bridged in H.D.'s experience. She regarded herself as a "student" of psychoanalysis, in the same category as Dr. J. J. Van de Leeuw, the "eminent scholar," educator, and theosophist who saw Freud in the hour immediately preceding her own (*T[ribute to] F[reud]*, pp. 5, 18, 20): "The Professor had said in the beginning that he classed me in the same category as the Flying Dutchman—we were students. I was a student, working under the direction of the greatest mind of this and of perhaps many succeeding generations" (*T. F.*, p. 18). Like Bryher, H. D. partially regarded analysis with Freud as a training in psychoanalysis that she could use to help other war-shocked people: "I had begun my preliminary research in order to fortify and equip myself to face war when it came, and to help in some subsidiary way, if my training were sufficient and my aptitudes suitable, with war-shocked and war-shattered people" (*T. F.*, p. 93) [pp. 21–22].

24. See also Sachs to Bryher, December 3, 1933: "Dorothy Townshend as third trustee is okay with me. She may be old fashioned in some ways but I'm sure she is straight."

25. Bryher to H.D., September 27, 1933.

26. Guest (1984) notes that "Barbara Low was a psychoanalyst practicing in London, a former analysand of Sachs. She had been a close friend of the Lawrences. . . . Lawrence gave Barbara the manuscript of *Sea and Sardinia* to pay for her training analysis with Dr. Ernest Jones. . . ." ( p. 203). Barbara Low's nephew, Stephen Guest, was in love with H.D.

27. Freud to H.D., March 5, 1934.

Dear H.D.!

. . . From Perdita's trip, I am getting postcards. The last came from Trinidad. Happy Girl!
Give my love to Bryher and don't forget me.

Yours affectionately Freud [p. 192].

28. Various writers have been less than complementary in describing the Schmideberg-Bryher relationship. Guest said that 1947 marked the "beginning of nearly ten years with Schmideberg as a companion, hostage, and finally a dependent" ( p. 295). Phyllis Grosskurth (1986), biographer of Melanie Klein, also described the relationship.

> At the end of the war Schmideberg and Bryher moved permanently to Switzerland, where Melitta visited them amicably from time to time. No one has been able to understand this strange three-sided relationship. Bryher was in the habit of collecting lame ducks, and one theory is that she took on Schmideberg, whose alcoholism became worse with the passing years. . . . Even after sharing a house with Bryher and Schmideberg for many years . . . [Perdita Schaffner, H.D.'s daughter] is still puzzled by the nature of the relationship. [p. 369].

In a footnote, Grosskurth passed along Freud's assessment. "Susan Friedman, who is editing the H.D.-Bryher letters, has recently found a letter dated Oct. 31, 1934, from Vienna, in which H.D. reveals that Freud had told her Schmideberg was a homosexual —'that poor dear charming fellow,' Freud described him" (p. 369).

29. "Through Nancy Cunard, she and H.D. had met members of the Harlem Renaissance and had begun supporting black avant-garde writing and filmmaking" (Benstock, 1989, p. 345).

30. In a letter to the authors on May 28, 1996, Sachs's attorney, David R. Pokross, explained the arrangements:

> In early May of 1940, I received a package of securities from Martin Freud, then living in London. I immediately called Dr. Sachs and told him of the property that I had received and asked him to explain the matter. He told me that these securities had been a gift by Bryher to him to support the publication in Vienna of the "Imago" and that Martin Freud managed the securities. Martin Freud feared in 1940 that the securities would be confiscated by the Nazis so he sent them to me on the instructions of Dr. Sachs.
>
> With the approval of Dr. Sachs I prepared a Trust document dated May 18, 1940 in which I declared myself as Trustee of the securities. Until the death of Dr. Sachs in 1946, he directed me as to the disposal of the Trust property. I recall that funds were used to publish the American Imago edited by Dr. Sachs. Following Dr. Sach's death, I have managed the investments of the Trust property and have largely used the income in accordance with the purpose and objects of the Trust.
>
> In particular, I have established at the Boston Psychoanalytic Society & Institute, Inc. a Fund in the name of Dr. Sachs to encourage and facilitate symposia managed by the Society. Most recently I have arranged with the help of Dr. Gifford to have a library at the Institute named in honor of Dr. Sachs.

31. *The Heart to Artemis: A Writer's Memoirs* (1962), The *Days of Mars: A Memoir, 1940–1946* (1972) and ten novels: *The Fourteenth of October* (1952a), *Beowulf* (1952b), *The Player's Boy* (1953), *Roman Wall* (1954), *Gate to the Sea* (1958), *Ruan* (1960), *The*

*Coin of Carthage* (1963), *Visa for Avalon* (1965), *This January Tale* (1966), and *The Colors of Vaud* (1969).

32. sgifford@warren.med.harvard.edu to dcmmm@ucla.edu, 18 April 1996.

# 2

# "The Story of Our Lives Becomes Our Lives"

1. Today these tools are simply called flexible curves. We have a pretty blue 12 inch "Mars curve," made by Staedtler, that promises to "meet all your special drawing needs," and help with the "easy drawing of curves, ellipses, parabolas and hyperbolas."

2. See, among many others, Foucault (1978, p. 43), Weeks (1977), Faderman and Eriksson (1980), Katz (1983), McIntosh (1968), and Lauritsen and Thorstad (1974).

> There is no question that the appearance in nineteenth-century psychiatry, jurisprudence, and literature of a whole series of discourse on the species and subspecies of homosexuality, inversion, pederasty, and "psychic hermaphrodism" made possible a strong advance of social controls into this area of "perversity"; but it also made possible the formation of a "reverse" discourse: homosexuality began to speak in its own behalf, to demand that its legitimacy or "naturality" be acknowledged, often in the same vocabulary, using the same categories by which it was medically disqualified [Foucault, 1978, p. 101].

3. See also Kristof (1995).

4. "About 2 million buraku people trying to 'pass' . . . lead ordinary lives in ordinary neighborhoods—on the surface" (Jameson, 1993, p. 24).

5. For descriptions of this moment of shock see Aarons (1995) and Dew (1994).

6. Eva Cantarella (1992) disagrees with the interpretations of the story of Sodom (Genesis 19:4-11) made by Boswell, namely, that Sodom was destroyed not for its homosexuality but because its citizens committed sexual violence against God's angels. She argues that "the Jewish aversion to homosexuality . . . derives from a perception of the need (obviously vital for any people, but particularly and dramatically felt by the Jews) to concentrate their efforts on procreation" (p. 202).

See also Romans 1: 26-27: "For this cause God gave them up unto vile affections: for even their women did change the natural use into what is against nature. And likewise also the men, leaving the natural use of the woman, burned in their lust one toward another; men with men working that which is unseemly, and receiving in themselves that recompense of their error which was meet."

7. See also Flaks (1992), Rosenbaum (1995).

8. Stoller (1985), an energetic examiner of how people think about and experience their sexual and gendered selves, once described his measures of optimal psychic function.

> When I am alone and not trying for clarity, I consider a person healthy if he or she gets along well with others—without a lot of anxiety, lying,

crippling psychologic symptoms, inhibitions, or hatred, open or disguised—takes responsibility for his or her actions, uses his or her talents effectively, and is dependable. This is a cliché-ridden, uninspiring, unpsychodynamic-sounding list of virtues; but then I am considering here only intrapsychic and interpersonal health. A description such as this one includes, perhaps, several heterosexual and homosexual people [p.102].

See also Mitchell (1981).

9. "Each society seems to have a limited range of potential storylines for its sexual scripts. . . . It may be that we are all acting out scripts—but most of us seem to be typecast. . . . To paraphrase Marx, people make their own identities, but they do not make them just as they please" (Epstein, 1987, quoted in Vicinus, 1989, p. 434 ).

10. On women and exercise in the late 19th century, including the transformative role of the bicycle in the 1890s, see also Vertinsky (1994, p. 76ff).

11. For an interesting discussion on these materials and their usefulness to psychoanalysis see Mack (1980).

12. Mitchell (1996) himself no longer holds that assumption.

13. Fuss (1993) examines this image in this very postmodern/metapsychological discussion.

# 3

# "She Forswore Her Womanhood": Psychoanalytic and Biological Theories of the Etiology of Female Homosexuality

1. See Weeks (1981): "The most commonly quoted European writers on homosexuality in the mid-1870s were Casper and Tardieu, the leading medical and legal experts of Germany and France, respectively, and both seemed to have been primarily concerned with the need to define the new type of 'degenerates' who were coming before the courts, and to test whether they could be held legally responsible for their acts" (p. 104).

See also Sulloway (1983):

> Widely known as the theory of "neuro-psychopathic degeneration," this general doctrine had been borrowed by Krafft-Ebing from the French psychiatrist Bénédict Morel (1857), whose influence pervaded psychiatric theory during the latter half of the nineteenth century. According to Morel's view, a predisposition to either insanity, perversion, or a host of other neurological disorders could be congenitally inherited from a 'tainted' relative, himself (or herself) the victim of severe alcoholism, syphilis, debauchery, epilepsy, mental illness, or a variety of other pathogenic agents of neuropsychopathic heredity. Prior to Krafft-Ebing, the more popular view, particularly that of educators, had been that homosexuality and most other perversions were acquired through seduction, bad example, vice, and similar environmental agents of corrupt habit formation [p. 284].

2. Karl Heinrich Ulrich had earlier described a special class of men, with whom he included himself, whom he called Urnings, whose nature he likened to such congenitally determined conditions as "left-handedness or a cleft palate."

> There is a class of born Urnings, a class of individuals who are born with the sexual drive of women and have male bodies. They are a subspecies of men whose Uranian love is congenital. . . . By congenital is meant sexual, organic and mental inheritance, not an inherited disease and not such inheritances as pyromania, kleptomania and alcoholism, but rather an inheritance such as Dionians [normal men] receive in their sexual drives towards women and vice versa [quoted in Dannecker, 1981, p.33].

3. For Ulrichs, lesbians were males in women's bodies and thus, being men, were "naturally" attracted to women. Ellis "believed the use of the dildo to be common, and played down the importance of clitoral sexuality" (see Weeks, 1977, p. 66).

4. Therefore, for Stoller, caught in his own binary conundrum, boys had more difficulty establishing gender identification since they had to shift from identifying with mother to identifying with father.

5. From a letter to Gisela Ferenczi, February 19, 1934, in Grossman and Grossman, 1965, p.193.

6. See the documentary film *Changing Our Minds: The Story of Dr. Evelyn Hooker*, directed by Richard Schmiechen, narrated by Patrick Stewart, and produced by David Haugland and James Harrison. It is a Frameline release (E-mail: Frameline@aol.com).

7. Magnus Hirschfeld was also impressed with Steinach's research. See Wolff, 1986, p. 181.

8. "There were three psychosurgery teams in West German: in Hamburg (D. Müller), in Göttingen (F. D. Roeder), and in Homburg (G. Dieckmann). In 1962 the first psychosurgical 'treatment' was carried out by Roeder on a man labeled as paedophile-homosexual. In 1979, Schorch and Schmidt estimated that, up to that time, operations had been performed on approximately 70 men labeled as sexually abnormal. The results of animal experiments, especially those using white laboratory rats, of the endocrinologist Günter Dörner served as the scientific basis for these operations" (Herrn, 1995, p. 51). See also Schmidt and Schorsch (1981).

9. In 1979, Inge Rieber, M.D. and Volkmar Sigusch, M.D., physicians at the Frankfurt University Medical School Institute of Sexual Science, published a Guest Editorial in which they criticized the psychosurgeries. They noted: "Because of the questionable theoretical basis and the extremely questionable present practice of the surgeons, we have demanded in a more detailed public statement that stereotaxic hypothalamotomies on humans with deviant sexual behavior be ceased immediately" (pp. 526–527).

In 1981, Schmidt and Schorsch of Hamburg University's Institute for Sex Research stated: "The neurophysiological bases for hypothalamotomies on humans with deviant sexual behavior appear dubious, the indications make use of questionable scientific and clinical categories and assumptions, few reliable data have been submitted for side effects, and follow-up studies are based on poor methodology. Restrictive regulations against this type of 'experimental therapy' are suggested." (p. 301).

Sigusch et al. (1982) concluded: "The motive and purpose of etiological research go hand in hand with the common discrimination against homosexuals in our society. It aims at preventing homosexual development by means of an endocrinological prophy-laxis. This, and nothing else, is the underlying interest in Dörner's research, which openly toys with the idea of endocrinological euthanasia of homosexuality" (p. 448).

See also Herrn (1995), who notes that the scientists named in the preceding para-graph ". . . protested against not only the inadmissible transfer to humans of the results of animal experiments, but also the surgery itself on the grounds that it deformed the personality of the patients" (p. 52).

[10.] In 1982, Sigusch et al. commented that Dörner "considers [homosexuality] to be a prenatal neuroendocrine maldifferentiation that can be diagnosed early enough dur-ing pregnancy, by examining hormone levels, to prevent by hormonal treatment. Dörner's aim is to eradicate homosexuality by means of radical endocrine intervention during fetal development" (pp. 445–446). Schmidt (1984) noted:

> In reply to our criticism (Sigusch et al., 1982), Dörner recently defended
> his position as follows. Should his ideas on the causes of homosexuality
> prove to be correct, in prospective studies, "it might be possible in the
> future, at least in some cases, to correct abnormal sex hormone levels dur-
> ing sexual brain differentiation in order to prevent the development of
> homosexuality.". . . Methods for diagnosing unusual hormone levels in
> male and female fetuses have been developed in his laboratories. His only
> reservation is that this treatment to correct the hormone levels and prevent
> homosexuality should be carried out only "if it is urgently desired by the
> pregnant mother" [p. 136].
>
>     Meyer-Bahlburg (1990/1991) notes: "Dörner (l976, l989) has even
> advocated prenatal endocrine screening and intrauterine sex hormone
> treatment of fetuses with inappropriate sex hormone levels in order to pre-
> vent later homosexuality" (p. 279).

[11.] Burr's (1993) summary of Dörner and Meyer-Bahlburg gives a different impres-sion of their positions than do Friedman and Downey.

> Of the scientists who have concentrated on hormonal or psychoen-
> docrinological studies of homosexuality, Günter Dörner, of Germany, is
> one of the best known. In the 1970s Dörner classified homosexuality as a
> "central nervous pseudohermaphroditism," meaning that he considered
> male homosexuals to have brains with the mating centers of women but,
> of course, the bodies of men. For decades endocrinologists had speculated
> that because male sex hormones are known to be responsible in human
> beings for masculine body characteristics and in animals for certain aspects
> of male sexual behavior, it follows that adult homosexual men should have
> lower levels of testosterone, or else higher levels of estrogen, in the blood-
> stream than adult heterosexual men, and that homosexual and heterosex-
> ual women should display the opposite pattern. This is known as the "adult
> hormonal theory" of sexual orientation, and Dörner claimed that some ini-
> tial studies bore it out.
>
>     In 1984 Heino Meyer-Bahlburg, a neurobiologist at Columbia
> University, analyzed the results of twenty-seven studies undertaken to test
> the theory. According to Meyer-Bahlburg, a score [20] of the studies in fact

showed no difference between the testosterone and estrogen levels of homosexual and heterosexual men. Three studies did show that homosexuals had significantly lower levels of testosterone. . . . Two studies actually reported higher levels of testosterone in homosexual men than in heterosexual men, and one unhelpfully showed the levels to be higher in bisexuals than in either heterosexuals or homosexuals.

As it came to be widely accepted that adult hormone levels were not a factor in sexual orientation, scientists shifted their attention to prenatal hormone exposure. . . . In an article published in 1990 . . . Heino Meyer-Bahlberg surveyed the work done so far on hormonal research in general and concluded: "The evidence available to date is inconsistent, most studies are methodologically unsatisfactory, and alternative interpretations of the results cannot be ruled out [pp. 58-59].

12. For a critical examination of Friedman (1988), see Schwartz (1993a).

13. Historian David McBride was a participant in the 1992 Symposium, "The Brain and Homosexuality" held at The Center for Lesbian and Gay Studies at CUNY. He discussed various theories about supposed African-American biological inferiority. See also Gould (1981) and Tavris (1992).

14. See Maccoby and Jacklin (1974), Hubbard, Henifin and Fried (1979), Lowe and Hubbard (1983), Bleier (1984), Fausto-Sterling (1985), Epstein (1988), Tuana (1989), Hubbard (1990), Longino (1990), Tavris (1992), Birke and Hubbard (1995), and Spanier (1995a).

15. Stephen Gould (1981) writes:

This chapter is the story of numbers once regarded as surpassing all others in importance—the data of craniometry, or measurement of the skull and its contents. The leaders of craniometry were not conscious political ideologues. They regarded themselves as servants of their numbers, apostles of objectivity. And they confirmed all the common prejudices of comfortable white males—that blacks, women, and poor people occupy their subordinate roles by the harsh dictates of nature [p. 74].

16. Tavris (1992) continues:

The neuroscientist Ruth Bleier . . . carefully examined Geschwind and Behan's data, going back to many of their original references. In one such study of 507 fetal brains of 10 to 44 weeks gestation, the researchers had actually stated that they found *no significant sex differences* in these brains. If testosterone had an effect on the developing brain, it would surely have been apparent in this large sample. Yet Geschwind and Behan cited this study for other purposes and utterly ignored its findings of no sex differences.

Instead, Geschwind and Behan cited as evidence for their hypothesis a study of *rats'* brains. The authors of the rat study reported that in male rats, two areas of the cortex that are believed to be involved in processing visual information were 3% thicker on the right side than on the left. . . . No one knows, [Bleier] said, what the slightly greater thickness in the male rat's cortex means for the rat, let alone what it means for human beings. There is at present no evidence that spatial orientation is related to asymmetry of the cortex, or that female rats have a lesser or deficient ability in this regard. And although Geschwind and Behan unabashedly used their limited findings to account for male "superiority" in math and art, they did not specifically study the incidence of genius, talent, or even modest giftedness in their sample, nor did they demonstrate a difference between the brains of geniuses and the brains of average people [pp. 49–50].

Tavris reviews assumed sex differences in verbal and math skills:

Janet Hyde, a professor of psychology at University of Wisconsin, and her colleague Marcia Linn reviewed 165 studies of verbal ability (including skills in vocabulary, writing, anagrams, and reading comprehension), which represented tests of 1,418,899 people. Hyde and Linn reported that at present in America, there simply are no gender differences in these verbal skills. They noted: "Thus our research pulls out one of the two wobbly legs on which the brain lateralization theories have rested.

Hyde recently went on to kick the other leg, the assumption of overall male superiority in mathematics and spatial ability. No one disputes that males do surpass females at the highly gifted end of the math spectrum. But when Hyde and her colleagues analyzed 100 studies of mathematics performance, representing the testing of 3,985,682 students, they found that gender differences were smallest and favored *females* in samples of the general population, and grew larger, favoring males, only in selected samples of precocious individuals.

What about spatial abilities . . . ? Many studies show no sex differences. Of the studies that do report sex differences, the magnitude of the difference is often small. And finally, there is greater variation *within* each sex than *between* them [pp. 51–52].

17. See Suppe (1994):

And the fact is that for all its methodological sophistication LeVay's research is conceptually crude. The binary labeling of regions of the brain or behaviors as "male-typical" or "female-typical" is unwarranted when the phenomena are known to exhibit considerable diversity [what LeVay calls 'exceptions' in the present sample (that is presumed heterosexual men with small INAH 3 nuclei, and homosexual men with large ones)]—being akin to trying to describe a population by a measure of central tendency without regard for spread. . . . The assumption that male homosexual orientation is to be equated with, or even strongly correlates with, female behavior is conceptually confused" [p. 231].

18. LeVay relied on hospital records for identifying his brain samples as "homosexual" or "heterosexual." Zicklin (1994) has pointed out, that this is not a reliable methodology.

What one decides to reveal to a record-keeper, what the record-keeper surmises one does not want to reveal but thinks should be included, what the record-keeper decides is meant by certain signs the person exhibits—all these may go into the act of fixing a label on a person, in the case of LeVay's subjects, the "homosexual" label or by default, the heterosexual one. . . . The designation of a sexual orientation that is made in a hospital setting in situations of extremis may bear only a tangential relationship to the truth of a person's sexual life. . . . Yet LeVay relied solely on such hospital designations for the determination of a principal variable in his study [pp. 9–10].

Suppe (1994) adds further criticism of LeVay's (1991) handling of his sample's identification as homosexual or heterosexual. Suppe focuses on the general tendency in research on sexual orientation to presume heterosexual identity in control groups and on LeVay's particular problem in this area.

19. "In a study that seeks to link sexual orientation with a specific brain structure, you would want to be able to assume that that brain structure was not being affected by other processes. Thus there are profound difficulties in Le Vay's (1991) use of homosexual men who died of AIDS as his homosexual sample. HIV infection itself is known to affect brain tissue, and this, not the subject's homosexuality, may be the determining factor in any brain structure measurements. Further, it is known that AIDS frequently lowers testosterone levels in males; again, it may be that the lowered testosterone and not the 'sexual orientation' is implicated in any brain findings" (Zicklin, 1994).

Le Vay responded to these criticisms by noting that he had included six heterosexual subjects who had AIDS and that the relationship of smaller INAH 3 in homosexual (AIDS) and larger INAH 3 in heterosexual (AIDS) held up. Byne (1994), a neuroanatomist, was not persuaded: "His inclusion of a few brains from heterosexual men with AIDS did not adequately address the fact that at the time of death virtually all men with AIDS have decreased testosterone levels as the result of the disease itself or the side effects of particular treatments" (p. 53).

LeVay (1993) again defended his use of homosexual AIDS subjects: "After publication of my study I obtained the brain of one gay man who died of a disease other than AIDS (he died of lung cancer). I examined this brain 'blind' along with three other brains from presumably heterosexual men of similar ages. Already during the analysis I correctly guessed which was the hypothalamus of the gay man; INAH 3 was less than half the size of the nucleus in the other three men" (p. 121).

20. As Suppe (1994) notes, "Since the borders of the nuclei are not well defined, there is a fair degree of subjectivity in demarcating the borders of these groups, hence determining their volume" (p. 230). A more objective procedure, and one that would decrease errors of judgment in "measuring" such a visually ambiguous area, would have involved counting the number of neurons.

21. "It should be emphasized that these differences were in the *averages*: some of the women and gay men had a large INAH 3, and some of the presumed heterosexual men had a small one" (Le Vay, 1993, p. 121). From a graphic display of the data, his conclusions would not strike the observer as obvious. The ranges of volume between homosexual and heterosexual men are almost identical, and the ranges of volume in the sample of six women approach the span of the other 2 groups.

22. For example, Charles Phoenix and his co-workers looked for a connection between prenatal testosterone exposure and increased aggression in rhesus monkeys. Aggression was measured by energy expenditure, a term proposed by Goy (1966) that encompasses behaviors associated with masculinity in monkeys—rough-and-tumble play, threat, play

initiations, and chasing play. Eight pregnant rhesus monkeys were injected with testosterone. Eight female monkey babies were born with masculinized external genitalia. The mean frequency of their behaviors was found to be intermediate between the two sexes. Phoenix (1978) concluded that prenatal testosterone had "masculinized" their nervous systems, thus "predisposing them to acquire predominantly masculine patterns of behavior" (p. 30).

Others have suggested, however, that such behaviors could also be understood as resulting from maternal training. The mother monkey, taking her cue from the masculinized external genitalia of her young, may have seen these female monkeys as males and trained them as she would train male offspring (see Fausto-Sterling, 1985, and Quadagno et al., 1977).

23. During the American Psychiatric Association's annual meeting in San Diego, California in May 1997, an allied APA organization, the Association of Gay and Lesbian Psychiatrists, hosted a presentation by the Intersex Society of North America (ISNA). One of the participants from ISNA said that there is no such thing as an individual child with an intersex condition. Whenever a child is born with an intersex diagnosis, the whole family becomes an intersex family because the entire family becomes involved in the complicated interventions and secrecies that are currently part of the treatment of intersex conditions.

24. See also Longino (1990), who comments on Slijper's work:

> She argued that the significant common factor was the experience of chronic illness with consequent hospitalization and frequent medical visits. She interprets the behavior of both groups as a deliberate challenge to the intrusion of medical authority into their lives as well as the expression of insecurity about their own well-being. It is, in her view, a response to their awareness and interpretation of their experience [p. 159].

25. Because of the duplication of samples of Money et al. (1984) and Mulaikal et al. (1987) it is difficult to tell exactly how many women there were. They do not make it clear which women were included in both studies.

26. For other recent criticisms of biological research into homosexuality see Fausto-Sterling (1995) and Gooren (1995).

27. Suppe (1994) noted that "after nearly 1,000 studies of homosexual etiology, we really haven't established much of anything positive about the causes of homosexuality" (p. 257).

4

## Assaults and Harassments: The Violent Acts of Theorizing Lesbian Sexuality

1. Quinodoz (1989) on lesbian relationships: "From the psychoanalytic point of view, the function performed by the [lesbian] partner can be considered from several complementary aspects: the partner represents a fetish; she constitutes the support neces-

sary for pathological projective identification; and, finally, she is used in the acting out of destructive envy" (p. 58).

2. Robert M. Friedman (1996), in his excellent review of the testicles in history and in the analytic literature, concludes that "the representation of male sexuality as purely phallic—with the testicles missing—is itself a reductionist distortion typical of an immature stage of male psychological development" (p. 249).

3. Laqueur (1990) discusses Freud's invention of the clitoral orgasm:

> Before 1905 no one thought there was any other kind of female orgasm than the clitoral sort. . . . The revelation by Masters and Johnson that a female orgasm is almost entirely clitoral would have been a commonplace to every seventeenth-century midwife and had been documented in considerable detail by nineteenth-century investigators. A great wave of amnesia descend on scientific circles around 1900. . . . There is nothing in nature about how the clitoris is construed. It is not self-evidently a female penis, and it is not self-evidently in opposition to the vagina [pp. 233–234].

4. Irigaray (1974): "[Woman] is left with a *void*, a *lack* of all representation, re-presentation, and strictly speaking of all mimesis of her desire for origin" (p. 42).

5. But Traub (1995), among others, sees a problematic essentialism in Irigaray's "geography of feminine pleasure," believing it to rely on synecdochical linking of body part to erotic desire and equating these with categorical identities.

6. McDougall (1980), for example, states:

> Several homosexual women who were my patients showed striking similarities in ego structure and oedipal background. Their violence was particularly evident, as was the complicated defensive struggle against it, especially when these violent feelings were directed to the sexual partner. Equally striking was the fragility of their sense of identity as expressed in periods of depersonalization, bizarre bodily states, and so on. . . . These analysands were expressing not only their almost symbiotic dependence on their partners, but also the terror and violent rage which the experience of separation and loss aroused [pp. 92–93].

And:

> Thus in spite of its reparative aspects, the homosexual situation is inevitably precarious. A sexual identity that disavows sexual reality and masks inner feelings of deadness can only be maintained at a costly premium. The homosexual pays dearly for this fragile identity, heavily weighted as it is with frustrated libidinal, sadistic, and narcissistic significance. But the alternative is the death of the ego [p. 138].

7. In 1988 Siegel wrote: "A series of coincidences placed me into the position of analyzing twelve women who thought they had "chosen" homosexuality as a lifestyle. I also saw several others in psychoanalytic psychotherapy" (p. xi). She described what she saw as "the dilemma facing analysts during the psychoanalytic treatment of deeply wounded female obligatory homosexuals" (p. 29).

In 1991, Siegel wrote, "During the last fifteen years I have conducted the analysis of twelve women who were obligatory homosexuals. I also saw several others in psychoanalytic psychotherapy" (p. 47).

Most of Siegel's patients were hardly obligatory homosexuals, if by obligatory it is understood that the woman is capable of feeling sexual attraction only toward women. The following is a brief summary of five of Siegel's 1988 patients. Carla, age 30, had been married and divorced, had three children, had been with men and, at the end of the treatment description, was with both men and women. Charlotte, aged 60, had one child and came into treatment after a previous analysis in which she had "stopped being a happy homosexual and became a frustrated woman looking for a man instead. I have now returned to a homosexual lifestyle" (p. 111). Treatment with Siegel, according to Siegel, had been successful in at least stirring up a wish for a male partner. Delilah, age 30, entered treatment at a time when she had not followed her long-time male partner to a city where he had moved; she thought she might be "homosexually inclined" but in her analysis with Siegel rejoins her old boyfriend. Serena, in her mid-40s, twice divorced, and with five children, was involved with both men and women, and, at the end of the analysis, was reportedly viewing her boyfriend's devotion in a more accepting light. Pepina, married, divorced, interrupted her analysis and her plans to move in with a female lover to pursue professional opportunities, and later wrote to Siegel that she had "found 'someone who will be a good father when we have a baby'" but also still wishes for a physically intimate connection to another woman (p. 143).

8. See also Limentani (1989).

9. In Shanghai in 1925 Mojing Dang (Rubbing Mirror Party) had 20 members. The women took marriage vows with one another in a ceremony. "This was not so much a matter of personal choice but of necessity because only by such a ceremony could they legally be allowed to live together as a couple" (Ruan and Bullough, 1992, p. 219).

Chinese sex manuals also described the delights of the double olisbos: "This was a short (8 to 10 inches) ribbed stick make of wood or ivory, with two silk bands attached to the middle. Each women put an end of the penis-like stick into her vagina and each held a ribbon which they alternated pulling in and out" (p. 221).

10. Eisenbud (1982): "A woman's limited response to a Lesbian lover may be related to this conditional acceptance of intimacy with mother. She must 'stay dressed' so to speak. Her inner self, her naked self, must not be seen by her Lesbian lover. She splits her feelings to defend herself from conflict between preoedipal and oedipal feelings and good and bad mother" (p. 89).

11. For a thoughtful and humorous discussion of ideas about "lesbian bed death" from 1979–1993, see Hall (1995).

12. Kaplan (1991):

> How does a child learn that her skin is an alive part if no one ever caresses it or rubs it or kisses it into aliveness? . . . The self-mutilator treats her skin with a conscious indifference, much as some surgeons have been trained to regard the human body—as though it were dead. However, unconsciously, she is recapturing and also remedying the unsatisfied longings of infancy. As a deadened piece of flesh is brought to life by the cutting edge of the razor and the sight of blood, the girl is also expressing the haunting complexity of her confused identifications with her mother. She is relieved when the "mother-blood" warmly flows over her. . . . As the bad, dirty

blood flows out, the daughter rids herself of her internal "bad" mother. . . . The selection of the skin surface as the site of mutilation is partly a compensation for the deprivation of skin contact during infancy. But more than that, the delicate cutter thinks of her skin as a container for the dangerous body substances . . . and all the insupportable arousals emanating from inside her body [pp. 379–383].

# 5

# Coming Out: The Necessity of Becoming a Bee-Charmer

1. Friedman (1988):

It would be clinically naive always to accept the reasons people give for coming out as the actual reasons motivating the behavior. Whereas emotionally healthy people come out for healthy reasons, people who suffer from psychopathology often come out for reasons that cannot be considered healthy, even given a generous margin of neutrality with regard to judgments about healthy and unhealthy. One common maladaptive, irrational reason for coming out is to satisfy masochistic needs. In these cases the sadistic aspects of homophobic society prove impossible for the masochistic person to resist. I am not suggesting that masochism provides a psychological model for coming out [pp. 148–149].

Eisenbud (1982):

The conditions that bring the woman of Lesbian choice into treatment are much the same as other women's: depression loss, identity crisis, problems with love, friendship, children, and work. For the lesbian woman many painful special issues remain as a consequence of her orientation, namely, isolation, concealment, restricted choice of love objects, sexual exploitation, splits in day living and night living, weekday and Sunday living, . . . difficulties of a devoted Lesbian partnership with social isolation and limited work, relations in the community, and adjustments to children and need for children [p. 103].

Morgenthaler (1988):

The coming out represents a process of consciousness in which the homosexual recognizes himself and presents himself as such. This process reveals whether or not homosexuality is consistent with the internalized image of one's own person and the societal reality. The greatest stresses to which homosexuals are exposed originate from the society in which they live. In general, society imputes to them the sexual role of unstable androgynes, slaves to their instincts. However, homosexuals, by nature, are by no means more carnal or less stable than heterosexuals. Their sexual role is defined, even though it is different from that of heterosexuals. To define this role for themselves, to form and maintain it, is the content of the conscious process of adult homosexuals, which represents the third turning of the switches in the development to homosexuality. If this step is successful, a reorientation in the life of the homosexual takes place [p. 67].

2. For a discussion of the need for, and effects of, secrecy, privacy, and lying see Rich (1975) and Bok (1983).

3. Sedgwick (1990):

Even at an individual level, there are remarkably few of even the most openly gay people who are not deliberately in the closet with someone personally or economically or institutionally important to them. Furthermore, the deadly elasticity of heterosexist presumption means that, like Wendy in *Peter Pan*, people find new walls springing up around them even as they drowse: every encounter with a new classful of students, to say nothing of a new boss, social worker, loan officer, landlord, doctor, erects new closets whose fraught and characteristic laws of optics and physics exact from at least gay people new surveys, new calculations, new draughts and requisitions of secrecy or disclosure. Even an out gay person deals daily with interlocutors about whom she doesn't know whether they know or not; it is equally difficult to guess for any given interlocutor whether, if they do know, the knowledge would seem very important [pp. 67–68].

4. See also Laufer (1965): "The narcissistic type of object choice (including homosexuality) need not be a sign of pathology in the early adolescent, whereas a continuation of such an object choice in late adolescence may be viewed as a sign of failure to give up these earlier means of narcissistic supply and as a hindrance to further emotional development" (p. 107).

5. African American lesbian writer and activist bell hooks points out the film's stereotypical images of black people: "The film is simply a modern plantation story with a white-lesbian twist" (cited in Mayne, 1996, p. 166).

6. Psychoanalytic discussions of the 1920 case include Irigaray (1974), Silva (1975), Harris (1991), Appignanesi and Forrester (1992), and Magid (1993).

Discussions of this case by lesbian therapists or lesbians making use of psychoanalytic theory include Klaich (1974), Merck (1986), Downing (1989), Russ (1993), and de Lauretis (1994).

7. Irigaray (1974) comments on Freud's dismissal of the patient:

So here we have the homosexual woman shown the door by her psychoanalyst, because she refuses to allow herself to be seduced by the father quite as much as he refuses to become the surrogate object of her desire, which in this case would mean his being identified with a *cocotte*, a woman of "bad reputation," who "lived simply by giving her bodily favours.". . . Freud's well-brought-up, middle-class superego did not permit him such lapses. Or even let him admit that a "beautiful and clever girl, belonging to a family of good standing" might throw over her father (whom Freud knows and likes and is *paid* by) in favor of a whore" [p 101].

8. We requested permission from Dr. Eissler to read the interview. In a letter to the authors dated March 3, 1997 he stated, "I am not permitted to reveal the patient's identity."

9. Klaich (1974) also discusses this case.

10. As do Limentani's (1989) comments in his discussion of homosexuality.

11. We were delighted with Judith Mitrani's reaction to reading an earlier version of this chapter. She suggested that, if analysts working with lesbian patients are frightened of the feelings and projections and alienated from their patients, they may defend by wearing the psychological equivalent of bee keeper suits, instead of engaging in the necessary bee-charming trial identification that allowed Idgie to enter the hive.

# 6

# Moratoriums and Secrets: Searching for the Love of One's Life

1. Moi (1994) rightly points out that Beauvoir's chapter on lesbianism is "exceptionally confused, structurally as well as thematically. . . . It is as if the very subject of lesbianism makes Beauvoir incapable of organizing her thought." Moi discusses Beauvoir's ambivalence about her own homosexual relationships. She also notes that "In spite of its confusion, Beauvoir's chapter on lesbianism does make a number of valuable political points. In France in 1949, it took courage even to raise the subject. There can be no doubt that Beauvoir in fact sees lesbianism as a perfectly valid existential choice . . . " (pp. 200, 203).

See also Butler (1986,1989) and Simons (1992).

2. For anthropological studies of the berdache, see Whitehead (1981), Williams (1986), Herdt (1991, 1996), Roscoe (1991), Blackwood (1993).

3. Some analytic readers will wonder about the sexual significance of Hannah's old emphasis on back alleys versus the dream of a new opening. Hannah had reported some past experiences with anal intercourse, and some of her material would probably have suggested to Siegel (1988) that Hannah's sense of her own vagina was less than optimally "internalized." I felt, however, that her back-alley moves were unconscious attempts to close or guard a (vaginal) opening that too early had been felt to be vulnerable to invasion. So the dream of the new opening, where there was no barrier and no fear, was not, to my mind, a newly found or mentalized vagina, but a lifting of defenses and inhibitions.

4. For another analytic case involving a patient's difficulty finding answers, see Trop and Stolorow (1992). In their discussions of this case, gay and lesbian psychoanalysts Mark Blechner (1993), Ronnie Lesser (1993), and David Schwartz (1993b) caution that an analyst's unexamined prejudice against homosexuality can collude with a patient's fear of being homosexual.

5. What must the Hannahs and Vivians of the 1960s have made of another of Bergler's (1951) notions: "What lesbians really act, unconsciously, is the passive baby-active Giantess game" (p. 338)?

6. For another and later atypical psychoanalytic response, see Gilberg (1978). In this "Brief Communication," Gilberg calls for the need for family involvement: "Helping the family recognize the homosexual adolescent as an integral part of the family and accept-

ing him as a person is important. His sexuality is only a part of him to be accepted, acknowledged and dealt with" (p. 356).

7. Wyler, in an amazing denial of the tragic irony of Hellman's play, insisted that Karen and Martha's relationship had nothing to do with lesbianism.

> "I wouldn't make a picture just about [lesbianism]. It simply wouldn't attract me. We're not out to make a dirty or sensational picture. . . . As I see it, it is a story that shows the effect of malicious gossip on innocent people."
>
> When the Hays Office [charged with keeping obscenity out of films] threatened to censor the film, Arthur Krim, then president of United Artists, backed up his director, guaranteeing that there would be no homosexuality, only a false charge by a malicious child. Krim, by the way, threatened to proceed with the film without approval from the Hays Office, and suggested that if the Code regulations could not allow the film to be shown, the regulations, and not the film, should be changed. His threat paid off, and the Code, on October 3, 1961, was revised so that "tasteful" treatments of homosexual themes were now permissible. Presumably suicide was what they meant by tasteful [Weiss, 1993, pp. 69–70].

The real-life Martha and Karen were Marianne Woods and Jane Pirie, two women who opened a boarding school in Edinburgh in 1809. The charges were brought against them by one of their pupils, who was the granddaughter of socialite Dame Gordon and the child of Gordon's son and a 15-year-old servant girl from India. Pirie and Woods sued Gordon for slander. They won their case 10 years later, but by that time their relationship and the school were destroyed. Faderman (1983) describes the issues of race, sex, and class that faced the judges in the case in *Scotch Verdict*.

Terry Castle (1993 ) examines the systematic negation of love between women in film and literature and the eerie ghost imagery that results from attempts to negate or deny. She also notes that, in many lesbian-themed books or films, the women characters are often found reading works about lesbians. In *The Well of Loneliness*, for instance, heroine Stephen Gordon reads Krafft-Ebing. In Hellman's *The Children's Hour*, characters read Gautier's *Mademoiselle de Maupin*.

8. "Between 1977 and 1982, seven anthologies were published consisting exclusively or largely of lesbian first-person narratives" (Zimmerman, 1984, p. 663).

See also Moraga and Anzaldúa (1981), Beck (1982), Jay and Glasgow (1990), Trujillo (1991), McKinley and L. Joyce DeLaney (1995), Zimmerman and McNaron (1996), and Ruff (1996).

9. See *Uncommon Uncommon Women*, Mount Holyoke's Lesbian Alumni Newsletter; the Society of Lesbian and Gay Anthropologists Newsletter; *LGSN*, the Lesbian and Gay Studies Newsletter of the Gay and Lesbian Caucus of the Modern Language Association; the American Association for Physicians for Human Rights; the Annual Women and Medicine Conference for Lesbian Physicians; the National Organization of Gay and Lesbian Scientists and Technical Professionals, Compuserve, America On-Line.

10. To mark the 25th Anniversary of Stonewall, in 1994 gay and lesbian organizations held marches in several cities, participated in sports events at the Gay and Lesbian Games in New York, and went by the tens of thousands to Disney World, Florida.

In Los Angeles, a high school student isolated or harassed or attacked because of homosexuality might be able to attend EAGLES (Emphasize Adolescent Gay and Lesbian Education Series), an alternative public high school program. See Boxall and Drummond (1994). In December 1993 the Massachusetts House and Senate banned discrimination against gay and lesbian students in public schools. See Appendix: Education.

[11.] The National Center for Lesbian Rights provides litigation, public policy advocacy, community education, resource publications and judicial training, including legal support for lesbians in custody battles. According to NCLR from 1985 to 1993 100 homosexuals gained rights in court by adopting a partner's biological child. NCLR also is a resource for gay, lesbian, bisexual, and transgender adolescents.

# 7

## What Sex Is an Amaryllis? What Gender Is Lesbian? Looking for Something to Hold it All

[1.] We are grateful to Donna Bassin, Adrienne Harris, Virginia Goldner, and Muriel Dimen for their help in untangling some of the organizational and conceptual muddles of this section. Harris (1991) has discussed gender by examining Freud's (1920) "The Psychogenesis of a Case of Homosexuality in a Woman." We rely on Harris's work for its substantive challenge to several psychoanalytic binaries, although we have different readings of some issues in Freud's case.

[2.] Genitals are, however, frequently a primary organizing principle for object representations in psychotic states. And it is in these states that internal objects most resemble static formal portraits. The patient suffers a painful inability to create or rediscover less sexualized representations.

Lansky (1989) also addresses the complicated origins and content of internal representations, by using photographic metaphors: "The paternal representation is not simple ideation, in the sense that a photograph is a record of the scene it captures, or even a composite version of that notion. Rather the 'representation' is a set of recollections or views of the paternal object that serves important defensive and screening functions for self-representation and other object representations considered in isolation and for the family as a whole" (p. 38). But Lansky undoes this assertion of complexity in internal representations by referring to *the* paternal imago.

# 8

## When the Psychoanalyst Is Lesbian: "A Certain Idealization of Heterosexuality"

[1.] For discussions of therapist disclosure of lesbian identity see Anthony (1982), Gartrell (1984), de Monteflores (1986), Kooden (1991), Isay (1991), and O'Connor and Ryan (1993).

# 9

## Homosexuality and Psychoanalytic Training

1. See also Abelove (1985).

2. Welch v American Psychoanalytic Association, No. 85 Civ.1651 (S.D.N.Y. 1985). See Flaks (1992) for a discussion of the ramifications of this settlement.

3. Robert Stoller wrote to the authors in response to our letter thanking him for his writing on homosexuality: "You are most kind to have written and to have sent on the material for your course outline. I get little feedback on my work and so am always pleased to learn that it can be useful. It was also good to hear that your Admissions Committee accepted you; I suspect that our Institute might be less understanding and more bound by 'the customary rules'" [September 20, 1989].

4. McDougall (1964) used clinical material from the same four patients (and "three others who, while not exclusively homosexual, were dominated by conscious homosexual wishes" (p. 171). See also McDougall, 1980, p. 96ff.

5. Socarides and others fought the resolution in several ways, including proposing an amendment that sought to insure "civil rights (as well as academic rights)" for all. See footnote 8 below.

6. The resolution continues:

> The American Psychiatric Association, of course, is aware that many other persons in addition to homosexuals are irrationally denied their civil rights on the basis of pejorative connotations derived from diagnostic or descriptive terminology used in psychiatry and deplores all such disaffirmation. This resolution singles out discrimination against homosexuals only because of the pervasive discriminatory acts directed against this group and the arbitrary and discriminatory laws directed against homosexual behavior.

This statement was approved by the Board of Trustees of the American Psychiatric Association at its December 14–15, 1973, meeting, upon recommendation of the Council on Professions and Associations. It was prepared by Robert L. Spitzer, M. D., with the approval of the Task Force on Nomenclature and Statistics. The Assembly of District Branches endorsed the statement at its meeting on November 2–4, 1973 (*American Journal of Psychiatry*, April 1974, 131:4, p. 497).

7. The Executive Council endorsed this statement on December 6, 1990, *Bulletin . . .* (1992), pp. 1216, fn1.

8. William B. Rubenstein, Director of the ACLU's Lesbian and Gay Rights Project thought the April 1992 decision "will help lesbians and gay men who choose to be psychoanalysts advance in their professional pursuits. This decision recognizes that a person's sexual orientation is not related to his or her ability to train or supervise psychoanalysis" (Hausman, 1992, p. 13).

But the story was not finished. At the May 1, 1992, Members Meeting, the New Business discussion time "was devoted entirely to a discussion of a presentation by Dr. Charles Socarides on the issue of homosexuality and psychoanalytic education, including a motion by Dr. Socarides that the action by council approving the addition of the phrase 'including training and supervising analysts' . . . be put aside until a secret balloting of members . . . could be implemented" (*Bulletin* of the American Psychoanalytic Association, 1992, p. 1223).

As a quorum was not present, no vote was taken.

Socarides and a group of members asked that the Council statement be set aside until a secret ballot of membership could be taken. In early December 1992, the Socarides group proposed the following amendment to the resolution on homosexuality:

> It is furthermore expected that the adoption of this Resolution should in no way be construed as limiting or prohibiting the free investigation and exploration of every aspect of human behavior and personality, including sexuality (its origins, meaning, and function) during the course of psychoanalytic treatment. As a guideline for the training analyst, this is understood to hold true whether the candidate is of homosexual or heterosexual orientation. It is in keeping with Freud's (1900) assertion that the "fundamental task" of psychoanalytic inquiry is the understanding of all human behavior in all its manifestations.
>
> In furtherance of this goal and in the spirit of civil rights (including academic rights) for all, the membership asserts that there shall be no exercising of censorship or abridgment of the freedom of speech, thought, and writing in connection with the presentation or publication of material on the subject of homosexuality or heterosexuality. Furthermore, analysands who wish to change from a homosexual orientation to a heterosexual one shall not be discouraged or impeded from realizing this goal.

[The Executive Committee found the proposed amendment] "inappropriate in that the original statement passed by Council is a simple, nondiscriminatory statement about selection and advancement. The Executive Committee sees no need to remind analysts of issues of analytic techniques, specifically about the importance of analytic neutrality" (*Bulletin* . . , 1993, p. 609).

The Council defeated the amendment. At the Members Meeting the vote was 173 to 92 against the Socarides amendment (p. 621).

9. Roughton cited the various steps the American had taken to ensure full acceptance of homosexual candidates as well as some of the problems that remain. This article prompted so many letters from Committee supporters and Committee critics, and members of the National Association of Research and Therapy of Homosexuality (NARTH), whose President is Charles Socarides, that TAP decided "to call a temporary halt to printing" the letters. "TAP has run out of space before its readers have run out of convictions" (TAP, 1997, Vol. 30/1).

10. Leaflet announcement provided by Paul Lynch, candidate member of the Committee on Issues of Homosexuality.

11. In his last years Fritz Morgenthaler, now deceased, openly identified as gay to his Swiss analytic colleagues. Italian Jungian analyst Vittorio Lingiardi (1997) has just published *Compagni D'Amore: From Ganymede to Batman, Identity and Myth in Male Homosexuality*.

# REFERENCES

Aarons, L. (1995), *Prayers for Bobby: A Mother's Coming to Terms with the Suicide of Her Gay Son*. San Francisco: HarperCollins.

Abelin, E. L. (1980), Triangulation: The role of the father and the origins of core gender identity during the rapprochement subphase. In: *Rapprochement*, ed. R. F. Lax, S. Bach & J. A. Burland. New York: Aronson, pp. 151–169.

Abelove, H. (1985), Freud, male homosexuality, and the Americans. In: *The Lesbian and Gay Studies Reader*, ed. H. Abelove, M. A. Barale & D. M. Halperin. New York: Routledge, 1993, pp. 381–393.

Abend, S. M. (1982), Serious illness in the analyst: Countertransference considerations. *J. Amer. Psychoanal. Assn.*, 30:365–379.

Adams, B. & Tate, T., ed. (1991), *That Kind of Woman*. New York: Carroll & Graf.

Alexander, F., Eisenstein, S. & Grotjahn, M. ed. (1966), *Psychoanalytic Pioneers*. New York: Basic Books.

Alexander, J., Kolodziejski, K., Sanville, J. & Shaw, R. (1989), On final terminations: Consultation with a dying therapist. *Clin. Social Work J.*, 17:307–324.

Allison, D. (1992), Survival is the least of my desires. In: *Skin: Talking About Sex, Class & Literature*. Ithaca, NY: Firebrand Books, 1994, pp. 209–223.

Anderson, B. S. & Zinsser, J. P. (1988), *A History of Their Own: Women in Europe from Prehistory to the Present, Vols. 1 & 2*. New York: Harper & Row.

Anthony, B. (1982), Lesbian client–lesbian therapist: Opportunities and challenges in working together. In: *Homosexuality and Psychotherapy: A Practitioner's Handbook of Affirmative Models*, ed. J. Gonsiorek. New York: Haworth Press, pp. 45–57.

Appignanesi, L. & Forrester, J. (1992), *Freud's Women*. New York: Basic Books.

Aptheker, B. (1989), The lesbian connection. In: *Tapestries of Life*. Amherst: University of Massachusetts Press, pp. 75–120.

Arens, K. (1995), H.D.'s Post-Freudian cultural analysis: Nike versus Oedipus. *American Imago*, 52:359–404.

Babcock, B. & Parezo, N. (1988), *Daughters of the Desert: Women Anthropologists and The*

*Native American Southwest, 1880–1980.* Albuquerque: University of New Mexico Press.

Balzac, H. (1835), *The Girl With the Golden Eyes.* New York: DeLuxe Editions, 1931.

Baruch, E. H. & Serrano, L. J. (1988), *Women Analyze Women.* New York: New York University Press.

Bassin, D. (1982), Woman's images of inner space: Data towards expanded interpretive categories. *Internat. Rev. Psychoanal.*, 9:191–203.

Bayer, R. (1987), *Homosexuality and American Psychiatry: The Politics of Diagnosis.* Princeton, NJ: Princeton University Press.

Bechdel, A. (1992), *More Dykes to Watch Out For and Dykes to Watch Our For: The Sequel.* Ithaca, NY: Firebrand Books.

Beck, E. T., ed. (1982), *Nice Jewish Girls: A Lesbian Anthology.* Watertown, MA: Persephone Press.

Bell, Anita (1961), Some observations on the role of the scrotal sac and testicles. *J. Amer. Psychoanal. Assn.*, 9:261–286.

Bell, A & Weinberg, M. (1978), *Homosexualities: A Study of Diversity Among Men and Women.* New York: Simon & Schuster.

Benjamin, J. (1988), *The Bonds of Love.* New York: Pantheon Books.

———— (1991), Father and daughter: Identification with difference: A contribution to gender heterodoxy. *Psychoanal. Dial.*, 1:277–299.

———— (1995), *Like Subjects, Love Objects: Essays on Recognition and Sexual Difference.* New Haven, CT: Yale University Press.

Bennett, P. (1993), Critical clitoridectomy: Female sexual imagery and feminist psychoanalytic theory. *Signs*, 18:235–259.

Benstock, S. (1986), *Women of the Left Bank. Paris, 1900–1940.* Austin: University of Texas Press.

———— (1989), Paris lesbianism and the politics of reaction: 1900–1940. In: *Hidden From History: Reclaiming the Gay and Lesbian Past*, ed. M. B. Duberman, M. Vicinus & G. Chauncey. New York: New American Library, pp. 332–346.

Berenbaum, A. & Snyder, E. (1995), Early hormonal influences on childhood sex-typed activity and playmate preferences: Implications for the development of sexual orientation. *Develop. Psychol.*, 31:31–42.

Berger, P. & Luckmann, T. (1966), *The Social Construction of Reality.* Garden City, NY: Doubleday.

Bergler, E. (1951), *Counterfeit-Sex: Homosexuality, Impotence, Frigidity.* New York: Grove Press.

Bernard, M. (1994), *Sappho, A Translation.* Boston: Shambhala.

Bernheimer, C. & Kahane, C., ed. (1985), *In Dora's Case.* London: Virago Press.

Bernstein, D. (1991), Gender specific dangers in the female dyad in treatment. *Psychoanal. Rev.*, 78:37–48.

———— (1993), Female genital anxieties, conflicts, and typical mastery modes. In: *Female Identity Conflict in Clinical Practice*, ed. D. Bernstein, N. Freedman & B. Distler. Northvale, NJ: Aronson, pp. 39–68.

———— Freedman, N. & Distler, B., ed. (1993), *Female Identity Conflict in Clinical Practice.* Northvale, NJ: Aronson.

Bertin, C. (1987), *Marie Bonaparte: A Life.* New Haven, CT: Yale University Press.

Bing, P. & Cohen, R., trans. & annot. (1991), *Games of Venus: An Anthology of Greek and Roman Erotic Verse from Sappho to Ovid*. New York: Routledge.

Birke, L. (1981), Is homosexuality hormonally determined? *J. Homosexual*, 6:35–49

———— & Hubbard, R., ed. (1995), *Reinventing Biology: Respect for Life and the Creation of Knowledge*. Bloomington: Indiana University Press.

Blackwood, E. (1993), Breaking the mirror: The construction of lesbianism and the anthropological discourse on homosexuality. In: *Psychological Perspectives on Lesbian and Gay Male Experiences*, ed. L. Garnets & D. Kimmel. New York: Columbia University Press, pp. 297–315.

Blechner, M. (1993), Homophobia in psychoanalytic writing and practice. *Psychoanal. Dial.*, 3:627–637.

———— (1995), The shaping of psychoanalytic theory and practice by cultural and personal biases about sexuality. In: *Disorienting Sexuality: Psychoanalytic Reappraisals of Sexual Identities*, ed. T. Domenici & R. C. Lesser. New York: Routledge, pp. 265–288.

Bleier, R. (1984), *Science and Gender*. Elmsford, NY: Pergamon.

Blos, P. (1979), *The Adolescent Passage: Developmental Issues*. New York: International Universities Press.

Blum, A. (in press), Assaults to the Self: The trauma of growing up gay. *Gender & Psychoanal.*.

———— Danson, M. & Schneider, S. (1997), Problems of sexual expression in adult gay men: A psychoanalytic reconsideration. *Psychoanal. Psychol.*, 14: 1–11.

Blum, H. P. (1971), On the conception and development of the transference neurosis. *J. Amer. Psychoanal. Assn.*, 19:41–53.

———— & Blum, E. J. (1986), Reflections on transference and countertransference in the treatment of women. In: *Between Analyst and Patient*, ed. H. C. Meyers. Hillsdale, NJ: The Analytic Press, pp. 177–192.

Blumstein, P. & Schwartz, P. (1983), *American Couples: Money, Work, Sex*. New York: William Morrow.

Boetti, A-M. S. (n. d.), Arachnee the spider. *Chrysalis*, 10:87–89.

Bok, S. (1983), *Secrets: On the Ethics of Concealment and Revelation*. New York: Vintage.

Bonaparte, M. (1951), *Female Sexuality*, trans. J. Rodker. New York: International Universities Press, 1953.

Boston Women's Health Collective, ed. (1992), *Our Bodies, Ourselves*. New York: Simon & Schuster.

Boswell, J. (1980), *Christianity, Social Tolerance, and Homosexuality: Gay People in Western Europe from the Beginning of the Christian Era to the Fourteenth Century*. Chicago: University of Chicago Press.

———— (1989), Revolutions, universals, and sexual categories. In: *Hidden from History: Reclaiming the Gay and Lesbian Past*, ed. M. Duberman, M. Vicinus & G. Chauncey. New York: Penguin/Meridian, pp. 17–36.

Boxall, B. & Drummond, T. (1994), Teens find a haven in L.A. program. *Los Angeles Times*, Jan. 10.

Breuer, S. & Freud, S. (1893–1895), *Studies on Hysteria. Standard Edition*, 2:21–47. London: Hogarth Press, 1955.

Brierley, M. (1932), Some problems of integration in women. *Internat. J. Psycho-Anal.*, 13: 433–448.

Brown, J. C. (1984), Lesbian sexuality in Renaissance Italy: The case of Sister Benedetta Carlini. *Signs*, 9:751–758.

———— (1986a), *Immodest Acts: The Life of a Lesbian Nun in Renaissance Italy*. New York: Oxford University Press.

———— (1986b), Lesbian sexuality in Medieval and early modern Europe, In: *Hidden from History: Reclaiming the Gay and Lesbian Past*, ed. M. B. Duberman, M. Vicinus & G. Chauncey. New York: New American Library, 1989, pp. 67–75.

Brown, R. M. (1973), *Ruby Fruit Jungle*. Plainfield, VT: Daughters.

Bryher (1918), *Amy Lowell: A Critical Appreciation*. London: Eyre & Spottiswoode.

———— (1920), *Development: A Novel*. London: Constable & New York: Macmillan.

———— (1923), *Two Selves*. Paris: Contact.

———— (1924) *A Picture Geography for Little Children, Part One: Asia*. London: Jonathan Cape.

———— (1925), *West*. London: Jonathan Cape.

———— (1929), *Film Problems of Soviet Russia*. London: POOL Productions.

———— (1952a),*The Fourteenth of October*. New York: Pantheon.

———— (1952b), *Beowolf*. New York: Pantheon.

———— (1953), *The Player's Boy*. New York: Pantheon.

———— (1954), *Roman Wall*. New York: Pantheon.

———— (1958), *Gate to the Sea*. New York: Pantheon.

———— (1960), *Ruan*. New York: Pantheon.

———— (1962), *The Heart to Artemis: A Writer's Memoirs*. New York: Harcourt, Brace & World.

———— (1963), *The Coin of Carthage*. New York: Harcourt, Brace & World.

———— (1965), *Visa for Avalon*. New York: Harcourt, Brace & World.

———— (1966), *This January Tale*. New York: Harcourt, Brace & World.

———— (1969), *The Colors of Vaud*. New York: Harcourt, Brace & World.

———— (1972), *The Days of Mars: A Memoir, 1940–1946*. New York: Harcourt Brace Jovanovich.

———— & Weiss, T. (1930), *The Light-Hearted Student*. Territet, Switzerland: Pool.

Bulletin of the American Psychoanalytic Association (1992), *J. Amer. Psychoanal. Assn.*, 40:1211–1225.

———— (1993), *J. Amer. Psychoanal. Assn.*, 41:603–621.

Burch, B. (1986), Psychotherapy and the dynamics of merger in lesbian couples. In: *Contemporary Perspectives on Psychotherapy with Lesbians and Gay Men*, ed. T. S. Stein & C. J. Cohen. New York: Plenum Medical, pp. 57–71.

———— (1987), Barriers to intimacy: Conflicts over power, dependency, and nurturing in lesbian relationships. In: *Lesbian Psychologies*, ed. Boston Lesbian Psychologies Collective. Urbana: University of Illinois Press, pp. 126–141.

———— (1997), *Other Women: Lesbian/Bisexual Experience and Psychoanalytic Views of Women*. New York: Columbia University Press.

Burlingham, D. (1973), The preoedipal infant-father relationship. *The Psychoanalytic Study of the Child*, 28:23–47. New Haven, CT: Yale University Press.

Burr, C. (1993), Homosexuality and biology. *The Atlantic*, 271(3):47–65.

Butler, J. (1986), Sex and gender in Simone de Beauvoir's *Second Sex*. In: *Simone de Beauvoir: Witness to a Century*, ed. H. V. Wenzel, special issue of *Yale French Studies* 72:35–49.

————— (1989), Gendering the body: Beauvoir's philosophical contribution. In: *Women, Knowledge, and Reality: Explorations in Feminist Philosophy*, ed. A. Garry & M. Pearsall. Boston: Unwin Hyman, pp. 253–262.

————— (1990), *Gender Trouble: Feminism and the Subversion of Identity*. New York: Routledge.

————— (1993), *Bodies That Matter*. New York: Routledge.

Byne, W. (1994), The biological evidence challenged. *Scient. Amer.*, May: 50–55.

Cabaj, R. & Stein, T., ed. (1996), *Textbook of Homosexuality and Mental Health*. Washington, DC: American Psychiatric Press.

Califia, P., ed. (1988), *Sapphistry: The Book of Lesbian Sexuality*. 3rd ed. Tallahassee, FL: Naiad Press.

Campbell, D. A., trans. (1982), *Greek Lyric, Vol. I*. Cambridge, MA: Harvard University Press.

Cantarella, E. (1992), *Bisexuality in the Ancient World*, trans. C. O. Cullilleánain. New Haven, CT: Yale University Press.

Caprio, F. S. (1954), *Female Homosexuality: A Psychodynamic Study of Lesbianism*. New York: Citadel.

Cass, V. C. (1979), Homosexual identity formation: A theoretical model. *J. Homosexual.*, 4:219–235.

————— (1984), Homosexual identity: A concept in need of definition. *J. Homosexual.*, 10:105–126.

Castle, T. (1993), *The Apparational Lesbian: Female Homosexuality and Modern Culture*. New York: Columbia University Press.

Cath, S. H., Gurwitt, A. R. & Ross, J. M., ed. (1982), *Father and Child: Developmental and Clinical Perspectives*. Boston: Little, Brown.

————— , ————— & Gunsberg, L., ed. (1989), *Fathers and Their Families*. Hillsdale, NJ: The Analytic Press.

Chasnoff, D. & Cohen, H. (1996), *It's Elementary: Talking about Gay Issues in School* (film). San Francisco, CA: Women's Educational Media.

Chasseguet-Smirgel, J. (1976), Freud and female sexuality: The consideration of some blind spots in the exploration of the "dark continent." *Internat. J. Psycho-Anal.*, 57:275–286.

————— (1984), The femininity of the analyst in professional practice. *Internat. J. Psycho-Anal.*, 68:169–178.

————— (1985), *Creativity and Perversion*. New York: Norton.

Chicago, J. (1996), *The Dinner Party*. New York: Penguin Books.

Chisholm, D. (1992). Lesbianism. In: *Feminism and Psychoanalysis: A Critical Dictionary*, ed. E. Wright. Oxford: Blackwell, pp. 215–220.

Chodorow, N. (1978), *The Reproduction of Mothering: Psychoanalysis and the Sociology of Gender*. Berkeley: University of California Press.

Chused, J. F. (1997), The patient's perception of the analyst's self-disclosure: Commentary on Amy Lichtblau Morrison's paper. *Psychoanal. Dial.*, 7:243–256.

Cleland, J. (1749), *Fanny Hill: Memoirs of a Woman of Pleasure*. New York: Putnam, 1963.

Cliff, J. (1972), You can get it if you really want. Irving Music Co.

Coleman, E. (1982), Developmental stages of the coming out process. In: *Homosexuality and Psychotherapy: A Practitioner's Handbook of Affirmative Models*, ed. J. Gonsiorek.

New York: Haworth Press, pp. 31–45.

Cook, B. W. (1979a), "Women alone stir my imagination": Lesbianism and the cultural tradition. *Signs*, 4:718–739.

—— (1979b), The historical denial of lesbianism. *Radical Hist. Rev.*, 20:60–65.

Corbett, K. (1993), The mystery of homosexuality. *Psychoanal. Psychol.*, 10:345–358.

—— (1996), Homosexual boyhood: Notes on girlyboys. *Gender & Psychoanal.*, 1:429–461.

Corinne, T. (1991), Notes on writing sex. In: *An Intimate Wilderness: Lesbian Writers on Sexuality*, ed. J. Barrington. Portland, OR: Eighth Mountain Press, pp. 212–215.

Cranz, G. (1980), Women in urban parks. *Signs*, 5:S79–S95.

Crastnopol, M. (1997), Incognito or not? The patient's subjective experience of the analyst's life. *Psychoanal. Dial.*, 7:257–280.

Crompton, L. & Robson, R. (1980/81), The myth of lesbian impunity: Capital laws from 1270 to 1791. *J. Homosexual.*, 6:11–25.

Cunningham, R. (1991), When is a pervert not a pervert? *Brit. J. Psychother.*, 8:48–70.

Curtis, H. C. (1989), Letter to the *Psychiatric News*. December 15.

Dalsimer, K. (1986), *Female Adolescence: Psychoanalytic Reflections on Literature*. New Haven, CT: Yale University Press.

Daly, M. (1978), *Gyn/ecology: The Metaethics of Radical Feminism*. Boston: Beacon Press.

Dannecker, M. (1981), *Theories of Homosexuality*. London: Gay Men's Press.

D'Augelli, A. R. & Hershberger, S. L. (1993), Lesbian, gay, and bisexual youth in community settings: Personal challenges and mental health problems. *Amer. J. Commun. Psychol.*, 21:421–428.

de Beauvoir, S. (1952), *The Second Sex*, New York: Vintage Paperback, 1974.

De Cecco, J. P. & Parker, D. A., ed. (1995), *Sex, Cells, and Same-Sex Desire: The Biology of Sexual Preference*. New York: Harrington Park Press.

de Lauretis, T. (1994), *The Practice of Love: Lesbian Sexuality and Perverse Desire*. Bloomington: Indiana University Press.

de Marneffe, D. (1995), Toddlers' reflections on bodies and gender. Presented Division of Psychoanalysis (39), American Psychological Association meetings, Santa Monica, CA.

de Monteflores, C. (1986), Notes on the management of difference. In: *Contemporary Perspectives on Psychotherapy with Lesbians and Gay Men*, ed. T. Stein & C. Cohen. New York: Plenum Press, pp. 73–101.

Deutsch, H. (1932), On female homosexuality. In: *The Psychoanalytic Reader*, ed. R. Fliess. Madison, CT: International Universities Press, 1948, pp. 208–230.

Dew, R. F. (1994), *The Family Heart: A Memoir of When Our Son Came Out*. New York: Ballantine Books.

Dewald, P. A., (1982), Serious illness in the analyst: Transference, countertransference and reality response. *J. Amer. Psychoanal. Assn.*, 30:347–363.

—— & Kramer, S., reporters (1976), Dialogue on "Family life and child development." *Internat. J. Psycho-Anal.*, 57:403–409.

Diamond, D. (1993), The paternal transference: A bridge to the erotic oedipal transference. *Psychoanal. Inq.*, 22:206–225.

Diamond, M. (1986), Becoming a father: A psychoanalytic perspective on the forgotten parent. *Psychoanal. Rev.*, 73:445–468.

Dijkstra, B. (1996), *Evil Sisters: The Treatment of Female Sexuality and the Cult of Manhood.* New York: Knopf.

Dimen, M. (1982), Seven notes for the reconstruction of sexuality. *Social Text,* 6:22–30.

———— (1986), *Surviving Sexual Contradictions: A Startling and Different Look at a Day in the Life of a Contemporary Professional Woman.* New York: Macmillan.

———— (1991), Deconstructing difference: Gender, splitting, and transitional space. *Psychoanal. Dial.,* 1:335–353.

———— (1995), On "our nature": Prolegomenon to a relational theory of sexuality. In: *Disorienting Sexuality,* ed. T. Domenici & R. Lesser. New York: Routlege, pp. 129–152.

Dittmann, R. W., Kappes, M. H., Kappes, M. E., Börger, D., Stegner, H., Willig, R. H. & Wallis, H. (l990a), Congenital adrenal hyperplasia I: gender-related behavior and attitudes in female patients and sisters. *Psychoneuroendocrinol.,* 15:401–420.

———— Kappes, M. E. & Kappes, M. H. (1992), Sexual behavior in adolescent and adult females with congenital adrenal hyperplasia. *Psychoneuroendocrinol.,* 17:153–170.

———— Kappes, M. H., Kappes, M. E., Börger, D., Meyer-Bahlburg, H. F. L., Stegner, H., Willig, R. H. & Wallis, H. (l990b), Congenital adrenal hyperplasia II: Gender-related behavior and attitudes in female salt-wasting and simple-virilizing patients. *Psychoneuroendocrinol.,* 15:421–434.

Domenici, T. (1995), Exploding the myth of sexual psychopathology: A deconstruction of Fairbairn's anti-homosexual theory. In: *Disorienting Sexualities: Psychoanalytic Reappraisals of Sexual Identities,* ed. T. Domenici & R. Lesser. New York: Routledge, pp. 33–63.

———— & Lesser, R., ed. (1995), *Disorienting Sexualities: Psychoanalytic Reappraisals of Sexual Identities.* New York: Routledge.

Doolittle, H. (H. D.)(1956), *Tribute to Freud.* New York: New Directions.

Dörner, G. (1979), Hormones and sexual differentiation of the brain. In: *Sex, Hormones and Behavior.* Ciba Foundation Symposium 62 (new series). New York.

———— (1989), Hormone-dependent brain development and neuroendocrine prophylaxis. *Exp. Clin. Endocrinol.,* 94:4–22.

———— Geier, T., Ahrens, L., Krell, L., Munx, G., Sieler, H., Kittner, E., & Muller, H. (1980), Prenatal stress as possible aetiogenetic factor of homosexuality in human males. *Endokrinologie,* 75: 365–368.

———— , Schenk, B., Schmiedel, B. & Ahrens, L. (1983), Stressful events in prenatal life of bi- and homosexual men. *Exp. Clin. Endocrinol.,* 81:88–90.

Downey, J., Ehrhardt, A., Shiffman, M., Dyrenfurth, I. & Becker, J. (1987), Sex hormones in lesbian and heterosexual women. *Hormones and Behavior,* 21:347–357.

Downing, C. (1989). *Myths and Mystery of Same-Sex Love.* New York: Continuum.

Drescher, J. (1995). Anti-homosexual bias in training. In: *Disorienting Sexuality: Psychoanalytic Reappraisals of Sexual identities,* ed. R. Domenici & R. C. Lesser. New York: Routledge, pp. 227–241.

———— (1996a), Psychoanalytic subjectivity and male homosexuality. In: *Textbook of Homosexuality and Mental Health,* ed. R. P. Cabaj & T. S. Stein. Washington, DC: American Psychiatric Press, pp. 173–189.

———— (1996b), Across the great divide: Gender panic in the analytic dyad. *Psychoanal. & Psychother.,* 13:174–186.

———— (1996c), A discussion across sexual orientation and gender boundaries: Reflections of a gay male analyst to a heterosexual female analyst. *Gender & Psychoanal.*, 1:223–237.

———— (in press), From preoedipal to postmodern: Changing psychoanalytic attitudes towards homosexuality. *Gender & Psychoanal.*

Duplessis, R. B. (1986), *H.D., The Career of that Struggle.* Bloomington: University of Indiana Press.

Ehrhardt, A. & Baker, S. W. (1974), Fetal androgens, human central nervous system differentiation and behavior sex differences. In: *Sex Differences in Behavior*, ed. F. Friedman & R. L. Van de Wiele. New York: Wiley, pp. 33–52.

———— Epstein, R. & Money, J. (1968), Fetal androgens and female gender identity in the early-treated adrenogenital syndrome. *Johns Hopkins Med. J.*, 122:160–167.

———— Evers, K. & Money, J. (1968), Influence of androgen and some aspects of sexually dimorphic behavior in women with the late-treated adrenogenital syndrome. *Johns Hopkins Med. J.*, 123:115–122.

Eisenbud, R.-J. (1982), Early and later determinants of lesbian choice. *Psychoanal. Rev.*, 69:85–109.

———— (1986), Lesbian choice: Transferences to theory. In: *Psychoanalysis and Women: Contemporary Reappraisals*, ed. J. L. Alpert. Hillsdale, NJ: The Analytic Press, pp. 215–235.

Elind, D. (1991), A review of *The House of Make-Believe. Readings*, June 6:8–11.

Ellis, H. (1938), *Psychology of Sex : A Manual for Students.* New York: Emerson Books.

Ellis, M. L. (1994), Lesbians, gay men and psychoanalytic training. *Free Associations.*

Epstein, C. F. (1988), *Deceptive Distinctions: Sex, Gender, and the Social Order.* New Haven, CT: Yale University Press.

Erikson, E. H. (1958), *Young Man Luther: A Study in Psychoanalysis and History.* New York: Norton, 1962.

———— (1963), *Childhood and Society.* New York: Norton.

———— (1968), *Identity: Youth and Crisis.* New York: Norton.

Etchegoyen, A. (1993), The analyst's pregnancy and its consequences on her work. *Internat. J. Psycho-Anal.*, 74:141–149.

Faber, D. (1980), *Lorena Hickock, E.R.'s Friend.* New York: Morrow.

Faderman, L. (1981), *Surpassing the Love of Men: Romantic Friendships and Love Between Women from the Renaissance to the Present.* New York: Morrow.

———— (1983), *Scotch Verdict.* New York: Columbia University Press, 1993.

———— (1991), *Odd Girls and Twilight Lovers: A History of Lesbian Life in Twentieth Century America.* New York: Columbia University Press.

———— ed. (1994), *Chloe Plus Olivia: An Anthology of Lesbian Literature from the Seventeenth Century to the Present.* New York: Viking.

———— & Eriksson, B. (1980), *Lesbians in Germany: 1890's–1920's.* Tallahassee, FL: Naiad Press, 1990.

Fanon, F. (1963), *The Wretched of the Earth.* New York: Grove.

Fast, I. (1984), *Gender Identity: A Differentiation Model.* Hillsdale, NJ: The Analytic Press.

Fausto-Sterling, A. (1985), *Myths of Gender: Biological Theories About Women and Men.* New York: Basic Books, 1994.

———— (1995), Animal models for the development of human sexuality: A critical evaluation. In: *Cells, and Same-Sex Desire: The Biology of Sexual Preference*, ed. J. P. De Cecco & D. A. Parker. New York: Haworth Press, pp. 217–236.

Fenichel, O. (1945), *The Psychoanalytic Theory of Neurosis*. New York: Norton.

Fenster, S., Phillips, S. & Rapaport, E. (1986), *The Therapist's Pregnancy*. Hillsdale, NJ: The Analytic Press.

Ferenczi, S. (1932), *The Clinical Diary of Sándor Ferenczi*, ed. J. Dupont, trans. M. Balint & N. Z. Jackson. Cambridge, MA: Harvard University Press, 1988.

Flagg, F. (1987), *Fried Green Tomatoes at the Whistle Stop Cafe*. New York: McGraw- Hill.

Flaks, D. K. (1992), Homophobia and psychologists' role in psychoanalytic institutes. *Psychoanal. Psychol.*, 9:543–550.

Flax, J. (1990), *Thinking Fragments: Psychoanalysis, Feminism, and Postmodernism in the Contemporary West*. Berkeley: University of California Press.

———— (1996), Taking multiplicity seriously. *Contemp. Psychoanal.*, 32:577–593.

Fliegel, Z. (1986), Women's development in analytic theory: six decades of controversy. In: *Psychoanalysis and Women: Contemporary Reappraisals*, ed. J. L. Alpert. Hillsdale, NJ: The Analytic Press.

Foster, J. (1956), *Sex Variant Women in Literature*. Tallahassee, FL: Naiad Press, 1985.

Foucault, M. (1978), *The History of Sexuality, Vol 1*, trans. R. Hurley. New York: Vintage Books, 1980.

Freeman, L. (1972), *The Story of Anna O*. Northvale, NJ: Aronson.

Freud, S. (1887–1902), *The Origins of Psychoanalysis: Letters, Drafts and Notes to Wilhelm Fliess*, ed. M. Bonaparte, A. Freud & E. Kris. New York: Basic Books, 1954.

———— (1900), *The Interpretation of Dreams. Standard Edition*, 4 & 5. London: Hogarth Press, 1953.

———— (1905a), Fragment of an analysis of a case of hysteria. *Standard Edition*, 7:7–122. London: Hogarth Press, 1953.

———— (1905b), *Three Essays on the Theory of Sexuality. Standard Edition*, 7:125–245. London: Hogarth Press, 1953.

———— (1918), *From the History of an Infantile Neurosis. Standard Edition*, 17:3–122. London: Hogarth Press, 1955.

———— (1919 ), "A child is being beaten." A contribution to the study of sexual perversions. *Standard Edition*, 17:175–204. London: Hogarth Press, 1955.

———— (1920), The psychogenesis of a case of homosexuality in a woman. *Standard Edition*, 18:145–172. London: Hogarth Press, 1955.

———— (1921), Group psychology and the analysis of the ego. *Standard Edition*, 18:65–143. London: Hogarth Press, 1955.

———— (1925), Some psychical consequences of the anatomical differences between the sexes. *Standard Edition*, 19:241–258. London: Hogarth Press, 1961.

———— (1930), Address delivered in the Goethe House at Frankfurt, *Standard Edition*, 21:2–5–212. London: Hogarth Press, 1961.

———— (1931), Female sexuality. *Standard Edition*, 21:221–243. London: Hogarth Press, 1961.

———— (1933a), Femininity. *Standard Edition*, 22:112–135. London: Hogarth Press, 1964.

———— (1933b), New introductory lectures on psycho-analysis. *Standard Edition*, 22:1–182. London: Hogarth Press, 1964.

———— (1937), Analysis terminable and interminable. *Standard Edition*, 23:216–253.

London: Hogarth Press, 1964.

Friedman, R. C. (1988), *Male Homosexuality: A Contemporary Analytic Perspective*. New Haven, CT: Yale University Press.

———— & Downey, J. (1993), Psychoanalysis, psychobiology, and homosexuality. *J. Amer. Psychoanal. Assn.*, 41:1159–1198.

Friedman, R. M. (1996), Testicles in male psychological development. *J. Amer. Psychoanal. Assn.*, 44:210–253.

Friedman, S. S. (1981), *Psyche Reborn: The Emergence of H. D.* Bloomington: Indiana University Press.

———— (1986), A most luscious *vers libre* relationship: H.D. and Freud. *The Annual of Psychoanalysis*, 14:319–343. New York: International Universities Press.

Friedrich, O. (1972), *Before the Deluge: A Portrait of Berlin in the 1920s*. New York: Harper & Row/HarperCollins, 1995.

Frommer, M. S. (1994), Homosexuality and psychoanalysis. *Psychoanal. Dial.*, 4: 215–233.

———— (1995), Countertransference obscurity in psychoanalytic treatment of homosexual patients. In: *Disorienting Sexuality: Psychoanalytic Reappraisals of Sexual Identities*, ed. R. Domenici & R. C. Lesser. New York: Routledge, pp. 65–82.

Frye, M. (1988), Lesbian "sex". In: *An Intimate Wilderness: Lesbian Writers on Sexuality*, ed. J. Barrington. Portland, OR: Eighth Mountain Press, 1991, pp. 1–8.

Fuss, D. (1993), Freud's fallen women: Identification, desire, and "A Case of Homosexuality in a Woman." In: *Fear of a Queer Planet*, ed. M. Warner. Minneapolis: University of Minnesota Press, pp. 42–68.

Gaddini, E. (1976), Discussion of "The role of family life in child development: On 'father formation' in early childhood." *Internat. J. Psycho-Anal.*, 57: 397–401.

Galenson, E. & Roiphe, H. (1976), Some suggested revisions concerning early female development. *J. Amer. Psychoanal. Assn.*, 24:29–57.

Garber, M. (1992), *Vested Interests: Cross Dressing and Cultural Anxiety*. New York: HarperCollins, 1993.

———— (1995), *Vice Versa: Bisexuality and the Eroticism of Everyday Life*. New York: Simon & Schuster.

Garnets, L. & Kimmel, D. (1991), Lesbian and gay male dimensions in the psychological study of human diversity. In: *Psychological Perspectives on Human Diversity in America*, ed. J. Goodchilds. Washington, DC: American Psychological Association.

———— ed. (1993), *Psychological Perspectives on Lesbian & Gay Male Experiences*. New York: Columbia University Press.

Gartrell, N. K. (1984), Issues in psychotherapy with lesbian women. Work in Progress Series. Wellesley, MA: Stone Center.

———— Loriaux, D. L. & Chase. T. M. (1977), Plasma testosterone in homosexual and heterosexual women. *Amer. J. Psychiat.*, 134:1117–1119.

Gaspar de Alba, A. (1996), Descarada/no shame: An abridged politics of location. In: *The Wild Good: Lesbian Photographs & Writings on Love*, ed. B. Gates. New York: Anchor Books Doubleday, pp. 217–223.

Gautier, A. (1835), *Mademoiselle de Maupin*. Chicago: Franklin.

Gay, P. (1988), *Freud: A Life for Our Time*. New York: Norton.

Gershman, H. (1983), The stress of coming out. *Amer. J. Psychoanal.*, 43:129–138.

Gilberg, A. L.(1978), Psychosocial considerations in treating homosexual adolescents. *Amer. J. Psychoanal.*, 38:355–358.

Glassgold, J. & Insenza, S., ed. (1995), *Lesbians and Psychoanalysis: Revolutions in Theory and Practice*. New York: Free Press.

Goffman, E. (1976), *Gender Advertisements*. New York: Harper & Row, 1979.

Goldberger, M. & Evans, D. (1985), On transference manifestations in male patients with female analysts. *Internat. J. Psycho-Anal.*, 66:295–309.

———— & Evans, D. (1993), Transferences in Male Patients with Female Analysts: An Update. *Psychoanal. Inq.*, 13:173–191.

Goldman, S. B. (1995), The difficulty of being a gay psychoanalyst during the last fifty years: An interview with Dr. Bertram Schaffner. In: *Disorienting Sexuality: Psychoanalytic Reappraisals of Sexual Identities*, ed. R. Domenici & R. C. Lesser. New York: Routledge, pp. 243–261.

Goldner, V. (1991), Toward a critical relational theory of gender. *Psychoanal. Dial.*, 1:249–272.

Goldstein, E. (1994), Self disclosure in treatment: What therapists do and don't talk about. *Clin. Social Work J.*, 22:417–433.

———— (1997), To tell or not to tell: the disclosure of events in the therapist's life to the patient. *Clin. Social Work J.*, 25:41–58.

Gonsiorek, J. C. (1993), Mental Health Issues of Gay and Lesbian Adolescents. In: *Psychological Perspectives on Lesbian and Gay Male Experiences*, ed. L. Garnets & D. Kimmel. New York: Columbia University Press, pp. 469–485.

Gooren, L. (1995), Biomedical concepts of homosexuality: Folk belief in a white coat. In: *Cells and Same-Sex Desire: The Biology of Sexual Preference*, ed. J. P. De Cecco & D. A. Parker. New York: Haworth Press, pp. 237–246.

———— Fliers, E. & Courtney, K. (1990), Biological determinants of sexual orientation. In: *Annual Review of Sex Research, Vol. 1*, ed. J. Bancroft, pp. 175–196.

Gould, S. J. (1981), *The Mismeasure of Man*. New York: Norton & Co.

Goy, R. W. (1966), Role of androgens in the establishment and regulation of behavioral sex differences in mammals. *J. Animal Sci.*, 25:21–35.

———— & McEwen, B. S., ed. (1980), *Sexual Differentiation of the Brain*. Cambridge, MA: MIT Press.

Grahn, J. (1984), *Another Mother Tongue*. Boston: Beacon Press.

Green, R. (1987), *The "Sissy Boy Syndrome" and the Development of Homosexuality*. New Haven, CT: Yale University Press.

Greenberg, J. R. (1995), Self disclosure: Is it psychoanalytic? *Contemp. Psychoanal.*, 31:193–205.

Greenson, R. (1968), Dis-identifying from mother: its special importance for the boy. *Internat. J. Psycho-Anal.*, 49:370–374.

Groddeck. G. (1923), *The Book of the It*. New York: Mentor Books, 1961.

Grosskurth, P. (1986), *Melanie Klein: Her World and Her Work*. New York: Knopf.

Grossman, C. M. & Grossman, S.(1965), *The Wild Analyst: The Life and Work of Georg Groddeck*. New York: Dell.

Guest, B. (1984), *Herself Defined: The Poet H. D. and Her World*. Garden City, NY: Doubleday.

Hacking, I. (1986), Making up people. In: *Forms of Desire: Sexual Orientation and the*

*Social Constructionist Controversy*, ed. E. Stein. New York: Routledge, pp. 69–88.

Hall, M. (1995), Not tonight dear, I'm deconstructing a headache: Confessions of a lesbian therapist. In: *Lesbian Erotics*, ed. K. Jay. New York: New York University Press, pp. 15–27.

Hall, R. [1928], *The Well of Loneliness*. New York: Avon Books, 1981.

Hamer, D. (1990), Significant others: Lesbianism and psychoanalytic theory. *Feminist Rev.*, 34:134–151.

Hanley-Hackenbruck, P. (1988), Psychotherapy and the "coming out" process. *J. Gay Lesbian Psychother.*, 1:21–39.

Hanscombe, G. E. & Forster, J. (1981), *Rocking the Cradle: Lesbian Mothers—A Challenge in Family Living*. Boston: Alyson Publications.

——— & Smyers, V. L. (1987), *Writing for Their Lives: The Modernist Women 1910–1940*. Boston: Northeastern University Press.

Harris, A. (1991), Gender as contradiction. *Psychoanal. Dial.*, 1:197–224.

Hart, J. & Richardson, D. (1981), *The Theory and Practice of Homosexuality*. London: Routledge.

Hart, L. ( 1994), *Fatal Women: Lesbian Sexuality and the Mark of Aggression*. Princeton, NJ: Princeton University Press.

Hartstein, N. B. (1996), Suicide risk in lesbian, gay and bisexual youth. In: *Textbook of Homosexuality and Mental Health*, ed. R. P. Cabaj & T. S. Stein. Washington, DC: American Psychiatric Press, pp. 819–837.

Hausman, K. (1989). Psychoanalysts asked to take stand on discrimination toward gays, AIDS patients. *Psychiatric News*, July 21, pp. 2, 13.

——— (1991), American Psychoanalytic Assn. opposes discrimination against homosexuals. *Psychiatric News*, August 2, p. 2.

——— (1992), American Psychoanalytic Association goes step further to eliminate bias against homosexual applicants. *Psychiatric News*, July 17, pp. 13, 16.

Heilbrun, C. (1988), *Writing a Woman's Life*. New York: Ballantine.

Helleday, J., Bartfai, A., Ritzén, E. M. & Forsman, M. (1994), General intelligence and cognitive profile in women with congenital adrenal hyperplasia (CAH). *Psychoneuroendocrinol.*, 19:343–356.

Hellman, L. (1934), The children's hour. In: *Six Plays by Lillian Hellman*. New York: Modern Library.

Henry, G. (1948), *Sexual Variants: A Study of Homosexual Patterns*. New York: Hoeber.

Herdt, G. (1989a), Introduction: Gay and lesbian youth, emergent identities, and cultural scenes at home and abroad. In: *Adolescence and Homosexuality*, ed. G. Herdt. New York: Haworth Press.

——— ed. (1989b), *Gay and Lesbian Youth*. New York: Harrington Park Press.

——— (1991), Representations of homosexuality: An essay on cultural ontology and historical comparison, Parts I and II. *J. Hist. Sexual.*, 1:481–504, 603–632.

——— ed. (1996), *Third Sex, Third Gender: Beyond Sexual Dimorphism in Culture and History*. New York: Zone Books.

Herman, J. W. (1992), *Trauma and Recovery: The Aftermath of Violence—From Domestic Violence to Political Terror*. New York: Basic Books.

Herrn, R. (1995), On the history of biological theories of homosexuality, In: *Cells, and Same-Sex Desire: The Biology of Sexual Preference*, ed. J. P. De Cecco & D. A. Parker.

New York: Haworth Press, pp. 31–56.

Heyward, C. (1989), Coming out and relational empowerment: A lesbian feminist theological perspective. Work in Progress Series, Wellesley, MA: Stone Center.

Holroyd, M. (1971), *Lytton Strachey: A Critical Biography*. Harmondsworth, Eng.: Penguin Books.

Hooker, E. (1957), The adjustment of the male overt homosexual. *J. Proj. Tech.*, 21:18–31.

Horney, K. (1924), On the genesis of the castration complex in women. *Internat. J. Psycho-Anal.*, 5: 50–65.

———— (1926), The flight from womanhood: The masculinity complex in women as viewed by men and by women. *Internat. J. Psycho-Anal.*, 7:324–339.

———— (1932), The dread of woman: Observations on a specific difference in the dread felt by men and by women respectively for the opposite sex. *Internat. J. Psycho-Anal.*, 13:348–360.

———— (1933), The denial of the vagina: A contribution to the problem of the genital anxieties specific to women. *Internat. J. Psycho-Anal.*, 14:57–70.

Horowitz, H. L. (1994), *The Power and Passion of M. Carey Thomas*. New York: Knopf.

Hubbard, R. (1990), *The Politics of Women's Biology*. New Brunswick, NJ: Rutgers University Press.

———— Henifin, M. S. & Fried, B., ed. (1979), *Women Look at Biology Looking at Women*. Cambridge, MA: Schenkman.

———— & Wald, E. (1993), *Exploding the Gene Myth*. Boston: Beacon Hill.

Irigaray, L. (1974), *Speculum of the Other Woman*, trans. G. C. Gill. Ithaca, NY: Cornell University Press, 1985.

———— (1977), *This Sex Which is Not One*, trans. C. Porter. Ithaca, NY: Cornell University Press, 1985.

Isay, R. (1989), *Being Homosexual: Gay Men and Their Development*. New York: Farrar, Straus & Giroux.

———— (1991), The homosexual analyst: Clinical considerations. In: *Affirmative Dynamic Psychotherapy with Gay Men*, ed. C. Cornett. Northvale, NJ: Aronson, pp. 177–198.

———— (1996), *Becoming Gay: The Journey to Self-Acceptance*. New York: Pantheon.

Jacoby, R. (1983), The Berlin institute: The politics of psychoanalysis. In: *The Repression of Psychoanalysis*. Chicago: University of Chicago Press, 1986, pp. 62–75.

Jameson, S. (1993), Japan's "Untouchables" suffer invisible stain. *Los Angeles Times*, January 2, pp. 24–25.

Jay, K. & Glasgow, J., ed. (1990), *Lesbian Texts and Contexts: Radical Revisions*. New York: New York University Press.

Jefferson, T. (1779), Bill Number 64, June 18, 1779. In: *Gay American History*, ed. J. N. Katz. New York: Meridian, 1992, pp. 23–24.

Jones, E. (1927), The early development of female sexuality. *Internat. J. Psycho-Anal.*, 8:459–472.

Kaes, A., Jay, M. & Dimendberg, E., eds. (1994), *The Weimar Republic Source Book*. Berkeley: University of California Press.

Kaplan, L. J. (1984), *Adolescence: The Farewell to Childhood*. New York: Simon & Schuster.

———— (1991), *Female Perversions: The Temptations of Emma Bovary*. New York:

Doubleday.

Karme, L. (1979), The analysis of a male patient by a female analyst: The problem of the negative oedipal transference. *Internat. J. Psycho-Anal.*, 60:253–261.

—— (1993), Male patients and female analysts: Erotic and other psychoanalytic encounters. *Psychoanal. Inq.*, 13:192–205.

Katz, J. (1980), This is how lesbians capture straight women and have their way with them. In: *The Coming Out Stories*, ed. J. Penelope & S. J. Wolfe. Watertown MA: Persephone Press, pp. 168–175.

Katz, J. N. (1976), *Gay American History: Lesbians and Gay Men in the U.S.A.* New York: Meridian, 1992

—— (1983), *Gay/Lesbian Almanac: A New Documentary*. New York, Harper.

Keller, E. F. (1985), *Reflections on Gender and Science*. New Haven, CT: Yale University Press.

Kestenberg, J. (1975), *Children and Parents: Psychoanalytic Studies in Development*. New York: Aronson.

Khan, M. (1964), The role of infantile sexuality and early object-relations in female homosexuality. In: *The Pathology and Treatment of Sexual Deviation: A Methodological Approach*, ed. I. Rosen. New York: Oxford University Press, pp. 221–292. Also In: *Alienation in Perversions*, ed. M. Khan. New York: International Universities Press, 1979, pp. 56–119.

—— (1983), *Hidden Selves: Between Theory and Practice in Psychoanalysis*. New York: International Universities Press.

Kirkpatrick, M. & Morgan, C. (1980), Psychodynamic psychotherapy of female homosexuality. In: *Homosexual Behavior*, ed. J. Marmor. New York: Basic Books.

Klaich, D. (1974), *Woman + Woman: Attitudes Toward Lesbianism*. New York: Morrow Quill, 1979.

Kleeman, J. (1976), Freud's views on early female sexuality in the light of direct child observation. *J. Amer. Psychoanal. Assn.*, 24 Suppl.: 3–27.

Klein, M. (1926), The psychological principles of early analysis. In: *Love, Guilt and Reparation and Other Works 1921–1945*. London: Hogarth Press, 1975, pp. 128–138.

—— (1928), Early stages of the oedipus complex. In: *Love, Guilt and Reparation and Other Works 1921–1945*. London: Hogarth Press, 1975, pp. 186–198.

Kleinberg, L. (1986), Coming home to self, going home to parents: Lesbian identity disclosure. Work in Progress Series, Wellesley, MA: Stone Center.

Kooden, H. (1991), Self-disclosure: The gay male therapist as agent of social change. In: *Gays, Lesbians, and Their Therapists*, ed. C. Silverstein. New York: Norton, pp. 143–154.

Krafft-Ebing, R. (1886), *Psychopathia Sexualis*. New York: Surgeons Book, 1925.

Kristof, N. (1995), Japanese outcasts better off than in past but still outcast. *New York Times Internat.*, November 30, pp. A1, A8.

Kulish, N. M. (1984), The effect of the sex of the analyst on transference: A review of the literature. *Bull. Menn. Clin.*, 48:95–109.

Kwawer, J. (1980), Transference and countertransference in homosexuality—changing psychoanalytic views. *Amer. J. Psychother.*, 34:72–80.

Lachmann, F. (1975), Homosexuality: Some diagnostic perspectives and dynamic considerations. *Amer. J. Psychother.*, 29:254–260.

Lansky, M. R. (1989), The paternal imago. In: *Fathers and Their Families*, ed. S. H. Cath, A. Gurwitt & L. Gunsberg. Hillsdale, NJ: The Analytic Press, pp. 27–45.

Laqueur, T. (1990), *Making Sex: Body and Gender from the Greeks to Freud*. Cambridge, MA: Harvard University Press.

Larkin, J. (1975), Some unsaid things. In: *Lesbian Poetry: An Anthology*, eds. E. Bulkin & J. Larkin. Watertown, MA: Persephone Press.

Laufer, M. (1965), Assessment of adolescent disturbance: The application of Anna Freud's diagnostic profile. In: *The Psychoanalytic Study of the Child*, 20:99–123. New York: International Universities Press.

——— & Laufer, M. E. (1984), *Adolescence and Developmental Breakdown*. New Haven and London: Yale University Press.

Lauritsen, J. & Thorstad, D. (1974), *The Early Homosexual Rights Movement (1864–1935)*. New York: Times Change Press.

Leavy, S. A. (1988), *In the Image of God: A Psychoanalyst's View*. Hillsdale, NJ: The Analytic Press, 1997

Leduc, V. ( 1965), *La Bastarde*. New York: Farrar, Straus & Giroux.

Leonard, M. (1966), Fathers and daughters: the significance of 'fathering' in the psychosocial development of the girl. *Internat. J. Psycho-Anal.*, 47:325–333.

Leopold, E. (l995), Beijing Women's Conference: What is gender? *Reuters World Report*, April 9.

Lerner, H. (1976), Parental mislabeling of female genitals as a determinant of penis envy and learning inhibitions in women. *J. Amer. Psycho-Anal. Assn.*, 24 Suppl.: 269–283.

Lesser, R. C. (1993), A reconsideration of homosexual themes. *Psychoanal. Dial.*, 3:639–641.

——— (1995), Objectivity as masquerade. In: *Disorienting Sexualities: Psychoanalytic Reappraisals of Sexual Identities*, ed. T. Domenici & R. Lesser. New York: Routledge, pp. 83–96.

Lester, E. P. (1990), Gender and identity issues in the analytic process. *Internat. J. Psycho-Anal.*, 71:435–444.

LeVay, S. (1991), A difference in hypothalamic structure between heterosexual and homosexual men, *Science*, 253:1034–1037.

——— (1993), *The Sexual Brain*, Cambridge, MA: MIT Press.

Lewes, K. (l988), *The Psychoanalytic Theory of Male Homosexuality*. New York: Simon & Schuster.

Lichtenberg, J. D. (1989), *Psychoanalysis and Motivation*. Hillsdale, NJ: The Analytic Press.

Lifshin, L., ed. (1982), *Ariadne's Thread: A Collection of Contemporary Women's Journals*. New York: Harper & Row.

Limentani, A. (1989), Clinical types of homosexuality. In: *Between Freud and Klein: The Psychoanalytic Quest for Knowledge and Truth*. London: Free Association Books, pp. 102–113.

———— (1992), Obituary: M. Masud R. Khan. *Internat. J. Psycho-Anal.*, 73:155–159.

Lindenbaum, J. (1985), The shattering of an illusion: The problem of competition in lesbian relationships. *Fem. Studies*, 11:85–103.

Lingiardi, V. (1997), *Compagni D'Amore: From Ganymede to Batman. Identity and Myth in Male Homosexuality*. Rome: Raffaollo Cortina.

Lipton, E. L. (1991), The analyst's use of clinical data, and other issues of confidentiality. *J. Amer. Psychoanal. Assn.*, 39:967–985.

Little, M. (1960), Countertransference. *Brit. J. Med. Psychology*, 33:29–31.

Longino, H. E. (1990), *Science as Social Knowledge: Values and Objectivity in Scientific Inquiry*. Princeton, NJ: Princeton University Press.

Loulan, J. A. (1990), *The Lesbian Erotic Dance*. San Francisco: Spinsters.

Lowe, M. & Hubbard, R. (1983), *Woman's Nature: Rationalizations of Inequality*. New York: Pergamon Press.

McAlmon, R. (1938), *Being Geniuses Together*. London: Hogarth Press, 1984.

McClure, R. & Vespry, A., ed. (1994), *The Lesbian Health Guide*. Toronto: Queer Press.

Maccoby, E. & Jacklin, C. N. (1974), *The Psychology of Sex Differences* Stanford, CA: Stanford University Press.

McDougall, J. (1964). Homosexuality in women. In: *Female Sexuality*, ed. J. Chasseguet-Smirgel, C. J. Luquet-Parat, B. Grunberger, J. McDougall, M. Torok, & C. David. Ann Arbor: Michigan University Press, 1970, pp. 171–212.

———— (1980), *Plea for a Measure of Abnormality*. New York: International Universities Press.

———— (1985), *Theaters of the Mind*. New York: Basic Books.

———— (1986), Eve's reflection: On the homosexual components of female sexuality. In: *Between Analyst and Patient: New Dimensions in Countertransference and Transference*, ed. H. Meyers. Hillsdale, NJ: The Analytic Press, pp. 213–228.

———— (1989), The dead father: On early psychic trauma and its relation to disturbance in sexual identity and in creative activity. *Internat. J. Psycho-Anal.*, 70:205–219.

———— (1991), Perversions in psychoanalytic attitude. In: *Perversions and Near-Perversions in Clinical Practice: New Psychoanalytic Perspectives*, ed. G. I. Fogel & W. A. Myers. New Haven, CT: Yale University Press, pp. 176–203.

McGuire, L. S., Ryan, K. O., & Omenn, G. S. (l975), Congenital adrenal hyperplasia. II. Cognitive and behavioral studies. *Behav. Genet*, 5:175–188.

McIntosh, M. (1968), The homosexual role. *Social Problems*, 16:182–192.

Mack, J. E. (1980), Psychoanalysis and biography: Aspects of a developing affinity. *J. Amer. Psychoanal. Assn.*, 28:543–562.

MacKay, A., ed. (1992), *Wolf Girls at Vassar: Lesbian and Gay Experiences 1930–1990*. New York: St. Martin's Press.

McKinley, C. R. & DeLaney, L. J., ed. (1995), *Afrekete: An Anthology of Black Lesbian Writing*. New York: Anchor Books.

Magid, B. (1993), A young woman's homosexuality reconsidered: Freud's "The psychogenesis of a case of homosexuality in a woman". *J. Amer. Acad. Psychoanal.*, 21:421–432.

Maggiore, D. J. (1988), *Lesbianism: An Annotated Bibliography and Guide to the Literature, 1976–1986*. Metuchen, NJ: Scarecrow Press.

Mahler, M. S., Pine, F. & Bergman, A. (1975), *The Psychological Birth of the Human Infant*.

New York: Basic Books.

Marcus, E. (1992). *Making History: The Struggle for Gay And Lesbian Equal Rights, 1945–1990, An Oral History.* New York: HarperCollins.

Marmor, J. (1980a), Overview: The multiple roots of homosexual behavior. In: *Homosexual Behavior: A Modern Reappraisal,* ed. J. Marmor. New York: Basic Books.

—— (1980b), Epilogue: Homosexuality and the Issue of Mental Illness. In: *Homosexual Behavior: A Modern Reappraisal,* ed. J. Marmor. New York: Basic Books, pp. 391–401.

—— ed. (1980c), *Homosexual Behavior: Modern Reappraisal.* New York: Basic Books.

—— (1996), Nongay therapists working with gay men and lesbians: A personal reflection. In: *Textbook of Homosexuality and Mental Health,* ed. R. Cabaj & T. S. Stein. Washington, DC: American Psychiatric Press, pp. 539–545.

Martin, A. (1993), *The Lesbian and Gay Parenting Handbook: Creating and Raising Our Families.* New York: HarperCollins.

—— (1994), Fruits, nuts, and chocolate: The politics of sexual identity. *Harvard Gay & Lesbian Rev.,* 1:10–14.

—— (1995), A view from both sides: Coming out as a lesbian psychoanalyst. In: *Disorienting Sexuality: Psychoanalytic Reappraisals of Sexual Identities,* ed. R. Domenici & R. C. Lesser. New York: Routledge, pp. 255–261.

Martin, A. D. & Hetrick, E. S.(1988), The stigmatization of the gay and lesbian adolescent. *J. Homosexuality,* 15:163–183.

Mayer, E. L. (1985), "Everybody must be just like me": Observations on female castration anxiety. *Internat. J. Psycho-Anal.,* 66:331–347.

Maylon, A. K. (1981), The homosexual adolescent: Developmental issues and social bias. *Child Welfare,* 60:321–330.

Mayne, J. (1996), Screening lesbians. In: *The New Lesbian Studies,* ed. B. Zimmerman & T. A. H. McNaron. New York: Feminist Press of City of New York, pp. 165–185.

Meisel, P. & Kendrick, W., ed.(1985), *Bloomsbury/Freud.: The Letters of James and Alix Strachey, 1924–1925.* New York: Basic Books.

Mencher, J. (1990), Intimacy in lesbian relationships: A critical re-examination of fusion. Work in Progress Series. Wellesley, MA: Stone Center.

Merck, M. (1986), The train of thought in Freud's "Case of Homosexuality in a Woman." In: *Perversions: Deviant Readings.* New York: Routledge, 1993, pp. 13–32.

Meyer-Bahlburg, H. F. L. (1990/1991). Will prenatal hormone treatment prevent homosexuality? *J. Child & Adolesc. Psychopharmacol.,* 1:279–283.

Meyers, H. (1986), Analytic work by and with women: The complexity and the challenge. In: *Between Analyst and Patient.* ed. H. Meyers. Hillsdale, NJ: The Analytic Press, pp. 159–176.

Mitchell, S. (1978), Psychodynamics, homosexuality, and the question of pathology. *Psychiat.,* 41:254–263.

—— (1981), The psychoanalytic treatment of homosexuality: some technical considerations. *Internat. Rev. Psycho-Anal.,* 8:63–80.

—— (1988), *Relational Concepts in Psychoanalysis: An Integration.* Cambridge, MA: Harvard University Press.

—— (1991), Contemporary perspectives on self: Toward an integration. *Psychoanal. Dial,* 1:121–147.

———— (1993), *Hope and Dread In Psychoanalysis*. New York: Basic Books.

———— (1996), Gender and sexual orientation in the age of postmodernism: the plight of the perplexed clinician. *Gender & Psychoanal.*,1:45–73.

Moi, R. (1994), *Simone de Beauvoir: The Making of an Intellectual Woman*. Oxford: Blackwell.

Money, J. & Ehrhardt, A. A. (1972), *Man & Woman, Boy & Girl: The Differentiation and Dimorphism of Gender Identity from Conception to Maturity*. Baltimore, MD: Johns Hopkins University Press.

———— & Lewis, V. (1966), IQ, genetics and accelerated growth: Adrenogenital syndrome. *Bull. Johns Hopkins Hosp.*, 118: 365–373.

———— Schwartz, J. & Lewis, V. (l984), Adult erotosexual status and fetal hormonal masculinization and demasculinization: 46, XX congenital virilizing adrenal hyperplasia and 46, XY androgen-insensitivity. *Psychoneuroendocrinol.*, 9:405–414.

Monnier, A. (1940), Our friend Bryher. In: *The Very Rich Hours of Adrienne Monnier*, ed. R. McDougall. Lincoln: University of Nebraska Press, 1996, pp. 204–206.

Moraga, C. & Anzaldúa, G., ed. (1981), *This Bridge Called My Back: Writings by Radical Women of Color*. Watertown, MA: Persephone Press.

Morgenthaler, F. (1988), *Homosexuality, Heterosexuality, Perversion*, trans. A. Aebi, ed. P. Moor. Hillsdale, NJ: The Analytic Press.

Morrison, A. (1990), Doing psychotherapy while living with a life-threatening illness. In: *Illness in the Analyst*, ed. H. Schwartz & A. Silver. New York: International Universities Press, pp. 227–250.

———— (1997), Ten years of doing psychotherapy while living with a life- threatening illness: self-disclosure and other ramifications. *Psychoanal. Dial.*, 7:225–241.

Moss, D. (1992), Introductory thoughts: Hating in the first person plural: The example of homophobia. *Amer. Imago*, 49:277–291.

Mulaikal, R. M., Migeon, C. J. & Rock, J. A. (l987), Fertility rates in female patients with congenital adrenal hyperplasia due to 21-hydroxylase deficiency. *New Eng. J. Med.*, 316:178–182.

Nardi, P., Sanders, D. & Marmor, J. (1994), Interview with Judd Marmor, M.D. In: *Growing Up Before Stonewall: Life Stories of Some Gay Men*. New York: Routledge, pp. 46–65.

Nestle, J. (1987), *A Restricted Country*. Ithaca, NY: Firebrand Books.

Nichols, M. (1987), Lesbian sexuality: Issues and developing theory. In: *Lesbian Psychologies*, ed. Boston Lesbian Psychologies Collective . Urbana: University of Illinois, pp. 97–125.

O'Brien, S. (1988). *Willa Cather: The Emerging Voice*. New York: Ballantine.

———— (1994), My Willa Cather: How writing her story shaped my own. *New York Times Book Review*, Feb. 20.

O'Connor, N. & Ryan, J. (1993), *Wild Desires and Mistaken Identities: Lesbianism & Psychoanalysis*. New York: Columbia University Press.

Ogden, T. (1987), The transitional oedipal relationship in female development. *Internat. J. Psycho-Anal.*, 68:485–498.

Person, E. (1980), Sexuality as the mainstay of identity: Psychoanalytic perspectives. *Signs*, 5:605–630.

———— (1985), The erotic transference in women and men: Differences and consequences. *J. Amer. Acad. Psychoanal.*, 13:159–180.

Phoenix, C. (1978), Prenatal testosterone in the non-human primate and its conse-quences for behavior. In: *Sex Differences in Behavior*, ed. R. Friedman, R. Richart & R. L. Vande Wiele. Huntington, NY: Krieger.

Pruitt, K. D. (1983), Infants of primary nurturing fathers. *The Psychoanalytic Study of the Child*, 38:257–277. New Haven, CT: Yale University Press.

Quadagno, D. M., Briscoe, R. & Quadagno, J. S. (1977), Effects of perinatal gonadal hor-mones on selected nonsexual behavior patterns: A critical assessment of the non-human and human literature. *Psycholog. Bull.*, 84:62–80.

Quinodoz, J-M. (1989). Female homosexual patients in psychoanalysis. *Internat. J. Psycho-Anal.*, 70: 55–63.

Quintanilla, M. (1994), Live to tell: Teenagers from L.A. schools pack first district- sanc-tioned gay prom. *Los Angeles Times*, May 22.

Rachman, A. W. (1993), Ferenczi and sexuality. In: *The Legacy of Sándor Ferenczi*, ed. L. Aron & A. Harris. Hillsdale NJ: The Analytic Press, pp. 81–100.

Reid, C. (1976), Introduction. *Lesbian Lives: Biographies of Women from The Ladder*. ed. B. Grier & C. Reid. Oakland, CA : Diana Press, pp. 21–24.

Remafedi, G. (1987), Adolescent homosexuality: Psychosocial and medical implications. *Pediatrics*, 79, 331–337.

———— Farrow, J. A. & Deisher, R. W. (1993 ), Risk factors for attempted suicide in gay and bisexual youth. In: *Psychological Perspectives on Lesbian & Gay Male Experiences*, ed. L. Garnets & D. Kimmel. New York: Columbia University Press, pp. 486–499.

Renik, O. (1994), Commentary on Frommer's paper. *Psychoanal. Dial.*, 4:235–239.

———— (1995), The ideal of the anonymous analyst and the problem of self-disclosure. *Psychoanal. Quart.*, 64:466–495.

Reuben, D. (1969), *Everything You Always Wanted to Know About Sex*. New York: McKay.

Rich, A. (1975), Women and honor: Some notes on lying. In: *Lies, Secrets and Silence*. New York: Norton, 1979, pp. 185–194.

———— (1976). "It is the lesbian in us . . ." In: *Lies, Secrets and Silence*. New York: Norton, 1979, pp. 199–202.

———— (1978), *Dream of a Common Language*. New York: Norton.

———— (1980), Foreword. In: *The Coming Out Stories*, ed. P. Stanley & S. Wolfe. Watertown, MA: Persephone Press, pp. xi-xiii.

Richards, A. K. (1992), Hilda Doolittle and Creativity: Freud's Gift. *The Psychoanalytic Study of the Child*, 47:391–406. New Haven, CT: Yale University Press.

Rieber, I. & Sigusch, V. (1979), Guest Editorial: Psychosurgery on sex offenders and sex-ual "deviants" in West Germany. *Arch. Sex. Behav.*, 8:523–527.

Riviere, J. (1924), Phallic symbolism. In: *The Inner World and Joan Riviere: Collected Papers,1920–1958*, ed. A. Hughes. London: Karnac Books, 1991, p. 52.

Robertiello, R. C. (1959), *Voyage from Lesbos: The Psychoanalysis of a Female Homosexual*. New York: Citadel.

Romm, M. (1965), Sexuality and homosexuality in women. In: *Sexual Inversion: The Multiple Roots of Homosexuality*, ed. J. Marmor. New York: Basic Books, pp. 282–301.

Roscoe, W. (1991), *The Zuni Man-Woman*. Albuquerque: University of New Mexico Press.

Rosenbaum, M. (1995), Comment. *Psychoanal. Psychol.*, 12:141.

———— & Muroff, M., ed. (1984), *Anna O: Fourteen Contemporary Reinterpretations.* New York: Free Press.

Roughton, R. (1996), Overcoming antihomosexual bias: A progress report. In: *The American Psychoanalyst*, 29:15–16.

Ruan, F. F. & Bullough, V. L. (1992), Lesbianism in China. *Arch. Sex. Behav.*, 21:217–226.

Ruff, S. S., ed. 1996), *Go the Way Your Blood Beats: An Anthology of Lesbian and Gay Fiction by African-American Writers.* New York: Henry Holt.

Rule, J. (1964), *Desert of the Heart.* Vancouver: Talonbooks.

Rupp, L. (1980), "Imagine my surprise": Women's relationships in mid-twentieth century America. In: *Hidden From History: Reclaiming the Gay and Lesbian Past*, ed. M. B. Duberman, M. Vicinus & G. Chauncey. New York: New American Library, 1989, pp. 395–410.

Russ, D. (1993), Freud's fallen women: Identification, desire and "A Case of Homosexuality in a Woman." In: *Fear of a Queer Planet*, ed. M. Warner. Minneapolis: University Minnesota Press, pp. 42–68.

Sachs, H. (1923), On the genesis of perversions. *Amer. Imago*, 48:283–293, 1991.

———— (1927), On the issue of lay analysis. *Internat. J. Psycho-Anal.*, 8:198–201.

Sahli, N. (1979), Smashing: Women's relationships before the fall. *Chrysalis*, 8: 17–27.

San Francisco Lesbian and Gay History Project (1989), "She even chewed tobacco": A pictorial narrative of passing women in America. In: *Hidden From History: Reclaiming the Gay and Lesbian Past*, ed. M. B. Duberman, M. Vicinus & G. Chauncey. New York: New American Library, pp. 183–194.

Sanville, J. (1991), *The Playground of Psychoanalytic Therapy.* Hillsdale, NJ: The Analytic Press.

Sautman, F. C. (1996), Invisible women: Lesbian working-class culture in France, 1880–1930. In: *Homosexuality in Modern France*, ed. J. Merrick & B. T. Ragan. New York: Oxford University Press, pp. 177–201.

Schafer, R. (1974), Problems in Freud's psychology of women. *J. Amer. Psychoanal. Assn.*, 22:459–485.

———— (1992), *Retelling a Life: Narration and Dialogue in Psychoanalysis.* Basic Books.

Schmidt, G. (1984), Allies and persecutors: Science and medicine in the homosexuality issue. *J. Homosexual.*, 10:127–140.

———— & Schorsch, E. (1981), Psychosurgery of sexually deviant patients: Review and analysis of new empirical findings. *Arch. Sexual Beh.*, 10:301–323.

Schwartz, A. (l986), Some notes on the development of female gender role identity. In: *Psychoanalysis and Women: Contemporary Reappraisals*, ed. J. Alpert. Hillsdale, NJ: The Analytic Press, pp. 57–79.

———— (1996), It's a queer universe: Some notes erotic and otherwise. *Psychoanal. & Psychother.*, 13:160–173.

Schwartz, D. (1993a), A psychoanalytic return to biology in the theorization of same-sex desire, Presented at meeting of the American Psychological Association, Toronto, August 21.

———— (1993b), Heterophilia—The love that dare not speak its aim. *Psychoanal. Dial.*, 3:643–652.

———— (1995), Current psychoanalytic discourses on sexuality: Tripping over the body.

In: *Disorienting Sexualities: Psychoanalytic Reappraisals of Sexual Identities*, ed. T. Domenici & R. Lesser. New York: Routledge, pp. 115–126.

———— (1996), Questioning the social construction of gender and sexual orientation. *Gender & Psychoanal.*, 1:249–260.

Schwartz, H. J. & Silver A-L., ed. (1990), *Illness in the Analyst: Implications for the Treatment Relationship*. New York: International Universities Press.

Sedgwick, E. K. (1990), *Epistemology of the Closet*. Berkeley: University of California Press.

———— (1993), *Tendencies*. Durham, NC: Duke University Press.

Shengold, L. (1989), *Soul Murder: The Effects of Childhood Abuse and Deprivation*. New Haven, CT: Yale University Press.

Shor, J. & J. Sanville (1979), *Illusion in Loving: Balancing Intimacy and Independence*. New York: Penguin.

Showalter, E. (1990), *Sexual Anarchy: Gender and Culture at the Fin de Siècle*. New York: Penguin.

———— Baechler, L. & Litz, A. W., ed. (1993), *Modern American Women Writers*. New York: Collier Books/Maxwell Macmillan.

Siegel, E. (1988). *Female Homosexuality: Choice Without Volition*. Hillsdale, NJ: The Analytic Press.

———— (1990), Review of Richard C. Friedman's *Male Homosexuality: A Contemporary Psychoanalytic Perspective*. In: *Psychoanal. Rev.*, 77:447–450.

———— (1991), The search for the vagina in homosexual women. In: *The Homosexualities and the Therapeutic Process*, ed. C. W. Socarides & V. D. Volkan. Madison, CT: International Universities Press, pp. 47–73.

Signorile, M. (1994), Independents: The post-Stonewall generation. *Out*, July/Aug: 86–93, 148–150.

Sigusch, V., Schorsch, E., Dannecker, M., and Schmidt, G. (1982), Guest editorial: Official statement by the German Society for Sex Research (Deutsche Gesellschaft für Sexualforschung e. V.) on the research of Prof. Dr. Günter Dörner on the subject of homosexuality. *Arch. Sex. Beh.*, 2:445–449.

Silva, J.(1975), Two cases of female homosexuality: A critical study of Sigmund Freud and Helene Deutsch. *Contemp. Psychoanal.*, 11:357–376.

Simons, M. A. (1992), Lesbian connection: Simone de Beauvoir and feminism. *Signs*, 18:136–161.

Sklar, K. K. (1985), Hull House in the 1890's: A Community of Women Reformers. *Signs*, 10:658–77.

Slijper, F. M. E. (1984), Androgens and gender role behaviour in girls with congenital adrenal hyperplasia (CAH), *Prog. Brain Res.*, 61:417–422.

Smedley, A. (1943), Silk Workers. In: *Portraits of Chinese Women in Revolution*. Old Westbury, NY: Feminist Press, 1976, pp. 103–110.

Smith, M. C. (1996), *Rose*. New York: Random House.

Smith-Rosenberg, C. (1975), The female world of love and ritual: Relations between women in 19th century America. *Signs*, 1:1–29.

———— (1985a), *Disorderly Conduct*. New York: Oxford University Press.

———— (1985b), Discourses of sexuality and subjectivity: The new woman, 1870–1936. In: *Hidden from History: Reclaiming the Gay and Lesbian Past*, ed. M. B. Duberman, M. Vicinus & G. Chauncey. New York: New American Library, 1989, pp.

264–280.

——— (1994), Women at the helm: Succession politics at the children's bureau, 1912–1968. *Social Work*, Sept.:551–559.

Socarides, C. (1963), The historical development of theoretical and clinical concepts of overt female homosexuality. *J. Amer. Psychoanal. Assn.*, 11:385–414.

——— (1968). *The Overt Homosexual*. New York: Grune & Stratton.

——— (1978), *Homosexuality*. New York: Aronson.

——— (1996), Adolescence. *Narth Bulletin* (National Association of Research and Therapy of Homosexuality), 4:14–15.

Spanier, B. B.(1995a), *Im/partial Science: Gender Ideology in Molecular Biology*. Bloomington: Indiana University Press.

——— (1995b), "Biological determinism and homosexuality," *NWSA J.*, 7:54–72.

Spezzano, C. (1994), Commentary on Frommer's paper. *Psychoanal. Dial.*, 2:241–245.

Spieler, S. (1984), Preoedipal girls need fathers. *Psychoanal. Rev.*, 71:63–80.

Spiers, H. & Lynch, M. (1977), The gay rights Freud, *Body Politic*, May.

Stafford, W. (1977), *Stories That Could Be True: The New and Collected Poems*. New York: Harper & Row.

Stanley, P. & Wolfe, S., ed. (1980), *The Coming Out Stories*. Watertown, MA: Persephone Press.

Star, S. L. (1980), How I spent at least one summer vacation. *The Coming Out Stories*. Watertown, MA: Persephone Press, pp. 229–234.

Stein, E. (1994), The relevance of scientific research about sexual orientation to lesbian and gay rights. *J. Homosexual.*, 27:269–308.

Stein, T. S. & Burg, B. K. (1996), Teaching in mental health training programs about homosexuality, lesbians, gay men, and bisexuals. In: *Textbook of Homosexuality and Mental Health*, ed. R. Cabaj & T. Stein. Washington, DC: American Psychiatric Press, pp. 621–631.

——— & Cohen, C.(1986), *Contemporary Perspectives on Psychotherapy with Lesbians and Gay Men*. New York: Plenum.

Stimpson, C. R. (1981), Zero degree deviancy: The lesbian novel in English. In: *Where the Meanings Are: Feminism and Cultural Spaces*. New York: Methuen, 1988, pp. 97–110.

Stoller, R. (1968), The sense of femaleness. In: *Sex and Gender: On the Development of Masculinity and Femininity*. New York: Science House, pp. 50–64.

——— (1976), Primary femininity. *J. Amer. Psychoanal. Assn.*, 24:59–78.

——— (1985), *Observing the Erotic Imagination*. New Haven, CT: Yale University Press.

——— (1988), Patients' responses to their own case reports. *J. Amer. Psychoanal. Assn.*, 36:371–391.

Strouse, J., ed. (1974), *Women and Analysis: Dialogues on Psychoanalytic Views of Femininity*. New York: Dell.

Sulloway, F. (1983), *Freud, Biologist of the Mind: Beyond the Psychoanalytic Legend*. New York: Basic Books.

Suppe, F. (1994), Explaining homosexuality: Philosophical issues, and who cares anyhow? *J. Homosexual.*, 27:223–268.

Swenson, C. (1994), Freud's "Anna O.": Social work's Bertha Pappenheim. *Clin. Social Work J.*, 22:149–163.

Szasz, T. (1970), *The Manufacture of Madness*. New York: Delta Books.

Tavris, C. (1992), *The Mismeasure of Woman: Why Women Are Not the Better Sex, the Inferior sex, or the Opposite Sex*. New York: Simon & Schuster.

Tessman, L. H. (1982), A note on the father's contribution to the daughter's ways of loving and working. In: *Father and Child: Developmental and Clinical Perspectives*, ed. S. Cath, A. Gurwitt & J. M. Ross. Boston: Little, Brown, pp. 219–238.

Thomas, D. (1957), *Collected Poems*. New York: New Directions.

Thompson, C. (1947), Changing concepts of homosexuality in psychoanalysis. *Psychiat.*,10:183–189.

Traub, V. (1995). The psychomorphology of the clitoris, *GLQ: A Journal of Lesbian and Gay Studies*, 2:81–113.

Trop, J. & Stolorow, R. (1992), Defense analysis in self psychology: A developmental view. *Psychoanal. Dial.*, 2:427–442.

Trujillo, C., ed. (1991), *Chicana Lesbians: The Girls Our Mothers Warned Us About*. Berkeley, CA: Third Woman Press.

Tsui, K. (1996), The cutting. In: *Breathless: Erotica*. Ithaca, NY: Firebrand Books, pp. 65–69.

Tuana, N., ed. (1989), *Feminism & Science*. Bloomington: Indiana University Press.

Tyson, P. (1986), Male gender identity: Early developmental roots. *Psychoanal. Rev.*, 73:405–425.

———— (1989), Infantile sexuality, gender identity, and obstacles to oedipal progression. *J. Amer. Psychoanal. Assn.*, 37:1051–1069.

Uyehara, L. A., Austrian, S, Upton, L. G., Warner, R. H., & Williamson, R. A. (1995), Telling about the analyst's pregnancy, *J. Amer. Psychoanal. Assn.*, 43:113–135.

Vance, C. S. (1984), *Pleasure and Danger: Exploring Female Sexuality*. New York: Routledge.

Vargo, S. (1987), The effects of women's socialization on lesbian couples. In: *Lesbian Psychologies*, ed. Boston Lesbian Psychologies Collective. Urbana: University of Illinois, pp. 161–173.

Vertinsky, P. (1994), *The Eternally Wounded Woman: Women, Doctors, and Exercise in the Late Nineteenth Century*. Chicago: University of Illinois Press.

Vicinus, M. (1984), Distance and Desire: English boarding school friendships, 1870–1920. In: *Hidden From History: Reclaiming the Gay and Lesbian Past*, ed. M. B. Duberman, M. Vicinus & G. Chauncey. New York: New American Library, 1989, pp. 212–229.

———— (1989), They wonder to what sex I belong. *The Lesbian and Gay Studies Reader*, ed. H. Abelove, M. A. Barale, & D. M. Halperin. New York: Routledge,1993, pp. 432–452.

Vida, J. (1991), Sándor Ferenczi on female sexuality. *J. Amer. Acad. Psychoanal.*, 19:271–281.

Weeks, J. (1977), *Coming Out: Homosexual Politics in Britain, from the Nineteenth Century to the Present*. London: Quartet Books.

———— (1981), *Sex, Politics & Society: The Regulation of Sexuality Since 1800*. New York: Longman.

———— (1991a), *Against Nature: Essays on History, Sexuality, and Identity*. London: Rivers Oram Press.

——— (1991b), Invented moralities. *History Workshop*, 32:151–166.

Weirauch, A. (1919–1921), *The Scorpion*, Berlin.

Weiss, A. (1992), *Vampires and Violets: Lesbians in Film*. New York: Penguin Books.

——— (1995), *Paris Was a Woman: Portraits from the Left Bank*. San Francisco: Harper.

Weiss, S. (1975), The effect on the transference of special events occurring during psychoanalysis. *Internat. J. Psycho-Anal.*, 56:69–75.

Wells, A. M. (1978), *Miss Marks and Miss Woolley*. Boston: Houghton Mifflin.

Whitehead, H. (1981), The bow and the burden strap: A new look at institutionalized homosexuality in native North America. In: *Sexual Meanings: The Cultural Construction of Gender and Sexuality*, ed. S. B. Ortner & H. Whitehead. London: Cambridge University Press.

Williams, W. L. (1986), *The Spirit and the Flesh: Sexual Diversity in American Indian Culture*. Boston, MA: Beacon.

Winnicott, D. W. (1958), *Collected Papers: Through Paediatrics to Psycho-Analysis*. New York: Basic Books.

——— (1961), Adolescence: Struggling through the doldrums. In: *The Family and Individual Development*. London: Tavistock, 1968, pp. 79–87.

——— (1965), *The Maturational Processes and the Facilitating Environment*. London: Hogarth Press.

——— (1971), *Playing and Reality*. New York: Basic Books.

Wolff, C. (1971), *Love Between Women*. New York: Harper & Row.

——— (1980), *Hindsight: An Autobiography*. London: Quartet Books.

——— (1986), *Magnus Hirschfeld: A Portrait of a Pioneer in Sexology*. London: Quartet Books.

Woolf, V. (1928), *Orlando*. New York: New American Library, 1960.

——— (1941), *Between the Acts*. New York: Harcourt, Brace.

Wrye, H. K. & Welles, J. K. (1994), *The Narration of Desire: Erotic Transferences and Countertransferences*. Hillsdale, NJ: The Analytic Press.

Young-Bruehl, E. (1988), *Anna Freud: A Biography*. New York: Summit.

——— ed. (1990), *Freud on Women: A Reader*. New York: Norton.

——— (1992), The biographer's empathy with her subject. *Acad. Forum*, 36:9–11.

Zicklin, G. (1994), Biological determinism and sexual orientation: Getting off the science/media bandwagon. Presented at CLAGS (Center for Lesbian and Gay Studies) Symposium Series, April 4, New York.

Zimmerman, B. (1984), The politics of transliteration: Lesbian personal narratives. *Signs*, 9:663–682.

——— (1990), *The Safe Sea of Women: Lesbian Fiction 1969–1989*. Boston: Beacon Press.

——— & McNaron, T. A. H., ed. (1996), *The New Lesbian Studies*. New York Feminist Press of City of New York.

# INDEX